David —

This is a great book in the John ~~Doe~~. It's always interesting to read about winds, and some prefer it to smell done. This one is easy to take, and I think a lot of fun —

love
Aunt Pat

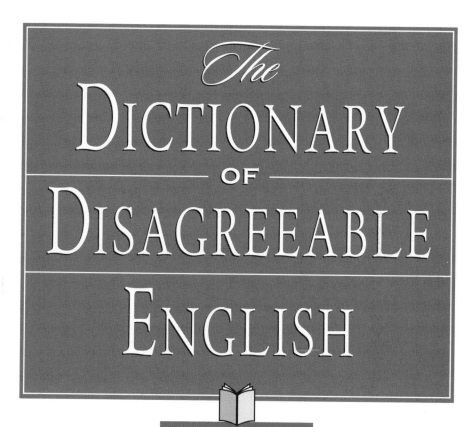

The DICTIONARY OF DISAGREEABLE ENGLISH

DELUXE EDITION

{ ROBERT HARTWELL FISKE }

THE GRUMBLING GRAMMARIAN

The

DICTIONARY

· OF ·

DISAGREEABLE

ENGLISH

DELUXE
EDITION

A CURMUDGEON'S
COMPENDIUM OF
EXCRUCIATINGLY
CORRECT GRAMMAR

WRITER'S DIGEST BOOKS

CINCINNATI, OHIO
www.writersdigest.com

ABOUT THE AUTHOR

Robert Hartwell Fiske is the author of *The Dictionary of Concise Writing* and *The Dimwit's Dictionary*, and the editor of *Vocabula Bound: Outbursts, Insights, Explanations, and Oddities*. He is the author of three Vocabula Books: *101 Wordy Phrases, 101 Foolish Phrases*, and *101 Elegant Paragraphs*. He is also the editor and publisher of *The Vocabula Review* (www.vocabula.com), a monthly online journal about the English language.

10   09   08   07   06   6   5   4   3   2

Distributed in Canada by Fraser Direct
100 Armstrong Avenue
Georgetown, ON, Canada L7G 5S4
Tel: (905) 877-4411

Distributed in the U.K. and Europe by David & Charles
Brunel House, Newton Abbot, Devon, TQ12 4PU, England
Tel: (+44) 1626 323200, Fax: (+44) 1626 323319
E-mail: postmaster@davidandcharles.co.uk

Distributed in Australia by Capricorn Link
P.O. Box 704, Windsor, NSW 2756 Australia
Tel: (02) 4577-3555

Library of Congress Cataloging-in-Publication Data

Fiske, Robert Hartwell.
    The dictionary of disagreeable English / Robert Hartwell Fiske.
  -- Deluxe ed.
      p. cm.
    Includes index.
    ISBN-13: 978-1-58297-418-7 (hardcover : alk. paper)
    ISBN-10: 1-58297-418-7
    1. English language--Usage--Dictionaries. 2. English language
--Grammar--Dictionaries. I. Title.
PE1464.F573 2006
423'.1--dc22

                                           2006004383

Cover designed by Claudean Wheeler
Interior designed by Lisa Kuhn
Illustrations by David E. Smith
Edited by Amy Schell
Production coordinated by Robin Richie

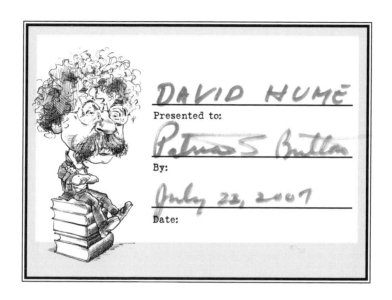

Presented to: DAVID HUME

By: Petrus S Butler

Date: July 22, 2007

DEDICATION

To my darling Ruth
Whose words are seldom ever wrong
Who speaks as if they're meant for song

OTHER WORDS
BY ROBERT HARTWELL FISKE

Inadequate though they may be, words distinguish us from all other living things. Only we humans can reflect on the past and plan for the future; it is language that allows us to do so. Indeed, our worth is partly in our words. Effective use of language—clear writing and speaking—is a measure of our humanness.

—The Dictionary of Concise Writing

Since how a person speaks and writes is a fair reflection of how a person thinks and feels, shoddy language may imply a careless and inconsiderate people—a public whose ideals have been discarded and whose ideas have been distorted. And in a society of this sort, easiness and mediocrity are much esteemed.

—The Dictionary of Concise Writing

As never before, people do as others do, speak as others speak, and think as others think. The cliché is king. Nothing is so reviled as individuality. We imitate one another lest we be left alone. We want to fit in, to be part of the crowd. We want groups to engulf us and institutions to direct us.

—The Dictionary of Concise Writing

Whatever the occasion, whether celebratory or funereal, quotidian or uncommon, people speak and write the same dimwitted words and phrases. No wonder so many of us feel barren or inconsolable: there are few words that inspire us, few words that move us, few words that thrill or overwhelm us. Persuasion has lost much of its sway, conviction, much of its claim.

—The Dimwit's Dictionary

Soon, it is clear, we will be a society unable to distinguish one word from another, sense from nonsense, truth from falsehood, good from evil. We will soon utter only mono- and disyllabic words, be entertained only by what pleases our peers, and adore whatever is easy or effortless.

—The Dimwit's Dictionary

It is not classism but clarity, not snobbery but sensibility that users of elegant English prize and wish to promote. Nothing so patently accessible as usage could ever be justly called invidious. As long as we recognize the categories of usage available to us, we can decide whether to speak and write the language well or badly. And we might more readily decide that elegant English is indeed vital were it more widely spoken by our public figures and more often written in our better books. Countless occasions where elegant English might have been used—indeed, ought to have been used—by a president or politician, a luminary or other notable, have passed with uninspired, if not bumbling, speech or writing.

—The Dimwit's Dictionary

Along with the evolution of language—the thousands of neologisms that new technologies and new thinking have brought about, for instance—there has been a concurrent, if perhaps less recognizable, devolution of language. The English language has become more precise for some users of it while becoming more plodding for others. Not a small part of this new cumbrousness is due to the loss of distinctions between words, the misuse of words, and other abuses of language.

—The Vocabula Review

A society is generally as lax as its language.

—The Vocabula Review

Well spoken is half sung.

—The Vocabula Review

TABLE OF CONTENTS

So true!

FOREWORD

There used to be various ways of telling whether a person was of discriminating taste, good breeding, refined sensibility. You could recognize gentility by clothes, hairdos, table manners; by the sports, films and foods someone preferred. Regrettably, our great democratic society, so worthy and desirable in many ways, has become such a leveler that most of these fine distinctions have been eroded, as if giving your bus seat to someone older, wearing a necktie, covering your mouth when yawning or sneezing, and speaking and writing correctly were signs of snobbish, undemocratic elitism. Being well groomed, well dressed, and well behaved have become obsolete, if not indeed politically incorrect.

Yet do we not want to distinguish ourselves, make good impressions, rise above the lowest common denominator? Is there no form of excellence left untarnished, unridiculed, unremembered—or, conversely, available to any boor who can afford designer clothes, four-star restaurants, or a trophy wife? One sure way remains for fastidiousness to shine forth without undue ostentation in the most ordinary, everyday situations; it is, you may have guessed it, language.

No damsel was ever in more distress, no drayhorse more flogged, no defenseless child more drunkenly abused than the English language today. And do not assume that it is attacked only from below, by what used to be called the great unwashed when looking washed was still held to be desirable. Given the sorry state of our education, the catastrophic neglect of book reading on all social levels, and the overwhelming indifference to all but material advancement and worldly success, no wonder that language gets it in the groin from all sides, not least from above. "Above" includes a variety of evils, from individuals who attended the best of schools and, whether through their own or their teachers' fault, learned nothing, to professional linguists of the descriptive or permissive persuasion, who find it more popular and remunerative to accept every change, however dumbing down and obfuscatory, they can lay their tape recorders on. Indeed, by endorsing it, they prove themselves edgy, with it, democratic, rather than courting unpopularity by being thought snobbish, pedantic, or, perish the thought, academic. As if many academics weren't the first to embrace mindless trendiness.

The fallacious but crowd-pleasing argument is that it is the people who use it that make a language, not the wizened fuddyduddies who desperately cling to antiquated niceties such as holding a door open for a lady, crossing the street on a green light, and knowing the difference between "between you and I" and "between you and me." It is not just a matter of convention and prudence; it is an aesthetic and moral choice. Rules of correctness are not some highbrow conspiracy; they strengthen the social fabric by making social intercourse more gracious, more efficient, and more satisfying.

Dictionaries, usually compiled by permissivists—which is to say copycats, cynics, lickspittles, or opportunists—are, by and large, no longer reliable guides, even when they aren't downright ignorant, as *The Dictionary of Disagreeable English* shows them to be. There is no evidence that Robert Hartwell Fiske is against reasonable change, that he hangs on by his fingernails to keep him from falling into a split infinitive. But he adheres admirably to rules that are practical, that facilitate understanding through logic and lucidity, or even just by a sense of decorum that makes speech more communicative and writing more elegant. Most people will understand from the context that you meant "imply" even though you barbarously said "infer." Multitudes, but not Mr. Fiske, will stand by, ignorant and unshuddering, when newscasters and celebrities, preachers and politicians, say "People were laying in the streets," and will comprehend, as Mr. Fiske will too, that a mass orgy is not what was meant. But isn't there something deeply satisfying, to speaker and hearer alike, when a person uses "prone" or "comprise" correctly, when a judge is said to be "disinterested" rather than "uninterested" when being scrupulously fair. After all, in the world we live in, judges have been known to be bored or even bribed.

Sad to say, some of our very best language authorities make undue concessions. The excellent Geoffrey Nunberg was willing, as long ago as 1983 in the *Atlantic Monthly*, to give up fighting for "disinterested" as a lost cause; the no less excellent Bryan Garner, in his new and very useful *Garner's Modern American Usage*, grimly concedes that "the battle over [using "hopefully" correctly] is now over." It is not over, should not be over, and I admire, indeed love, Mr. Fiske for making no such concession but throwing down the gauntlet (not gantlet) at anyone who jumps on this defective bandwagon.

Rules may be there, as some say, to be broken. Sure, if anything is gained thereby. But what if not? The time may be at hand when picking your nose in church, breaking wind at the dinner table, and talking during a concert will be accepted and universally practiced. What enormousness (not enormity) of loss that will be. Even if nobody is there to hear you—let alone correct you—when you say "more preferable," or "flout" for "flaunt," is there no satisfaction to yourself in knowing better? Is it not preferable to be on the side of the angels even if angels do not exist? But unlike angels, people who know better do exist, and would you not want to share their wisdom, partake of their esteem, and, who knows, perhaps even earn a better job on account of it?

John Simon

John Simon is the theater critic of New York *magazine and music critic of* The New Leader. *He is the author of several books on theater, film, language, literature, and poetry. Born in the former Yugoslavia, he lives in New York City with his wife, books, and CDs.*

INTRODUCTION:
THE DECLINE OF THE DICTIONARY

You're much too much, and just too "very, very"
To ever be in Webster's Dictionary.

LAXICOGRAPHERS ALL

The slang-filled eleventh edition of "America's Best-Selling Dictionary," *Merriam-Webster's Collegiate Dictionary* (Frederick C. Mish, editor in chief), does as much as, if not more than, the famously derided *Webster's Third International Dictionary* to discourage people from taking lexicographers seriously. "Laxicographers" all, the Merriam-Webster staff reminds us that dictionaries merely record how people use the language, not how it ought to be used. Some dictionaries, and certainly this new Merriam-Webster, actually promote illiteracy.

Several years ago, the editors of *The American Heritage Dictionary* ("America's Favorite Dictionary") caused a stir by deciding to include four-letter words in their product. Since the marketing strategy of including swear words has now been adopted by all dictionary makers, Merriam-Webster, apparently not knowing how else to distinguish its dictionary from competing ones that erode its marketing share, has decided to include a spate of slang words in its eleventh edition. There's nothing wrong with Merriam-Webster's trying to distinguish its product, of course, but when it means tampering with the English language—by including idiotic slang and apparently omitting more useful words—it's reprehensible.

Merriam-Webster proclaims it has added some ten thousand words to its *Collegiate Dictionary* (though there is some reason to question the staff's ability to count well; see note 7, page 19). To do so, as a company spokesman admitted, "some words had to be kicked out" of the earlier edition. More interesting than this new edition would be a book of the words abandoned. Were they sesquipedalian words that few people use or know the meaning of; *disyllabic* words that few people use or know the meaning of? It's quite true: People are increasingly monosyllabic; after all, many people today prefer *dis* (included in the *Collegiate* tenth and eleventh) to *disparage* or *disrespect* or *insult*. And now, in the eleventh, there is also the equally preposterous *def*, another word, Merriam-Webster assures us, for *excellent* or *cool* (which among many younger people today is also spelled *kool* and *kewl*, and though both words may have as much—or as little—currency as *def*, neither, curiously, Merriam-Webster saw fit to include in its compilation).

What word did Merriam-Webster decide to omit to make room for the all-important *def*? What word did they decide to omit to make room for *funplex* (an entertainment complex that includes facilities for various sports and games and often restaurants)? What word did they omit in order to add *McJob* (a low-paying job that requires little skill and provides little opportunity for advancement)? What words did they omit in order to add *headbanger* (a musician who performs hard rock), *dead presidents* (United States currency in the form of paper bills), *phat* (highly attractive or gratifying), and *Frankenfood* (genetically engineered food)? Frankly, I rather like the coinage *Frankenfood*. But if people do not enjoy or feel comfortable eating genetically altered foods, which I suspect is likely, the word will be fleeting. Almost all slang, the people at Merriam-Webster should know, is ephemeral. Most of the slang added to the eleventh edition will never see the twelfth—or ought not to. Consider this paragraph from the Merriam-Webster web site:

> *Many new words pass out of English as quickly as they entered it, the fad of teenagers grown to adulthood, the buzzwords of the business meetings past, the cast-off argot of technologies superceded* [sic]*, the catchy phrases from advertisements long forgotten. It is likely that many such ephemeral coinages will never be entered in dictionaries, especially abridged dictionaries where space (or time or money or all of the above) are at a premium. That does not mean, however, that the words did not exist, simply that they did not endure.*[1]

Odd that Mish and his minions would then agree to the addition of so much slang to the eleventh edition. (Odder still, perhaps, that slang like *far-out* and *groovy*, even though the popularity of these words has been much reduced over the years, are still entries in the Collegiate.[2]) But, as I say, it's a marketing strategy. It's not lexicography. These slang terms are not meant to improve the usefulness of their product; they're meant to help sell "America's Best-Selling Dictionary." Slang, Merriam-Webster believes, sells.

A CATALOG OF CONFUSIONS

Lexicographers are descriptivists, language liberals. The use of *disinterested* to mean *uninterested* does not displease a descriptivist. A prescriptivist, by contrast, is a language conservative, a person interested in maintaining standards and correctness in language use. To prescriptivists, *disinterested* in the sense of *uninterested* is the mark of uneducated people who do not know the distinction between the two words. And if there are enough uneducated people saying *disinterested* (and I'm afraid there are) when they mean *uninterested* or *indifferent*, lexicographers enter the definition into their dictionaries. Indeed, the distinction between these words has all but vanished owing largely to irresponsible writers and boneless lexicographers.[3]

Words, we are told, with the most citations are included in the Merriam-Webster dictionaries. Are then words with the fewest omitted, or in danger of being omitted? *Merriam-Webster's Collegiate Dictionary* includes *alright*,[4] but what word was not included, or was "kicked out," so that an inanity, an illiteracy like *alright* could be kept in? *Boeotian* is not defined in *Merriam-Webster's*; nor is *diaskeuast* defined; nor *logogogue*; nor *nyctophobia*; nor *myriadigamous*; nor *ubiety*; nor *womanfully*;[5] nor hundreds of other words that a college student might find infinitely more useful than the entry, the misspelling and definition of, *alright*.

All it takes for a solecism to become standard English is people misusing or misspelling the word. And if enough people do so, lexicographers will enter the originally misused or misspelled word into their dictionaries, and descriptive linguists will embrace it as a further example of the evolution of English.

Merriam-Webster's laxicographers, further disaffecting careful writers and speakers, assign the meaning *reluctant* to the definition of *reticent*. *Reticent* means disinclined to speak; taciturn; quiet. *Reluctant* means disinclined to do something; unwilling; loath. Because some people mistakenly use *reticent* to mean *reluctant*, dictionaries now maintain *reticent* does mean *reluctant*. Dictionaries are complicit with other purveyors and vendors of mangled writing, muddled speech.

There are many other examples of Merriam-Webster's inexcusably shoddy dictionary making. For example, according to the dictionary's editors:

- **accidently** is as valid a spelling as **accidentally**
- **bemuse** means the same as **amuse**
- **enormity** means the same as **enormousness**
- **flaunt** means the same as **flout**
- **fortuitous** means the same as **fortunate**
- **get** is pronounced **GET** or **GIT**
- **hone in** means the same as **home in**
- **impactful** is listed as an adjective of **impact**
- **incent** means **incentivize**, itself ungainly
- **infer** means the same as **imply**
- **less** means the same as **fewer**
- **miniscule** is a variant spelling of **minuscule**
- **mischievous** is pronounced **MIS-chi-ves or mis-CHEE-vee-es**
- **nuclear** is pronounced **NU-klee-er** or **NU-kya-ler**
- **peruse** means not only to examine carefully but to read over in a casual manner
- **predominate**, a verb, is also an adjective meaning **predominant**
- **publically** is a variant spelling of **publicly**
- **replete** means the same as **complete**
- **sherbert** is as valid a spelling as **sherbet**
- **supercede** is a variant spelling of **supersede**
- **tho** is a variant spelling of **though**
- **transpire** means the same as **occur**
- **where** means **that** [6]

Merriam-Webster's Collegiate Dictionary, like other college dictionaries, actually promotes the misuse of the English language. Dictionaries are ever more a catalog of confusions, a list of illiteracies. Dictionaries acknowledge the errors that people make; by acknowledging them they, in effect, endorse them; by endorsing them, they are thought correct by the dull, duped public. Ultimately, all words will mean whatever we think they mean, indeed, whatever we want them to mean.

It's true that *Merriam-Webster's* does offer some usage notes,[7] but "usage notes" is a misnomer for *Merriam-Webster's* are largely otiose. In virtually every instance, the editors at Merriam-Webster use these notes to underscore their descriptive bent and to rebut those who believe in maintaining standards of language use:

- **couple:** *The adjective use of **a couple**, without **of**, has been called nonstandard, but it is not.*

- **enormity:** ***Enormity,** some people insist, is improperly used to denote large size. They insist on **enormousness** for this meaning, and would limit **enormity** to the meaning "great wickedness."*

- **me:** ***Me** is used in many constructions where strict grammarians prescribe **I**. This usage is not so much ungrammatical as indicative of the shrinking range of the nominative form.*

- **nuclear:** *Though disapproved of by many, pronunciations ending in \-kye-ler\ have been found in widespread use among educated speakers including scientists, lawyers, professors, congressmen, U.S. cabinet members, and at least two U.S. presidents and one vice president.*

- **so:** *The intensive use of **so** is widely condemned in college handbooks, but is nonetheless standard.*

Even a usage note that does uphold the differences in meanings between commonly misused words is written begrudgingly:

- **mitigate:** ***Mitigate** is sometimes used as an intransitive where **militate** might be expected. Even though Faulkner used it and one critic thinks it should be called an American idiom, it is usually considered a mistake.*

And here is a definition followed by its usage note, a Merriam-Webster model of helpless confusion:

- **literally** *1. in a literal sense or manner: ACTUALLY <took the remark ~> <was ~ insane> 2. in effect: VIRTUALLY <will ~ turn the world upside down to combat cruelty or injustice - Norman Cousins>*

  Usage: *Since some people take sense 2 to be the opposite of sense 1, it has been frequently criticized as a misuse. Instead the use is pure hyperbole intended to gain emphasis, but it often appears in contexts where no additional emphasis is necessary.*

NO LONGER HARMLESS

Some months ago, in *The Vocabula Review*, I offered the following TVR Poll:
Dictionaries should be much more prescriptive, far less descriptive, than they now are.

- *Yes! More than that, laxicographers promote the dissolution of the English language (and even society) with their misguided liberality: 19%*

- *Quite so. Dictionary compilers need to maintain, and perhaps even decide, distinctions between words; they need to guide us on matters of usage: 27%*

- *A mix of guidance and license is probably the best course—it's also the commonest course: 22%*

- *Lexicographers are necessarily descriptivist for their job is simply to record how people use the language: 28%*

- *Obviously, we all must bow to the definitions and spellings found in the dictionary: 4%*

As you see, 68 percent of the respondents rejected the strong descriptivist idea of dictionary making.[8] Still more heartening to me is that only 4 percent of the people who participated in this poll believe that the definitions and spellings a dictionary offers are those we are necessarily bound to. More than that, though, the new Merriam-Webster is a sign that dictionaries, at least as they are now being compiled, have outlived their usefulness. Dictionaries are no longer sacrosanct, no longer sources of unimpeachable information. Dictionaries are, indeed, no longer to be trusted.

That a president can ask *Is our children learning?*, a basketball star can use the word *conversate*, a well-known college professor can say *vociferous* when he means *voracious*, and another can scold a student for using the word *juggernaut* because she believes it means *jigaboo* is disturbing. But these are precisely the sorts of errors, if enough people make them, that the staff at Merriam-Webster will one day include in their dictionaries:

- **child** *(pl. or sing.) children.*

- **conversate** *to exchange thoughts or opinions in speech; to converse.*

- **vociferous** *1. marked by or given to vehement insistent outcry. 2. voracious.*

- **juggernaut** *1. a massive inexorable force, campaign, movement, or object that crushes whatever is in its path. 2. (usu. offensive) jigaboo; black person.*

Over the last forty and more years, linguists and lexicographers have conspired to transform an indispensable reference work into an increasingly useless, increasingly dangerous one. Lexicographers are no longer harmless.

Robert Hartwell Fiske

editor@vocabula.com

NOTES

1 From the Merriam-Webster web site: "Passing Fancies" (www.m-w.com/service/realwords.htm). This web page, I discovered only recently, has been removed from the Merriam-Webster web site—perhaps in response to this article, an earlier version of which appeared in *The Weekly Standard* and *The Vocabula Review* in August 2003.

2 Merriam-Webster does publish a number of "specialty dictionaries," including *Merriam-Webster's Biographical Dictionary, Merriam-Webster's Geographical Dictionary, Merriam-Webster's Dictionary of English Usage, Merriam-Webster's Dictionary of Synonyms*, and *The Merriam-Webster Dictionary of Quotations*, but it has not published a dictionary of slang. Since the editors at Merriam-Webster are so enamored of slang, let them publish a specialty dictionary of it.

3 Lexicographers often try to justify the inclusion of a solecism, such as *disinterested* in the sense of *uninterested*, in their dictionaries by citing examples from authors who have used the word incorrectly. The obvious response to this is that authors—well known or not—are not immune from misusing and misspelling words and have forever done so. In the seventeenth century, *disinterested* did have the meaning "without interest or concern," but for the last three hundred years, the word has meant "impartial or without bias."

4 Though Merriam-Webster's is very likely the most descriptivist dictionary on the market today (see Appendix A), many of my criticisms of it are also applicable to other popular college dictionaries. *The American Heritage College Dictionary, The Oxford American College Dictionary, Webster's New World College Dictionary, Microsoft Encarta College Dictionary*, and *Random House Webster's College Dictionary*, for instance, all include, and thereby endorse, the solecism *alright.*

5 *Boeotian*: of or like Boeotia or its people, who were reputed to be dull and stupid; *diaskeuast*: someone who makes revisions; *logogogue*: one who legislates over the use of words; *nyctophobia*: an abnormal fear of darkness or nighttime; *myriadigamous*: pertaining to someone who marries all kinds; *ubiety*: the condition of being in a particular place; *womanfully*: with the characteristic grace, strength, or purposefulness of a woman.

6 Of course, it's in the financial interest of dictionary makers to record the least defensible of usages in the English language, for without ever-changing definitions—or as they would say, an evolving language—there would be less need for people to buy later editions of their product.

7 Merriam-Webster boasts that its eleventh edition contains "4,000 usage notes" though its staff may have miscounted. The book itself has 1,623 pages, so we might expect an average of two or three usage notes a page, but this is hardly what we find. Perhaps, by "usage notes," Merriam-Webster also means synonyms (or "syn" as it abbreviates the word). The editors at *The American Heritage College Dictionary* may count more carefully—or better know the meaning of the word *usage*—for they speak of their 300 usage notes, and the *Microsoft Encarta College Dictionary* advertises its 600.

8 This TVR Poll is not scientific and reflects the opinions of only those *Vocabula* readers who chose to participate.

IMPRECATION

Liber scriptus proferetur—
dictionaries have had their day
in quo totum continetur—
dictionaries have had their day
unde mundus judicetur—
dictionaries have had their day

Dies irae, dies irae, dies irae

ABBERATION

Misspelling of **aberration**. • New employment data will either corroborate recent evidence showing the economy is improving, or indicate that last month's job gain was an **abberation**. USE **aberration**. • Hedman had been a player in search of one, redemptive moment that would grant him forgiveness in the eyes of the fans after his **abberation** in Munich. USE **aberration**.

> ***Abberation*** *is how aberrant users of the English language spell **aberration***. *The language has its deviants, its descriptive linguists, its dictionary makers.*

ABROGATE

Misused for **arrogate**. • Yet, cocooned as they are in their superstitions, the eco-warriors **abrogate** for themselves the right to break the law. USE **arrogate**. • With an astonishing arrogance, the law in this case has **abrogated** to itself the right to decide on whether one twin should survive. USE **arrogated**.

> ***Abrogate*** *means to abolish; to annul.* ***Arrogate*** *means to appropriate; to take or claim without justification; to assign something to another in an unwarranted way.*
> *If we ignore the distinctions between words, we begin to ignore or disapprove of the distinctions between people; individuality, which, even now, is not favorably regarded, will become increasingly frowned upon, eventually unlawful, perhaps.*

ABSORBTION

Misspelling of **absorption**. • Total energy **absorbtion** coefficients are used for the calculation of deposited dose by a given energy fluence. USE **absorption**. • These wheels are used to achieve higher top speed and better shock **absorbtion**. USE **absorption**. • In broccoli for example, cooking increases iron **absorbtion** from 6% to 30%. USE **absorption**.

***Absorption,** not **absorbtion,** is the process of absorbing or of being absorbed; the state of being engrossed.*

ACCELERATE

Solecistic for **exhilarate.** • For a lot of these Wadsworth seniors, *Grease* will be an **accelerating** experience, but also close to four years of hard work. USE **exhilarating.** • It is an evolving, **accelerating** experience like none other that has come before. USE **exhilarating.** • The old Minerva would have felt sorry for the bickering couple, but she felt **accelerated** by their pain. USE **exhilarated.**

> **Accelerate** *means to increase the speed of; to cause to occur sooner than expected.* **Exhilarate** *means to cause to feel refreshed and energetic; to invigorate. SEE ALSO* **exhileration.**

ACCIDENTLY

Misspelling of **accidentally.** • Immediately smitten, Guido, who gets a job as a waiter, arranges to **accidently** bump into Dora over the next several days, but eventually realizes that she's engaged—albeit unhappily—to a Fascist official. USE **accidentally.** • If a thrown ball **accidently** touches a base coach, or a pitched or thrown ball touches an umpire, the ball is alive and in play. USE **accidentally.**

> *At least two well-known dictionaries do recognize the spelling* **accidently***. But let this be a further reminder that dictionaries merely record how people use the language, not necessarily how it ought to be used. Some dictionaries, we can reasonably infer, actually promote illiteracy. If we were to rely exclusively on dictionary pronouncements, we'd be altogether undone. SEE ALSO* **incidently; publically.**

ACROSST

Misspelling of **across.** • Do you think of countless sold records and happy fans from **acrosst** the world? USE **across.** • I was not sure what was actually being aborted until I came **acrosst** this web site. USE **across.** • These people do not work directly in the Rice Psychology Department, but many of them are **acrosst** the street at UT-Houston Medical School. USE **across.**

> *Among the ill-read and the ill-bred,* **across** *is spelled* **acrosst***.*

A

'I don't mind tellin' you, Godwin,' pursued Andrew presently, in a cautious voice, laying an open hand against his trousers-pocket, 'as I've been a-doin' pretty good business lytely. Been growin' a bit--see? I'm runnin' round an' keepin' my heyes open understand? Thoughts I, now, if I could come acrosst a nicet little openin', somethink in the rest'rant line, that's what 'ud sewt me jest about down to the ground. I'm cut out for it--see?'

—**George Gissing, *Born in Exile*, 1892**

ACT OUT

Idiotic for **misbehave** (or similar words). • When children can't use words to say what they feel, they may hit, bite, or **act out** in other ways. USE **misbehave**. • A common explanation is that it's because blacks **act out** more or because blacks are from low-income backgrounds. USE **behave badly**. • Children often **act out** irrationally and impulsively, and only later think about the consequences. USE **behave**.

> *Act out is drivel for misbehave or behave badly. Psychologists and other social scientists create nonsensical terms like this to try to add an aura of credibility and mystery to their largely self-evident studies. **Act out** does properly mean to perform as if in a play. SEE ALSO **aggress; consequate**.*

ADAPTION

Solecistic for **adaptation**. • We also provide a lot of counseling and hand-holding on **adaption** to the community and finding activities for them. USE **adaptation**. • Soldier Ride is outfitting every soldier who's participating with a bike and the prosthetic **adaption** that's needed. USE **adaptation**. • The **adaption** of Stoker's *Dracula*, which is being released as a four-issue mini-series, is, as of issue two, well worth the price of admission. USE **adaptation**.

> *The noun **adaptation** is preferable to **adaption**; the adjective **adaptive**, preferable to **adaptative**.*

> Its publication just happens (oh, yes?) to coincide with the opening on Broadway last month of "Spama-lot," a musical adaption of "Monty Python and the Holy Grail."
>
> **—Ann Geracimos, *The Washington Times***

AD FEMINAM

Idiotic for **ad hominem**. • In 1998, Crittenden subjected the pro-working mother book, *A Mother's Place*, by journalist Susan Chira, to a startingly **ad feminam** thrashing in *National Review*. USE **ad hominem**. • Butler's defenders branded it an **ad feminam** attack on an innovative thinker whose reputation was surpassing Nussbaum's own. USE **ad hominem**.

*Latin for "to the man," **ad hominem**—attacking the character or motives of an opponent rather than debating the policy or position—obviously does not refer to men alone. **Ad feminam** is thus no more needed than the sexist **womyn** and **her-story**. The notion—which to some **ad feminam** is also supposed to convey—that women are being attacked, not for their positions or character, but solely because they are women, might be articulated, if articulated it need be, far more sensibly with other words.*

ADIEU

Misspelling of **ado**. • Without further **adieu**, let us see what they are serving up on this final stretch towards the end of the season. USE **ado**. • With no more **adieu**, I grabbed my submachine gun and sprinted out into the hall. USE **ado**. • And now, without further **adieux** here is my own personal recipe for absinthe. USE **ado**.

*Occasionally, **ado** (or even **a duo**) is used in place of **adieu**: • Sometime in early September we bid **ado** to the Green River. USE **adieu**. • The second round of Indian summer is about to wish us **a duo**. USE **adieu**.*

*   *Adieu (plural: adieux), meaning to God (I commend you), today is used largely to mean goodbye or farewell. **Ado** means trouble or bother; fuss. **A duo** is a duet; a pair or two allied people or things.*

ADJECTIFY

A

Idiotic for **describe** (or similar words). • Where the opinion-makers and media moguls **adjectify** every political action these days as "vaguely reminiscent of the sixties," I prefer to think of them as "clearly foreshadowing the millennium." USE **describe**. • I think that I'm going to change the name in a totally undefined way: I'm going to use the gjwalberg.com, then **adjectify** it with a nonsensical statement. USE **define**. • It also uses the term "community" to **adjectify** programs in justice as well, so that we have community corrections, community policing, etc. USE **portray**.

> As not every phrase can be reduced to a single word, so not every noun should be made into a verb. **Adjectify**—which apparently means to use as an adjective—sounds dreadful, and its meaning is questionable in nearly every context. If meaning it must have, **adjectify** should mean to modify; to qualify, limit, or specify the meaning of. **Adjectify**, at least in the preceding examples, seems to mean to describe or define. And **adjectify** sounds like it means to dehumanize or objectify. A few words whose meaning is apparent are better than one word whose meaning is not.

In its sense of to use a proper name as an adjective, **adjectify** is irreplaceable; whole sentences need to be reworked: • And academics love to **adjectify** luminaries in their fields. • A search of the Nexis database reveals him to be the most **adjectified** Chief Executive of recent years.

ADJURE

Misused for **abjure**. • There should also be a commitment on both sides to **adjure** violence against non-combatant civilians and a willingness to pursue the democratic process. USE **abjure**. • At the moment the government takes not in consideration, like in eastern Europe to **adjure** the communism and to build up a capitalistic society. USE **abjure**.

And **abjure** is sometimes misused for **adjure**: • In the name of the Lords of the Dead, I command you; with the Three Sigils of the Dreamless Ones, I **abjure** you; by the pleasure of the Dread Majesties of Night, I order you. USE **adjure**.

> **Adjure** (ah-JOOR) means to command or enjoin solemnly; to appeal to or entreat.
> **Abjure** (ab-JOOR) means to renounce under oath; to repudiate.

ADOPT

Misused for **adapt**. • Maybe you'll need a little time to **adopt** to the Indian English, but that's all. Use **adapt**. • On the basis of this point, there is no reason why Western companies cannot successfully **adopt** to Japanese practices. USE **adapt**. • Universities and other traditional institutions of education must therefore also change and **adopt** to new conditions and societal needs. USE **adapt**.

> To **adopt** means to take into one's own family through legal means; to choose and follow a course of action; to take up and use as one's own; to take on or assume. To **adapt** means to make suitable or fit for a specific use.

ADULTRY

Misspelling of **adultery**. • Apparently he has said he committed **adultry** and cheated on his wife and now he is being charged with sexual assault. USE **adultery**. • Does chatting and flirting in a chatroom count as **adultry**? USE **adultery**.

> Those who write **adultery**, like those who commit it, do indeed need to know how to spell it. SEE ALSO **marrage**.

ADVERTIZE

Misspelling of **advertise**. • Be the first to **advertize** and your ad will be right here at the top. USE **advertise**. • It normally takes about sixty to ninety days from the start of **advertizing** for a new position until a new hire comes on board. USE **advertising**. • There's an **advertizement** at every turn, which gets annoying, but I guess that's the price you pay for freeware. USE **advertisement**.

> In the United States, **advertise** is spelled with an **s**; in Britain, with a **z**. Generally, **ise** is the ending used in Britain, and **ize**, the ending used in the United States (though there are exceptions: **advertise, apprise, chastise**, and others).

ADVICE

Solecistic for **advise**. • We will only **advice** them to join those colleges that will be ready to offer quality education. USE **advise**. • If you have a wheelchair please **advice** us at least five days in advance so we can arrange suitable accommodation. USE **advise**.

A

Advice (ad-VIS)—*opinion or counsel—is a noun;* **advise** (ad-VIZ)—*to offer opinion or counsel—a verb. SEE ALSO* **device**.

AEROBIC

Idiotic for **Arabic**. • This has a brass dial with silver chapter ring and Roman and **Aerobic** numerals, signed "Lanrie Carlisle." USE **Arabic**. • Notes in a scale are identified using **Aerobic** numbers 1-2-3-4-5-6-7 and the chords in a key use roman numbers I-II-III-IV-V-VI-VII. USE **Arabic**.

Only people unfamiliar with both fitness and world affairs could possibly confuse **aerobic** *with* **Arabic***, but flabby xenophobes there are.*

AESTHETIC

Misused for **anesthetic**. • Hyaluronic Acid is also used for lip enhancement (definition of upper lip) and augmentation (fuller lips); this is carried out under dental block using local **aesthetic**. USE **anesthetic**. • Topical local **aesthetic** preparations such as EMLA cream or Ametop gel are used in reducing the pain of venepuncture and intravenous cannulation in both children and adults. USE **anesthetic**.

An **anesthetic** *is a substance that reduces sensitivity to pain during a medical procedure. And* **aesthetic***, as an adjective, refers to art or beauty and the appreciation of them. SEE ALSO* **ascetic**.

He said surgical, aesthetic, nursing and physiotherapy staff had all worked together to get him home as soon as possible.

He said he had been deeply worried about having a general aesthetic and had been delighted to be offered the epidural in his spine.

—Jane Elliott, BBC News

Ms. Elliott does manage to use the word **anaesthetic** *(the British spelling) once in her article but, dulled by her own writing perhaps, not before using* **aesthetic** *twice.*

AFFECT

Misused for **effect**. • As for the world-wide **affects** of volcanic eruptions, this only happens when there are large explosive eruptions that throw material into the stratosphere. USE **effects**. • Eventually, these gases escaped and produce a runaway greenhouse **affect**. USE **effect**. • The primary **affect** on property values will come from the aerosols associated with the spray. USE **effect**. • Now breathe deeply for the full **affect**. USE **effect**.

And **effect** is misused for **affect**. • The vice president had become self-conscious about the condition of his teeth and aides believed it was directly **effecting** his campaign performance. USE **affecting**. • Leslie says she teaches because it gives her a natural high to know she has the power to positively **effect** all who enter her classroom. USE **affect**. • Global warming will **effect** many aspects of daily life in the future. USE **affect**.

*Though both **affect** and **effect** may be either a noun or a verb, it is usually the verb **affect** that is confused with the noun **effect**. **Affect** as a verb means to influence or have an effect on; as a noun, **affect** means an emotion or emotional response. **Effect** as a verb means to bring about or accomplish; as a noun, **effect** means a result or an influence. The word **affect** is much less often used as a noun than it is as a verb. All the same, it is often misused for, or perhaps misspelled, **effect**.*

AFFIDAVID

Misspelling of **affidavit**. • You will be required to sign an **affidavid** stating you paid for the lot but never received it and to file a police report alleging fraud against the seller. USE **affidavit**. • Cindy Shook's **affidavid** was discounted by the court as unbelievable. USE **affidavit**. • Martin Coonce died on March 1, 1909, and Sarah Coonce subsequently filed an **affidavid** for relief under the Widow's Pension Act of 1908. USE **affidavit**.

*More than a misspelling, **affidavid** signals that ineptitude and ignorance overwhelm us; today, entertainment is all; learning how to spell correctly or write well interests us no more than does civility and justice, honesty and integrity, yet how we use language is inseparable from how we view the world.*

A

'I am not a swearer in of people, man.'

The visitor, clearly anything but reliant on this assurance, doggedly muttered 'Alfred David.'

'Is that your name?' asked Lightwood.

'My name?' returned the man. 'No; I want to take a Alfred David.'

(Which Eugene, smoking and contemplating him, interpreted as meaning Affidavit.)

'I tell you, my good fellow,' said Lightwood, with his indolent laugh, 'that I have nothing to do with swearing.'

'He can swear AT you,' Eugene explained; 'and so can I. But we can't do more for you.'

—Charles Dickens, *Our Mutual Friend*, 1864–1865

AFFLICT

Misused for **inflict**. • Other times we choose to **afflict** voluntary suffering on ourselves (as in a fast or long march). USE **inflict**. • She hoped for a different world for her daughters and wanted her sons to understand the issue and not **afflict** any pain on the women in their lives. USE **inflict**. • Jeryl L. Beckett, 28, 208 S. Summitt, died at 2:45 P.M. Monday, March 3, 1997, of a **self-afflicted** gun wound. USE **self-inflicted**.

This distinction is increasingly unobserved, for dictionaries are, not at all helpfully, offering one word as a synonym for the other. Both words mean to mete out or impose pain or suffering, but the object used with **afflict** *is most often an animate one, whereas the object used with* **inflict** *is inanimate. You* **afflict** *a person with pain, or* **inflict** *pain on a person. What's more,* **inflicted** *is usually followed by* **on** *or* **upon***;* **afflicted***, by* **by** *or* **with***.*

AFFLUENT

The pronunciation of **affluent** *is (AF-loo-ent), not (ah-FLOO-ent).*

AGGRAVATE

Solecistic for **annoy** (or similar words). • What is most needed from us, instead, may be the simple quality of steadfastness—the persistent, open-hearted willingness to simply hang in there with the clients who most confuse, **aggravate**, or discourage us. USE **annoy**. • Most of the time, swapping human contacts for electronic ones looks as though it's saving us time, money, and **aggravation**. USE **irritation**. • The first set of people I **aggravated** Tuesday were those of you who get angry when I don't stick to financial topics. USE **irritated**. • Skunks stink up campus and **aggravate** students. USE **upset**. • He sincerely regrets all the **aggravation** the school, teachers, parents have been put through. USE **exasperation**. • Every women knows that satisfying a man is easy, but **aggravating** him takes a special talent! USE **exasperating**.

Aside from the added amusement of "Every **women** knows," the online advertisement for *How to Aggravate a Man Every Time*, a book, offers another example; it's too dear: • Learn the best **aggravating** tricks, such as: take over the remote control, make the most of PMS, make friends with his ex-girlfriends....

*The modern (as well as, apparently, historical) view is that **aggravate** may mean, along with to make worse or exacerbate, to irritate or annoy. If people who use **aggravate** to mean annoy also had knowledge of its sense of to make worse and could occasionally use it in that sense, perhaps careful writers and speakers of the English language would be less inclined to carp—while, of course, never agreeing to capitulate.*

*Let us, if need be, create distinctions between words where, perhaps, there have been none. We have words aplenty that mean to annoy; the only other words that mean to aggravate are **worsen** and **exacerbate**, itself often ridiculously confused with **exasperate**. SEE ALSO **exasperate**.*

AGGRESS

Idiotic for be **aggressive** (or similar words). • Freudian theory would suggest that the desire to **aggress** would be subconscious, not a product of cognitive processes. USE **be aggressive**. • When we are **aggressed against**, it is our right to face up to the aggression, to confront the aggression. USE **attacked**. • The neighbors were getting nervous because of the crowd of people passing in their hall, and a group of volunteers was **aggressed** by a drunken man. USE **assailed**. • We don't see ourselves responsible, because it wasn't we who **aggressed** them, but they came and **aggressed** the community. USE **assaulted**.

*A wholly useless construction, **aggress** is far less specific than attack, assault, assail, accost, be aggressive, and other words. SEE ALSO **act out; enthuse**.*

A

AGREEANCE

Idiotic for **agreement**. • In **agreeance** with the Monterrey Consensus, Guinea believes there should be an increase of Foreign Direct Investment (FDI), especially in the continent of Africa. USE **agreement**. • All present members were in **agreeance** that if a problem arises and the by-laws are not adhered to, the current officers might seek legal counsel if necessary to resolve the conflict. USE **agreement**.

* **Agreeance** is an obsolete word. Almost anyone who uses it today instead of **agree-ment** is being ignorant, not as some linguists have maintained, inventive or clever.*

AIDE

Misused for **aid**. • Support garments used after liposuction can help decrease swelling and **aide** in general comfort. USE **aid**. • As a Psychologist with thirty years experience, I will be your personal coach, I will carefully listen, help steer you to healthy sources to **aide** in your growth, guide you in setting up a plan of action and personal goals, and provide support during your voyage of re-discovery. USE **aid**. • Polk and Salem housing authorities receive grant to **aide** seniors and the disabled. USE **aid**.

* To **aid** is to help, assist, or support someone; to promote or encourage. An **aide** is a person who assists; an assistant or helper.*

A.K.A.

Idiotic for **that is** (or similar words). • From the data, he saw evidence that computer investments were improving business efficiency, a.k.a. productivity. USE **that is**. • RUF Commander, Dennis Mingo a.k.a. Superman has disappeared from Makeni. USE **also known as**. • "My face is still in Chicago," Oprah announces as she ushers me (a.k.a. the poor slob) into the suite. DELETE a.k.a. • Sharon Adl-Doost, a.k.a. The Lunch Lady, may be the most famous cafeteria worker in the country, if not the world. USE **well known as**.

An abbreviation for also known as, **a.k.a.** *has no place in written language and little in spoken language. Only a writer manqué would use* **a.k.a.**

Nonsoaps have the same ability to clean as their sudsy counterparts, but they do so using synthetic detergents (a.k.a. "syndets").

—**Leah Wyar,** *Health*

Magazine writers sound laughably alike. Most of them would have written this sentence (and those that precede and follow this sentence) much as Ms. Wyar has, and not one of them would have thought not to use **a.k.a.**

ALBUM

The pronunciation of **album** *is (AL-bum), not (AL-blum).*

ALIMENT

Misused for **ailment**. • While well drawn, *Altered Beast* suffers from an **aliment** known as image break-up. USE **ailment**. • Thumb fatigue is a painful **aliment** that is becoming increasingly common among dental professionals. USE **ailment**.

Though **ailment** *(AIL-ment) is far more commonly used than* **aliment**, *the words are sometimes misused. An* **ailment** *is a mild illness; whereas* **aliment** *(AL-ah-ment) is food or something that nourishes.*

As some people confuse **ailment** with **aliment**, so they use the nonword **ailmentary** instead of **alimentary**: • Alcohol cannot be called a food for it enters the **ailmentary** canal and is not changed or digested in any way. USE **alimentary**. • With the help of strong muscular walls and the stones and grit, the gizzard grinds the food into a pulp before it passes further along the **ailmentary** canal. USE **alimentary**.

ALLEGED

A

Alleged means suspected but not proved of having committed, or of being, a crime; supposed. *("In the fall of 2002, after receiving reports of **alleged** wrongdoings by one of the twenty participants in the honor program, the state Department of Environmental Management launched an investigation focusing on five boats, four of which were randomly chosen."; "Saying it has found no concrete evidence of a crime, the Nevada County Sheriff's Office has forwarded its investigation of an **alleged** rape at Bear River High School to the district attorney's office."; "Hononegah High School officials and Rockton Police are investigating two reports of **alleged** criminal sexual abuse.")*

Often **alleged** is improperly or needlessly used. *("Twelve **alleged** white supremacists face racketeering charges under a hefty federal indictment made public Wednesday afternoon.")* If these people are indeed white supremacists, they cannot be alleged to be though perhaps the charges against them are allegations. *("The **alleged** threat was posted on www.horror.com's message board Monday night, officials said.")* If this posting is indeed a threat, it is not alleged. *("Jesse James Miller is being charged with the **alleged** murder of Derek Edward Miller of Peoria.")* If Derek Edward were murdered, the murder is not alleged though Jesse James may be the alleged murderer.

ALLITERATE

Misused for **illiterate**. • An additional 35 million are **alliterate**—they can read a few basics with difficulty, but that is about all. USE **illiterate**. • *The Washington Post* dubbed independent publishing a "bright and vital spot" in "this **alliterate** culture," pointing out that niche publishers are succeeding where others have failed by closely targeting books to specific audiences. USE **illiterate**. • Not only is it managing to dent established titles but has also succeeded in converting a sector of the **alliterate** population to the reading habit. USE **illiterate**.

*Alliterate, a verb, means to use or contain alliteration (the repetition of the same sounds at the beginning of words) in speech or writing. **Illiterate**, an adjective, means unable to read and write; violating established standards of speech or writing. SEE ALSO **literately**.*

ALLUDE

Misused for **elude**. • Oak Ridge police are still searching for a man wanted on drug charges after he **alluded** capture last Monday. USE **eluded.** • I recognize him, but his name **alludes** me. USE **eludes.** • Detective Lincoln Rhymes, the foremost criminalist in the NYPD, is put on the trail of a cunning professional killer who has continually **alluded** the police. USE **eluded.**

Allude means to mention indirectly. *Elude* means to escape capture or detection; to dodge. SEE ALSO *refer*.

The sow, dubbed Babe by the Boston press, became famous as she alluded capture for two days by local police.
—**Jeanne Miles, *The Caledonian-Record***

Herb Clay, 53, has been charged with alleged possession of a controlled substance, resisting a peace officer and fleeing or attempting to allude a peace officer, East St. Louis police have confirmed.
—**Krista Wilkinson, *Edwardsville Intelligencer***

This point obviously did not allude McDonald's officials when they presented the McCaf idea to Freeman in September.
—**Julie O'Shea, *Mountain View Voice***

To misuse *allude* for *elude* is common, and can mean only that the writers who do so—as well as their writing—are themselves common.

ALLY

Misused for **allay**. • Only a comprehensive, independent and public inquiry will **ally** fears about their safety, and get to the root of this issue. USE **allay.** • Officials have further sought to **ally** concerns that the United States seeks to be a colonial power in Iraq, going so far as to dub General Jay Garner as the "senior civilian administrator," rather than "military governor." USE **allay.**

The verb **ally** (ah-LIE) means to unite for a specific purpose; to relate. **Allay** (ah-LAY) means to quiet or calm; to lessen or alleviate.

A

ALMOND

The pronunciation of **almond** is (AH-mend), not (AL-mend).

ALOT

Idiotic for **a lot**. • Programming is **alot** of fun and even more so if you can work on a program that is used by many people all over the world. USE **a lot**. • I saw **alot** of him last season and know what he is capable of. USE **a lot**. • **Alot** of people don't realize that you produced **alot** of Tupac's *All Eyez on Me* album. USE **A lot**.

Some people misspell the word even worse: • So in a sense **allot** of people are blind to tradition and think tradition in any form is evil. USE **a lot**. • I guess it's frustrating because boxing will lose **allot** of fans over this decision even many of Oscar's critics had him winning the fight. USE **a lot**. • One thing **allot** of people don't realize is that Vince McMahon is right in your ear, he can talk to you at any given moment. USE **a lot**.

Some people—not a few college students among them—cannot even manage to spell two words, four letters, correctly. SEE ALSO **alright**.

ALOT

Misspelling of **allot**. • You still agreed to the Software License Agreement and like it or not must wait for Omega to **alot** resources to fix the Y2K problem, if and when they choose to do so. USE **allot**. • In addition, the Queen had ordered the governor to **alot** land for Swiss settlers at these branches in Virginia. USE **allot**.

Allot means to assign, apportion, or distribute. **Alot** means nothing at all.

ALPHABETICALIZE

Solecistic for **alphabetize**. • Find it quickly with our **alphabeticalized** list of all the Gateway sites. USE **alphabetized**. • There is an **alphabeticalized** directory of articles on the Parish Center main page available to guide viewers to any topic of interest. USE **alphabetized**. • How hard is it to **alphabeticalize** some files and put them in the right order on the shelf? USE **alphabetize**.

*The verb meaning to arrange words or names in alphabetical (or alphabetic) order is **alphabetize**, not **alphabeticalize**.*

Selecting the data and sorting it by their last name and then re-selecting the data and sorting it by first name will give you a list alphabeticalized by first names.
—**University of California at Berkeley**

*Though the good people at the University of California may know how to arrange first and last names, they seem not to know that **alphabeticalize** is analphabetic.*

ALRIGHT

Idiotic for **all right**. • It looks **alright** from this view, but Pooh's Bridge, near Hatfield, England, was recently condemned and rebuilt. USE **all right**. • "**Alright**, close No. 2 and 3," says the manager of the Mt. Hermon ski resort, Israel's only winter wonderland, as the sight of cable cars with legs and skis dangling from them disappears into sky soup. USE **All right**. • The next morning, I knew that everything would be **alright**. USE **all right**.

*The inclusion of **alright** in dictionaries is indefensible. If many more popular misspellings—of which there are scores—were also entries, dictionaries would be censured by people more sensible than the makers of them.*

ALTER

Misused for **altar**. • A religious **alter** was created, with candles representing God, the Spirit of Guidance, and each major religion. USE **altar**. • The main sacrificial **alter** is now closed due to vandals. USE **altar**.

A

And, of course, **altar** is sometimes misused for **alter:** • The popular TV teenager Lizzie McGuire hits the big screen with *The Lizzie McGuire Movie* complete with her animated **altar** ego. USE **alter.**

*An **altar** is a platform where offerings or sacrifices to a god are made; a table or stand used in a religious service. To **alter** is to make different; to adjust or resew a garment for a better fit; an **alter ego** is a second side of oneself, a counterpart.*

ALTERATE

Idiotic for **alter** (or similar words). • You must not **alterate** the button in any way. No changes to the graphics of the button or its size are allowed. USE **alter.** • The only way of getting a glimpse of it is shutting down normal perception and entering **alterate** states of consciousness, when the sense of unity with Ultimate Reality can be experienced. USE **altered.** • In order to **alterate** this field, the user has to change a display setting for the composition window. USE **alter.**

*Some people have a fondness for adding suffixes like **-ate** or **-ity** or **-ster** to words that they don't know the correct forms of, or that they hope to add some small significance to. **Alterate** is a barbarism. SEE ALSO **documentate**.*

ALTERIOR

Solecistic for **ulterior.** • A change of name upon marriage, dissolution, or divorce normally meets the court's requirements, provided no **alterior** motive is present. USE **ulterior.** • And yet it is this fact, this **alterior** position of the other, that draws the reader's care. USE **ulterior.** • The fee should be sent via Paypal, but really if you'd prefer an **alterior** method I'm open to suggestions. USE **ulterior.**

***Ulterior** means beyond that which is evident or disclosed; lying beyond or outside; subsequent. **Alterior** means nothing at all.*

ALTERNATE

Misused for **alternative.** • Under the **alternate** bid submitted on Wednesday of last week, the fund's investors would have received just 5% of the roughly $4.6 billion their stakes were worth at the beginning of the year. USE **alternative.** • This **alternate** route adds

36 miles to your trip so be prepared. USE **alternative**. • The natural method involves abstaining from intercourse or using **alternate** methods of birth control during fertile periods. USE **alternative**.

Commentators on English usage have long complained about people confusing ***alternate*** *with* ***alternative***. ***Alternate*** *as a verb means to occur in succession or to move back and forth; as a noun, it means a person acting for another, a substitute; as an adjective, it means every other. The adjectival* ***alternate***—*it ought to be clear by now—does not mean, as* ***alternative*** *does, providing a choice between two or more things; nor does it mean, as* ***alternative*** *does, relating to an undertaking or institution that appeals to nontraditional interests. As a noun,* ***alternative*** *is a choice between two, or more than two, possibilities.*

ALTHO

Idiotic for **although**. • **Altho** it is covered with a water-tight roof and all doors and windows are closed, the Goodyear-Zeppelin is so large that sudden changes of temperature cause clouds to form inside the hangar—and rain falls. USE **although**. • Morse is my favorite mystery **altho** I like almost any of the U.K. mysteries. USE **although**.

So, too, is **tho** idiotic for **though**: • Chrome's music score **tho** should really get some kind of an official award. USE **though**. • On the other hand, **tho**, I've never actually seen one in that condition. USE **though**.

Spelling ***although*** *or* ***though*** *with fewer letters ought to impress no one. It's not cute, it's not clever, it's not stylish, it's not smart. SEE ALSO* ***tho; thru***.

What are the appropriate ways to use *although*?

Although is a conjunction meaning "even though" or "though" or "despite the fact that" or "regardless of the fact that" (the last two, wordy phrases that ought never to be used). Many people use the word **while** where **although** (**even though** or **though**) is preferable; that is, **while** is best used, and least often misunderstood, in a temporal sense.

A

ALTOGETHER

Misused for **all together**. • I keep seeing improvement from the girls and with districts next week, now is the time to put it **altogether**. USE **all together**. • The fifth and sixth grade select chorus sang **altogether** one song called "Where do the Stars Go?" USE **all together**.

*Unlike **alright** and **alot**, **altogether** is a perfectly good word though it does not mean **all together**. **Altogether** means wholly or completely; in all; on the whole. **All together** means together; in a group; all at once.*

ALUMNUS

Misused for **alumna**. • As an **alumnus**, she can attest to the educational and athletic experience a student-athlete can receive at Bellarmine. USE **alumna**. • My speech professor told me she was an **alumnus** of Moraine and many of the alumni return to teach at Moraine. USE **alumna**. • Margaret is a senior at West Virginia Wesleyan College and is an **alumnus** of Upward Bound. USE **alumna**.

*Though many people today use **alumnus** to mean males and females alike, **alumnus** is a male graduate of a school, college, or university; **alumna**, a female graduate. **Alumni** are the male or the male and female graduates of a school, college, or university; **alumnae**, the female graduates.*

Alumni is also misused for **alumnus**: • He is an **alumni** of Cal State LA where he studied Biology and Chemistry. USE **alumnus**. • She is an **alumni** of Lincoln University, earning both her bachelor's and master's degrees in Secondary Education with a Mathematics emphasis. USE **alumna**.

AMBIVALATE

Idiotic for **be ambivalent**. • They **ambivalate** about making love, and planning to see each other again. USE **are ambivalent**. • Most of us vacillate and **ambivalate** about type on occasion. USE **are ambivalent**.

***Ambivalate**, another stillborn word from the social sciences, is meant to mean to vacillate between opposing interests, desires, or views, which of course, is what the flourishing **be ambivalent** has long meant. SEE ALSO **consequate**.*

AMBIVALENT

Misused for **ambiguous.** • Although it clearly was not the intention of the Administration to force the change for existing or already authorized projects, it is true that the language is **ambivalent.** USE **ambiguous.** • If we are of serious intent we should have watertight wording, not **ambivalent** wording. USE **ambiguous.**

And **ambiguous** is misused for **ambivalent:** • Even today when I look at photographs of the boat I have **ambiguous** feelings—a love-hate relationship! USE **ambivalent.** • **Ambiguous** feelings in Poland, for example, about military commitment in Iraq reflect the contradictory pulls of these impulses. USE **Ambivalent.**

Ambiguous means unclear; capable of being understood in more than one way. *Ambivalent* means having two different or contradictory feelings or views about someone or something. The meanings of these two words are decidedly different. Let us not waste the words we have under the false rubric, the artificial idealism, of liberalism or democracy, which as espoused by some, asserts one word may mean much the same as another. Neglecting or not knowing the distinctions between words can lead only to ambiguity and ambivalence at best, anarchy and turmoil at worst.

AMELIORATE

Misused for **alleviate.** • The liberal Democratic model assumes that society can and should be adjusted to **ameliorate** suffering, especially of the underprivileged and the newcomers. USE **alleviate.** • One of the simplest and most efficient means to **ameliorate** pain and suffering is through the use of analgesics or pain medication. USE **alleviate.**

You do not *ameliorate* pain or suffering; you *alleviate* it. *Ameliorate* means to make better; to improve. *Alleviate* means to lessen; to make more bearable.

AMEND

Confused with *emend.* To *amend* is to make better or improve; to correct or revise ("Lubbock County Commissioners had to *amend* the county's sexually oriented business regulations based on a recent supreme court ruling"). To *emend* is to make improvements or corrections, often to literary text ("Calligraphers are free agents; they *emend* texts, and elongate graphs and employ variant or archaic forms for artistic ends").

AMENDABLE

Idiotic for **amenable**. • Defensor was **amendable** to Lacson's suggestion and added he was willing to shoulder the cost in the spirit of cooperation. USE **amenable**. • Change is never easy and the membership must be **amendable** to change. USE **amenable**. • Organizations that are more idea-driven than dollars-and-cents driven can be more **amendable** to compromise. USE **amenable**.

> *Amendable* has a meaning different from that of *amenable*. *Amendable* means able to be changed or improved for the better; correctable; alterable. *Amenable* means responsive to suggestion, advice, or authority; willing. Those unaware of the distinction deserve the D.

AMIABLE

Misused for **amicable**. • Following the public lecture, there will be **amiable** discussion over lunch with the speakers and registered faculty. USE **amicable**. • Following the divorce, he and the mother maintained an **amiable** relationship and were able to effectively manage his visitations with the children. USE **amicable**.

Amicable is also misused for **amiable**: • We seek an **amicable** person to assist our receptionist with general office duties. USE **amiable**.

> *Amiable* means friendly; cordial; likeable. *Amicable* means showing goodwill or friendliness. *Amiable* is generally used to describe people; *amicable*, to describe occurrences, situations, or the relationships between people.

AMONGST

Solecistic for **among**. • But we knew **amongst** ourselves that we could get the job done. USE **among**. • He ranked fourth on the team, and first **amongst** defensive linemen, with both his 81 tackles and 57 solos. USE **among**. • It does appear that awareness is up **amongst** consumers. USE **among**.

> *Amongst*, like *amidst* and *whilst*, is an archaic term, as pretentious as it is silly. Use *among, amid, while*. SEE ALSO *between*.

The team's offensive player of the year award for the second consecutive year was shared amongst two worthy recipients.
—*Willimantic Chronicle*

However could this Chronicle *writer use the affectation* **amongst** *with the word* **two** *alongside it—a high-flown word in a low-brow sentence.*

AMORAL

Misused for **immoral.** • There's nothing inherently **amoral** or scandalous about manifesting your sexuality for a mass audience, especially when your job is to entertain. USE **immoral.** • AIDS is not a punishment or a retribution for **amoral** practices, but a problem which faces modern humankind: in 2002 in the world there were 3.2 million children infected with the virus. USE **immoral.**

*Amoral means unconcerned with or incapable of distinguishing between right and wrong; beyond the scope or morality. **Immoral** means not conforming to the accepted standards of right and wrong; wicked; lewd.*

AMOUNT

Misused for **number.** • Buy a qualifying **amount** of books and save 10% on all your subsequent purchases of non-discounted books. USE **number.** • All these methods will get you a minuscule **amount** of terrorists and a maximum **amount** of drug dealers instead. USE **number.** • In addition, actions taken to eliminate the **amount** of immigrants who are consuming U.S. jobs have created an underground economy and consequently lowered the wages for Americans as well as immigrants. USE **number.**

*The word **number** is used with that which can be easily counted (or count nouns); the word **amount** with that which cannot easily be (or mass nouns). SEE ALSO **less; much.***

A

What was interesting to me, during the recall, was the amount of people that came out to hear Schwarzenegger.

—U.S. Senator Dianne Feinstein

*If Senator Feinstein thinks of these people as a mass of people, "the masses," perhaps, and not as individuals, she might be able to convince us that **amount** is the correct word; if not, then not.*

AMPERSAND

I am in the habit of using *&* instead of *and*. Does this meet with your approval, and if not, why not?

*Use an ampersand **(&)** only in proper names—business names, book titles, and the like—that use it themselves; never use it in place of the word **and**. Aside from the hurried, the only people inclined to use **&** in place of **and** are those who have scant sense of self and scant sense of style, and believe using **&** somehow swells them both.*

- *The complete first **&** second season is available now on a DVD 4-volume set.*

- *The Goldman Sachs Foundation announces $2.5 million in grants for international education projects in Europe, Africa, Asia **&** South America.*

- *Read about our responsibilities and find passport information, visa regulations, travel tips, **&** voting procedures.*

- *My idea is also to turn you on to writers' efforts, flaws **&** fortes, **&** my interviews reveal some of the passion, adventures **&** everyday labor that goes into making a book happen.*

AN

Misused for **a.** • After **an historic** day of grand jury testimony, Clinton called on the country—and independent counsel Kenneth W. Starr—to move on from the embarrassing episode. USE **a historic.** • **An hallucination** may be a sensory experience in which a person can see, hear, smell, taste, or feel something that is not there. USE **A hallucination.** • Search for **an hotel** in France. USE **a hotel.** • This is what I would call **an human** interest story. USE **a human.**

*The correct form is **a historic**, not **an historic**. Similarly, **a hallucination** and **a hotel** and **a human** are correct; **an hallucination** and **an hotel** and **an human** are not. Conversely, **a heirloom** (like **a herb**, **a heir**, and **a heiress**) is incorrect. Since the **h** of **heirloom** is not pronounced, we say **an heirloom**. **A** is used before a consonant sound; **an** before a vowel sound. It's true that the correct wording was once **an historic**, but not since we have been pronouncing the **h** in this word and others. SEE ALSO **historic**.*

At this point, the broken consensus represents, more than anything else, an historic opportunity.
—**Laura Carlsen,** *CounterPunch*

Gengaro's all-star pitching effort had an huge effect on the whole team.
—**Michael Cheung,** *Yale Daily News*

Potential banned activities include implanting human embryos in animal bodies, attempting to fertilize an human egg with animal sperm and conceiving children by harvesting eggs and sperm from fetuses.
—**Sheri Hall,** *The Detroit News*

*There is no reason to—and every reason not to—use **an** before an aspirated **h**. Surely these writers do not say **an istoric, an uge, an uman**, but using **an** before these words suggests that they do and that we, their readers, should. You can be certain that Carlsen, Cheung, and Hall, like so many of their colleagues, do not read their own words. We, too, perhaps should not read them.*

ANAL RETENTIVE

I have noticed recently that it has become somewhat of a complement to call someone *anal retentive*. I find this description quite derogatory. Do you have suggestions for alternative descriptions or adjectives?

You mean **compliment**, *and* **something of a** *is better than* **somewhat of a**. *An anal retentive person, like me, is likely to point out your errors, whereas another might not bother.* **Anal retentive,** *though, is a charmingly apt description of someone who is exacting, orderly, meticulous, or fastidious.*

AND ETC.

Solecistic for **etc.** • The money pays for trips to day camp, uniforms, training videos on topics such as drug awareness and youth protection, snorkeling gear, life jackets, fishing equipment, scholarships, **and etc.** DELETE **and.** • Many other advanced functions for mail service like anti-spam, auto-reply, mail block, forward, search **and etc.** are all in WMS-2208R's feature list. DELETE **and.**

> *The expression* **and etc.** *is redundant; use* **etc.**—*sometimes misspelled* **ect.**—*alone.*
> *SEE ALSO* **et al.; etc., etc.**

ANECDOTE

Misused for **antidote.** • The best **anecdote** to a full day of shopping is sitting down to an unforgettable meal. USE **antidote.** • The assassination attempt upset the late King Hussein, who threatened to sever diplomatic relations with Israel unless the Jewish state provided the **anecdote** countering the chemical agent. USE **antidote.** • The **anecdote** to violence is not turning our schools into prisons. USE **antidote.** • Extracts of jewelweed have been shown in clinical studies to be an effective **anecdote** to poison ivy and oak rashes. USE **antidote.**

*An **anecdote** is a short, interesting, or amusing story about a person or event. An **antidote** is a medicine that counteracts the effects of a poison; something that neutralizes an unpleasant situation or feeling.*

ANGEL

Misused for **angle**. • The recommended numbers of lines and **angels** in the PIJ mesh are 100 and 11, respectively. USE **angles**. • The sum of two **angels** of a triangle is less than or equal to their remote exterior angle. USE **angles**.

And **angle** is misused for **angel**: • Fully one third of the **angles** in heaven were deceived by satan. USE **angels**. • The scene is a large village view with the **angles** on high and scripture verses scattered in the sky. USE **angels**.

*An **angel** is a celestial being; a seraph; a lovable, gentle person. An **angle**, a figure made by two lines or planes diverging from a common point; a scheme.*

ANNOYMENT

Idiotic for **annoyance**. • If you hide this bauble on one of your pages, you do risk major **annoyment** to any of your visitors who lack a sense of humor. USE **annoyance**. • This portion of the site contains a few ramblings for your enjoyment/**annoyment**. USE **annoyance**. • The **annoyment** level goes up as the fun quotient drops during tourist season but on an average day you almost always see someone you know. USE **annoyance**. • What are these words that men mistakenly repeat over and over that are a source of **annoyment** and can actually make you appear to be stupid because you lack a vocabulary? USE **annoyance**.

*__Annoyment__, an archaic variation of **annoyance**, has no place in today's English usage, where words for being annoyed are already superabundant.*

ANXIOUS

Misused for **eager**. • The fifty people whose lives were changed when fire ravaged their homes at the Maryel Manor senior housing complex two months ago are **anxious** for things to return to the way they used to be. USE **eager**. • I'm not **anxious** to fly, but I have to be in California. USE **eager**.

Anxious is best reserved for feelings of dread, apprehension, or uneasiness; let's not use it as a synonym for *eager*.

ANY MORE

The expression *not any more* has always meant "no longer the case" as in "you can't buy that here *any more*." However, I often hear people saying things like, "Gas is so expensive *any more*." I don't think this a proper use of *any more*; what say you?

Anymore (not *any more*) is used in the sense of "today" or "nowadays" when the sentence in which it appears is negative: "Gas isn't so expensive anymore." **Anymore** in a nonnegative sentence like "Gas is so expensive anymore" is fairly common among speakers in the midwestern and western United States. People who care about how they speak, and about being understood, would do well to shun this dialectal usage.

ANYMORESO THAN

Solecistic for **any more than.** • And let's not forget that being Jewish is no guarantor of appropriate behavior **anymoreso than** any other religious affiliation. USE **any more than.** • It is not beyond the limits of your intelligence to comprehend the differences between truth and deception, **anymoreso than** between right and wrong. USE **any more than.** • HumanKin do not want to destroy magical things **anymoreso than** OtherKin want to destroy human things. USE **any more than.** • Why should we be exposed to these egotistical and amateurish Karaoke singers **anymoreso than** all these poorly conditioned and ill-trained backyard wrestlers? USE **any more than.**

Any more than, not *anymoreso than*, is the correct wording.

ANYWAYS

Solecistic for **anyway.** • What is a blog **anyways**? USE **anyway.** • What time is it, **anyways**? USE **anyway.** • **Anyways**, I guess the best thing about birthdays is you get to hear from people you haven't heard from for a while. USE **Anyway.**

Labeling **anyways**—like **anywheres, somewheres,** and **nowheres**—dialectal, as many dictionaries do, is too kind; let them label it what it is: uneducated. SEE ALSO **in regards to**.

He was executed somewheres around December 1974.
—**Howard Dean, politician**

This ignominious s may fell anyone who pronounces it—the best of us, perhaps, more easily than the rest of us.

APPRAISE

Misused for **apprise.** • There is a thermocouple, which is a heat probe, connected to a digital controller, that keeps me **appraised** of the exact salt temps and can be used to control the temperature automatically, though I don't regularly use this feature. USE **apprised.** • Obviously, we cannot keep up with day-to-day changes, if any, in the methodology unless the vendor keeps us **appraised** of the changes and that is why we will cease showing numbers on his system. USE **apprised.**

*The word **appraise** means to evaluate or estimate; **apprise** to inform or notify. To use **appraise** when **apprise** is meant not only may confuse your audience but also may eventually eliminate from the language a unique word.*

And throughout it all Laing executives held meetings in residents' homes and City Councilman Alex Padilla's office to keep the neighborhood appraised of progress.
—**Gregory J. Wilcox, *Los Angeles Daily News***

APPRECIATE

A

Idiotic for **value** (or similar words). • I **appreciate** you, and what you do. USE **value**. • I know I've said it time and again, but I do **appreciate** you my friend. USE **treasure**. • He's dedicating a lot of time to make sure our national finance effort is as strong as I know it's going to be. I **appreciate** you, Mercer. USE **thank**. • There are not enough words in the world to tell you how much I love you, how much I **appreciate** you, or how much I want to thank you. USE **admire**. • She keeps me straight on all my links and I **appreciate** her very much. USE **respect**. • Tell your brothers that you **appreciate** them, but they need to back off. USE **love**.

> You can **appreciate** an attribute or occurrence ("I appreciate her thoughtfulness"; I appreciate your coming"), but not a person ("I appreciate you"; "I appreciate so many folks enduring the rain").
>
> Using **appreciate** in the sense discouraged here is the mark of people who have no notion of eloquence and style, little understanding of the limits of language, and scant insight into themselves or their audience.

> Thank you for your interest in Patrick Henry College. We appreciate you.
>
> **—The Trumpet of Liberty, Patrick Henry College**

APROPOS

Solecistic for **appropriate**. • They've had three years to get it right and the timing could not be more **apropos**. USE **appropriate**. • The setting will be **apropos**, since the museum currently has forty-eight paintings by fifteen Highwaymen artists on exhibit in its art gallery. USE **appropriate**.

> **Apropos** (ap-rah-POE) means in regard to; relevant. **Appropriate** means suitable or fitting.

ARCHITECT

Idiotic for **design** (or similar words). • Advanced modeling tools based on Visio enable developers to **architect** applications, design databases, and model business processes. USE **devise**. • You'd never ask an interior designer to **architect** a house, and you probably wouldn't go with an architect's opinion of a color scheme for the walls of your living space. USE **design**. • Howard Alan's vision is to **architect** buildings that are of the continuous present. USE **engineer**. • They were faced with the dilemma of how to **rearchitect** the existing site and deliver a high-quality application to their customers on a timely basis. USE **redesign**.

> *To **architect** is an absurdity. Not everyone can concoct an effervescent verb from some stolid noun. Though nouns do indeed occasionally become verbs, **architect** is hardly a good candidate, for many other words already provide the definitions, and more exacting ones at that. A word not born of need begets only noise.*

ARTIC

Misspelling of **arctic**. • But by the afternoon, the wind rolled in like a blast straight from the **Artic**. USE **Arctic**. • However, to advocate the exploitation of the **Artic** National Wildlife Refuge and other protected spaces in the United States is irresponsible. USE **Arctic**. • In the film, Adam plays Henry, an **artic** wildlife veterinarian who spends his spare time breaking the hearts of female tourists. USE **arctic**.

> ***Arctic** is spelled with two **c**'s: **arc**, **tic**. Only the hopelessly insular spell the word with one **c**. The pronunciation of **arctic** is (ARK-tik), not (AR-tik).*

AS

Misused for **because** or **since**. • Very little goes to waste, **as** almost the entire creature is edible. USE **since**. • Enthusiastic capitalists are rarely conflicted about turning away from an open palm, **as** most believe that the U.S. economy offers everyone a fair shot and therefore losers are just plain losers. USE **since**. • That does not happen now, however, **as** there is just too much mail. USE **because**. • The situation may be worse **as** 12 of the 43 schools surveyed did not respond. USE **since**.

> ***As** instead of **because** or **since** is sometimes ambiguous for the word **while**, and therefore is best not used casually. What's more, **as** is decidedly colloquial; it is used by everyday, uninspired writers and speakers.*

A

ASCETIC

Misused for **acetic**. • While the accident was contained to the southbound lanes, traffic was halted on all four lanes because of some spillage of **ascetic** acid solution, which was described to city-county Emergency Operations Center dispatchers as "paint thinner." USE **acetic**. • Citric acid seems to be the most dominant acid flavor, and I do not detect much in the way of **ascetic** acid. USE **acetic**.

And, yes, **acetic** is misused for **ascetic**: The mummies in question are the remains of an obscure cult of mountain-dwelling Buddhist monks known as the Yama-bashi—literally "he who lives in the mountain"—famous for their extremely **acetic** lifestyle. USE **ascetic**.

Acetic *means like, containing, or producing vinegar or acetic acid.* ***Ascetic*** *means self-denying or austere.*

ASCETIC

Misused for **aesthetic**. • Installation of a new storm door takes about two hours and may greatly improve the **ascetic** beauty at the front entrance of your home. USE **aesthetic**. • The flowers are not just for **ascetic** pleasure, but have amazing flavoring qualities. USE **aesthetic**. • Citizens Against Ugly Street Spam is a non-profit organization formed to fight against the proliferation of advertising signs placed along roadways for the sole purpose of advertising at the expense of the **ascetics** of the community. USE **aesthetics**.

Ascetic means pertaining to or characteristic of an ascetic; rigid in self-denial or devotions; austere; severe. ***Aesthetic****, which might easily mean the opposite of* ***ascetic****, relates to aesthetics or what is beautiful; artistic; pleasing in appearance; attractive. SEE ALSO* ***aesthetic***.

ASCRIBE

Misused for **subscribe**. • The Iraqi people did not **ascribe** to Saddam's thoughts, nor did the majority of them support his regime. USE **subscribe**. • Those in the center, on the other hand, believe the extremists are ideologically arrogant and are likely to **ascribe** to the philosophy espoused in the famous Indian legend, The Blind Men and the Elephant. USE **subscribe**. • I know that some well-known popular bands **ascribe** to this theory, so I suspect that there is some truth to it. USE **subscribe**.

To **ascribe** is to attribute something to; to assign as a quality. To **subscribe** is to support or believe in; to pledge money; to sign one's name to a document; to sign up and pay for a regular publication or service. SEE ALSO **prescribe**.

If legislators truly ascribe to the notion that "less government is preferable to more," a fresh look at the state and federal funding of unemployment compensation would seem an ideal fit.

—**Jon Zahm,** *The Illinois Leader*

Scribbler Zahm, a scribe indeed. Trust no one who does not know the meaning of his words. A person who does not know the meaning of his words does not know the meaning of his sentences and may not know the meaning of himself.

ASSAY

Confused with **essay**. To **assay** is to determine the content or quality of; to analyze or evaluate ("To predict their deleterious effects, various in vivo or in vitro tests have been proposed to **assay** the xenoestrogenic activity"). To **essay** is to try out; attempt ("Such a ball can cramp a batsman, making it difficult for him to **essay** a positive stroke").

ASSENT

Misused for **ascent.** • The door had locked behind him and the small aircraft was beginning its **assent** into space. USE **ascent.** • Theme Park Inc. promises to include an on-going narrative based around your projected **assent** up the corporate ladder. USE **ascent.** • Another steep **assent** puts you on top of the world amongst scenic high lakes, meadows, and snow-capped peaks. USE **ascent.**

Assent *means agreement or consent.* **Ascent** *means the act of rising or climbing; an upward slope; an advancement in status.*

ASSERTATION

A

Misused for **assertion**. • I would dispute your **assertation**. USE **assertion**. • I can't say enough that this **assertation** is categorically, absolutely and unconditionally wrong. USE **assertion**. • Given Miller's **assertation** that he knew of "at least three" teams willing to pay Boozer's $10.97 million salary, it appears that other teams have called to inquire about the forward. USE **assertion**.

> *Assertation*, *a thoroughly obsolete word used by fearfully modern people, is incorrect for* *assertion*. *Assertation—like the equally preposterous* *documentate* *(instead of document) and* *opinionation* *(instead of opinion)—is spoken or written by people who do not know the words they use, by people who do not read, by people who believe adding a syllable or two to a word adds to its meaning: humanity lies elsewhere.*

ASSIDUOUS

Misused for **acidulous**. • Duchamp himself developed a profound and **assiduous** wit throughout his artistic career, to the extent that his works have been described as forms of wit themselves. USE **acidulous**. • I enjoyed *Armageddon*, but it can't really be viewed as an **assiduous** commentary on the danger posed by asteroids and comets. USE **acidulous**.

> *Assiduous means diligent; persistent.* *Acidulous means tart or sour in taste or manner.*

ASSUME

> *Confused with* *presume*. *To* *assume* *is to suppose something to be so, and is based on possible evidence; to* *presume* *is to believe something to be so, and is based on probable evidence.*

ASSUME

Idiotic for **as soon**. • Last year was Lowe's worst in the majors, so it was somehow fitting that it was also a season Varitek would just **assume** forget. USE **as soon**. • Although it was fast becoming the entertainment and gambling Mecca of the world, the city was dogged by an image as a haven for crooks, thieves, and any other unsavory characteristic a city would just **assume** not be associated with. USE **as soon**.

Assume, instead of **as soon**, *is mind-numbingly stupid. SEE ALSO* **wearas**.

The Red Sox want Rodriguez to re-structure his contract, and Scott Boras would just assume wash some of the slime off his skin before allowing that to happen.

—Eric Wilbur, *The Boston Globe*

Sports writers at The Boston Globe, *though they may know the difference between a football and a baseball, don't know the difference between* **assume** *and* **as soon**, *for the first sentence example shown in this entry was also composed by a* Globe *sports writer.*

ASTERISK

The pronunciation of **asterisk** *is (AS-tah-risk), not (AS-tricks) or (AS-trick).*

AS TO

Solecistic for **about** (or similar words). • Suddenly expectations and preconceptions **as to** how things should be done and what steps could be taken disappear, often leaving the displaced family members feeling confused. USE **of**. • For example, testing of a graphics library will require a very different approach **as to** that of a calendar manager. USE **from**. • Depending on the night, the meal, and the energy of the evening, I also made distinctions **as to** the drink best suited to the occasion. USE **in**.

As to the phrase **as to whether**, delete **as to**. • If your browser is not secure, or there is any question **as to whether** or not it is, please download Netscape Navigator, Microsoft Internet Explorer, or an equivalent browser. DELETE **as to**.

*Except when used to begin a sentence, **as to** is if not solecistic then certainly sloppy for a more precise **about** or **of**, **for** or **with**, **from** or **to**, **on** or **in**. This phrase, midsentence, identifies a philistine, a person who, though he writes, doesn't much care to.*

A

ASTRONOMY

Misused for **astrology**. • We are raised in a highly Western civilized religion based society where it is wrong and evil to believe in psychics and **astronomy** and horoscopes. USE **astrology**. • An official in the Presidential Security Service is paid to prepare **astronomical** horoscopes of the leaders of the nation. USE **astrological**.

* **Astrology** is the study of the positions of the sun, moon, and stars so as to foretell the future or determine human affairs. **Astronomy** is the scientific study of the universe. SEE ALSO **cosmology**.*

ATHLETE

*The pronunciation of **athlete** is (ATH-leet), not (ATH-ah-leet).*

AUGUR

Misused for **auger**. • For the past several weeks Goldstake field crews have been correlating mapped diamond and **augur** drill hole and surface trench data with the actual sites on the property. USE **auger**. • Ten inches from the ground in each of the posts, make a hole 3 inches by 1 inch, by boring three holes with an inch **augur** and clearing them out. USE **auger**.

And **auger** is often used where **augur** should be: • Recent developments **auger** well for the public availability of a new class of drugs that appear to alleviate deficits in learning and memory and may also show promise in the treatment of schizophrenia. USE **augur**. • We do not **auger** future events, but rather focus upon present circumstances. USE **augur**.

*An **auger** is a tool used to make holes; as a verb, it means to bore or drill. An **augur** is a soothsayer, prophet, or diviner; as a verb, it means to predict or presage. **Augury** is an omen or the interpretation of omens.*

AURAL

Misused for **oral**. • Feedback was in the form of weekly tutorials and **aural** remarks during reviews and written comment and marks for assessment of the students' work. USE **oral**. • The other class participants observe and offer both written and **aural** comments and suggestions. USE **oral**.

*Aural means heard through the ears; relating to the ears or hearing. **Oral** means uttered by the mouth; relating to the mouth or speaking. People who confuse **aural** with **oral**, though pronounced alike, may not know their ears from their mouth. SEE ALSO **verbal**.*

AUTHENTIFICATION

Solecistic for **authentication**. • The Justice Ministry has been found to be testing a high-tech voice **authentification** system for surveillance of some violent and sexual offenders released on either bail or probation. USE **authentication**. • A certificate of **authentification** signed by the late Maris comes with the etching. USE **authentication**.

*The verb is **authenticate**, and the noun is **authentication**, not **authentification**.*

AVENGE

*Confused with **revenge**. **Avenge** (a verb) implies getting even for a previous wrong or injustice, one often done to a third party ("Arshad believed he had to **avenge** a stain on his family's honor"; "Inmates had feared the guards would try to **avenge** the death of their colleague"). **Revenge** (a verb or a noun) implies a mean-spirited or malice-driven retaliation ("The Independent reported that Kulwant Singh did this in **revenge** after being spurned by Amex"; "A man was charged with shooting another man to death apparently out of **revenge**, just days after the victim had been acquitted of murdering the suspect's cousin").*

AVERSE

Misused for **adverse**. • In addition, dosage guidelines and **averse** effects of these therapies are presented. USE **adverse**. • Natural doesn't necessarily mean allergy-free, of course—fruits and plants can cause **averse** reactions on sensitive folk,

A

just like the man-made stuff—but consider this: Everything your skin absorbs ends up in your bloodstream. USE **adverse**. • Despite the **averse** weather most caught well from the start with only four blanks recorded over the two days. USE **adverse**.

And **adverse** is sometimes used for **averse**: • Risk **adverse** market participants need to know the most likely cost of environmental response and most likely value of the impaired property. USE **averse**.

*The word **adverse** means antagonistic or adversarial; unfavorable or harmful.*
***Averse** means having a feeling of distaste, repugnance, or aversion; disinclined.*

AWAY

Misspelling of **aweigh**. • As *USS Cowpens* arrives for the International Fleet Review, crew members man the rails while the 7th Fleet Band plays "Anchors **Away**." USE **Aweigh**.

***Aweigh** (used of an anchor), not **away**, means hanging clear of the bottom. Similarly, you **weigh**, not **way**, anchor. ("Ground tackle can become so firmly snagged on an underwater cable or pipe that attempting to **way** anchor can cause the boat to capsize.")*

AWESOME

Idiotic for **excellent** (or similar words). • Our **awesome**, super child cross stitch will blow you away and help you to get more of what you deserve. USE **first-rate**. • These **awesome** calendars feature photos and illustrations and remind us of special occasions. USE **superlative**. • We went to Fire and Ice to eat which was **awesome** and then we drank and drank and drank. USE **excellent**.

***Awesome** ought to be used to mean inspiring awe, fear, or admiration; extremely impressive or intimidating. In the informal sense of excellent, it is a very poor choice of words indeed. More than that, people who use **awesome** to mean excellent are, in fact, describing something that is, to keener minds, invariably mediocre or ridiculous.*

A WHOLE NOTHER

I am aware of school children and public speakers splitting *another* in two: *a whole nother thing* is one example. What is the linguistic explanation for this error?

*Among educated speakers, **a whole nother thing** is sometimes used jocularly—though the humor of this phrase and others like it often escapes me. Perhaps a clever person thought of this arrangement as an example of tmesis, a rhetorical figure in which one word is made into two (**another** > **a nother**) or a word or phrase is added between parts of a compound word or between syllables of a word (**a whole nother**).*

A delightful example of tmesis is found in the song "Wouldn't It Be Loverly" from My Fair Lady:

> *Oh so loverly sittin'*
> *Abso-bloomin-lutely still.*
> *I would never budge*
> *Til Spring crept over the window sill.*

*Among uneducated or slang-loving speakers, **a whole nother thing**, however, is just another example of dull-witted, ungrammatical English.*

B

BACK SLASH

Confused with **forward slash**. The forward slash (or slash) is the name of the **/** character on a computer keyboard. It leans forward. The **back slash** is the name of the **** character, which leans backward.

BACKWARDS

Misused for **backward**. • Each state can be selected in order or random, so a **backwards** step or a jump of several steps is as simple to implement as a single step forward. USE **backward**. • It follows the lives of seven disparate people: a rock musician and his teenage groupie, two ruthless corporate sharks, an innocent **backwards** youth and his older brother, and a mysterious (and disarmingly droll) shaman. USE **backward**.

*As an adverb, either **backwards** or **backward** is correct. As an adjective, only **backward** is correct. SEE ALSO **forwards**.*

BAD

Solecistic for **badly**. • In Britain you will never find a paper that speaks **bad** about that country. USE **badly**. • During pregnancy her calories will increase, but only if she eats **bad** will she get fat or crave even junkier foods. USE **badly**.

***Bad** is an adjective; **badly**, an adverb. Sensory verbs like **feel, taste**, and **smell** are followed by the adjective **bad**, not the adverb **badly**: ("If the water is safe but smells **bad**, there are steps you can take to reduce or eliminate the problem"; "Remember that lots of people say mean things because they feel **bad** about themselves."; "Anytime potential government benefits flow to friends and relatives it looks **bad**.") SEE ALSO **feel badly**.*

BALEFUL

Misused for **baneful**. • Locutional sloppiness and hyperbole reign in health advocacy literature, where advocacy has displaced scholarship and the only allowable peer review or criticism is that which arraigns authors for underemphasizing the baleful effect guns have on society. USE **baneful**.

> **Baleful** means menacing or ominous, portending evil; **baneful**, the stronger though less often used word, harmful, destructive, or fatal. The distinction between these two words should be observed.

BASICLY

Misspelling of **basically**. • Basicly, the philosophy is this: If you have a strong team then you should trade down some of your talent for youth during the offseason. USE **Basically**. • The IRW library allows reading basicly any type of color data (palette, images) in basicly any color space. USE **basically**.

> The much written and spoken **basically** is used by people who do not think; **basicly**, by people who do not think well or spell well.

BATE

Misused for **bait**. • A bated electric fence has a foodstuff attached to the wire fence strand that, when the deer sniffs or licks it, will shock them. USE **baited**. • Felipe Ortiz, 48, fishing in Colombia, cast a line into the teeth of a gale and suffocated when the bated hook blew back into his throat. USE **baited**.

And **bait** is misused for **bate**: They produce an outstanding selection of finely crafted guards that can be combined with epee, generic schlager, and baited rapier blades. USE **bated**.

> To **bate** is to abate; to lessen or moderate; to restrain; to flap the wings furiously; to blunt. To **bait** is to entice or lure; to torment; to tease; to feed an animal. As a noun, **bait** is food used to trap or lure an animal; an enticement. The idiom is **bated breath**, not **baited breath**.

BATHOTIC

B

Solecistic for **bathetic**. • Originally, I had planned some scathing comments on the death of the much-beloved-by-the-media John-John. But I've decided to leave the **bathotic** commemoration to just the title of this issue and be done with it. USE **bathetic**. • From its hyperbolic style and **bathotic** self-importance many might conclude that the piece in question is a spoof of the kind familiar to readers of this paper. USE **bathetic**.

*The adjective of **bathos** is **bathetic**, not **bathotic**.*

BEAUROCRAT

Idiotic for **bureaucrat**. • The only difference is that the person who earned it will decide how it is spent instead of some **beaurocrat** in Washington. USE **bureaucrat**. • I am the expert when it comes to motorcycles, not some **beaurocrat** who's never even been near a bike. USE **bureaucrat**. • He was an academic **beaurocrat**; he taught at the academy three times a week. USE **bureaucrat**.

__Bureaucrat__ (from French bureau, office, *and Greek,* krates, ruler) *alone, is the spelling.*

We don't need beaurocrats to tell us what to teach!
—*Oxford University Press*

Does the Oxford English Dictonary *consider **beaurocrat** to be an acceptable variant spelling of **bureaucrat**? The* New Oxford American Dictionary *(2005) does allow* **agritainment, trustafarian, phishing,** *and* **ginormous**; *perhaps* **beaurocrat** *is also an entry. According to these lexicographers, all words, all spellings, all usages are allowable.*

BEAUTIFY

Misused for **beatify**. • Showing the frailty that marked her last days, Pope John Paul II **beautified** late nun Mother Teresa in Vatican City Sunday, October 19, for of up to 300,000 people, one of its largest crowds ever. USE **beatified**.

*Beautify means to make beautiful. **Beatify** means to declare a deceased person to be in heaven and entitled to public veneration; to make blissfully happy.*

In order to encourage us in becoming holy, our Holy Father has canonized and beautified more persons during his pontificate than any of his predecessors on the Chair of Peter.

—**Bishop Paul S. Loverde, *Arlington Catholic Herald***

It's true that beatification happens rarely, but not so rarely that Bishop Loverde and the Catholic Herald *shouldn't know the difference between **beatify** and **beautify**.*

BECKON CALL

Solecistic for **beck and call**. • If your significant other has a load of homework or tests, don't expect that person to be at your **beckon call**. USE **beck and call**. • Many of Cox's customers have become unwilling and unknowing cyborgs at the **beckon call** of people all over the world. USE **beck and call**.

*A **beck** is a gesture of beckoning; a wave or nod. To be at someone's **beck and call** is to be always ready to fulfill a wish. **Beckon call** is as incorrect, as ridiculous, as **for all intensive purposes** (instead of **for all intents and purposes**), **assume** (instead of **as soon**), **off the beat and path** (instead of **off the beaten path**), and **wearas** (instead of **whereas**).*

BEHEADED

Why is someone *beheaded*, and not *deheaded*?

The **be-** in **behead** (from ME biheden and OE beheafdian) is a prefix meaning "away from" or "cut off or away." This use of **be-** is also found in less known words like **bedeal** (to deprive; bereave), **benim** (to take away; bereave), **beshear** (to shear or shave or cut off), and **bereave** itself. The prefix **de-** (as in **decapitate**) means "remove from."

BEING THAT

Solecistic for **since** (or similar words). • There is an especial irony in Bush criticizing Syria and Iran as illegitimate dictatorships, **seeing that** it was the United States which destroyed Syria's young parliamentary democracy in 1949. USE **since**. • This is a grand scale project, **being that** it is a full curriculum covering math, science, social studies, language arts, physical education, art, and more! USE **in that**. • **Being that** the *Stockton Record* story never ever released the public information as to what revitalization idea did cause Stockton to win the State Enterprise Zone award, things have been changed. USE **Considering that**. • **Being as how** the year is 2003 and this is the "land of opportunity," I am both supportive of the ruling and shocked at how many people are against it. USE **Given that**.

> **Being that**, like **seeing that, seeing as (how)**, and **being as (how)**, is uneducated English. Literate alternatives to these expressions include **because, considering that, given that, in that**, and **since**.

BELIE

Misused for **betray** (or similar words). • Stress interviews can **belie** trouble within a company, such as a difficult boss, long hours or impossible workload. USE **reveal**. •

The Return of the King's weaknesses do stem from exaggerations and intrusions that **belie** the screenwriters' misinterpretation of Tolkien's convictions. USE **betray**.

> *Belie means to give a false impression of; to contradict; to show to be false or wrong. Betray means to show unknowingly; to disclose; to reveal.*

BEMUSE

Misused for **amuse**. • This play will delight and **bemuse** you with its nimble humor. USE **amuse**. • Breakfast treats such as "Nuddy Nubble Abblestuffel," "Phantasmagoria," and a "Humpty Dumpty" house specialty continue to **bemuse** and entertain our guests. USE **amuse**.

Many people, clumsy writers all, will use **bemuse** and **amuse** together, perhaps to increase their chances of, with one word or the other, saying what they mean to: • Back when he was living in Moe, Greg Domaszewicz used to **amuse** and **bemuse** friends with tales of flying saucers and alien abductions. • Enjoy this collection of poems which will alternatively **amuse**, **bemuse**, and give you pause for thought.

> *Bemuse means to confuse or stupefy; to absorb in thought. Amuse is to entertain; to cause to laugh or smile.*

BETWEEN

> *Confused with **among**. **Between** is most often used with two objects or people ("Some of it is spewed by journalists who feign expertise in the Middle East, but couldn't tell you the difference **between** a Sunni or a Shiite"; "Some people might wonder about the connection **between** ethics and diversity"); **among** with three or more ("Terry was **among** about 200 or so people who turned out for The TechExec"; "Rafe Esquith of Hobart Boulevard Elementary School was **among** ten people honored by President Bush Wednesday"). **Between** is also the correct word to use if, no matter how many people or things are being discussed, one person or thing is being considered in relation to one other person or thing ("Even **between** provinces, there are differences in the way statistics are kept"; "The common link **between** the three destinations—and the perfume itself—is the watery floral accord"). SEE ALSO **amongst**.*

I wish he had said here that "between you and I " is too often heard. Me is not a bad word, I say.

B

Perhaps there's strife because there's some type of anger or disagreement among the boyfriend and girlfriend.

—Dr. Alvin Poussaint, Harvard Medical School

*The redoubtable Dr. Poussaint misspoke; the strife, doubtless, is **between** the boyfriend and girlfriend.*

BIANNUAL

*Confused with **biennial**. **Biannual** means twice a year; semiannual ("If you tried, you probably couldn't come up with a more rigorous test of a relationship than producing a **biannual** poetry journal"). **Biennial** means once in two years or lasting two years ("Crop producers in Manitoba are advised to be on the lookout next year for **biennial** wormwood, a native weed that appears to be making a comeback"). SEE ALSO **bimonthly**.*

BIMONTHLY

*Confused with **semimonthly**. Because **bimonthly** is commonly used to mean either twice a month or every other month, it may be better to use twice a month or every other month. **Semimonthly** also means twice a month, but some people may not know this word for it is seldom used.*

*The same holds for **biweekly** and **biyearly**: biweekly may be used to mean either twice a week or every other week, and **bimonthly** may be used to mean either twice a month or every other month. **Semiweekly** means twice a week, and **semimonthly** means twice a month. SEE ALSO **biannual**.*

BIZARRE

Misused for **bazaar**. • For not only did they provide us with the use of their property for this charity **bizarre**, but they also are allowing us the use of their extensively stocked dungeon and their private clinic. USE **bazaar**. • It was like having a Middle Eastern **bizarre** right here in the middle of the Forest Mountains. USE **bazaar**.

> ***Bizarre*** *means weird or very odd; unexpected; fantastic or grotesque. A **bazaar** is a market or street of shops, especially in Middle Eastern countries; a shop that sells a variety of goods; a sale of various items, often to raise money for a club or group.*

BLATANT

Misused for **flagrant**. • Moreover, to open it up to other Clinton scandals would put Lowell at the center of a **blatant** conflict of interest. USE **flagrant**. • Sometimes **blatant** injustice is committed in the name of security requirement or under the pretext of saving one's own country or even humanity. USE **flagrant**.

And **flagrant** is misused for **blatant**: • Straight-laced companies might have discouraged such **flagrant** displays of color, but not Yahoo! Kimo. USE **blatant**. • Having worked for them for the better part of a decade, I witnessed how managers told **flagrant** lies to get Apple's business. USE **blatant**.

> ***Blatant*** *means offensively loud or clamorous; conspicuous or obtrusive.* ***Flagrant*** *means glaringly offensive or deplorable; scandalous.*

BLESSING IN THE SKY

Misused for **blessing in disguise**. • Triple H was a terrible champion in 2003, and it was a **blessing in the sky** when he finally lost to Bill Goldberg later in the year. USE **blessing in disguise**. • And like a **blessing in the sky**, I found out that Lennie, an ex-officemate, actually emcees professionally through her blog. USE **blessing in disguise**.

> *The correct expression is **blessing in disguise**.*

BLINDSIGHTED

Misused for **blindsided**. • They say they're trying to improve our education, but they are being **blindsighted** by their own selfishness. USE **blindsided**. • Brokers, never knowing the current risk appetite of a given carrier can not afford to be **blindsighted** by a competitor. USE **blindsided**. • It's so easy to be **blindsighted** by romance, but the rose-colored glasses eventually have to come off. USE **blindsided**.

Blindsight, a noun, is the ability of blind people to respond to stimuli they are unable to see. *Blindside,* a verb, is to be attacked or struck, literally or figuratively, from an unseen or unexpected direction. Why do you suppose some people say *blindsighted* when they mean *blindsided*? Is it not because they neither read nor listen well? Is it not because they feel one word is as good as another? Is it not because dictionary makers and descriptive linguists promote and applaud blind choice, blind chance?

B

BOAT PEOPLE

I'm an editor with the *Daily Press* in Newport News, Va., and I'm requesting your assistance on a delicate newsroom issue. Recently, the Associated Press published a chronology on the Haitian uprising, in which the term *boat people* was used to describe the immigrants who traveled by boat to the United States. While I realize that term has been used since the 1970s when Vietnamese people came to the U.S. via boats, I feel that there is no room for its use in today's media, unless for historical references. What is your position on this topic?

The flight of the Vietnamese by boat is not likely to recur, but refugees elsewhere still occasionally leave their land by boat. Though **boat people** originally referred to Vietnamese who fled their country by sea, today—since the word is still being used to define similar occurrences—it refers to any refugees fleeing their country by boat. **Boat people**, then, has two definitions: (1) refugees who, in small boats, fled South Vietnam after the invasion by the North Vietnamese; (2) any refugees who leave their land by boat in an effort to immigrate elsewhere.

Of the six dictionaries I evaluated in the Fiske Ranking of College Dictionaries (Appendix A), Oxford American (*OA*) and Webster's New World (*NW*) define **boat people** best, most completely. American Heritage (*AH*) defines the word worst—that is, not at all.

I'm an editor with *The Morning Call* in Allentown, Pa., and I'm interested in an issue you discussed. I noticed that you merely defined the term *boat people* instead of answering the question. You didn't take a position on whether the phrase is appropriate or offensive. Again, what is your take on the term?

*Was she asking if I found the term **boat people** offensive? Maybe so. I thought she was asking my opinion of the term's correct definition and whether **boat people** is appropriate to use when describing non-Viet-namese immigrants.*

*No, I do not find **boat people** offensive if it designates refugees who emigrate from their country via small boats. You might also describe them as "refugees who emigrate from their country via small boats." If the term is used to suggest another meaning, then perhaps, in those instances, the person who uses the term is being offensive.*

BOUGHT

Misused for **brought**. • The lack of an appropriate memorial was **bought** to my attention by the Birmingham Air Raids Remembrance Association. USE **brought**. • They have been duping the people since the president was **bought** to power. USE **brought**. • These itinerant winemakers **bought** with them a wealth of viticulture and viniculture knowledge. USE **brought**.

*Bought is the past tense of buy; **brought** is the past tense of bring. SEE ALSO **boughten**.*

BOUGHTEN

Idiotic for **bought**. • If using store **boughten** veggies that are waxed, such as cucumbers and zucchini, it is best to peel them. USE **bought**. • Stocker cattle, either **boughten** or carried over from the previous year's calf crop, should also be culled. USE **bought**.

*The past tense of **buy** is **bought**, not **boughten**, which is nonstandard, or more accurately, uneducated English. SEE ALSO **bought**.*

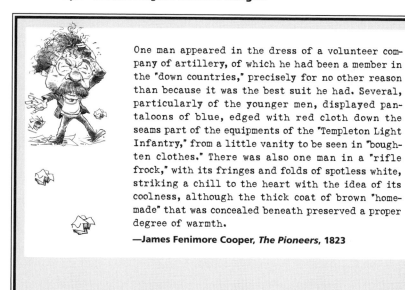

One man appeared in the dress of a volunteer company of artillery, of which he had been a member in the "down countries," precisely for no other reason than because it was the best suit he had. Several, particularly of the younger men, displayed pantaloons of blue, edged with red cloth down the seams part of the equipments of the "Templeton Light Infantry," from a little vanity to be seen in "boughten clothes." There was also one man in a "rifle frock," with its fringes and folds of spotless white, striking a chill to the heart with the idea of its coolness, although the thick coat of brown "homemade" that was concealed beneath preserved a proper degree of warmth.

—James Fenimore Cooper, *The Pioneers*, 1823

BRAGGADOCIOUS

Idiotic for **boastful** (or similar words). • We're full of it. We're vain. We're **braggadocious**. USE **conceited**. • As for that **braggadocious** young associate, his days at the firm were numbered. USE **bigheaded**. • He knew that being **braggadocious** would bring people to his fights and give black people pride. USE **arrogant**.

*Though the noun **braggadocio** (a braggart) is a word, the adjective **braggado-cious** is not. Let us admire those who use the word **braggadocio**, and mock those who use **braggadocious**.*

I don't want to sound braggadocious, but I do have the biggest buildings in the city.
—**Donald Trump, businessman**

BREATH

Misused for **breathe**. • The enriched oxygen seems to **breath** new life into tired aging skin, making it look more youthful and have a glow. USE **breathe**. • They possessed the equipment to **breath** in water and on land, and were one of the first amphibious animals. USE **breathe**.

*The verb is **breathe** [BREETH]; the noun is **breath** [BRETH].*

BREECH

Misused for **breach**. • Although we will do our best to work with our customers in the event of a **breech** of policy, we will also take a firm line when necessary to protect our other customers and network. USE **breach**. • The vibrations created by the marching and the shouts of the people caused a **breech** in the wall large enough for Israel's army to march through. USE **breach**.

And **breach** is misused for **breech**: • Super heated Plasma from the reactor is injected into the **breach** of the rifle where it is contained and focused by a magnetic field. USE **breech**. • If there is a **breach birth** the baby would take its first breath while its head was still in the birth canal. USE **breech birth**.

*A **breach** is an act of breaking the law, terms of an agreement, or expected conduct; a break in relations; a gap in a wall or barrier. A **breech** is the part of a firearm at the back of the barrel; the buttocks; the lower part of a pulley block. A **breech birth** occurs when a baby's buttocks or feet are delivered first.*

BREECH

B

Solecistic for **broach.** • I really respect that kind of honesty, and have **breeched** the subject at times to encourage fellow pioneers to bring some integrity to the table in such matters. USE **broached.** • When discussing changes in the current severance package, **breech** the topic within the context of changes of other benefit plans. USE **broach.** • Since we've **breeched** the subject, I have to say the Associated Press poll shows John Kerry doing better with women by 1 percentage point than Al Gore did with women. USE **broached.**

> **Breech** the noun has several meanings; as a verb, it has two meanings, both rarely used and little known: to put (a boy) in **breeches**; to provide a gun with a **breech**. **Broach** the verb has several definitions, but the one that's mistaken for breech means to raise for discussion.

BRIDAL

Misused for **bridle.** • Featuring a horse with saddle and **bridal**, proud foal, posable rider, bucket, bag of oats, brush and trophy, this collection provides quality play for the imaginative young rider. USE **bridle.** • They take one incident at a time in isolation and not only don't they put them together, they **bridal** at the idea that they should be put together or dismiss the idea out of hand. USE **bridle.**

> **Bridal** as a noun means a wedding or marriage ceremony; as an adjective, it means relating to a bride or wedding ceremony. **Bridle**, as a noun, means a horse's harness, and **bridle path** is a trail used for horseback riding; as a verb, **bridle** means to harness or restrain, or to show anger or resentment.

BRING

Misused for **take.** • Please keep copies of all documents you **bring** to your interview for your own records. USE **take.**

And **take** is misused for **bring:** • I know you're leaving for a final now so you won't want to carry this, but don't forget to **take** it when you come in on Monday. USE **bring.**

> Use **bring** to indicate movement toward the person who is speaking or being spoken to; use **take** to indicate movement away from the person who is speaking or being spoken to.

Where has the word *take* gone? Before moving east many years ago I had never heard anyone say, "*Bring* this over there" or "*Take* that over here." To me, the difference in the meaning of *bring* and *take* is as great as the difference between *up* and *down*. For many years it just seemed to be local usage by various groups but now no one ever *takes* anything somewhere, they always *bring* it there.

I've tried to raise my kids to *take* things there and *bring* things here. If I'm at the table they have to *bring* the plates to the table, but if we're all at the table, they have to *take* the plates to the sink. If we're in the process of leaving the house they may *bring* their friend along, but if we haven't left yet, they may *take* their friend with us. I just get blank stares when I try to explain this difference. Could you please, please give me a clear rule on the use of these words?

Your explanation is as good as, perhaps better than, any I have read.

*Use **bring** when the action comes toward whoever is (understood to be) speaking, or wherever the speaker is speaking from (even if implied).*

*Use **take** when the action goes away from whoever is (understood to be) speaking, or wherever the speaker is speaking from (even if implied).*

- *But they have been forced to tell their guests to **bring** a gas bill with them if they want to get into Holyrood.*

*The action is toward the people doing the telling, so **bring** is correct.*

- *The first-prize winner could **take** home more than $20,000.*

*The action is away from wherever the prize is awarded, so **take** is correct.*

- *Looking for an extra-special place to **take** the family this summer?*

*The action is away from one's home, so **take** is correct.*

*Few people, however, bother to distinguish between **bring** and **take**, and fewer still, today, have any notion of their being, or of there ever having been, a distinction between these words' meanings. Still, the distinction should be observed, especially by those who value clarity, precision, and elegance in language.*

BROACH

B

Misused for **brook**. • Believing themselves to be divinely inspired, they **broach** no dissent, and will argue with vehemence that they've been led by God. USE **brook**. • I will **broach** no arguments on the subject. USE **brook**. • They **broach** no nonsense from petty officialdom and would rather spend an hour by the roadside than pay a bribe to a policeman. USE **brook**.

> **Broach** means to start a discussion about; to bring up; to announce. To **brook** is to put up with; to endure; to tolerate. **Brook** is usually used with the word **no**: "brook no dissent."

CACHET

Misused for **cache**. • The brother of the political head of KLA was just arrested with a large **cachet** of arms and some $800,000 in cash, the first such arrest by NATO. USE **cache**. • With home-baked cake and a secret **cachet** of sweets, the bedrooms live up to the Latin name, meaning "everything is a dream." USE **cache**.

And **cache** is misused for **cachet**: • Slate talks about the brand name **cache** of Starbucks coffee, BMW cars and Godiva chocolates for the middle class to outwardly demonstrate status. USE **cachet**.

Cachet (kah-SHAY) is a mark that indicates something is authentic, genuine, or superior; a distinction; a seal on a document; a commemorative design or motto stamped on an envelope; a medicinal wafer or capsule. Cache (KASH) is a hiding place for storing supplies, weapons, valuables, or other items; the items stored.

Because few people know the meaning of these two words, and fewer still the difference in their pronunciations, we can be sure that dictionaries will soon offer (KASH) as a variant pronunciation of cachet, and (kah-SHAY) as a variant of cache. Dictionaries: the new doomsday books. SEE ALSO loathe.

```
I think if Arnold had not been an action hero,
and, say, he had been in ten movies where he was
the super villain, it may have hurt his celebrity
cache a little bit.
```
—John Orman, political science professor

```
We've been working very closely within Iraq to try to
find cachets of cash, as we have found to date.
```
—Juan Zarate, U.S. Department of Treasury

Professors and government officials, equally untaught, do not know the difference between cachet and cache.

CACOPHONY

Idiotic for **mess** (or similar words). • Without a way to organize, house and label wires, the desk, baseboards and nooks behind the monitor or PC tower can become a **cacophony** of cluttered cables. USE **jumble**. • My kahlua pork sandwich ($6.95) was a **cacophony** of flavors—tender pork chunks roasted in banana leaves accompanied by sweet mango pico and cilantro spread made interesting by the addition of musky rye seeds. USE **mix**. • Our city has become part of the **cacophony** of cities each with their own ordinances that conflict in substance with each other. USE **confusion**.

C

> *The word **cacophony** refers to noise—not to cables, not to flavors, not to cities—discordant, jarring noise. The meaning of **cacophony** is easily understood: the prefix **caco-** means bad, and the suffix **-phony** means sound. You might speak of "a cacophony of criticism" or "a cacophony of color," but in this sort of example, **cacophony** suggests a metaphorical dissonance.*

> Legitimate business needs to have clear rules of the road. We really have a cacophony of laws.
> **—Trevor Hughes, Network Advertising Initiative**

CADILLAC

Misused for **catalytic**. • We were a strong competitor throughout the competition, but then the **Cadillac** converter fell off, which hurt our emissions and place in the overall standings. USE **catalytic**. • 1997 Pontiac Trans Am WS6 (ram air) convertible, automatic black leather interior, red exterior with black top. A/C, ABS, cruise, cassette with 12-disk CD changer, keyless entry, always covered, second owner and 3" pipe from **cadillac** converter full-master exhaust. USE **catalytic**.

> ***Cadillac** (KAD-il-ak) is the name of a car. **Catalytic** (kat-il-IT-ik), an adjective, means of or involving a catalyst. A **catalytic converter**, a device attached to automobile exhaust systems, converts harmful gases to harmless products.*

CALLUS

She had all the privledges a young woman could want. She lived this life to the fullest until a brutal attack on her sister by the son of one of the wealthiest families in the country showed her that her world was cold, callus and cruel.

—Angela Winters, author

Angela Winters—we are doubtless informed by Angela Winters—is the "national bestselling author of several romance and romantic suspense novels and short stories." Maybe so, but her novels might be replete with misspellings if these two sentences are any indication.

CALVARY

Misused for **cavalry.** • After months of anticipation, members of the 278th Armored **Calvary** Regiment said goodbye to loved ones. USE **Cavalry.** • The troops will be opposing the 1st **Calvary** Division, working as an enemy force during extremely lifelike fighting. USE **Cavalry.** • Beck said the charge, which wiped out the remaining Confederate troops at Fort Collier and effectively ended the 1864 battle, was the largest **calvary** charge in American history. USE **cavalry.**

Calvary is the place where Jesus was crucified; calvary, with a lowercase c, is any representation of the crucifixion of Jesus; intense anguish or suffering. Cavalry is an army's combat troops, whether on horses or in armored vehicles. SEE ALSO crucifiction.

CAN

*Confused with **may.** **Can** expresses ability to do something ("The system incorporates a seven-inch camera shaped like a fish and connected to a cable that **can** be lowered up to 60 feet below the ice"; "In the classroom and out, male teachers are living* *proof that men **can** be just as smart—and nurturing—as women"). **May** expresses possibility or permission to do something ("Fencing along the Line of Control by India **may** hamper the peace process between two countries"; "You **may** attend only one grocery distribution site per seven days"). The words today are often used interchangeably, but the consequence of this is that the meaning of the sentences in which they are used is sometimes unclear and confusing. SEE ALSO **might**.*

CANNON

Misused for **canon.** • Other fans of The Force have taken it upon themselves to distill it into a religious **cannon**, taking the film scripts as their scripture. USE **canon.** • The female writer's "battle for self-creation" and her struggle for a permanent spot in the literary **cannon**, involves her in a revisionary process. USE **canon.** • If jazz is to remain a living music any sort of inventive reinterpretation of its musical **cannon** is necessary and should be welcomed. USE **canon.**

> *A **cannon** is a piece of artillery; an automatic or laser gun; the loop on the top of a bell by which it is hung. **Canon** is a body of rules or principles; a decree issued by a church; a body of religious writings; the list of Roman Catholic saints; a Roman Catholic prayer; a complete set of artistic or literary works; a musical composition.*

CAN'T HELP BUT

Solecistic for **can't help ...-ing.** • We **can't help but go** back past the electric motor, past the telephone, all the way back to the first controlled fire, when our awed ancestors tried to figure out how to use a new tool. USE **can't help going.** • I **couldn't help but glance** into the room as Hartley worked her magic. USE **couldn't help glancing.** • With the stores chock-full of cupids, chocolates, and hearts of every size and description, I **can't help but smile and think** that all of those mushy poets, songwriters, and sentimentalists were on to something really good for us. USE **can't help smiling and thinking.** • As hopes of victory faded, Hyde **couldn't help but complain** bitterly about being sold out by Senate Republicans. USE **couldn't help complaining.** • Tymberly Wes Fields **can't help but laugh** when she thinks about her job. USE **can't help laughing.**

> *Popular though the expression is, **can't help but** is less defensible (since some critics maintain it is a double negative) than **can't help ...-ing**, which also sounds better—and sound counts for something.*

CANTOR

Misused for **canter.** • The horses are well trained and responsive to all levels of riders, whether you want to walk, trot, **cantor**, or gallop. USE **canter.** • I know the tempos and rhythms that horses trot or **cantor** or gallop in, and I know the adagio nature of certain wire acts or trapeze acts. USE **canter.**

*A **canter** is a slow, easy pace of a horse. A **cantor** is the singer of the liturgy in a synagogue.*

CAN'T SEEM TO

Solecistic for **seem unable to.** • Everyone at this photo shoot so obviously loves Melissa Etheridge that they **can't seem to** keep their hands off her. USE **seem unable to.** • Unlike Karen, who **can't seem to** get to Grace's office before 11 a.m. and complains at only having four hours for lunch, Megan is always striving to perfect her craft. USE **seems unable to.**

*Though **can't seem to** is considered acceptable idiomatic English, it sounds awkward; **seem unable to** is more logical and sounds more euphonious.*

CANVAS

Misused for **canvass.** • Extensive public workshops and meetings were held in 1998 to **canvas** the public's views about solid waste management. USE **canvass.** • In formulating Esap, Chidzero was determined to **canvas** opinion far and wide, drawing upon the expertise of as many as possible, and to be aware of the detailed circumstances impacting upon all facets of the economy. USE **canvass.** • The meeting was designed to **canvas** views of trends in the nuclear and regulatory fields against the background of changing economic and decision-making processes. USE **canvass.**

*Canvas is a strong, heavy, unbleached cloth; **canvass** is a survey; as a verb, it means to survey or question.*

CAPITOL

Misused for **capital**. • Additional words in the function name should begin with a single **capitol** letter. USE **capital**. • Newark is the **capitol** of stolen cars. USE **capital**. • The one city that didn't own a public utility was Kutztown, Pa., which is located between Philadelphia and Harrisburg, the **capitol** of the state. USE **capital**. • God has declared in his Word that whosoever wrongfully takes the life of an unborn child shall be guilty of a **capitol** crime. USE **capital**. • The whole point of capitalism is unabashed growth, the accumulation of **capitol**, wealth and power. USE **capital**.

And **capital** is misused for **capitol**: • There were trees and limbs strewn all around the **capital** building, too. USE **capitol**.

> The word **capital** has several meanings: a city, usually the seat of government of a country; principal or chief; a capital letter; a city or town associated with a particular industry or activity; wealth; a valuable resource; and so on. The word **capitol** has but one meaning: a building that houses a state legislature.

CAREEN

Misused for **career**. • Drivers cruise—or **careen**—down Woodland Hills as an alternative to Loop 323. USE **career**. • Is the band's decision to keep its follow-up down and dirty an effort to keep from **careening** too quickly toward pop stardom? USE **careering**.

> **Careen** (kah-REEN) means to lean to one side; to lurch from side to side; to tilt a ship in order to clean or maintain the bottom of the hull ("A missile struck the Ch-47 Chinook and sent it **careening** into an Iraqi field"; "A pirate's least favorite part about coming to land was **careening**, or beaching the ship and cleaning the hull"). **Career** (kah-RIR) means to rush; to move at full speed ("While his friends fine tune their parallel parking, 17-year-old James Sutton will be **careering** around race tracks at speeds in excess of 150 mph").

CARET

Misused for **carat**. • The gold detail is antiqued in 24 **caret** gold leaf. USE **carat**. • Until last summer, they had never sold a two **caret** diamond and they had wondered why. USE **carat**.

And **carat** is misused for **caret**: • Leave the text **carat** in the field where you entered the ID. USE **caret**. • The **carat** (^) symbol acts as a dynamic left alignment position for all of the lines that contain it within a given text object. USE **caret**. • Use the **carat** symbol to indicate powers; for example, type as x^2 or as x^(1/3). USE **caret**.

*A **caret** (^) is a symbol traditionally used to indicate where text is to be inserted in a document, but also used in mathematical and computer-related notation. A **carat** is a unit of weight for precious stones and pearls; (also spelled **karat**) a unit of measure of the purity of gold.*

Carrot is also misused for **carat**: • The Gold Paralympic medals are made out of solid silver with a 24 **carrot** gold coating. USE **carat**.

*A **carrot** is a plant or vegetable; an inducement.*

CATTERWALL

Misspelling of **caterwaul**. • And the left won't respond as they only want issues to **catterwall** about, not solutions. USE **caterwaul**. • We are getting little to no sleep as she keeps us up all night with her moaning and **catterwalling**. USE **caterwauling**. • Since 1980, the life expectancy rate among men and women is ten years higher despite the **catterwalling** that we're all getting fatter. USE **caterwauling**. • If she left him out there, he'd raise the dead with his **catterwalling**, and if she let him in, well, God knew what would happen. USE **caterwauling**.

*As a verb, **caterwaul** means to wail or moan like a cat in heat; to make a shrill, jarring sound. As a noun, it is a harsh, cacophonic noise. **Catterwall** is an unacceptable spelling.*

Maria. What a catterwalling doe you keepe heere? If my Ladie haue not call'd vp her Steward Maluolio, and bid him turne you out of doores, neuer trust me.

—William Shakespeare, *Twelfth Night*

CELEBRATE

Misused for **celibate**. • The idea of young girls forced into a state of chastity and working with so-called **celebrate** priests is also questioned in the film. USE **celibate**. • Some undertake strict vows to remain **celebrate** throughout life, never to accept service from others and in this way lead a life of extreme hardship. USE **celibate**. • Many gay people never make it past acknowledging themselves as gay; they may remain **celebrate** throughout their lives or they may cave in to society and live a life that is not natural to them. USE **celibate**.

> *Celebrate*, *a verb, means to commemorate with festivity; to honor or mark with a celebration.* *Celibate* *is an unmarried person; one who vows to abstain from sexual intercourse.*

CEMETERY

Misused for **seminary**. • I once heard Dr. David A. Seamands from Asbury Theological **Cemetery** say that woman's ministry is fine and should not be discounted because of an obscure verse (1 Cor. 14:34–35) in the Bible. USE **Seminary**. • He was a graduate of Wheaton College and Westminster Theological **Cemetery**, Philadelphia. USE **Seminary**.

> *A* *cemetery* *is a graveyard. A* *seminary* *is a school that trains candidates to be priests, ministers, or rabbis.*

CENTURION

Misused for **centenarian**. • Aristophus was called Aris (pronounced Ayres) and lived to be a **centurion** in an age when this was rare. USE **centenarian**. • **Centurion** Lizzie Leonard of Tourlestrane died peacefully in Enniscrone last Thursday January 10. USE **Centenarian**. • More than one million of these baby boomers are expected to live to be **centurions**, living to be 100 years old and older. USE **centenarians**.

> *Centurion* *is the commander of a century in the Roman army; one who has scored or achieved 100 in any way.* *Centenarian* *is a person who is 100 years old or older.*

CHAFF

Misused for **chafe.** • Perhaps their new confidence in their ability to make decisions and tendency toward criticalness causes them to **chaff** at authority. USE **chafe.** • While you appreciate the vast history and resources of the Council, you also **chaff** at their sometimes stifling procedures, directives and politics. USE **chafe.**

> *Chaff is the husks of grain separated in threshing; anything worthless; strips of metal used to confuse enemy radar; good-natured teasing. **Chafe** means to rub in order to make warm; to wear away or make sore by rubbing; to become annoyed or irritated because of some constraint.*

CHAISE LOUNGE

Solecistic for **chaise longue.** • Just take a peek into any interior design magazine, and you will see touches such as Wenge dining tables, Italian marble floors and micro-suede **chaise lounge.** USE **chaise longue.** • Place upholstered chairs or a **chaise lounge** in the bedroom to provide a more inviting and personal feeling in the room. USE **chaise longue.** • Beautiful, sunny days were made for this elegant **chaise lounge.** USE **chaise longue.**

> *Chaise longue (shaz LONG) is French for long chair. Lazy, lolling Americans, however, prefer **chaise lounge** (shaz LOUNJ), doubtless for lounge chair.*

CHALK FULL

Misused for **chock full.** • It's a great family film about little-league baseball that is **chalk full** of baseball action and delivers a powerful possitive message. USE **chock full.** • It is hard to tell the West Orange-Stark Lady Mustangs are not **chalk full** of seniors on their roster, especially on Monday against the Ozen Lady Panthers. USE **chock full.**

> *Chock full (chock full) means as full as possible. **Chalk** is a limestone composed of calcite from sea shells and used for writing on a blackboard.*

CHILDISH

Misused for **childlike**. • To win his love you should assume a sweet and **childish** behavior. USE **childlike**. • The music and the choreography are a fine balance between **childish** awe and adult dreams, and never lapse into nauseous sentimentality. USE **childlike**.

> **Childish** means immature; infantile. **Childlike** means naive; innocent; guileless.

C

CLEAN

Idiotic for **cleanliness** (or similar words). • Add one cup to each gallon of warm water and sponge mop, then allow to dry for a fresh smelling **clean** that kitchens and bathrooms deserve. USE **cleanliness**. • A **clean** you can smell; a **clean** you can trust. USE **cleanliness**.

> Evidence that some people—marketers and advertisers more than most—have contempt for their audiences is their using the abomination **clean**. Some words are to be cherished, some to be questioned, and some, like the noun **clean**—and whoever uses it—to be disdained.

> SuperMat clean is a clean you can see.... SuperMat clean is a clean you can feel.... SuperMat clean is a clean you can hear.
>
> **—Kleen-Tex Industries**
>
> ---
>
> KleenTex is a company you can tease. ... KleenTex is a company you can mock. ... KleenTex is a company you can scorn.

CLICHÉ

Solecistic for **clichéd**. • Despite the **cliché** theme of a shameless trip to Vegas, there are enough random elements thrown in to keep the film interesting. USE **clichéd**.

• The obvious weakest link among the boys in Korn is the lead singer Jonathan Davis, who not only cannot hold a note, sing a melody, or hit any decent range, but also writes some of the most **cliché** lyrics in modern rock. USE **clichéd**. • Anything from gospel choirs to pop music to show tunes—I hate to be so **cliché**, but it's true. USE **clichéd**.

*The adjectival form of **cliché** is **clichéd**. If we would rely less on speaking, writing, and even behaving in **clichés**, we would have less need to use the word, however it might be formed. SEE ALSO **copyright**; **prejudice**.*

Most people in the U.S. picture the classic and cliche woman-flat-on-back kind of labor.

—Susan Ashmore, *American Baby*

*From someone who uses **woman-flat-on-back** as a compound adjective—often a sign of an unaccomplished, a clunky, writer—we cannot very well hope for **clichéd** instead of **cliché**.*

CLICK

Misused for **clique**. • It is not uncommon to go places and see that certain social **clicks** exist; and most of the members of the **click** find it difficult to interact with members of other **clicks**. USE **cliques; clique, cliques**. • I have probably insulted or upset every little social **click** that exits in modern society today, but that was not my intention. USE **clique**.

*A **clique** (KLEEK) is a small, exclusive group of people; a coterie. A **click** (KLICK) is a slight, sharp sound; the press of a computer mouse button; a part of a mechanical locking device; a sound made by the tongue against the soft palate.*

CLIMATIC

Misused for **climactic**. • From his first walk-on to his **climatic** battle scene, classical stage actor John Vickery plays the kind of villain that *Lion King* fans will happily boo. USE **climactic**. • By the time this becomes a plot point, Gibson has teamed up with his own clone and begun the **climatic** attack on Drucker's headquarters.

USE **climactic**. • The final confrontation between Sabrina and Amanda may seem **anti-climatic** for some players. USE **anti-climactic**.

And **climactic** is misused for **climatic**: • The travel agent shall not be responsible for any injuries, damages or losses caused to traveler in connection with terrorist activities, social or labor unrest, mechanical or construction difficulties, diseases, local laws, **climactic** conditions, abnormal conditions or developments, or any other actions, omissions or conditions outside the travel agent's control. USE **climatic**.

C

Climatic means of or relating to climate. *Climactic* means relating to or constituting a climax.

The climatic battle is indeed a big, clever pay-off.

—Mike Ward, Richmond.com

But until the climatic battle scenes and predictable reunion of mother and daughter, the missing in "The Missing" refers more to the absence of Maggie's father in her life.

—Mike Ward, Richmond.com

*However many times Mike Ward uses it, **climatic battle** will never be correct.*

CLOTHS

Misused for **clothes**. • All the doctor has to do is go over the area with a sort of brush, without the patient ever even taking his **cloths** off. USE **clothes**. • We got by with black and white TVs, hanging our wet **cloths** on a line to dry, washing dishes by hand and throwing our potato peels in a pail instead of down the drain. USE **clothes**.

Cloth is a fabric such as cotton, silk, or wool. *Clothes* are wearing apparel and are usually made of *cloth*.

So maybe the quarterback of the football team is not hiding the Batmobile in the basement of his student-housing building. Maybe he doesn't wear the Flash's red spandex jumpsuit under his street cloths. But that doesn't mean he is not a superhero.

—Heather Mathews, Portland State University *Vanguard*

He may be a hero, but she, Ms. Mathews, does not seem to be. Heroes aren't simply noble warriors or sports figures, they are also common people who are uncommonly aware of how they use the language. They are the people who, despite weak-willed lexicographers, descriptive linguists, peer-fearful adolescents, and others as pitiable, know the distinctions between words and observe them.

COLLABORATE

Misused for **corroborate**. • As our feedback reflects, we applaud some comments that **collaborate** our views on the proposals for further enhancement of relay services across the nation. USE **corroborate**. • At this point, we really only have Daniel's word and to back it up, it would be necessary to find Aerojet employees or White Sands people who could **collaborate** his statement. USE **corroborate**.

*Whereas **collaborate** means to work together to accomplish something, **corroborate** means to confirm the truth of something. If people fail to enunciate their words, if they do not distinguish their liquid l's from their liquid r's, dictionary makers will one day dictate that these two words sound alike and mean the same.*

COLLISION

Misused for **allision**. • The Canadian Navy said that the damage was likely from a **collision** with a dock, but had not happened while the Victoria was in Canadian possession. USE **allision**.

*A **collision** (kah-LIZH-en) occurs when one object or person hits, and is hit by, another object or person. An **allision** (ah-LIZH-en) occurs when only one of the objects (usually a ship) is moving.*

COLUMNIZE

Idiotic for **write.** • Anyway, let me know what your interests are, and if you want to **columnize** with us! USE **write.** • Whenever something frightening happens, columnists like me hasten to **columnize** about the anxieties of absentee parents; wire services follow the tragedy daily; and there is a hue and cry over the need for better regulation of the day-care profession. USE **write.**

*Whatever is the point of **columnize**? Will we soon also have to endure **paragraphize** and **articleize**? Columnists write columns, articles; only the least able, or the most Corinthian, of them would say **columnize**.*

COMMITED

Misspelling of **committed.** • Witnesses say the assault was **commited** in front of neighbors and a school bus full of children in a LaVerne neighborhood. USE **committed.** • Hastert says the U.S. must stay **commited** to Iraq and that it would be very irresponsible to pull coalition forces out prematurely. USE **committed.**

*There are two **t**'s in **committed** and **committing**, but only one in **commit** and **commitment**.*

COMMODITIZE

Idiotic for **commodify** (or similar words). • I think this is where we start to find the sense of the deal as part of AOL's strategy to deploy and **commoditize** interactive services. USE **commodify.** • Thus IBM needs to **commoditize** enterprise software, and the best way to do this is by supporting open source. USE **commodify.** • Standardization tends to **commoditize** a product or technology. USE **commodify.**

*
Commodify means to turn into or treat as a commodity—which is also what **commoditize** is meant to mean. In other words, **commoditize** is likely a word born of error and ignorance, perhaps of people mispronouncing **commodify**. This is not,*

*as descriptive linguists might maintain, an example of the evolution of English; it's an example of its devolution, its—when one word isn't distinguished from another (in this instance, a good, useful word from a bad, useless one)—**commodification** (not **commoditization**). And the commodification of the language can result only in the commodification of the people who use the language.*

COMPARABLE

*The pronunciation of **comparable** is (KOM-per-ah-ble), not (kom-PAIR-ah-ble).*

COMPASSIONATED

Idiotic for **compassionate** (or similar words). • We provide a 24-our dignified, **compassionated** and dedicated funeral service. USE **compassionate**. • Dr. Hobson has a special interest in diseases of the breast and his sensitive and **compassionated** approach endears him to our breast patients who often face serious illnesses. USE **compassionate**. • Through house-to-house gatherings called Hope Parties, we are helping **compassionated** people like you learn more about this crisis, and providing opportunities to make a difference in the life of a hurting child. USE **compassionate**.

*Though **compassionated**, in the sense of pitied or sympathized with, was used by Mary Wollstonecraft Shelly, Anne Brontë, Charles Dickens, Sinclair Lewis, Frederick Douglass, Herman Melville, Abraham Lincoln, and others in the past, it is not used today, in the sense of **compassionate**—except by people who do not read Shelly, Brontë, Dickens, Lewis, Douglass, Melville, Lincoln.*

I've got a record, a record that is conservative and a record that is compassionated.

—U.S. President George W. Bush

COMPLAISANT

Misused for **complacent**. • It is vital for all of us to be most careful that we don't become **complaisant**; that we aren't willing to live with the good instead of striving for the best. USE **complacent**. • Have we become so smug, so **complaisant**, so sure that it can't happen here, that we can sit idly by and watch as it does, in fact, happen here? USE **complacent**.

Complacent means self-satisfied or contented; *complaisant*, eager to please.

C

COMPLECTED

Solecistic for **complexioned**. • The victim claims that two dark **complected** males stole her tote bag from her. USE **complexioned**. • Hyperpigmentation and hyperpigmented lesions are more prominent components of photoaging in darker **complected** individuals. USE **complexioned**.

Complected is informal, substandard usage; *complexioned*, standard.

COMPLIMENT

Misused for **complement**. • Gamma Telecom has today announced the launch of Gamma Access, a new value added service to **compliment** its expanding wholesale termination services. USE **complement**. • We **compliment** each other, so the cumulative result is greater than two individual funny performances. USE **complement**. • Orange is the **compliment** of blue, yellow is the **compliment** of purple, green is the **compliment** of red. USE **complement**.

And **complement** is misused for **compliment**: • Watt was trying to be funny: Watt was actually paying them a **complement**. USE **compliment**. • So while we can't recommend *Our Lady of the Assassins*, we take some delight in the backhanded **complement** the film pays to Catholicism. USE **compliment**.

A *compliment* is a remark of praise or admiration; an act that shows respect or tribute. A *complement* is something that adds value or completes; one of two things that makes a whole; a quantity of people or things that completes a group or unit.

COMPRISE

Misused for **compose**. • Together, these four parts **comprise** the NGWS runtime architecture. USE **compose**. • Altogether 1,548 digitized segments **comprise** the shoreline system of the study area. USE **compose**.

And **compose** is misused for **comprise**: • The album **composes** eleven songs, mostly mellow sounding albeit sometimes romantic but never boring. USE **comprises**. • The business immigrant category for Canada **composes** three components: self-employed immigrants, entrepreneurial immigrants, and investor immigrants. USE **comprises**.

> The distinction is thus: The whole **comprises** the parts ("The United States **comprises** fifty states"); the parts **compose** the whole ("Fifty states **compose** the United States").

Comprises is also far better than the wordy **is comprised of** or **is composed of**: • The list this year **is comprised of** 335 law firms. USE **comprises**. • The hydrogen atom **is composed of** a proton (which serves as the nucleus) and an electron. USE **comprises**.

COMPULSORY

Misused for **compulsive**. • The Code also sets out what are not disabilities such as substance abuse, **compulsory** gambling, self-imposed body adornments or normal deviations in height, weight and strength. USE **compulsive**. • Sven Hassel must be characterized as a **compulsory** liar, with a habit to dress up in uniforms, with lots of medals. USE **compulsive**.

> **Compulsory** means obligatory; mandatory. **Compulsive** means something that is compelling; obsessive.

CONCAVE

> Confused with **convex**. **Concave** means curved inward like the inside of a ball ("Mike Russell said his daughter, delivered by Caesarean section, didn't turn pink and her stomach was **concave**, so sunken it appeared to touch her backbone"). **Convex** means curved outward like the surface of a ball ("Unlike traditional tooth-

brushes that have a **concave** or flat bristle surface, the new Curvex toothbrush has a patented **convex** head and tapered bristle array that is designed to better contact the surfaces of teeth, front and back "). A cave is **concave**; a mound, **convex**.

CONCENSUS

Misspelling of **consensus**. • The **concensus** in Ottawa is the banks have not made that case, despite extensive public relations campaigns and behind-the-scenes lobbying. USE **consensus**. • **Concensus** is a sportsmanlike approach to group decision-making, which avoids the win/lose situation sometimes caused by voting. USE **Consensus**.

People would do well to remember that the only **c** in **consensus** is the one that begins the word.

CONFIDENT

Misused for **confidant**. • He was a **confident** to his sister, three years his junior. USE **confidant**. • A **confident** to the Queen in the early years of her reign, he had been suffering from liver cancer. USE **confidant**.

Confident means assured; full of confidence. A **confidant** is a trusted friend with whom one shares intimacies.

CONFLICTED

Solecistic for **torn** (or similar words). • Many such parents feel **conflicted** about segregating their children in special classes but think they have no alternative. USE **have conflicting feelings**. • The single most important element to a successful production of *Julius Caesar* is to see Brutus as a truly honorable, yet **conflicted** soul whose actions belie his intentions. USE **torn**. • My guess is that you have underlying and perhaps, **conflicted** feelings about the way this change occurred. USE **conflicting**. • A **conflicted** relationship with a partner often means there is a nonexistent sex life. USE **uneasy**. • Our western science and religion is **conflicted**, reflecting our Judaic and Christian mix of philosophy, theory, and practice. USE **in conflict**.

And some people apparently use **conflicted** to mean war-torn or embattled: • RON-CO involvement in humanitarian demining in **conflicted** countries evolves from 20 years experience with worldwide development and humanitarian assistance contracts. USE **embattled.** • The war on drugs cannot alone explain why the U.S. is sending 60 Black Hawk and Huey helicopters to this **conflicted** nation. USE **war-torn.**

If the people who use **conflicted** *instead of* **conflicting, torn,** *or* **uneasy** *mean to suggest they also are* **afflicted**—*with what horror one can only wonder—there may be reason to forgive this usage. If not, then not.*

CONFUSED

The pronunciation of **confused** *is (kon-FYOOZD), not as some would have it, (kon-FYOOZ-ed).*

CONGENIAL

Misused for **congenital.** • DiGeorge's syndrome is a **congenial** defect resulting in absence of a thymus. USE **congenital.** • Of these chronic defects include **congenial** heart disease, anomalities of the urinary tract and genitals, and spina bifida. USE **congenital.** • It may not be easy, given that once a **congenial** liar, always a **congenial** liar. USE **congenital.**

Congenial *means compatible; having the same qualities or interests; agreeable.* **Congenital** *means existing from birth; inherent or well established.*

Jake and Alyssa (Arp) Laughlin shared the story of their baby son, Cole, and his struggle with a congenial heart defect.

—North Scott Press

The staff at North Scott Press should be humiliated by their having used **congenial** *instead of* **congenital,** *for it rather strikingly suggests that the concern they have for the people in their stories is no greater than the care they take in writing their stories.*

CONGENIAL

Misused for **genial**: • My **congenial** taxi driver, Mohsen, insisted that we approach the Old City from a little-used side road that provided the most dramatic vista. USE **genial**. • It requires a **congenial** climate and suitable soil for the seed to grow into a tree. USE **genial**.

Genial means affable or friendly; mild and favorable to growth.

C

CONGRADULATE

Misspelling of **congratulate**. • Over 3000 wrestlers signed already; **congradulation** to all of you. USE **congratulation**. • Pro K-9 would like to **congradulate** Officer McClure and Officer Nelson and their K-9 partners Oky and Nash. USE **congratulate**.

*Despite how it is often pronounced, **congratulate** is spelled with a **t**, not a **d**.*

CONNOTATE

Solecistic for **connote**. • I think the difference between the words denote and **connote** is one of those important distinctions people need to know about words. USE **connote**. • The reference to "God's eyes" is an Old Testament term used to **connotate** divine oversight of God in the life of an individual or group of people. USE **connote**. • Obviously, therefore, a white elephant in India's cultural context can never **connotate** redundancy, as it would in the West. USE **connote**.

*Connotate is, or ought to be, obsolete. **Connote**, to suggest or imply meaning in addition to the explicit meaning, is the word to use. SEE ALSO **denotate**.*

CONNOTE

*Confused with **denote**. **Connote** means to refer to implicitly; to suggest ("I had grown up in a culture where academic titles are at a premium and **connote** awe and respect"). **Denote** means to refer to explicitly; to mean ("The showy red flowers will **denote** the school building as a drug-free building").*

CONSCIENCE

Misused for **conscious**. • We are faced with a number of situations whose full understanding goes beyond our **conscience** thoughts. USE **conscious**. • First, an eating disorder is an illness that affects several of the United States population because society has driven many people to be **self-conscience** about their appearance. USE **self-conscious**.

And **conscious** is sometimes misused for **conscience**: • It is based on the honor system, so let your **conscious** be your guide. USE **conscience**.

> *Conscience, in brief, is the inner sense of right or wrong that influences one's actions and behavior; equally briefly, **conscious** (an adjective) means having an awareness of oneself and one's environment.*

CONSEQUATE

Idiotic for **discipline** (or similar words) • When our students say or do something profoundly antisocial, we must not only **consequate** the behavior and insist on alternatives, but address the values and norms that make such behavior possible. USE **punish**. • The school personnel should discuss the nature of their existing systems to **consequate** undesired behavior. USE **discipline**. • You also should not wait until you get home to **consequate** the behavior, as this diminishes the effectiveness of the intervention. USE **censure**.

> *Like the equally counterfeit to **consequence**, to **consequate** means (1) to discipline, penalize, or punish; to reprimand or scold; (2) its user is a social scientist or a professor of education—a fraud or a fool. SEE ALSO **consequence**.*

They are not going to change unless you consequate their behavior.

—Dr. Phil McGraw, television personality

Those in the business of social behavior, like Dr. Phil, need to make up preposterous words so that their counsel is not so easily understood; were it, their authority might be readily dismissed.

CONSEQUENCE

Idiotic for **discipline** (or similar words) • Be willing to **consequence** defiant or resistant individuals. USE **punish.** • With these ideas in mind, Fay concludes that the most effective way to **consequence** is to: Lock in the empathy and then lower the boom. USE **discipline.** • My probation officer may choose to **consequence** me for not showing up. USE **discipline.**

Not yet in many dictionaries, the politically correct, though completely inane and pathetic, to **consequence** *is increasingly used by psychologists and human resource personnel, themselves often inane and pathetic. SEE ALSO* **consequate.**

CONSUL

Confused with **council.** **Consul** *is a government official who represents his country's business interests in a foreign country ("French Vice* **Consul** *Olivier Arribe is in this city on a goodwill visit with Utah's political, religious, business and education leaders").* **Council** *is a legislative body or group of delegates who administer, discuss, consult, or advise ("Harpersville Town* **Council** *members will ask Mayor Gloria Tate to resign Monday following her arrest last week"). SEE ALSO* **council.**

CONTEMN

Misused for **condemn.** • The Armenian president thanked the House of Representatives for its preceding decision to **contemn** the Armenian genocide by the Turks. USE **condemn.** • When the French captured the Castle of St. Andrews, Knox as a prisoner was **contemned** to row in the French galleys for nineteen months. USE **condemned.**

To **condemn** *(kon-DEM) is to censure or express disapproval of; to convict or sentence; to doom; to declare unsuitable for public use ("I* **condemn** *this vicious attack and extend my sympathies to the families"; "The district has not yet filed to* **condemn** *the property through eminent domain, but has notified Vavrina it intends to do so"; "Eddie Crawford, 56, was* **condemned** *to die in 1983 for the death of his two-year-old niece"). To* **contemn** *(kon-TEM) is to treat with scorn or contempt; to despise ("Such forms do not teach students to write well; they teach students to* **contemn** *all writing"; "He must have learned to* **contemn** *euphony and symmetry, with it benison of restfulness, and to delight in monotony of orchestral color and monotony of dynamics and monotony of harmonic device").*

CONTEMPTIBLE

Misused for **contemptuous**. • Flaubert had a pessimistic view of life, and he was **contemptible** of middle-class society. USE **contemptuous**. • He socked me hard in the stomach. I doubled over, but that **contemptible** smile never left my face. USE **contemptuous**.

And **contemptuous** is misused for **contemptible**: • Manzotti's interpretation does expose the novel's **contemptuous** intentions with regard to the genealogy of the Pirobutirro family, but an additional layer of interpretation is also possible. USE **contemptible**.

*Contemptible means deserving contempt; disgraceful. **Contemptuous** means showing contempt; disdainful. The indignation or contempt that people who use these words feel is wholly lost when the words are confused—a very good reason not to confuse them.*

CONTINUOUS

Misused for **continual**. • He also criticizes the **continuous** equipment failures and the poor design of the delivery elevators, which sometimes leave crushed books. USE **continual**. • But after **continuous** self-reflection and adjustments, we now stand firmly on the road of reform. USE **continual**. • The ongoing concern over crippling attacks necessitates the **continuous** upgrade of anti-virus software to ensure maximum protection in the enterprise. USE **continual**.

*Continuous means without interruption, whereas **continual** means recurring at intervals. Though a distinction that is perhaps seldom observed, such subtlety can only enrich our writing.*

CONTRETEMPS

*The pronunciation of **contretemps** is (KON-trah-tan), not (KON-trah-temps).*

CONVERSATE

Solecistic for **converse** (or similar words). • Receive bulletins about news articles and **conversate** with our readers. USE **converse**. • Despite this busy workload, he still manages to make time to **conversate** with others. USE **talk**. • San Diego Mommies is a place for local mommies and mommies-to-be to congregate and **conversate** about anything and everything under the sun. USE **chat**. • I am looking for an intelligent young man who loves to cook and **conversate**. USE **communicate**.

> Over the last few years, this ridiculous word has cleaved to young adults, sports figures, and, now, others ill advised. Any dictionary that eventually adds this word born of imbecility to its pages is a dictionary to be disdained. As it is, we ought to consider whether we can gainfully consult a dictionary that includes the comical, the infantile **humongous**. SEE ALSO **humongous**.

C

CONVEY BACK

Solecistic for **convey**. • If you are not convinced the deaf person has understood the content of the conversation or question, ask the person to **convey back** to you a condensed version. DELETE **back**. • They typically **convey back** to the property owner the results of those meetings. DELETE **back**. • I want to **convey back** to the author or web designer my appreciation of what they have given me. DELETE **back**.

> You **convey to**; you do not **convey back to**. SEE ALSO **re- back**.

CONVINCE

Is there really no difference in meaning or usage of the two verbs *convince* and *persuade*? More and more, I find *convince* used where the intended meaning is clearly *persuade*.

That's because many people do not observe the distinction between the two words, and that in part is due to dictionaries that use one word to define the other. Buy your dictionary deliberately.

There is a difference between **convince**—which as you note, is being used where **persuade** is better suited—and **persuade**. **Convince** means create belief in; **persuade**, induce or talk into. We are **convinced of** or **convinced that**, and **persuaded to**.

COPULATION

Though not a common error—what unspeakable progeny would we know if it were?—misusing **copulation** *(the act of sexual intercourse) for* **cooperation** *(a joint effort) does happen: "losing its candor, valor and taste in schools and the spirit of academic* **copulation** *is fastly evading...."*

COPYRIGHT

Solecistic for **copyrighted.** • Baker and others said they sympathized with efforts by the recording and motion picture industries to protect **copyright** material, but insisted on their own rights to protect the privacy of subscribers. USE **copyrighted.**

The adjectival form is **copyrighted,** *not* **copyright.** *SEE ALSO* **cliché; prejudice.**

CORD

Misused for **chord.** • It is simply a mathematical representation of a word which can also relate to a musical **cord.** USE **chord.**

And sometimes **chord** is misused for **cord:** • Have your fireplace checked by a chimney sweep annually or after burning one **chord** of wood—whichever comes first. USE **cord.** • The central nervous system is made up of a brain, a spinal **chord** and nerves. USE **cord.** • He discovered that this charge could be transferred to cork using an electrical **chord.** USE **cord.**

A **chord** *is usually three or more musical notes played or sung together in harmony. A* **cord** *is a thick string or thin rope; something that acts as a tie; a measure of wood cut for fuel; a ribbed fabric; an insulated electrical cable.*

CORE

Misused for **corps.** • The Marine **Core** is only for the real men of the United States of America. USE **Corps.** • Within the ROTC **core** of cadets, experienced cadets take on leadership responsibilities and roles inside the detachment. USE **corps.**

Core *(KOR), as a noun, is the central or innermost part of something; the most important part; the central part of an apple or other fruit; a section of the earth's* *strata; the main memory of a computer; the central part of a nuclear reactor. As an adjective,* **core** *means principal or central.* **Corps** *(KOR) is a group of people involved in some organization; a military force or branch of the armed forces.*

COSMOLOGY

Misused for **cosmetology.** • You'll enjoy the best food, finest fashions, all the attentions of an esthetician, **cosmologist,** hairdresser and personal trainer. USE **cosmetologist.** • Late in the afternoon of November 17, 1993, Hales drove to Sylvina's Hair Emporium in Laurel, where his wife of twenty five years, Donna Elaine Hales, worked as a **cosmologist,** to drive her home after work. USE **cosmetologist.**

And **cosmetology** is misused for **cosmology:** • I recently read an article—I think it was in the *Journal of Astrology and Cosmetology*—that a new asteroid had been discovered and was being named Xantisuia. Use **Cosmology.**

Cosmetology *is the study of cosmetics and the application of them.* **Cosmology** *is the scientific study of the universe. SEE ALSO* **astrology.**

COULD

Please denote the usages of *could* vs. *might.*

A few thoughts: As **can** is confused with **may,** so **could** is confused with **might. Could** signifies ability, and **might,** possibility; however, both words are used when requesting per-

mission ("**Could** I tell you something?" "**Might** I ask you for your autograph?"). **Might** (like **may**) is the polite way of asking permission, and **could** (like **can**), the popular way.

There is, I am loathe to say, the expression **might could** (as well as similar combinations), which some people use instead of **might** or **could.**

COULD CARE LESS

Solecistic for **couldn't care less.** • Then you end up with a site that makes you happy but which everyone else on the planet **could care less** about. USE **could not care less.** • What could be more fascinating than knowing what really matters to American women—what they adore, detest and **could care less** about? USE **couldn't care less.**

*However it is meant, whatever the speaker's intention, the phrase **could care less** means just the opposite of the one it is so often misused for. Though hardly elegant English, **couldn't care less** means that apathy reigns in regard to whatever is being discussed; **could care less** clearly means that there is still interest.*

COULD OF

Solecistic for **could have.** • Defensively, I thought we played as well as we **could of** at this stage. USE **could have.** • If she did not have a gun, she **could of** got hurt. USE **could have.** • He **could of** told us what went on with that woman. USE **could have.**

*Because **could've** (like **should've** and **would've**) is the term many people say, **could of** (**should of**, **would of**) is the term many people write ("The football season is over. **Could of, should of, would of,** are all irrelevant points right now").*

COUNCIL

Misused for **counsel.** • The Adviser shall give **council** to the president and **council** on matters concerning PHC. USE **counsel.** • Lawyers for Oba Chandler argued before the Supreme Court this morning that their client had ineffective **council** in his murder trial. USE **counsel.**

And **counsel** is misused for **council:** • Syria asked the UN Security **Counsel** to condemn the act of aggression which, they say, has no justification at all. USE **Council.**

*A **council** is a group of people, legislative body, or body of delegates that deliberates over matters. **Counsel** is advice or a person who gives advice, such as a lawyer. SEE ALSO **consul.***

COUPON

The pronunciation of **coupon** *is (KOO-pon), not (KYOO-pon).*

COURSE

C

Misused for **coarse**. • Later, Stalin, in his rude and **course** manner, would develop that which Lenin began, as shown in dealings with Roosevelt and with Hitler. USE **coarse**. • The foundation may consist of rock, **course**-grained material (sand and gravel), fine-grained material (silt and clay), or a combination of all three. USE **coarse**. • Light gray hair tumbled over her **course** face and it was obvious she was never a beauty. USE **coarse**.

And **coarse** is misused for **course**: • September 11 dramatically altered the **coarse** of events. USE **course**. • If you are one of those who wants to know more about golf **coarse** equipment this is the place to look. USE **course**. • The tip of Mud Island and its shrimp boat wreck soon passed by and we were free to leave the channel and set a more direct **coarse** to Rockport. USE **course**.

Course means a route or direction; a duration of time; a mode of action or behavior; the manner in which something develops; a mealtime dish or set of dishes; an area of land where a game or sport is played; a series of lectures or medical treatments. Coarse means rough in texture; consisting of large particles; not fine or elegant in structure; of inferior quality; rude or vulgar.

CREDIBLE

Misused for **credulous**. • Teach us not to be gullible, and **credible**, swallowing every line that comes along. USE **credulous**. • I have asked Dr. Wilkinson more than once to name an ancient writer who was not, on occasion, **credible**, gullible and superstitious. USE **credulous**.

Credible means believable, plausible. Credulous means believing too readily, gullible.

CRITERION

Misused for **criteria**. • Product designers have to consider a number of **criterion** to determine the best shielding solution for their product. USE **criteria**. • If we classify "the election defaults" as "not a candidate," quorum would satisfy these **criterion**. USE **criteria**.

Criterion is singular; ***criteria***, or ***criterions***, plural. SEE ALSO ***phenomenon***.

CRUCIFICTION

Misspelling of **crucifixion**. • This is the account of the **crucifiction** of Jesus as written by John. USE **crucifixion**. • After the **crucifiction**, the Apostles begin spreading the teachings of Jesus, first in Judea and Galilee, then to the gentiles in Greece, Rome and elsewhere. USE **crucifixion**.

Crucifixion refers to the execution of Jesus on a cross at Calvary; execution on a cross; extremely painful suffering. If you believe Jesus did not die, that he simply lost consciousness, you might make a case for spelling the word ***crucifiction***; otherwise, ***crucifixion*** is correct. SEE ALSO ***Calvary***.

I understand that these questions admit of no other answers than such as go to show, that if there be any evidence of the resurrection of Jesus, sufficient to support it, if there were no evidence to counterbalance it, such evidence is not capable of being counterbalanced. You will perceive that our reasoning must issue in the truth of the resurrection, unless we assume the extravagant notion, that the people who lived in Jerusalem and its vicinity, at the time of the crucifiction of Jesus, were not brought over to believe it.

—Hosea Ballou, *A Series of Letters In Defence of Divine Revelation*, 1820

CRUMBLE

Confused with **crumple**. To **crumble** is to break apart or disintegrate ("That day, terrorists foolishly thought that they could cause America **to crumble** by destroying the financial towers and the innocent people within them"). To **crumple** is to crinkle; to collapse; to be upset ("If you made a typo and had to **crumple** up a piece of paper and rewrite a memo, you would not be expected to pay for that sheet of paper out of your own pocket"; "Mr. Bush's face **crumpled**, and he stuttered the reply: 'Oh, I'm so sorry'").

C

CURRANT

Misspelling of **current**. • It is appropriate for young and fit individuals and is adapted to the athlete's **currant** needs. USE **current**. • This internal command is used to display and change the **currant** time. USE **current**. • Electrical **currant** is equal to the flow of water, and voltage is equal to the pressure. USE **current**.

Current, as an adjective, means at the present time; contemporary; circulating; prevalent. As a noun, it means the flow of air or water; the flow or amount of electricity; a general tendency or course. *Currant* is a small, seedless raisin; a shrub.

{ 103 }

DAIRY

Misspelling of **diary**. • "It's a wonder I haven't abandoned all my ideas," Anne wrote in her **dairy**, "they seem so absurd and impractical." USE **diary**.

And **diary** is misused for **dairy**: • Under the compact, a commission of **diary** farmers and bureaucrats sets the minimum farm price that processors must pay for milk. USE **dairy**.

*The adjective **dairy** means of or relating to milk and milk products. The noun **diary** is a journal of one's own thoughts, feelings, and experiences; a book of such writing.*

DALMATION

Misspelling of **dalmatian**. • This page is dedicated to all **dalmations**. I love all **dalmations** and hope you will too. USE **dalmatians**. • One of the newest additions to the Disney Series is this adorable set of salt and pepper shakers from the recent Disney movie *102 Dalmations*. USE **Dalmatians**.

*__Dalmation__ persists as a common misspelling of **dalmatian**.*

DEBACLE

*The pronunciation of **debacle** is (di-BAHK-el), not (DEB-i-kel).*

DEBONE

*Confused with **bone**. As shell means to remove the shell from, so **bone** means to remove the bones from. Because people, for decades, have mistakenly used **debone** to mean to remove the bones from, most dictionaries now include this definition* *with no qualifying remarks—further evidence that the word **dictionary** will, before long, mean rubbish; rot; claptrap; tripe; offal.*

DECANT

Misused for **descant.** • It has an optional brass quintet, percussion, organ fanfare at the beginning, then five stanzas (one in four part for choir), soprano **decant** on the last stanza. USE **descant.** • Kurt can also **decant** on early-modern and modern Europe, the early-modern Atlantic world, comparative European imperialism, and modern south Asia. USE **descant.**

*To **decant** (di-KANT) is to pour liquid from one container to another, usually so as not to disturb the sediment ("Conventional wisdom has it that fine wines should be **decanted** before serving in order to let the wine breathe"). To **descant** (DES-kant) is to discourse on a subject; to sing or play melodiously ("She **descants** on, among other things, her own upbringing as a mass-media consumer"). As a noun, a **descant** is a comment or criticism; a melody or counterpoint sung or played above the basic melody.*

DECIMATE

Misused for **destroy** (or similar words). • A trial enabled the company to **decimate** the workforce at its Taupo mill this year—one hundred more jobs are at risk next year. USE **reduce.** • Bulldogs **decimate** Cougars. USE **thrash.** • Inexperience and injury may **decimate** some wrestling teams, but the Bears have held their ground through a difficult start to the season despite some new faces. USE **defeat.** • If he doesn't go for the deal, we'll just **decimate** him. USE **crush.**

*Originally, **decimate** meant to kill one person in ten. Today, the word has come to mean to kill or destroy a large part of. One cannot correctly, as in these illustrations, use **decimate** to mean, simply, kill or destroy, or (even more absurdly) damage or defeat.*

Sugar and citrus producers say eliminating tariffs could decimate farmers in the Sunshine State.
—**Tamara Lush,** *St. Petersburg Times*

Why do students decimate their bodies with alcohol one night a year?
—**Adam Pulver,** *The Tufts Daily*

*Examples of the absurd use of **decimate** are abundant. People who do not distinguish **decimate** from **destroy** or **damage** or other words also do not distinguish their writing.*

DE FACTO

*Confused with **de jure**. **De facto** (di-FAK-toe) means existing in fact though not in law ("Hill is even serving as **de facto** mayor of the district where his battalion is stationed"). **De jure** (dee-JOOR-ee) means by right or law ("He was also incensed that Sharansky had voted for a new law that would give Orthodox rabbis **de jure** control over religious conversions inside Israel").*

DEGRADATE

Idiotic for **degrade.** • Materials used in cars, airplanes, tools, constructions, electronic equipment can **degradate** gradually or fail suddenly. USE **degrade.** • It's electric generating capacity may **degradate** gradually between 0-20% over its useful life. USE **degrade.** • We seem to **degradate** psychiatry and psychiatric patients no less than we denounce the legislation of mind expanding drugs. USE **degrade.**

Occasionally, **degradate** is meant to mean something other than **degrade:** • Are we to **degradate** to the stone age to adopt a code of religiousness that many of us do not want? USE **revert.** • This is a read for men and women; its tough, but tough is what it takes to get people to communicate, instead of **degradate.** USE **separate.**

To **degrade** *is to treat with contempt or disrespect; to lessen in rank or in value; to wear down, decompose, or deteriorate.* **Degradate** *is nonsense.*

"It is a larned word, no doubt; but she must persevere until she's able to masther it. I wouldn't for three tenpennies that the priest would hear one of you call me Dinny; it would degradate me very much in his estimation. At all events, if my mother cannot manage the orthography of Dionysius, let it be Denis, or anything but that signature of vulgarity, Dinny."

—**William Carleton,** ***Going to Maynooth, Traits and Stories of the Irish Peasantry,*** **1881**

DELEGATE

Misused for **relegate.** • We can read this verse in a couple of seconds, and it's a summation that the beast was speaking, it was eventually slain, and finally, it was **delegated** to hell. USE **relegated.** • Black people were **delegated** to an inferior role in life. USE **relegated.** • The problem here is the Public's access to and their channel time allotments on Channel 12 have been **delegated** to third place within the PEG equation. USE **relegated.**

> To **delegate** *is to authorize another person to act as one's representative; to entrust a task or responsibility to another. To* ***relegate*** *is to assign to a particular place or position, class or category; to assign to an inferior position; to banish. Watch this word. One day soon, our worst dictionaries will tell us that* ***delegate*** *does mean* ***relegate.***

DELIBERATIVE

Misused for **deliberate.** • But the status quo is unacceptable to me and to the governor, so we are going to make thoughtful, **deliberative** changes in personnel, practices and programs. USE **deliberate.** • He doesn't usually react or respond in a visceral way, he's very **deliberative.** USE **deliberate.** • I think he's going to go about this in a very **deliberative** fashion. USE **deliberate.**

Deliberate—*which means thoughtful, premeditated, considered, not impulsive*—*does not mean* **deliberative**—*which means relating to discussion or consideration. There are deliberate people, deliberate lies, deliberate attempts, but deliberative bodies, deliberative sessions, deliberative processes.*

DELUSION

Confused with **illusion**. *An* **illusion** *is a false perception of reality; something that tricks the mind ("Beware of the* **illusion** *of perfection"; "Are we interested in security or just the* **illusion** *of it?"). A* **delusion** *is a false belief held despite strong evidence that indicates its falsity ("The* **delusion** *of grandeur was reinforced by his nickname, King James"; "It can cause hallucination,* **delusion** *and disorganized speech patterns, otherwise known as thought disorders"). SEE ALSO* **illusion**.

DEMUR

Misused for **demure**. • The always delicate and **demur** Helen Hunt graced the stage to hand out the Best Actor award and I was happy to see Roberto Benigni win for the second time in the evening. USE **demure**. • During athletic competitions, Armour, a Memphis, Tenn., native, is anything but **demur**. USE **demure**. • With her flaming red hair this model could be a **demur** woman or a cabaret dancer complete with black stockings and garter. USE **demure**.

Demur, a verb, means to object; to have scruples; to hesitate. Demure, an adjective, means modest, reserved, decorous; affectedly shy or modest.

DENOTATE

Solecistic for **denote**. • Synths also **denotate** the nightmarish moment of the action. USE **denote**. • In real situations labels can be names for the objects or may **denote** specific features or functions of them. USE **denote**. • Letters i, j, k, l, m, n often **denotate** subscripts of arrays. USE **denote**.

Denotate is also sometimes used for **detonate**: • The alleged al-Qaeda plot to build and **denotate** a "dirty" bomb is a grim reminder of the widespread proliferation of nuclear materials. USE **detonate**. • TNT is less powerful, harder to **denotate**, more difficult to make, but cheaper, less poisonous, unaffected by dampness, and less dense. USE **detonate**.

*As **connote** is preferable to **connotate**, so **denote** is to **denotate**. **Denote** means to signify or refer to explicitly; to be a sign of; indicate. It does not mean, as **detonate** does, to explode or cause to explode. SEE ALSO **connotate**.*

DEPRAVATION

D

Misused for **deprivation**. • At times, members of 1st Battalion, 7th Marines battled Hussein's Republican Guard troops, sand storms, the searing Iraqi sun, slow mail, sleep **depravation** and no days off. USE **deprivation**. • India has gone through decades of want and **depravation**. USE **deprivation**. • He is also a graduate of Ranger School, a rigorous school that includes sleep and food **depravation**. USE **deprivation**.

Annie Dillard says in her *The Writing Life*, "The writing life is colorless to the point of sensory depravation."
—**Philip Yancy, as quoted in ChristianityToday.com**

*If we believe Dillard wrote **deprivation** and Yancy said **deprivation**, we must wonder at how deprived of depravity, or old-fashioned fun, perhaps, the good people at Christianity Today are.*

DEPRIVE

Misused for **deprave**. • It is said that they are the most evil race in the Warhammer World because they derive pleasure in performing the most **deprived** acts just because it causes suffering to others. USE **depraved**. • Fifteen years after thousands were killed in a poison gas leak, survivors and relatives of victims sued the company on Monday for "**deprived** indifference to human life." USE **depraved**.

To **deprive** is to take something away from; to deny. To **deprave** is to make immoral or corrupt.

DESSERT

Misused for **desert**. • At points we hit totally barren **dessert**, no vegetation to be seen whatsoever. USE **desert**. • So why do we lock them up for thirty years?—probably not to protect us from them, but for retribution or just **desserts**. USE **deserts**. • Taliban military forces **desserted** the capital of Kabul today, after a series of stunning military victories by opposition forces. USE **deserted**.

*Dessert has one meaning: a usually sweet dish that is served at the end of a meal. The noun **desert** means barren or arid land with sparse vegetation; desolate; deserved reward or punishment. The verb means to abandon or withdraw from.*

DESTRUCT

Solecistic for **destroy** (or similar words). • A port was **destructed**. USE **obliterated**. • Aboriginal communities were **destructed** and displaced, which has had an indelible effect on their cultural practices and existence. USE **destroyed**. • If quarantined disease organisms are detected, the cut flower must be reconditioned, **destructed** or returned to the shipper. USE **destroyed**.

*Though obsolete, the verb **destruct** is in use today by people insufficiently familiar with the English language. Of course, **autodestruct** and **self-destruct** are popularly and correctly used, as is, in computer terminology, the **destruct** class object.*

DEVICE

Misused for **devise**. • He **deviced** a new plan based on the contemporary Gothic pointed arch, and "ribs" that would support the ceiling. USE **devised**. • They have to **device** a strategy so that the visitor comes again and again. USE **devise**.

*Device (di-VIS)—a contrivance; plan; scheme; technique; trick—is a noun; **devise** (di-VIZ)—to contrive; plan; invent—a verb. SEE ALSO **advice**.*

DIDN'T (HADN'T; SHOULDN'T) OUGHT

Solecistic for **ought not to.** • You **didn't ought to** make me do something like that. USE **ought not to.** • Now, maybe all this **shouldn't ought to** be true. USE **ought not to.** • He was searched, and though nothing was found, it was decided that he **shouldn't ought to** return to the store. USE **ought not to.** • We **hadn't ought to** fool ourselves or fool the public in the sense that if we charge ourselves for the demolition debris for the high school we will be adding about $1,250,000 to the high school project. USE **ought not to.**

*These expressions are illiteracies. Use **ought not to**. SEE ALSO **ought not**.*

D

DIERESIS

What's your take on *The New Yorker*'s use of the diaeresis? I'm no expert, but reelection with an umlaut on the second *e* looks odd to me.

*It looks no more odd than it is. The dieresis, which is rarely used today (though occasionally in **naïve**), is placed atop the second of two juxtaposed vowels to indicate two separate sounds are to be pronounced. And though two sounds are found at the beginning of **reelection**, no one (except perhaps the recently reelected U.S. president, the lexicographers at Merriam-Webster's, and the editorial staff at The New Yorker) is likely to pronounce the word ree-LEK-shen.*

*The hyphen, far more often than the dieresis, is used in this country to indicate two sounds, but more often still to separate a prefix from a word stem or to distinguish one word from another (**re-create** from **recreate**, for instance).*

DIFFERENTIAL

Misused for **difference.** • The consensual relationships that are of concern are those romantic and/or sexual relationships in which both parties appear to have consented, but where there is a definite power **differential** between the two parties.

USE **difference**. • With thirty-five seconds left, FBCA turned the ball over, but with a five second **differential** between the shot clock and game clock they elected to play tough defense. USE **difference**.

Differential is not simply a synonym for difference, and in the examples shown here, difference is the word wanted. Differential is often used in regard to differences in price and mathematics.

There's a minor advantage when you look at polls toward one or the other, depending on which issue, but apart from Iraq, which has fallen on the list of concerns, there really isn't a big differential between the candidates.

—Ron Brownstein, political analyst

*Brownstein evidently believes that **differential**, instead of **difference**, makes his vapid thought a more inviting sentence.*

DIFFERENT THAN

When did the British *different to* and the American *different from* (now, often, different than) part company?

The Old English Dictionary *records examples of **different to** from 1526, **different from** from 1590, and **different than** from 1644.*

***Different than** is peculiarly an American expression and the least supportable of the three; **different to** is widely used in Britain though not in the United States; and **different from** is popular in both British and American English.*

DIFFUSE

Misused for **defuse**. • After confirming a bomb report, DeBenedet scans the possible explosive, secures the area and decides whether to detonate or **diffuse** the bomb. USE **defuse**. • Taiwan's newly elected president is steering a moderate political course to **diffuse** tension between his nation and mainland China. USE **defuse**. • If you encounter a bear, Do Not Run! Slowly back away to try to put distance between you and the bear to **diffuse** the situation. USE **defuse**.

Diffuse means to spread over a wide area, disseminate; to make less brilliant, soften. As an adjective, it means widely spread or scattered; verbose or unclear. Defuse means to remove the fuse from (a bomb); reduce the danger or tension in.

DILEMMA

*Misused for **predicament** (or similar words). A **dilemma** offers a choice between two equally unappealing outcomes ("The constant **dilemma**—how to abide by all the state-regulated nutrition standards yet still offer students a meal that won't end up trashed—became the main point of discussion at the El Centro Elementary School District board meeting Monday"). A **predicament** does not suggest a choice of any kind, simply a bothersome or vexing problem ("It's hard to know which is the better analogy for our **predicament** in Iraq: Vietnam or Israel").*

DIS

Solecistic for **disrespect** (or similar words). • This issue addresses five other means of **dissing** employees: buck passing, procrastination, inattentiveness, impatience and public reprimands. USE **disrespecting**. • Watch Letterman stir up trouble with a Top 10 list or by **dissing** the soft drink Dr Pepper as "liquid manure." USE **disparaging**. • Franzen, despised and envied by all writers for his talent, his luck, his good looks, and his marketing acumen, essentially **dissed** the Oprah award for being lowbrow. USE **dismissed**.

*Haven't we all had quite enough of this prefix aspiring to be a word? Are we to allow **un** and **anti, non** and **pre** to follow? People are increasingly mono- and disyllabic as it is; let's rail against this foolishness, this affront, this **dis**.*

If you speak in monosyllables, you likely think in monosyllables. Complex thoughts, well-reasoned arguments, a keen understanding of self are all then lost.

DISABILITATE

Solecistic for **debilitate**. • Sleep disorders like apnea, narcolepsy and insomnia can be dangerous and **disabilitating**. USE **debilitating**. • Many who suffer from a **disabilitating** illnesses swear that this wonderful machine has changed their life. USE **debilitating**. • Also, note that microwave and lower frequency EMF weapons are in wide use today as so called non-lethal weapons to disorient and **disabilitate** people. USE **debilitate**. • Back pain can cause severe suffering and **disabilitate** anybody. USE **debilitate**.

*Disabilitate, an apparent muddle (or blend as a linguist might say) of **disability** and **debilitate**, is incorrect for **debilitate**, which means to enfeeble or enervate.*

DISBURSE

Misused for **disperse**. • Arrested and charged with failure to **disburse**, unlawful assembly, and failure to give their names (some had given their names, however), bail was set at $2,000 for most rescuers. USE **disperse**. • An explosion at 10:12 P.M. Tucson time outside the Hut, 305 N. Herbert Ave., sent spectators running and activated nearly five hundred extra police officers in full riot gear to **disburse** the crowd. USE **disperse**.

And **disperse** is misused for **disburse**: • The National Heritage Foundation is the entity that will hold and **disperse** funds. USE **disburse**.

*Disburse means to pay out; expend. **Disperse** means to spread or distribute over a wide area; to scatter in different directions; to cause to vanish or disappear.*

DISCOMFORTURE

Idiotic for **discomfiture**. • However, the reason for your obvious **discomforture** is unclear to even someone as smart and learned as I am. USE **discomfiture**. • The women just now are discussing the relative merits of men and women much to the **discomforture** of the men. USE **discomfiture**.

*Discomforture has no known meaning. The actual word, **discomfiture** (or **discomfort**), means frustration or embarrassment.*

DISCONNECT

Solecistic for **gap** (or similar words). • In other words, there's a **disconnect** between Dubya's policies and his governance. USE **disparity**. • We identified a $1.1B projected shortfall and continued to track the **disconnect** between projected and actual sales for subsequent months. USE **variance**. • There is an apparent **disconnect** between OO community and systematic reuse community. USE **misunderstanding**. • Throughout this decade there has developed a widening **disconnect** between what we expect our national defense forces to do, and the resources supplied to accomplish those missions. USE **gap**. • A communications **disconnect or** gap exists between our operations commanders and our logisticians. DELETE **disconnect or**.

D

*In this brash but silly sense of a gap, misunderstanding, miscommunication, or disparity, **disconnect** is to be reviled. Even if we must concede to its usage as a noun in the sense of a computer modem or electrical line disconnection, let that be the end of it. All further development of this word produces only grotesqueries.*

DISCRETE

Misused for **discreet**. • Our goal is to provide you with a simple, secure and **discrete** method of obtaining Viagra from the privacy of your own home. USE **discreet**. • Condom King has twelve different name brands in an assortment of styles; you pick the desired quantity, pay once and have them mailed to your home **discretely** on a monthly basis. USE **discreetly**. • The individual briefing must be provided as inconspicuously and **discretely** as possible. USE **discreetly**.

*The homonyms **discrete** and **discreet** are often confused. Whereas **discrete** means distinct or separate, **discreet** means circumspect or prudent.*

DISCRIMITORY

Solecistic for **discriminatory**. • It is illegal in the U.S. to make any **discrimitory** remarks, and post pictures of people without written and direct permission. USE **discriminatory**. • No hate related, pornographic or **discrimitory** sites will be allowed. USE **discriminatory**. • He grew up in a tough neighborhood, and succeeded in becoming a doctor despite **discrimitory** circumstances. USE **discriminatory**.

*The fast-paced occasionally mispronounce **discriminatory**, and the slow-minded often misspell it.*

Non-discrimitory policy: St. Marys School recruits and admits students of any race, color, or ethnic origin to all the rights, privliges, programs, and activities.

—Clyde St. Mary's Catholic School

*Since it—in large, bold type—proclaims its **non-discrimitory** policy, St. Mary's must attract people who neither understand nor care that the word is **discriminatory**; who neither understand nor care the word is **privilege**; who neither understand nor care the word is **St. Mary's**— nondiscriminating people all.*

DISCUSS (EXPLAIN) ABOUT

Solecistic for **discuss** (**explain**). • Captain Erickson introduced himself and **explained about** what it means to become a commissioned officer in the Air Force. DELETE about. • Our guide **discussed about** the types of methods that are used in the factory. DELETE about. • One speaker also **mentioned about** marketing. • DELETE about. • The two men **discussed about** Greek–Turkish relations, the Cyprus issue, developments in the Middle East, and the crisis in Southern Serbia. DELETE **about**. • Here is where you can **discuss about** the polls and see their results. DELETE **about**. • As HIV/AIDS is still considered a social taboo, no one is willing to **discuss about** it openly. DELETE **about**.

*You may **talk about**, but you may not always **discuss about**. This misusage is fairly common among people still learning the English language, but people who have spoken the language all of their lives also use this disturbing solecism. SEE ALSO **discussed**.*

DISCUSSED

Misused for **disgust**. • She didn't feel pity for him, she felt **discussed**. USE **disgust**. • She figured that she better try and please him even though she felt **discussed** for him. USE **disgust**.

*How, we must wonder, do the people who spell **disgust discussed** spell the past tense—**discusseded**? Yes, it appears so: "I was **discusseded** not just by some of that woman's policies, but also by the fact that people are using the thing to spam."*

D

DISGUARD

Solecistic for **discard**. • As the new energies approach, many people feel a need to **disguard** the old and get themselves together. USE **discard**. • This was the first book I read after I became a Christian—a true story that I will never forget, and a book that I will never **disguard**. USE **discard**. • Clean and **disguard** stems of mushrooms and put in a Ziploc bag. USE **discard**.

*Discard means to get rid of, throw away, or reject; **disguard** is useless nonsense.*

DISINTEREST

Misused for **indifference** (or similar words). • For Washingtonians, pop culture is a threat, a Pied Piper leading Americans down the road to **disinterest**. USE **apathy**. • The lack of fights is not a result of **disinterest** from nationally based promoters. USE **uninterest**. • Finally, there was lots of talk at Cannes this year about the lack of a Hollywood presence, whether due to the festival's inattention or industry **disinterest**. USE **indifference**.

*Disinterest means without bias or impartial; it does not now mean uninterest or indifference. To use **disinterest** in the sense of **uninterest** is to forsake the word itself and, in effect, is a diminution of the foremost way in which we maintain our humanity: using language effectively.*

We have let the liberal paradigm define the debate, and the result is the false stereotyping of Conservatives as disinterested in the suffering of this nation's at-risk kids.

—U.S. Representative Tom DeLay

As middle school and high school children are tested before they are allowed to graduate, so perhaps elected officials ought to be tested before they are allowed to serve.

DISPARATE

Misused for **desperate**. • In retaliation to its military and political losses in different corners of the country, the TPLF regime is taking **disparate** measures such as killing and imprisoning of civilians in the country. USE **desperate**. • It is a known fact that **disparate** people do **disparate** things and our government has played a major role in our lives being in a **disparate** state. USE **desperate**.

Disparate means distinct or different. Desperate means so overwhelmed by hopelessness or anxiety as to behave rashly or violently; frantic; having a great need; extremely difficult, dangerous, or serious.

DISPLACE

Misused for **misplace**. • A weak attack or defense will only serve to create an air of **displaced** confidence on the part of your partner. USE **misplaced**.

To misplace is to mislay; to bestow confidence or some other quality on a person or idea undeserving of it. To displace is to move from a usual place; to force to leave a country; to supplant; to remove from a position.

DISPREFER

Idiotic for **dislike** (or similar words). • It's interesting as a spelling pronunciation, preferred by some speakers, **dispreferred** by others. USE **not**. • They never spontaneously produce them; in fact, they strongly **disprefer** them. USE **object to**. • In a pinch, you can fax it to me at 011-44-1865-279299, but I **disprefer** faxes because of deficient legibility. USE **dislike**. • Other things being equal, we should **disprefer** blogs to journalism. USE **prefer journalism to blogs**.

> Among linguists and their lackeys, **disaffected** as they often are from sense and thoughtfulness, **disprefer** actually does exist. No sentence is improved, none made true or clear, by using **disprefer** instead of some other wording.

D

The findings demonstrate that children disprefer learning a different, unrelated meaning for a known word when that word is used in a linguistic context that fails to bias strongly for a new meaning.

—Devin Casenhiser, Department of Linguistics, University of Illinois at Urbana-Champaign

This one sentence, scarcely intelligible as it is, should dissuade all of us from having much faith in linguists and their pronouncements. If linguists want to use a word like **disprefer**, let them first learn how to write a readable sentence.

DISSEMBLE

Misused for **disassemble**. • If the engine happens to be going through a rebuild, it would be best to have this done before all components are installed even though you can install this kit without having to **dissemble** the entire engine. USE **disassemble**. • They codenamed Weems the Modular Man due to the ability to **dissemble** and reassemble his body, and due to the number of detachable components of his body. USE **disassemble**.

Dissemble *means to disguise or hide behind a false appearance; to feign.* **Disassemble** *means to take apart; to break up.*

People that had been trained in some instances to disassemble--that means not tell the truth.

—U.S. President George W. Bush

Like others who speak before sizeable audiences, Bush has a responsibility to speak well. The worse a person speaks, the smaller his audience deserves to be.

DISSENT

Misused for **descent**. • Her **dissent** into madness is hastened by his cruelty. USE **descent**. • It occurs when one's best friend moves out of state and you are left behind, when a person is left in the wake of unrequited love, or when a seemingly healthy marriage finds itself in a steep **dissent** toward divorce. USE **descent**.

And occasionally **descent** is misused for **dissent**: • Duke's political **descent** and felony plea have alienated even longtime supporters in America, including those who once saw him as the ticket to the mainstream. USE **dissent**. • When is political **descent** unpatriotic? USE **dissent**.

> **Dissent** *is a difference of opinion or belief from that commonly held; nonconformity.* **Descent** *means a descending; a downward slope; a way down; a decline into an undesirable state; ancestry or lineage.*

DIVERT

Misused for **avert**. • If ever there was a time for peaceful demonstrations to **divert** war, now is that time. USE **avert**. • Negotiators from both sides said Monday that a last-minute deal could **divert** a strike. USE **avert**. • Her small breasts peeked through the foaming ocean and Helen had to **divert** her eyes. USE **avert**.

And **avert** is confused for **divert:** • Rosario said the need for the parapet is to **avert** the river waters from overflowing into the Pantal area community, especially during high tide and typhoons. USE **divert.**

> **Avert** means to turn away; to ward off or prevent. **Divert** means to turn aside; to distract the attention of; to entertain or amuse.

DOCUMENTATE

Solecistic for **document.** • These data are **documentated** by three machine-readable portable document files. USE **documented.** • We provide fully **documentated** results with a publication quality print and stained gel (wet or dry). USE **documented.** • During this expedition we were able to closely **documentate** the breeding and the birth of these frogs. USE **document.**

> Not only a noun, **document** is also a verb. Aside from **document**, the English language admits the words **documentary, documentation, documental, documentable, documenter, documentalist, documentarian,** and even **documentarist**. Barred is **documentate**.

DOMESTICATED

Misused for **domestic.** • I have selected three rituals that are clear examples of **domesticated** violence. USE **domestic.** • Supernaturalists have generally displayed a willingness, if not an eagerness, to suffer and die, and to cause others to suffer and die, to defend, maintain and extend their doctrinal dominions against all enemies, foreign or **domesticated,** actual or hallucinated. USE **domestic.**

> Both **domestic** and **domesticated** refer to tame animals. **Domestic** also means relating to family or home life; relating to a country's internal affairs; native to or made in a particular country. **Domesticated** also means adapted to domestic or home life; naturalized.

DOMINATE

Misused for **dominant.** • The cumulative actions of the **dominate** group, in this case Whites, far outweigh the cumulative actions of the oppressed group, in this case Blacks. USE **dominant.** • Certain actions are recognized as **dominate** behavior;

deep growling tones are aggressive while high-pitched whining tones are submissive. USE **dominant**.

Dominate, to rule or control through superior power or authority, is a verb; *dominant*, exercising authority or control, an adjective. SEE ALSO *predominate*.

There is significantly more rainfall in the south, making agriculture the dominate economy.

—**Kathy Stephenson,** *The Salt Lake Tribune*

DONE

I have noticed in spoken and written communication the increasing use of the word *done* instead of *finished* or *completed*. Are these words completely interchangeable, or are there nuances of meaning which might cause one word to be preferred over the others?

Today, they are all interchangeable. Some years ago, officiators of language usage decried the use of **done** to mean either **finished** or **completed**, but few people today are undone by **done**.

When speaking of a thoroughly cooked meal, **done** is the best word to use. If you want your writing to have a more elegant tone, **finished** or **completed** is still the better word to use.

DOSE

Misused for **douse**. • He was **dosed** with water, chased by dogs and threatened to be shot. USE **doused**. • It's basically fried white rice, onions, red pepper, and black beans, liberally **dosed** with hot sauce. USE **doused**. • He said the family at first attempted to **dose** the fire with water, but once a bedroom door was opened, the flames "took off." USE **douse**.

> To **douse** (DOUS) is to immerse, to plunge into liquid; to wet thoroughly; to extinguish (a fire). To **dose** (DOS) is to give someone a specified quantity of medicine; to prescribe (medicine) in certain amounts.

D

DO TO (DO TO THE FACT)

Solecistic for **due to** (or similar words) • **Do to** a current departure from Los Angeles for a weekend press event, she will not be available today for the interview. USE **Owing to**. • Amare, as you all know, ended up being the ninth overall pick in the 2002 NBA Draft, the only high schooler chosen in the first round, largely **do to the fact that** both Anthony and Bosh decided to give college a year. USE **because**. • **Do to the fact** some individuals desire to spam others, all email features were eliminated. USE **Since**.

> Although **due to** is the expression meant in these examples, it is ungrammatical. **Do to** is astonishingly incorrect; **due to**, more commonly incorrect. Instead of **do to**, use **due to**; instead of **due to**, use, at least in these examples, **owing to**, **because**, or **since**. SEE ALSO **due to**.

DOUBT THAT

Misused for **doubt whether**. • We **doubt that** anything on this year's MTV Video Music Awards will top that special moment in 1999 when Diana Ross copped a feel from Lil' Kim, but we'll be watching just in case. USE **doubt whether**. • And given the thoroughness of our inventory work, we **doubt that** any such evidence will be forthcoming. USE **doubt whether**. • In fact, we **doubt that** Iraq will take the sensible steps necessary to obtain the lifting, or the suspension, of sanctions as long as Saddam Hussein remains in power. USE **doubt whether**.

Arcanum though it may be, the idiom is **doubt whether** *unless the sentence is a negative one, whereupon* **doubt that** *is correct. The conjunction following* **doubt** *or* **doubtful** *is* **that** *in negative or interrogative statements, and* **whether** *or* **if** *in positive statements.*

DOUBTLESSLY

I should like to ask why anyone would use the word *doubtlessly*. The usage with which I am familiar is *doubtless* as both adverb and adjective. The *-ly* seems to me to be redundant.

Yes, you are right, though many people may be unfamiliar with this distinction. All six collegiate dictionaries in the Fiske Ranking of College Dictionaries (Appendix A) record **doubtlessly** *as an adverb, as they do* **doubtless***. Not one of these books suggests that* **doubtlessly** *is awkward and that* **doubtless** *is the better adverb to use.*

Other adverbs also do not use an **-ly** *ending:* **seldomly**, **thusly***, and* **muchly***, for example.*

DOUSE

Misused for **dowse**. • This phenomena, often hinted at, but rarely spoken of openly in the trade, is something akin to an ability to **douse** for water. USE **dowse**. • According to records, he could **douse** for gold and silver, cure sick horses, and speak with animals. USE **dowse**.

Douse (DOUS) means to drench; to immerse or plunge into liquid. **Dowse** *(DOUZ) means to search for water or minerals with a divining, or dowsing, rod.*

DOWNTALK

Idiotic for **disparage** (or similar words). • A lot of people **down talk** our military; they don't realize that if we don't have this, they can't talk at all. USE **vilify**. • Why **down talk** religion? Religion is a faith, a belief. USE **denigrate**. • So many uninformed people **down talk** the tapes and equipment, and others call themselves "Eight Track Nuts" to describe their interest in the format. USE **sneer at**. • Also, I've seen other car forums where people **downtalk** Japanese cars yet praise the Elise, and it just makes me wonder, since the B18C and 2ZZ are both Japanese engines. USE **ridicule**. • The Fed as a whole does not like to **downtalk** the economy, but the data is not matching what their yak has been saying. USE **criticize**.

And sometimes **downtalk** is used instead of **talk down to**: • Anderson himself doesn't exactly **downtalk** his class of women, but he does try to explain things in housewife terms. USE **talk down to**.

> One word or two, **downtalk** is as much as some people can manage. Words like **vilify** and **denigrate**, **malign** and **defame** may be unknown or misused by people who know and use **baby talk**.

DRIBBLE

Misused for **drivel**. • The diatribe given by that pro-union guy at The Twilight Zone was nothing short of intellectual **dribble**. USE **drivel**. • Salepeople talk **dribble**. USE **drivel**.

> **Dribble** is drool; the bouncing of a basketball. **Drivel**, which also means drool, is more often used to mean silly talk, nonsense.

DRUG

Misused for **dragged**. • Who **drug** up the past? USE **dragged**. • I've been kicked, beat, and **drug** through the dirt by many a man and want someone who knows how to treat a woman. USE **dragged**. • Our girls are not part of this presidential process, and I'm not going to let them get **drug** in. USE **dragged**.

> **Dragged**, not **drug**, is the past tense of **drag**.

I think if you felt that your name was going to be drug through the mud and it would do great damage to your career, it would last a long period of time, one might make that decision.
—**Johnnie Cochran, attorney**

I mean, that seems to be a category all in itself to me, that, yes, your name is going to be drug through the mud, but you've got an accusation that's so severe that most of us consider one of the worst crimes.
—**Jann Carl, correspondent with *Entertainment Tonight***

*Two minutes after Cochran used the word **drug**, an illiteracy in the sense used here, Ms. Carl, being interviewed on the same program, did as well. The only impression Cochran and Carl were likely to have made is how inarticulate, how easily influenced they are.*

DUE

Misused for **do**. • If you also reduce the core voltage of the CPU, you could probably get away with just one large heat sink and **due** away with the fan altogether. USE **do**. • As it stands now, the university will have to make **due** with half that amount. USE **do**. • Since boats are a luxury item (not a necessity), consumers can **due** without them. USE **do**. • It's always good to see people **due** something for America, and ask for nothing in return. USE **do**.

*Though pronounced the same, these two words differ in meaning, spelling, and part of speech. As an adjective, **due** has several meanings: payable immediately; owed; appropriate; expected at a certain time; adequate; and so on. As a verb, **do** has many meanings: to perform; to work on; to fulfill; to carry out; to solve; to produce; to exert; and so on.*

With Floyd batting .391, the Mets have been able to
make due with Mike Piazza batting .198.
—Lee Jenkins, *The New York Times*

*When he mistakes one word, one meaning, for another,
Jenkins himself does not make **do**. He makes doo-doo.*

D

DUEL

Misused for **dual**. • Each team is allowed three foreign players, but Skinnon, an
Italian-American who has **duel** citizenship, counts as an Italian. USE **dual**. • Unlike
Final Fantasy 7, you can use a **duel** shock controller and you will feel every bit of
vibration. USE **dual**. • For **duel**-use facilities, high collateral damage refers to significant effects on the environment, facilities and infrastructure that are not related to
war-making ability. USE **dual**. • A **duel** diagnosis patient is someone who has both
a drug problem as well as some sort of mental issue along with it. USE **dual**.

And **dual** for **duel**: • U.S. President George Bush, who was once challenged to a
dual by Ramadan, has welcomed the Iraqi's capture. USE **duel**.

*A **duel** is a combat with deadly weapons, usually to settle a point of honor; a con-
test between two persons or groups. **Dual** means consisting of two parts; having
two purposes.*

The affair caused rifts within families. People
fought duals over it. There was talk of civil war.

—*NPR Writer's Almanac*

*A compelling account of the Dreyfus Affair, a story of cou-
rageous behavior by some and despicable behavior by others, has as its denouement, a mistake that unsettles every
reader more attentive than the writer.*

DUE TO

Misused for **owing to** (or similar words). • **Due to** the transformer fire at our 31st Street and 23rd Avenue location, we have to merge our offices. USE **Owing to.** • The Crusaders' game against Bulloch Academy on Friday night was postponed at half **due to** a lightning storm. USE **because of.** • Pakistan had to cancel the South Asian Federation Games **due to** India's refusal to participate. USE **because of.** • Business suffers and commuters work longer **due to** poor rail services. USE **owing of.** • The plan was intended to be used through 2010, but **due to** rapid growth, it became outdated. USE **because of.**

*Traditionalists and stylists have long railed against using **due to** as a preposition. If **due to** can be replaced by **attributable to**, the phrase is perfectly good; if not, use **because of** or **owing to**. You could not say "**Attributable to** the transformer fire...."; **owing to** or **because of** is the correct phrase. You could, however, use **attributable to** in this sentence: "She said her success was entirely **due to** the devotion of her fans."*

*The correct use of **due to** is normally found after some form of the verb **to be**, whether stated, as in "The only changes **were due to** injuries after Greg Williams beat out Jomo Legins for one starting safety spot after two games," or elliptic, "Despite a month-long delay **[that was] due to** equipment and software installation glitches, 258 testing sites around the stations had no visible problems with the testing procedure."*

*__Due to__ also, of course, means scheduled to ("It is **due to** dock with the sixteen-nation orbital platform early on Monday") or expected ("He is **due to** arrive October 19"). SEE ALSO **do to (do to the fact).***

EACH OTHER

Misused for **one another**. • Since voters approved an $82-million bond issue last October, Paul Yelensky has been busy linking the twenty-seven elementary schools, seventeen junior high schools, four high schools and the Utica school board office to **each other** and the Internet. USE **one another**. • Testimony from a former Los Angeles police officer to investigators looking into police corruption has opened a window into an ominous world where allegedly corrupt cops brazenly rewarded **each other** for their actions. USE **one another**.

And in this next example, the writer doesn't quite know what to do: • After their long distraction, the two presumptive nominees finally get to concentrate on **one another**, and they are losing no time trying to define **each other**. USE **each other**.

Each other *is properly used when only two are being referred to;* *one another*, *when three or more are. It is a distinction worth observing. Although some texts and commentators suggest the distinction between* *each other* *and* *one another* *is artificial, more important than a phrase's historical, or even present-day, usage is maintaining clarity. Along with observing and maintaining, let us then strive for better comprehension and clarity by, if need be, devising distinctions between words.*

EBULLIENT

The pronunciation of *ebullient* *is (i-BOOL-yent), not (EB-yah-lent).*

ECONOMICAL

Misused for **economic**. • The European Information Technology Observatory analyses the current European ICT-Market and contains a statistical and **economical** forecast for the next years. USE **economic**. • This resulted in a gradual decline and four hundred years of **economical** downfall. USE **economic**.

*Even though **geographic** and **geographical**, **pharmacologic** and **pharmacological**, **theoretic** and **theoretical**, and other such pairs are synonymous, **economic** does not necessarily mean **economical**. **Economic** means pertaining to an economy or the science of economics; thrifty, inexpensive, cost effective. **Economical** has only the latter definition.*

ECSCAPE (EXCAPE)

Misspelling of **escape**. • He should just sit in jail to **ecscape** again and kill once more? USE **escape**. • He may be able to **ecscape** me, but he won't be able to **ecscape** everyone else. USE **escape**. • Many people come to our chat rooms because the need to **excape** from the every day life and have some fun. USE **escape**. • The Reset Button on this page or the Esc (**Excape**) Key on the Keyboard will clear all entries. USE **Escape**.

***Escape** is the correct spelling, and (i-SKAPE), not (ek-SKAPE) or (eks-SKAPE), the correct pronunciation.*

ECSTACY

Misspelling of **ecstasy**. • Gospel trio The Emotions are filmed in rapturous **ecstacy** in a decrepit storefront church. USE **ecstasy**. • Human life must know **ecstacy**. USE **ecstasy**.

***Ecstacy** is not a variant spelling of **ecstasy**; it is a misspelling. So-called variant spellings are nothing other than misspellings.*

EDIFY

Confused with **enlighten**. To **edify** is to instruct or improve, especially morally or spiritually ("It could mean a thing like bad language, dirty stories, unkind remarks, and gossip, anything that does not **edify** or build someone up"). **Enlighten** means to furnish knowledge or insight to; to make clear; to inform ("The media's role is to **enlighten** the public").

ELDER (ELDEST)

Misused for **older** (**oldest**). • This building has the distinction of being not only the **eldest** building in the city but in southern Illinois. USE **oldest**. • And if the younger ox wanted to "slack off" the **elder** animal would keep him going so the job would be completed. USE **older**.

E

Elder is properly used when referring to two people; **eldest** when referring to three or more people. **Older** is used when referring to two people, animals, or objects; **oldest** when referring to three or more.

When speaking of an individual, **elder** signifies relatively advanced age as well as accomplishment ("As an **elder** statesman among rodeo athletes, Woolman also would like the top competitors to be able to focus more on major rodeos so they can travel less and win more"). Advanced age alone is better expressed with **older** or **elderly** ("That would leave more shots for people in high risk groups like the **elderly** and children").

ELICIT

Misused for **illicit**. • Love making for pleasure exists only in a fantasy world—either with porno flicks, an **elicit** affair between a teacher and student, or a fling between two emotional desperadoes. USE **illicit**. • Anyway, it appears that the label is really nothing but a pathetic front for untold **elicit** and illegal operations. USE **illicit**. • And the entertainment industry said, let's make television shows and movies that promote profanity, violence and **elicit** sex. USE **illicit**.

Elicit is a verb meaning to draw out or evoke; **illicit** is an adjective meaning unlawful or improper.

EMAIL

Do you favor *email* or *e-mail*? I see both usages, and it seems to me that the former, non-hyphenated usage is more common. To me the hyphenation makes better logical sense, however, since the *e* is not a prefix in the usual sense, but the abbreviation of an entire, long word.

And I know *The New Yorker*, to cite one authoritative publication, still keeps the hyphen.

This is largely a matter of house style. The editors at The New Yorker *may have decided to use* **e-mail**, *but* Wired *apparently prefers* **email**.

The Chicago Manual of Style, *always a few years behind and struggling hopefully for modernity, also recommends* **e-mail**. *But since they, for years, have recommended that their readers use the spellings found in* Merriam-Webster's Collegiate Dictionary, *I suspect the manual will fall into hopeless desuetude.*

I prefer **email** *for at least two reasons:*

- **Email** *is as understandable as* **e-mail**; *that is, very few people misunderstand what the nonhyphenated word means or would pronounce it EM-ail.*

- *Many compound words evolve from two words to a hyphenated word to a single word:* **electronic mail, e-mail, email**. *By god, the language does evolve.*

I prefer **email** *to* **e-mail**, *and I find no fault with* **ebusiness**, **ebooks**, *and* **ecommerce**. *Yet I may not be so eager to write* **eindustry** *or* **emanufacturing**; *here, using the hyphen seems necessary, for without, the word may not be immediately readable.*

Four of the six dictionaries in the Fiske Ranking of College Dictionaries list the word as **e-mail** (**email**)—*that is, they prefer the hyphenated spelling but allow the nonhyphenated.* Merriam-Webster's Collegiate Dictionary *and* Webster's New World College Dictionary *allow* **e-mail** *only; neither* mentions the spelling **email**, which to my mind, further illustrates how dictionaries are a hotchpotch of inconsistencies and absurdities.

Electronic mail, of course, is not alone in its evolution to becoming one word. Many words have changed similarly. For instance, **lowercase** (the bottom or lower drawer in a cabinet that housed the small letters of metal type in a compositor's shop) was initially two words. **Lower case** became **lower-case**, became **lowercase**.

In the computer field, where a wholly unknown term may be widely known within months, we have **data base, data-base, database**, and **on line, on-line, online**, to name but two that have evolved speedily.

E

EMBARASS

Misspelling of **embarrass**. • They're not going to come up with anything that's going to **embarass** DHHR, because that's who they work for. USE **embarrass**. • If I am wrong about this, I would totally **embarass** the both of us and possibly ruin our friendship. USE **embarrass**.

Embarrass has two **r**'s and two **s**'s, which is likely the easiest way to remember how the word is spelled for those who seem unable to.

EMBETTERMENT

Idiotic for **betterment** (or similar words). • You are struggling sometimes to see some sign of **embetterment**, but know that the improvements are not too far behind the resolution you have made. USE **betterment**. • The primary objective of the Foundation, then, is the introduction and cultivation of ethical and spiritual principles centered on individual **embetterment**. USE **improvement**. • These two actions, taken together on the same day, made a powerful statement: the **embetterment** of persons with disability was now a global priority. USE **betterment**.

Embetterment is the product of careless people confusing *embitterment* with *betterment*, the word they surely mean to use.

EMIGRATE

Misused for **immigrate**. • Bush announced Friday that his government would tighten a ban on American tourism and other restrictions against the island, and would allow more Cubans to **emigrate** to the United States. USE **immigrate**. • Subsequently, these peoples are drawn to urban centers, even being compelled to **emigrate** to them, suffering readily observable consequences for their quality of life and for their ability to preserve their specific identity. USE **immigrate**.

Some people, perhaps not clever enough to distinguish between **emigrate** and **immigrate**, prefer using **out-migrate** and **in-migrate**: • Given the level of attractiveness, as long as a region's relative wage is below its long-run level, native and foreign workers are assumed to **out-migrate**. USE **emigrate**. • That shortage encouraged African Americans to **in-migrate** from southern cities into the larger industrialized cities of the north in search of that elusive "better life." USE **immigrate**.

*People who **emigrate** leave one place or country for another; those who **immigrate** arrive at one place or country from another.*

EMINENT

Misused for **imminent**. • Anyone reading one of her romances is in **eminent** danger of addiction. USE **imminent**. • Lester Brown, president of the Worldwatch Institute based in Washington, D.C., said the solution to **eminent** water shortages can be found in a water-pricing policy that reflects the real value of water and in research into energy-efficient irrigation technologies. USE **imminent**.

And **imminent** is misused for **eminent**. • One **imminent** scholar of its recent history, Charles Cruickshank (1979), says that deception is the art of misleading an enemy into doing something or not doing something so that his strategic or tactical position will be weakened. USE **eminent**. • City Manager Ted Staton said the city is trying to find a solution to appease fraternity members but it ultimately could use its power of **imminent** domain to obtain the house. USE **eminent**.

Eminent means lofty; renowned or distinguished. Eminent domain is the right of a government to take private property. Imminent means impending or about to occur. SEE ALSO immanent.

ENARMORED

Misspelling of **enamored**. • When he becomes **enarmored** of a young bride-to-be (Madge Bellamy) who is visiting a neighboring estate, Legendre resorts to black magic to make her his own. USE **enamored**. • For those, like myself, who are **enarmored** by the Tucson poet, it is a refreshing visit to an old friend who also has strong connections to Mexico. USE **enamored**.

> **Enamored** (i-NAM-erd), not **enarmored** (i-NAR-merd), means to be captivated or charmed by; to be in love with.

ENCOURAGEABLE (INCOURAGEABLE)

Misspelling of **incorrigible**. • You drove in silence to my condo in Gold Coast where you would prove to be the most **incourageable** and thankless of all my progeny. USE **incorrigible**. • The five words that describe me best are: feisty, stubborn, strong, **incourageable**, independent. USE **incorrigible**. • You're **encourageable**. How could you have spent so much of your time chasing skirts with all that other stuff happening around you? USE **incorrigible**.

> **Incorrigible** refers to someone who's not improvable or manageable. **Encourageable** (or **incourageable**), a word only to the witless, refers to someone who's simply not able.

ENDUE

Misused for **endure** (or similar words). • Pasteuria spores can **endue** long periods of drought. USE **endure**. • Riders begin the ride in snow, **endue** 110 degree heat in the canyons and traverse the American river. USE **endure**.

> **Endue**, not a common word, means to endow with a quality or faculty; to put on or assume; to clothe. **Endure** means to undergo; to carry on despite suffering or hardship.

ENERVATE

Solecistic for **energize** (or similar words). • Even the hurricanes, the torrential downpours, skies solid black with furious clouds, could do nothing but **enervate** and invigorate me. USE **energize**. • Fashion is photography's Frankenstein monster; a hideous parody of the photographic art rudely constructed with bits and pieces discarded from other art forms, which seeks not to elevate, illuminate, invigorate, **enervate** or inspire but exists only to serve its own purpose: to sell a rather ordinary garment at a grossly inflated price. USE **energize**. • Mitchell plays his curmudgeonly role with a vitality and energy that seems to **enervate** the rest of the cast. USE **invigorate**.

*Enervate, an antonym for **invigorate** or **energize**, means to weaken or enfeeble, to debilitate or deplete the energy of.*

That aspect of it in particular is not to my taste, although on the whole, I believe it's been a very successful and enervating and exciting convention.
—Ben Affleck, actor

*Not only did Affleck embarrass himself by saying **enervating** when he meant **invigorating** (or **energizing**), he, embarrassing himself further, chided one or two people who questioned his use of the word.*

ENORMITY

Solecistic for **enormousness** (or similar words). • Ms. Hall believes that God's **enormity** and universality are best communicated through science, which the characters in *Joan of Arcadia* will discuss at least as often as they talk about religion. USE **enormousness**. • The idea of testing athletes was dropped because of cost and the **enormity** of the task of administering tests in a truly random manner. USE **enormousness**. • Many regional projects, breathtaking in their **enormity** and vision, are acting as magnets to the international real estate industry. USE **enormousness**.

*Enormity means monstrous wickedness. **Enormousness** means very great in size, number, or degree; immensity. Though these two words were once synonyms, **enormity** in the sense of **enormousness** has been archaic for some centuries.*

And the enormity of the honor that you have bestowed upon him is still sinking in.
—**Lynne Cheney, wife of U.S. Vice President Dick Cheney**

Enough of this misusage. **Enormity** *is a word like no other; let us not disembowel it by using it as a synonym for* **enormousness***, which of course, is sated with synonyms.*

ENSURE

E

Misused for **assure.** • They have the best track record and they **ensured** us of the broadest distribution of television viewers. USE **assured.** • How can you **ensure** us that the Beijing declaration on commitments for children will be realized and implemented? USE **assure.** • I want to **ensure** you that I will get a satisfactory answer and bring it to the House. USE **assure.**

As there is a distinction between the words **insure** *and* **ensure***, so there is between* **assure** *and* **ensure***. To* **assure** *is to declare confidently; to promise or guarantee. To* **ensure***, to make certain. In Britain,* **assure** *means to* **insure***, to cover by insurance. SEE ALSO* **insure***.*

ENTHUSE

Solecistic for **excite** (or similar words). • A renewed doctrinal, theological and spiritual proclamation of the Christian message, aimed primarily to **enthuse** and purify the conscience of the baptized, cannot be achieved through irresponsible or indolent improvisation. USE **galvanize.** • Book Fairs provide a wide selection of books that **enthuse** children, parents and teachers alike. USE **animate.** • Good interpersonal and time management skills are essential, as is the capacity to **enthuse** others. USE **motivate.** • It can be a way in for some boys, and whatever we can we use as a hook to **enthuse** boys and girls. USE **stimulate.**

What's worse, **enthuse** is sometimes used to mean talk excitedly or be excited: • Scientists can stand up and **enthuse** about their work but it's really important that they question it, too. USE **talk excitedly.** • Angel's free-kick apart, there was precious little else to **enthuse** about in the opening 45 minutes, with the half-time whistle being greeted by boos from sections of the Holte End. USE **be excited.**

*Enthuse, a malformation capable only of misshaping whatever sentence it appears in, is one of those words that reveal more than its users may suppose. Aside from expressing its irregular meaning, **enthuse** exposes its users as slapdash speakers and indifferent writers. SEE ALSO **aggress**.*

ENTOMOLOGY

Misused for **etymology** • A Gemini Mercury and an Aquarian Mercury will talk for hours sharing perspectives on world peace, the digital divide or the **entomology** of words, while a Virgo Mercury and a Capricorn Mercury may go over details of the work to be accomplished in the next week. USE **etymology.** • By systematically teaching students stems of words, their meanings, and their uses, students are able to internalize the **entomology** of words, often revealing hidden meanings and stimulating thought and discussions about words. USE **etymology.**

What's worse, some people misspell **entomology entymology** and misuse it for **etymology:** • Upon successful completion of this unit, the learner will be able to trace the **entymology** of words. USE **etymology.** • If Yiddish dies, Yinglish dies with it, and where would we be without an **entymology** of words like schlemiel, schmuck, putz, yold, bullvan, yenta, shmooze, schlep, schpiel, yentz, chutzpah, meshuga, schlemazel, mazel tov, and if you can think of others, add them to the list. USE **etymology.** • Trent. Uncertain **entymology.** May have been given to those known for traveling, one who lived near one of various rivers named Trent in England or from a town named Trent near Dorset. USE **etymology.**

*Entomology is the study of insects; **etymology** is the study of the origins of words.*

ENVIOUS

Misused for **enviable.** • The tax law change raises the amount farmers can deduct for certain farm-related purchases, while placing some producers in the **envious** position of deciding whether they want to pay income tax at all—at least for now. USE **enviable.** • Either way, we need not peer too closely into the world of George Lucas to see he leads a normal life with a normal family but with a particularly unique and **envious** job. USE **enviable.**

Enviable means evoking feelings of envy. *Envious* means feeling, showing, or characterized by envy. Most often, it is people who are *envious*, things that are *enviable*.

EPICENTER

Misused for **center**. • At the **epicenter** of the clergy sex abuse scandal that brought unprecedented changes and multimillion-dollar settlements to the Roman Catholic church, Massachusetts Catholics were hoping—but not hopeful—that the next pope would help to reform a church some believe is out of step. USE **center**. • Pocatello is a secret arts **epicenter** with a long, and colorful, literary tradition. USE **center**.

The **epicenter** *is the point on the earth's surface directly above the origin of an earthquake. It does not mean the most central point or the center of center.*

E

EPIGRAPH

Misused for **epitaph**. • In the south-eastern side the Cemetery hosts, among others, the tomb of Andrea Costa with an **epigraph** written by poet Giovanni Pascoli. USE **epitaph**. • The **epigraph** on his tombstone, which Conrad had used for the title page of *The Rover*, reads, "Sleep after toyle, port after stormie seas, Ease after warre, death after life, does greatly please." USE **epitaph**.

An **epigraph** *is an inscription on a statue or building; a motto or quotation at the beginning of a literary work. An* **epitaph** *is an inscription on a tomb or gravestone and in memory of the person buried there; a literary piece commemorating a deceased person.*

EPITHET

Confused with **insult** *(or similar words). An* **epithet** *need not be a disparaging or abusive term, though, because many people think it must be, it often is ("If you wonder where this came from, consider their* **epithet** *'sand nigger'"; "A government official used the word 'niggardly,' which is not a racial* **epithet** *but happens to sound like one, and was forced to resign"). An* **epithet** *can also be an innocuous term or name used to describe a person or thing; a descriptive title ("The 'iron' in the* **epithet** *'Iron Chancellor' given to Germany's Otto von Bismarck is a way of describing absolute military power"; "Oddest of the bacterial bunch was the West Nile Isle Virus—a deceptively exotic* **epithet** *that concealed a legacy of astonishing doom").*

EPITOME

*The pronunciation of **epitome** is (i-PIT-ah-mee), not (EP-i-tome).*

EQUALLY AS

Misused for **as**. • Newer categories of antidepressant drugs are **equally as** effective as older-generation antidepressants and roughly equal numbers of patients drop out of clinical trials because of side effects, according to a new evidence report comparing drug treatments for depression. USE **as**. • If Windows applications which include macro programming languages are run on an OS/2 machine, then the OS/2 machine is **equally as** susceptible to macro viruses as a Windows machine. USE **as**. • A banana and whole-wheat bagel would be cheaper and **equally as** nutritious. USE **equally** or **as**.

*Since the word **as** means equally, **equally as** is redundant.*

I can't make a distinction because they're both equally as bad, and equally as evil, and equally as destructive.

—U.S. President George W. Bush

*Both **both** and **as** (and perhaps the **and**s) turn Bush's otherwise capably spoken sentence into near blather.*

I am equally as excited about sending a cashmere sweater to someone who I know doesn't expect it as I am about making a hefty donation to my favorite charity, A Better Chance.

—Oprah Winfrey, *O, The Oprah Magazine*

*To all the glitter of this magazine, grammar is sometimes sacrificed. The **equally** in **equally as** is as unnecessary as the picture of Winfrey on each month's cover.*

EQUIVOCABLE

Idiotic for **equivocal**. • At this time it is **equivocable** whether or not the presumptive myoblast and the satellite cell are functionally identical and at the same stage of myogenic differentiation. USE **equivocal**. • Emotions and dispositions are in no way **equivocable**. USE **equivocal**. • As an aside, Joan Rivers, on Johnny Carson, said she was always **equivocable** about the women's movement. USE **equivocal**.

*Equivocable is in no lexicon. Equally idiotic is **equivocably** for **unequivocally**. Many people, as the next few examples make clear, think **equivocably** means **unequivocally**—allowing no doubt; unambiguously.*

I can state most **equivocably** that we are committed to our membership and zoos in general by way of publications. USE **unequivocally**. • However, what I can **equivocably** state is many thousands of hours of solo are required. USE **unequivocally**. • Regarding a flat earth, the Bible doesn't **equivocably** state that it is flat. USE **unequivocally**.

Others think **equivocable** means **equivalent**: Jim was also awarded the lot at a value $25,000 and Sue was awarded an **equivocable** amount of cash of $25,000 from the parties' savings.

ERUPTION

Misused for **irruption**. • This study establishes that the **eruption** of crows and ravens in the last decade or so is very large. USE **irruption**. • This is the second front of the Revolution: an **eruption** of meaningful content and innovative design that puts the means of production to use for something other than a fast buck. USE **irruption**. • There has been an **eruption** of silent film on video and cable, jointly produced by the Smithsonian Institution and the Library of Congress. USE **irruption**.

And **irruption** is sometimes misused for **eruption**. • Located at the base of the 11,000 foot high Irazu Volcano, the area has been nearly destroyed by **irruptions** and earthquakes three separate times. USE **eruptions**.

*An **eruption** is a sudden, violent outburst; an explosion; a rash or blemish on the skin; the emergence of a tooth through the gums. An **irruption** is a sudden, violent entrance; a bursting in; a rapid and irregular increase in number.*

ESOTERIC

Confused with **exoteric**. **Esoteric** means understood only by a chosen few or the initiated; recondite; private ("The Constitution of the United States is not some **esoteric** document, written to be understood only by people with high IQs and postgraduate education"). **Exoteric** means understood by the public or uninitiated; external; popular ("It is an **exoteric** music; that is, it's meant to be easily comprehended and performed by anyone with little musical training").

ESPECIAL

Confused with **special**. **Special** means distinctive; peculiar; individual; uncommon ("I have a **special** interest in blue eye fluorescence"). **Especial** means exceptional or outstanding ("Such issues have posed **especial** difficulties in Africa, the region with the highest incidence of poverty, as well as in Latin America").

 What is the difference between *special* and *especial*? *The New Yorker* seems to prefer the latter. Is that just an affectation, or is there a real distinction?

Journalists and other writers have forsaken the word **especial**, using **special** almost exclusively. **Special** means particular or specific to someone or something. That The New Yorker uses the word **especial** is to be applauded—so long as by it they mean more than **special**; preeminent; outstanding or exceptional. What's more, to be **special** is hardly a compliment; it may mean you are simply ordinary, or that you are decidedly unordinary. Are we not, today, all drearily **special**? I'd far rather be cranky or foolish or unbearable. And so should you.

ESPECIALLY

The pronunciation of **especially** is (i-SPECH-ah-lee), not (ek-SPECH-ah-lee).

ET AL.

Misused for **etc.** • It also reminded the U.N. that there are a ton of issues on which the U.N. wants the U.S.'s help: AIDS, the sex trade, **et al.** USE **etc.** • Allegations are that he was told to go on leave due to a host of issues, such as the issue of temple demolition, row over the issue of headship in the department of general surgery **et al.** USE **etc.**

Et al. *means "and other people";* ***etc.*** *means "and other things." SEE ALSO* ***and etc.***

ETC., ETC.

E

Solecistic for **etc.** • There is an entrepreneur in Texas that has some land upon which he has placed various "wild" animals such as sheep, deer, wild pigs **etc., etc.** DELETE **etc., etc.** • There was news about Iraq, about Afghanistan's leader visiting the States, **etc., etc.** USE **etc.** • They made all the usual boasts: Vibram soles, nubuk upper leather, Gore-Tex for waterproofing, anti-microbial lining, **etc., etc.** USE **etc.** • Now I'm a good liberal, too, and I believe that helping people, respecting diversity, saving the environment, **etc., etc.**, are good things. USE **etc.**

After ***like, such as, for instance***, *or* ***for example***, *the expression* ***etc.*** *is superfluous—nevermind* ***etc., etc.***, *which, of course, is always unnecessary, always a mark of callow writers and inept editors.*

EVERYDAY

Misused for **every day.** • Hieroglyphics were not for **every day** writing. USE **everyday.** • Do you find yourself overwhelmed with the **every day** tasks of running your business? USE **everyday.**

And **every day** is misused for **everyday:** • The odd thing is that though I see her **everyday**, I doubt I'd recognize her if I ran into her at the mall. USE **every day.**

Everyday, *as an adjective, means common or ordinary.* *Every day*, *as an adverbial phrase, means each day. Almost all language, whether written or spoken, is today everyday. The misuse of these two terms, a fair example of that.*

EVIDENCE

I have been taught that the word *evidence* is uncountable. To my surprise, I have seen quite a few news articles, mostly outside the United States, use the plural form--*evidences*. I'm not sure whether such use is acceptable in today's English. What do you think?

Only as a verb (to attest or prove; to indicate clearly) acting on a singular noun can **evidences** be considered correct:

- We at Carroll celebrate the award, recognizing the energy, dedication, and achievement on the part of Bruce, which this award **evidences**.

- This tournament **evidences** the positive impact that the new West Boulevard YMCA will have in this 'Y' community.

But **evidences** as a noun (a thing or things that help form a conclusion; an indication or sign) is insupportable:

- Sometimes, when the water recedes, so do the **evidences** of all but the trashiest of the trash—but that doesn't mean it isn't there.

- By now, the defense is leading and the prosecutors are seeking for more **evidences** to support the charges against Michael Jackson.

- In my own life, I've seen too many **evidences** of healing through prayer to doubt Owens' claim.

- Guns, illegal drugs and other **evidences** that have been kept at the evidence custodian of the prosecutors' offices are already blighted or decaying.

Indeed, **evidences** is used by people—whether from Pakistan or Virginia—insufficiently familiar with the English language.

EVOKE

Misused for **invoke**. • This is a country of profound religiosity and personal piety—a place where small charismatic and Pentecostal places of worship with names like the "Temple of Fire End Time Church" seem to inhabit every corner and where someone like Taylor, a Baptist, could **evoke** God's name at every turn with a straight face—and, for a time, get away with it. USE **invoke**. • One must even stir the porridge in the proper direction, so as not to **evoke** evil spirits. USE **invoke**.

And **invoke** is misused for **evoke**: • As the dollar slides, dire prognostications of an investors' strike **invoke** comparisons between the U.S. economy and Enron. USE **evoke**. • The first winter storm of the year might **invoke** memories of last year's treacherous winter. USE **evoke**.

> To **invoke** means to call on God or another for help or support; to cite as pertinent or as an authority; to summon an evil spirit; to ask for solemnly. To **evoke** means to elicit or call to mind; to provoke a feeling; to recreate with the imagination.
> **Evoke** does not mean **invoke** though some dictionaries, mimicking the public misusage of this word, now insist it does.

E

EXALT

Misused for **exult**. • Those that finish the journey will **exalt** in their triumph, and rightly so. USE **exult**. • As parents we are delegated to the sidelines, to watch as our children **exalt** in tackling new sports and activities. USE **exult**. • As we share stories, we **exalt** in the joy of completed journeys, solved problems and happy endings. USE **exult**.

And **exult** is used for **exalt**: • Because of his obedience, Jesus was **exulted** to a position of fame second only to Jehovah himself. USE **exalted**.

> To **exalt** is to hold someone in high regard; to raise someone to a high standard; to make noble or glorify. To **exult** is to celebrate; to show jubilation.

EXASPERATE

Misused for **exacerbate**. • Poor illustrations of the white shark also abounded, **exasperating** the problem. USE **exacerbating**. • During the flight you should drink plenty of nonalcoholic beverages (alcohol at any time can cause dehydration and swelling of sinus membranes, and when flying it will just **exasperate** the effects of dry cabin air). USE **exacerbate**. • The only two alternatives in this case are to raise taxes or cut spending—both of which serve to **exasperate** rather than temper recessions. USE **exacerbate**.

> **Exasperate** *(ig-ZAS-pah-rate) means to annoy greatly or make angry;* **exacerbate** *(ig-ZAS-er-bate) to aggravate or make worse.*
> *A dictionary that records that both words mean to aggravate or increase the severity of is a dictionary to shun—or shed. SEE ALSO* **aggravate**.

A mother of five, Christine continued to gain weight with each pregnancy, exasperating a weight problem she says she had her whole life.
—Caritas St. Elizabeth's Medical Center

EXCEED

Misused for **accede**. • And given that his Honour was not going to **exceed** to the wishes the child had expressed, he took the view that it was an appropriate case given the age and maturity of the child to speak to the child. USE **accede**. • Henry did have a third child, a son, named Edward VI, who **exceeded** to the throne after his father's death, but he died at the age of fifteen. USE **acceded**.

> **Exceed** *means to surpass; to go beyond what is required or expected.* **Accede** *means to give one's consent to; concede or agree to a request, demand, or treaty; to come into an office or position of authority.*

EXCELL

Misspelling of **excel**. • They've come a long way since taking the court together in the third grade, but they're still going strong, mesh beautifully and **excell** in a sport they both love. USE **excel**. • According to Police, the daughter of the businessman, who did not **excell** in her studies, was denied a prefectship. USE **excel**.

> *Though the noun* **excellence** *is spelled with two l's, the verb* **excel** *has but one l.*

EXCEPT

Misused for **accept**. • You never know, so please **except** my apologies. USE **accept**. • But, I'll **except** your eternal gratitude, friendship, and patronage in return. USE **accept**. • All major credit cards are **excepted**. USE **accepted**. • We **except** all ad offers. USE **accept**.

*The confusion between **except**—which means excluding or otherwise than—and **accept**—which means to receive something offered or to agree to something—is most often due to a lapse of carefulness rather than a lack of comprehension. Carelessness, however, is easily just as harmful as confusion.*

EXCEPTIONABLE

E

Misused for **exceptional**. • Transicoil LVDT pressure transducers provide high accuracy and **exceptionable** reliability at moderate prices. USE **exceptional**. • You will treasure this print, not only for its **exceptionable** beauty but also for the memory of Nelson, Sarazen, and Snead. USE **exceptional**.

__Exceptionable__ means objectionable; __exceptional__ means something quite different: uncommon or extraordinary.

EXHILERATION

Misspelling of **exhilaration**. • Or if the child who for the first time bravely put his whole head under the rolling wave before it crashed, would in later years remember the **exhileration** he felt. USE **exhilaration**. • This was a more exciting journey where the atma (soul) soared to new heights and there was a sense of **exhileration** instead of the peace and calm and contentedness of Muar! USE **exhilaration**.

__Exhilaration__, not __exhileration__ (and certainly not __acceleration__) is the correct spelling. SEE ALSO __accelerate__.

EXISTANCE

Misspelling of **existence**. • The same reports were seized on by environmentalists as evidence that **co-existance** was impossible and growing crops such as GM rape would cause contamination. USE **co-existence**. • The alleged **existance** of biological, chemical and nuclear weapons that posed an imminent danger to the western world was one of the main reasons for the U.S.-led war that toppled the Iraqi Leader. USE **existence**.

*Existence (three **e**'s: beginning, middle, and end), not **existance**, is the correct spelling.*

EXOTIC

*Confused with **erotic**. **Erotic** means of or relating to sexual desire; amatory ("But those images of the city may soon have to make way for a new project called Erotichesky Peterburg, or **Erotic** Petersburg, that aims to highlight the city's sensual pleasures"). **Exotic** means foreign; strikingly strange or fascinating ("However, selling and keeping the more **exotic** creatures such as Burmese pythons and Gila monsters could become illegal under a proposed Lake County Health Department ordinance").*

EXPATRIOT

Misused for **expatriate**. • Integration of political refugees is an important issue in Switzerland, a small country with a large number of **expatriot** residents. USE **expatriate**. • We open with Adolfo Olaechea, a fifty-two-year-old Peruvian **expatriot** living in London, England. USE **expatriate**. • "April is the cruelest month," begins T. S. Eliot's most famous poem, and it is ironic that, as an **expatriot**, he never had to suffer the agony of the Internal Revenue Service and April 15 in America. USE **expatriate**.

*Expatriots (people who no longer love or support their country) are likely few, but the number of **expatriates** (people who—though they may love their country—live in another) ever increases.*

Joerg, a German expatriot and local windsurfing pro, had suggested a ride through El Choco.
—**Steven Mark, *The Seattle Times***

*Mr. Mark means **expatriate**. Misusing the language may merit a smack in the face.*

EXPIATE

Misused for **expatiate**. • The wise man from America **expiated** at length on two issues: first, that everyone should live according to his means and second, that there should be an international division of labor. USE **expatiated**. • It would be a mistake, we think, to **expiate** on what may be the merit of these paintings, or to do more than point out that many of them are very summary in their impressionistic statement of the pictorial facts. USE **expatiate**.

> To **expiate** (EK-spee-ate) is to atone for sins; to make amends. To **expatiate** (ek-SPA-shee-ate) is to speak or write at length.

Assorted obscure Southern musicians--a guy named "16 Horsepower" was a favorite--and not-so-obscure writers (Harry Crews) pontificate, ruminate, meditate and expiate on their rural home-country from the farms, honky-tonks, churches, jails and junkyards of the Southland.

—Roger Moore, *Orlando Sentinel*

EXPIRE

Idiotic for **retire** (or similar words). • CNN.com will **expire** this article on 06/12/2003. USE **remove**. • He thought that T13 should probably vote to **expire** the document if there were no issues with this action. USE **retire**. • Authors wouldn't be able to **expire** documents, only to request that the documents be **expired**. USE **delete; deleted**.

> **Expire** means to end or terminate; to cease to be valid; to die; to exhale. Let us disabuse information technology professionals and their peers of the belief that **expire** should also mean to retire, remove, or delete.

EXPLICIT

> Confused with **implicit**. **Explicit** means distinctly stated; definite ("A row erupted today over an **explicit** new booklet on puberty aimed at nine-year-old schoolchil-

dren"). **Implicit** *means implied; suggested or understood; without question ("The letter contained an **implicit** threat that Democrats had sufficient strength to block the bill under Senate rules").*

EXPRESSO

Misspelling of **espresso**. • While 90 percent of the coffee sold in cafés was **expresso**, it represented only 5 percent for Starbucks. USE **espresso**. • Since then, the Wykoop House has been purchased by Saugerties couple Wendy Ricks and Mark Colligan, who plan to turn it into an **expresso** bar, Internet café and gourmet ice cream shop. USE **espresso**.

*The word is spelled **espresso** (i-SPRES-oh), not **expresso** (ex-PRES-oh).*

EXTANT

Misused for **extent**. • These efforts demonstrate the **extant** to which Kao-tsung cherished certain types of jade, and, by implication, the impact that his personal taste had on the content of the palace collection. USE **extent**. • Another indication of the **extant** of the problem is the support market for sprays, dips, etc. to rid your pet of unwanted parasites. USE **extent**. • We will prosecute any and all violators to the full **extant** of the law. USE **extent**.

And **extent** is sometimes misused for **extant**: • From this perspective, one could say that, of the currently **extent** species, man must be one of the oldest, having had the time to adapt to most environments. USE **extant**. • This tune is a simplified phrase from one of the **extent** fragments of ancient Greek music. USE **extant**.

*Extant means still in existence; not extinct. **Extent** means range, size, breadth, or scope of something.*

EXTRACT

Misused for **exact**. • However, uncertainty certainly is not **extracting** a toll from the American housing market. USE **exacting**. • We have taken it upon ourselves to promise to **extract** vengeance for them. USE **exact**. • It is not a time for demonstrating the coalition's power or **extracting** revenge from a beaten despot. USE **exacting**.

To **exact** is to demand (a payment); to inflict. To **extract** is to remove or draw out; to obtain by force; to obtain by mechanical or chemical action; to derive information from a source; to deduce.

EXTRAORDINARY

The pronunciation of **extraordinary** is (ek-STROR-di-nair-ee), not (ek-strah-OR-di-nair-ee).

EXTREMIFY

Idiotic for **hyperbolize** (or similar words). • Indeed, a relatively small portion of senators extremify their public ideology during this decade. USE **exaggerate**. • To extremify the example: if I'm having a debate with someone who is speaking in Latin, what would it profit me to attempt to answer them in English? USE **give an extreme**.

In using **extremify**, people acknowledge their inability to think well. We use incorrect words, counterfeit words, simple assemblages, when we cannot think of the better built words available to us.

E

FARTHER

Misused for **further**. • Elsewhere, Parker goes even **farther** with Paul McCartney's "My Love," eliminating all the vocal parts and playing the melody on sax. USE **further**. • Earlier this week, he stunned the court by musing about the possibility of breaking the company into three parts, going even **farther** than the government had proposed. USE **further**.

Further is also misused for **farther**: • The field in this type of magnet is zero at dead center, but grows linearly as you move **further** away from the center. USE **farther**.

Farther refers to physical distance; *further* refers to extent or degree.

FATEFUL

Misused for **fatal**. • The representative of Fiji added that most deaths and **fateful** injuries would have been preventable if suitable intervention had been developed. USE **fatal**. • In order not to fall prey to this **fateful** disease, I learnt that prevention is the best tool. USE **fatal**.

*Fatal means resulting in death; disastrous. **Fateful** means determined by fate; prophetic; significant. Several dictionaries maintain that **fatal** also means **fateful**, but the true meaning of this is that dictionaries are increasingly defective and unreliable.*

FAWN

Misused for **faun**. • Claude Débussy (1862–1918), whose style is called Impressionist, used tone color and nontraditional scales in his *Prelude to the Afternoon of a Fawn* (1894). USE **Faun**. • I like to characterize the period following 9/11 as a "Pan Period" because silhouettes during the past four seasons since the fall of '01 have been dominated by a juxtaposition that rivals the body of the mythic **fawn**. USE **faun**.

And **faun** is misused for **fawn:** • Fans of classic rock will **faun** over this album while guitar enthusiasts will perhaps adore it. USE **fawn.**

*A **fawn** is a young deer; to **fawn** is to act servilely or obsequiously; to attempt to please. A **faun** is a god in Roman mythology, half man and half goat.*

FEARFUL

Misused for **fearsome.** • We were either viewed as the pitiful refugees or we were looked at as the horrible and **fearful** terrorists. USE **fearsome.** • Nigerian gangs in South Africa have now became the most **fearful** immigrants in South Africa. USE **fearsome.** • Their bond was so strong that when they crossed over, it made them the most powerful and **fearful** vampires known to man or vampire. USE **fearsome.**

*Though many dictionaries declare that **fearful** and **fearsome** are synonyms, dictionaries—it must be remembered—merely record how people use the language.*
*It is far better to use **fearful** to mean afraid or frightened, and **fearsome** to mean causing fear. If we allow one word to mean much the same as another, we have fewer words that matter. If we have fewer words, nuance and knowledge are lost.*

F

FEEL BADLY

Misused for **feel bad.** • And when she loses, I think she'll **feel very badly.** USE **feel very bad.** • I **feel badly** because I understand Connie is upset with me because I think we joked about her departure from CBS. USE **feel bad.** • Our resident Sexdoc Dr. William Fitzgerald has advice for a woman whose husband is constantly making her **feel badly** about her body—in and out of bed. USE **feel bad.**

*The distinction should be maintained between **feel bad** and **feel badly**. The former is meant to describe emotional or physical condition; the latter, touch. SEE ALSO **bad**.*

FELICITATE

Confused with **facilitate.** • Lord Shiva created Lord Brahma to **felicitate** the process of creation and bestowed him with all these eighteen learnings. USE **facilitate.** • The newly launched offerings are designed to provide an effective solution to the increasing challenges of risk measurement and management faced by banks the world over and to **felicitate** the adoption of quantitative techniques and international best practices in risk management. USE **facilitate**.

> *Facilitate (fah-SIL-i-tate) means to make easier;* **felicitate** *(fi-LIS-i-tate), a less common word, means to congratulate.*

FETCH

How and why did the word *fetch* become popular with the U.S. stock market media? Example: "Xerox fetched $10 at today's closing." My third-grade teacher taught us that this word was not acceptable English.

Fetch, in the sense of "to go after and bring back," though perfectly good English, may seem informal and folksy to some. It does to me, as perhaps it did to your teacher. The meaning "to sell for a certain price" has no stigma even though the U.S. financial market does.

FINELY

Misused for **finally**. • Ronald Reagan was quoted as saying, "Those that have known freedom and lost it, have never regained it," and we are seeing the loss of our freedoms **finely** come to fruition. USE **finally**. • It looks like I can **finely** stop complaining about the cold and start complaining about the heat. USE **finally**. • When war **finely** began, the republicans, under the name of "unconditional Union men," took complete control of the new state. USE **finally**.

> *Both adverbs,* **finely** *means in a fine manner, discriminatingly, or in small parts, and* **finally** *means in conclusion or conclusively.*

FIRST OFF

Solecistic for **first**. • **First off**, design a simple letterhead that you'll use throughout your packet pages. USE **First**. • **First off**, I want to thank everyone for being here this morning. USE **first**. • Jerry, **first off**, this is a great forum, and thanks for providing us all with such great info. USE **first**.

> **First off**—like **first of all** and **in the first place** and **first and foremost** and **firstly**—is a thoughtless expression that people use only because they hear others using it. The **off** is completely meaningless. At least people seem to have the great good sense not to say **second off**. SEE ALSO **start off (out)**.

FISCAL

> Confused with **physical**. **Fiscal** (FIS-kel), of or relating to finances or revenue, and **physical** (FIZ-i-kel), of or relating to the body or material world, are as different in meaning as they are in spelling.

F

FIXING TO

I believe that *fix'n to* is a Southern expression. I also believe that it is grammatically incorrect even if properly spelled *fixing to*, but I do not know exactly why it is improper.

The expression **fixing to** means "planning to (do something)" or "on the verge of (doing something)." Perhaps you have trouble understanding why **fixing to** is improper because—dislike it though you may—it is not improper; it is, as you say, Southern.

Much regional English sounds incorrect to people from other areas, and indeed much if it can be called incorrect. Some of these expressions, however, like **fixing to**, though they sound incorrect are, instead, merely informal or casual. Still, anyone who wishes to make a favorable impression on others would be well advised to shun the regionalism **fixing to**.

FLACCID

*The pronunciation of **flaccid** is (FLAK-sid), not (FLA-sid).*

FLARE

Misused for **flair.** • Wahlberg shows plenty of **flare** in the sensational exposé *Boogie Nights*! USE **flair.** • Jane is an accomplished actress who has a natural talent and **flare** for performing. USE **flair.** • Glasgow's music seems to be a mixture of the best parts of everywhere else. Dirt from Detroit, cheekiness from Chicago, style from Paris and **flare** from New York. USE **flair.** • With precision **flare** and panache she has demonstrated before hundreds of thousands of spectators across the globe. USE **flair.**

> *Flair means natural ability or aptitude; style; flamboyance. Flare, as a verb, means to blaze brightly; to burst out in anger. As a noun, it means a flame.*

FLAUNT

Misused for **flout.** • Why is Ted Kennedy a "pseudo-Catholic"? He claims to be a Catholic but **flaunts** the rules of the church he belongs to. USE **flouts.** • Companies regularly **flaunt** the laws, collecting and disseminating personal information. USE **flout.** • North Korea continues to **flaunt** international law by speeding ahead with their nuclear program with no consequences whatsoever. USE **flout.** • Leave it up to the Rocky Mountain volleyball team to **flaunt** convention. USE **flout.**

> *To **flaunt** is to show off or exhibit ostentatiously; to **flout** is to disobey or show contempt for.*

That flaunts industry convention, in which agents provide a package of services for a commission. It also flaunts the law, at least in a technical sense.

—Loren Steffy, *Houston Chronicle*

*Steffy **flaunts** his unfamiliarity with the difference in meaning between **flaunt** and **flout**.*

FLOTSAM

*Confused with **jetsam**. **Flotsam** is the wreckage from a ship or its cargo found at sea; odds and ends; people who live on the fringes of society ("The federal government is considering several measures to reduce the flotilla of **flotsam** that's clogging seas around northern Australia, the vast bulk of it coming from countries to our North"; "Police never enter The Zone, an urban wasteland peopled by society's **flotsam**"). **Jetsam** is cargo thrown overboard to lighten a ship in distress; such material washed ashore; discarded items ("**Jetsam** was the luggage, furniture and fittings thrown overboard to lighten the ship when it was being shipwrecked").*

FLOUNDER

Misused for **founder**. • Staff writer P. J. Connelly muses over Apple's ill-fated Open-Doc and wonders why a **floundering** ship would toss women and children overboard to stay above water. USE **foundering**. • Sparks fly when Dawson manages to talk Rose out of jumping overboard, but tragedy awaits as the unsinkable ship hits an iceberg and begins to **flounder**. USE **founder**. • Unfortunately, while the business thrived, the marriage **floundered**; in late 1997, Pete and Linda divorced after thirty-three years together. USE **foundered**.

*To **flounder** is to move clumsily or thrash about; to struggle confusedly. To **founder** is to fill with water and sink; to cave in; to fail or collapse.*

FLUSH OUT

Misused for **flesh**. • We also appreciate the need for business executives to **flush out** an idea before proceeding into anything too robustly and quickly. USE **flesh out**. • I take these masks, using them for comic effect or using them to **flush out** story or create atmosphere. USE **flesh out**. • Frequent brainstorming sessions between the contractor and customer can **flush out** details, and new ideas can be implemented immediately. USE **flesh out**.

*To **flesh out** is to realize; to fill out or give substance to. To **flush out** is to force an animal or person into the open.*

FONT

Misused for **fount**. • He was a **font** of stories about ancient feuds, ward fights, canny pols, and the funny and desperate moments the political life dishes out. USE **fount**. • So it's no wonder that the Democrats seek one of their own, a **font** of wisdom who can divine what is wrong and point the way forward. USE **fount**.

And from a Ph.D. candidate at Michigan State University: • It was agreed that responses to each question would not exceed ten pages in length using a 12 point Times Roman **fount** with one-and-one-half spacing and one inch margins. USE **fount**.

*In the United States, a **font** (FONT) is a set of type of one face and size, and a **fount** (FOUNT) is a fountain, or a source of something, knowledge, for example. These are two different words, with two different pronunciations and two different meanings. Let the laxicographers mix them up if they must; let the rest of us understand that it is language, and our ability to use it, that best identifies us as human. The less well we use the language, the less thoughtful, cogent, and communicative we likely are—indeed, the less humanity we likely have.*

FOR ALL INTENSE OF (INTENSIVE) PURPOSES

Solecistic for **for all intents and purposes**. • For all intense purposes asthma is behind me unless I come upon a stressful situation or dust. USE **For all intents and purposes**. • While many may shun from any comparison to the men, the fact is that the WUSA, **for all intensive purposes**, will be imitating the structure of MLS. USE **for all intents and purposes**. • Only in this play a cookie is a biscuit because **for all intense purposes** the play is delivered in a foreign language. USE **for all intents and purposes**. • We have been waiting since 6 March 2004 and we have not seen it, so may we presume that **for all intense of purposes** we are never going to see it? USE **for all intents and purposes**.

***For all intents and purposes** means in effect or virtually. **For all intense (intensive) (of) purposes** is a meaningless mash.*

FOR AWHILE

Misused for **for a while**. • They've been around **for awhile**, they happen with some frequency in these parts and as long as you're willing to crouch idiotically beneath a friendly desk, you're as prepared as humanly possible. USE **for a while** or **awhile**. • Just need to get away from it all and take it easy **for awhile**? USE **for a while** or **awhile**. • Considered to be the logo for the Louisiana Tech Drumline, the name was dropped **for awhile**. USE **for a while** or **awhile**.

> **Awhile**, *an adverb, means for a short time or* **for a while**, *and hence, does not need the* **for** *preceding it. Using one phrase for the other ought to be frowned upon.*

FORCEFULLY

Misused for **forcibly** • Hong Kong is a colony that Great Britain **forcefully** took from China about 150 years ago when China was weak and intimidated by the strengths of the Western World. USE **forcibly**. • On Monday, Thai police arrested more than 200 Pak villagers who had **forcefully** broken into the Government House compound on Sunday. USE **forcibly**. • In all territories, members of minority groups have been **forcefully** evicted from their homes, violently attacked, robbed, threatened, dismissed from their jobs and, in some cases, killed. USE **forcibly**.

> *To the diminution of us all, the meanings of these two words often trespass on each other:* **forcefully** *means with force or power, effectively;* **forcibly** *most often describes actions involving physical force. Both* **forceful** *and* **forcible** *mean having or using force or strength, but the former is reserved for metaphorical or abstract force (such as a* **forceful** *speaker), whereas the latter is reserved for physical or exceptional force (such as a* **forcible** *eviction).*

FOREBEAR

Misused for **forbear**. • Equity, however, enters injunctions or decrees directing someone either to act or to **forebear** from acting. USE **forbear**. • I'm going to **forebear** from writing a long, goofy column today and instead will just extend my thanks to Mark for his dedication. USE **forbear**. • Due to the weakness of their faith and their utter lack of wisdom, they were not able to **forebear**. USE **forbear**.

> **Forbear**, *a verb, means to refrain from or resist; to control oneself under provocation.* **Forebear**, *a noun, is an ancestor. Ignore all dictionaries that would have you believe* **forbear** *is also a noun having the same meaning as* **forebear**.

FOREGO

Misused for **forgo**. • NASA officials decided Friday to **forego** any extra inspections on shuttle *Endeavor's* twin orbital maneuvering engine pods. USE **forgo**. • The researchers looked at the proportion of young people who reported **foregoing** medical care, their reasons for doing so, and their risk for health problems. USE **forgoing**. • What better way to fund the government than to **forego** all those deductions and all that loophole lawyering? USE **forgo**.

> **Forego** *means to precede; to go before.* **Forgo** *means to do without; abstain from; renounce. Some dictionaries offer the spelling* **forego** *as a variant of* **forgo***, but this is only because so many people have confused the words for so long—and dictionaries merely compile people's language usage, however incorrect or cretinous.*

FOREWARN

Misused for **warn**. • I will **forewarn** readers that the following is a discussion of feminists and liberals, some of whom are adolescents attending public high schools. USE **warn**. • We're trying to be proactive and **forewarn** students that if they plan to drink they need to go somewhere else. USE **warn**. • I want to **forewarn** potential ticket buyers: I'm not going to be playing an acoustic version of "Thunder Road." USE **warn**.

> *To* **warn***—to notify or make aware of in advance—renders the word* **forewarn** *unnecessary, useless. People often use the phrase* **warn in advance***, which many know is a silly redundancy, but to* **forewarn***, which means to warn in advance, is equally silly, equally redundant.* **Forewarn in advance***, were someone to use it, would be irrefutably foolish.*

FORMERLY

Solecistic for **formally**. • Many companies embark on a strategic planning process, either **formerly** or informally. USE **formally**. • Customer Solutions **formerly** announces the release of a new and innovative approach to bag tags and label product design, development and distribution. USE **formally**.

> **Formerly** *means at an earlier time, erstwhile, once;* **formally***, officially, properly, or ceremoniously.*

FORTE

Confused with **forte**. **Forte** *(FORT) means one's strong point; the strongest part of the blade of a sword.* **Forte** *(FOR-tay) is a musical notation meaning loud or forceful.*

When did *forte* (FOR-tay) become acceptable as a substitute for the proper pronunciation (FORT) in the sense of "someone's strong suit"?

It is not acceptable—despite what your dictionary may tell you. **Forte** *(pronounced for-TAY), as you know, is a musical instruction meaning loud or forceful.* **Forte** *(pronounced FORT), one's strong suit; the strongest part of a sword's blade.*

Misguided, impressionable people think the words, though spelled the same, are pronounced they same. They are two different words (one of French derivation, one of Italian), and they have two different pronunciations.

F

FORTUITOUS

Misused for **fortunate** (or similar words). • Some of these days, now that we are a dominant, if not the dominant power in the world, we may have to make good without Allies or time or **fortuitous** circumstances to assist us. USE **fortunate**. • State employees looked on today's results not only as **fortuitous** for themselves, but the services they provide as well. USE **fortunate**.

> **Fortuitous** *means happening by chance, accidental or unplanned. It does not mean—despite the efforts of a good many people—**fortunate** or **lucky**.*

FORWARD

Misused for **foreword** • Cynthia teams up with Roopster Roux to write the **forward** for *Roopster Roux Presents... Modern Day Fairy Tales.* USE **foreword**. • As he points out in the **forward** of the book, you will find the inches and centimeters approach to measurements used in his illustrations. USE **foreword**.

*Authors often confuse **forward** with **foreword**. **Forward** has a number of meanings, most of which people are familiar with. Among its meanings, however, is not a preface or introductory remarks in, say, a book; this meaning belongs to **foreword**.*

FORWARDS

Misused for **forward**. • The paddle tip describes a figure-of-eight pattern and each stage of the cycle produces **forwards** movement. USE **forward**. • Each click will accelerate the clock in a **forwards** direction. USE **forward**.

*As an adverb, either **forwards** or **forward** is correct. As an adjective, only **forward** is correct. SEE ALSO **backwards**.*

FOURTY

Misspelling of **forty**. • The Pats enter the holiday break in second place in the East division with a 20-13-0-1 record and **fourty**-one points. USE **forty**. • **Fourty**-two-year-old Rick Armbruster of Alanson was last seen in a bar in Indian River on October 11. USE **Forty**.

***Forty**, not **fourty**, is the correct spelling.*

The game features fourty maps, fifty enemy creatures, three difficulty levels, and high quality
graphics and sound effects.
—Jen Edwards, *Brighthand*

*Anyone who can count to one hundred should know the correct spelling of **forty**. Edwards and the people at Dull-head apparently neither can nor do.*

FOWL

Misused for **foul**. • If it has **fowl** smell, you should reject that wine. USE **foul**. • I believe that while even Potter's author shows murder as a **fowl** act young people just don't need to read about any more violence. USE **foul**.

And **foul** is misused for **fowl**: • They used these assays in seven TMJ patients who had described recent contact with domestic **foul** (chickens, pigeons, etc) or pet birds (canaries, etc), plus ten other TMJ patients who had no close contact with birds (controls). USE **fowl**.

> **Fowl** *is any of several large, domestic birds used for food; the flesh of these birds.* **Foul** *means offensive to the senses; stinking; filthy; putrid; obscene; abominable; inclement; not according to the rules of a game; dishonest.*

FROM WHENCE

F

Misused for **whence**. • If the children represent where society is going, then the elderly represent **from whence** we came. USE **whence**. • But I kept thinking about what I'd seen on the sunporch that morning when I wandered in to look out over Lake Margrethe, **from whence** our weather usually comes. USE **whence**.

> **From whence** *is redundant for* **whence**, *which means from what place, from where.*

FULSOME

Misused for **abundant** (or similar words). • As White House aides expressed their glee when Independent Counsel Kenneth Starr resigned last month, one top official broke ranks, offering Starr **fulsome** praise. USE **gushing**. • At no point in his broadcasts did Jones disclose that there was a financial consideration underpinning his **fulsome** editorial support. USE **enthusiastic**. • European leaders marked Reagan's death with unusually **fulsome** praise. USE **effusive**.

> **Fulsome** *means insincere, offensive, or odious, not, as is meant in these examples, abundant, effusive, or enthusiastic.*

Under certain circumstances, after the sampling part of that process is taken... it's supposed to go forward with a more fulsome process.
—**Theodore Olson, attorney for George W. Bush**

Full or *complete* is what Olson meant, not *fulsome*, which means insincere or offensively flattering. If someone is to make such an error, it's best not to do so, as Olson did, before the U.S. Supreme Court.

FUN

Is the use of the noun *fun* as an adjective (as in "We had a fun time") truly permissible nowadays?

All six of our largely descriptivist dictionaries in the Fiske Ranking of College Dictionaries (Appendix A) allow **fun** in the sense of enjoyable or amusing although several of these dictionaries do concede that fun as an adjective is "informal."

Why do you suppose people use the adjectival **fun**, a mean, monosyllabic word, when they might use **entertaining** or **amusing** or **enjoyable** or **pleasurable** or **pleasant** or any one of a dozen other words?

The reason is that most people are linguistically lazy and find it comforting to speak as their peers do. Few people read good literature, from which they might indeed learn to speak, now and then, less casually. If we were to encourage individuality and thoughtfulness, we might also begin to hear people occasionally say "We had a merry time."

GAFF

Misused for **gaffe**. • Ironically, that refusal to disclose his background leads to his professional demise, when an innocent verbal **gaff** in a classroom is instead viewed as a deliberate racist comment. USE **gaffe**. • Gifford chatted about some of the politically incorrect remarks he had heard on TV over the years, seemingly inspired by Rush Limbaugh's recent **gaff** on TV. USE **gaffe**.

> A **gaffe** is a social blunder; an embarrassing mistake. A **gaff** is a large hook on a pole used to land large fish; a pole attached to a ship's mast used to extend a sail; a metal spur attached to the leg of a fighting cock; a climbing hook used by workers.

GAMBIT

Misused for **gamut**. • This video runs the **gambit** of instructional techniques used against various weapons and in real situations. USE **gamut**.

And **gamut** is misused for **gambit**: • Readers who relish a powerfully written amateur sleuthing romantic fantasy will want to peruse Candace Sams' opening **gamut** in what the audience will hope is a long running series. USE **gambit**.

> **Gambit** is an opening move in the game of chess in which a piece is sacrificed to get an advantage; an opening maneuver or remark intended to gain an advantage. **Gamut** is a full range of something; all recognized musical notes. To **run the gamut** is to go through the complete range of something.

GAMBOL

Misused for **gamble**. • But, wealthy men were **gamboling** away their homes and livestock against futures in the tulip growing industry! USE **gambling**. • Initial intentions are to offer the developed product to major gaming sites for a portion of the advertising revenues as well as develop interest in the **gamboling** industry. USE **gambling.**

*To **gambol** is to skip or leap about playfully; to frolic. To **gamble** is to play games of chance; to bet; to take a risk or put at risk.*

GAUNTLET

Misused for **gantlet.** • If the odds are against her, they're against him as well and the **gauntlet** of bullets they run on the way to Phoenix is spectacular. USE **gantlet.** • Prince, who is told by Eastwood that he is coming, sets up an incredible police **gauntlet**, hundreds of cops who riddle the bus as it roars into the city. USE **gantlet.** • The new year is just around the corner, but first you have to get through the **gauntlet** of activities. USE **gantlet.**

And **gantlet** is misused for **gauntlet:** • A loss next week will provide the opportunity for him to throw down the **gantlet** publicly. USE **gauntlet.** • For heavy degreasing or cleaning jobs, where your hands are likely to be submerged in solvent, use thicker, over ten mil, gloves with a **gantlet.** USE **gauntlet.**

*A **gantlet** (GANT-lit) is a form of punishment in which a person had to run between two rows of men who struck him with clubs or sticks; a severe trial or ordeal; two railroad tracks that converge into one so that one rail of each track is within the rails of the other. A **gauntlet** (GONT-lit) is a medieval glove covered with metal plates; a fortified glove with a flared cuff; a challenge. **Take up the gauntlet** and **throw down the gauntlet** mean, respectively, to accept a challenge and to issue a challenge.*

GENTILE

Misused for **genteel.** • When men open the doors for ladies and girls, they exhibit a respect for women and encourage their daughters to behave in a feminine and **gentile** fashion. USE **genteel.** • Compared to the strongly etched drama of Shakespeare, Jane Austen's books were more refined, **gentile** and civilized and as such Patrick Doyle's score is more elegant and restrained than the tempestuous moods he created for *Henry V* or the exuberant sunniness of *Much Ado About Nothing.* USE **genteel.**

And **gentile** is also misused for **gentle:** • After the history our people have had, leave it to the Japanese to be forever kind and **gentile.** USE **gentle.**

Gentile *(JEN-tile) means any person not a Jew; a Christian; somebody who is not Mormon; someone who does not believe in God.* **Genteel** *(jen-TEEL) means well-mannered and refined; excessively or pretentiously refined.* **Gentle** *(JEN-til) means kind; considerate; tender.*

GIFT...(WITH)

Idiotic for **give** (or similar words). • **Gift** her a soft Pashmina wrap to keep her cozy and she will know that you really care. USE **Give**. • Keep them all for yourself or **gift** them for the holidays. USE **give**. • Keeping alive this charming tradition, not only gives family and friends an opportunity to **gift** the bride, but also to share some personal, intimate moments while the bride ends her single life and begins on her road to marriage. USE **buy a gift for**. • If you have one specific cause in mind you can **gift** stocks and shares to CAF naming the charity you wish to benefit from the proceeds. USE **donate**.

Though **gift** *as a verb is an antiquated form, the use of it today is nonsense, even offensive. When we have words like* **give** *and* **donate** *or* **make a gift of**, **gift** *the verb is patent commercialese for* **buy** *or* **purchase**. *SEE ALSO* **shop (it) against**.

G

GODSPEED

I am a seminarian from the Philippines and I'd like to ask what does the expression *God speed* mean?

Godspeed *is an expression of good fortune or success to a person beginning a journey or venture. It derives from the fifteenth-century phrase* **God spede you**, *meaning "God prosper you."*

GOOD

Solecistic for **well**. • I tried to play my heart out and did the best I could; we really all did **good**. USE **well**. • He is funny and sings **good** enough to give us a pleasant performance. USE **well**. • What programs run **good** with other programs? USE **well**. • Currently the 2-in-1 Comfort Shorty is my favorite pen/stylus combo: It looks **good**, it writes **good** and it has a nice price. USE **well**. • Here in the mountains, the radar doesn't work too **good**. USE **well**.

> **Well**, not **good**, is the word that accompanies the verbs shown in the examples. **Well** may be used as an adjective or an adverb. **Good** is always an adjective and should never modify a verb.
>
> With sensory verbs like **feel**, **taste**, **smell**, and linking verbs like **be**, **appear**, and **seem**, **good** is the word to use: ("At the starting line, you could tell she wasn't feeling too **good**."; "We felt **good** about ourselves last year when we beat them twice."; "Corn yields appear **good**, but harvesting is still behind its average pace."; "Our first obligation is to ensure that the water tastes **good**.")
>
> People who use **good** where **well** should be are soulless speakers.

GORILLA

Misused for **guerilla**. • Kelly ran his pizza operation in a very competitive arena where **gorilla** marketing played a major role in controlling his market share. USE **guerilla**. • There is no way for a country to defend itself against the U.S. other than fight using **gorilla** warfare. USE **guerilla**.

> A **gorilla** is a large and powerful ape; a person who is regarded as, or who looks like, a gorilla; a thug. A **guerilla** is a member of a band of volunteer soldiers bent on defeating a more established enemy; a terrorist. As an adjective, **guerilla** relates to unconventional marketing practices (**guerilla marketing**); drama about political or social issues that is usually performed outside (**guerilla theater**).

GOURMAND

> Confused with **gourmet**. A **gourmand** (goor-MAND) is a lover of food who likely eats to excess ("They savoured French words with all the gusto of a Parisian **gourmand**"). A **gourmet** (goor-MAY) is a connoisseur of food and drink; an epicure ("Thailand is a **gourmet's** paradise"). As an adjective, **gourmet** means of or relating to fine foods ("Add **gourmet** food to the point-and-click world of Amazon.com").

There was a fat gourmet named Finney
Who hated to see people skinny
Which I think best explains
Why he left his remains
To a cannibal tribe in New Guinea
—**Graham Lester**

Lester's limerick is worthy of Lear
*But his use of **gourmet**—*
*Instead of **gourmand**—*
May make us sneer.

GRADUATED

Solecistic for **graduated from**. • The study showed 83 percent of Latinos and 80 percent of blacks failed the tenth-grade math exam, which will be a requirement to **graduate** high school in 2003. USE **graduate from**.

*The use of **graduated**, instead of **graduated from** (or, perhaps, **was graduated from**), displays a remarkable lack of learning. More than many solecisms, **graduated** taints the talker and, with each new reader, ridicules the writer.*

G

After graduating high school in 1985, Kravits received an acting scholarship to the University of Maryland and spent the next six years doing theater in Washington, D.C., before moving to New York City, where he acted in commercials and small theater productions.
—**Jason Lynch and Allison Singh Gee, *People***

Two people are apparently not enough to write a grammatically correct sentence at People *magazine, where the writing is so often reminiscent of someone who never did* **graduate from** *high school.*

GRAMMER

Misspelling of **grammar.** • They can't wait to take the field against former Pop Warner teammates, friends and **grammer** school classmates. USE **grammar.** • I've found a few things to teach **grammer**, parts of speech, and that sort of thing for her grade level. USE **grammar.**

Grammar is the correct spelling.

This site has a great deal of information about the basics of English grammer.
—**Mid-Continent Public Library**

*The basics of English **grammar** surely include knowing how to spell the word.*

GRANITE

Misused for **granted.** • Prior to this experience of observation and teaching, I took for **granite** lessons, never once stopping and questioning where they came from. USE **granted.** • Literacy is clearly very valuable as it helps us complete many activities we take for **granite**, such as using the Internet, filling out applications, earning our driver's license, looking up phone numbers and voting. USE **granted.**

*Granite is a very hard igneous rock often used in buildings. To **take for granted** is to assume something is true without question, or to fail to appreciate the worth of someone or something.*

Despite their easy Primary race, Smith and Caiola said they aren't taking anything for granite.

—**Jeff Werner, *Yardley News***

Werner's prose is very badly wrought, but damn good rock.

GRIZZLY

Misused for **grisly** • When a popular youth pastor is accused of a **grizzly** crime, MacLaren won't rest until she finds the truth. USE **grisly**. • Although a bit **grizzly** in light of recent events, it presents a fascinating case study to pose to high school and university students. USE **grisly**. • There hasn't been a national tragedy in my memory that wasn't coupled with **grizzly**, awful humor, told at the expense of the most injured, often within hours of the injury itself. USE **grisly**.

And **grisly** is sometimes misused for **grizzly**: • Managing to glance back you see it, it is in fact a giant **grisly** bear snarling ferociously and wanting to destroy you. USE **grizzly**. If Joe liked a person, he would often be treated to a joke and a complimenting slap on the back by one of Joe's greasy, **grisly** bear sized paws. USE **grizzly**.

Grizzly means grayish; a North American brown bear. ***Grisly*** *means causing horror or disgust.*

GROCERY

*The pronunciation of **grocery** is (GRO-sah-ree), not (GRO-shree).*

GROW

Idiotic for **increase** (or similar words). • We merged Navision Software and Damgaard to **grow** the business, to take us closer to our goal. USE **expand**. • The coupons and strategies on this page are just a fraction of the useful strategies that may be used to **grow** profits. USE **increase**. • Implicit in that act was the determination that we would **grow** our business with all of our partners based on trust, teamwork, honesty and mutual respect. USE **build**. • These are just two examples of our plans to diversify and **grow** income from our existing and new customer base. USE **earn**.

This is an example of a word whose meaning has hypertrophied into something ugly and ungainly.

Instead of spreading the wealth, we are growing the disparity.

—U.S. Representative Carolyn Maloney

Growing a business or the economy is quite bad enough, but if Representative Maloney also feels we can grow a disparity, it may be time to stunt her career.

GUESSTIMATE

Idiotic for **guess** (or similar words). • If you would like a **guesstimate** of time required for your site, we would be happy to give you one. USE **estimate**. • Yet with just a few moments of thought you can make a surprisingly good **guesstimate**. USE **guess**. • They were asked to guess what the contents were and **guesstimate** how many objects were in the envelope. USE **guess**. • We know that at this time you may not know the exact style or quantities, but a **guesstimate** of the extent of your participation will help us in the planning. USE **estimate**.

> *Guesstimate is a perfectly ridiculous merger that people who are uncomfortable with using **guess** will turn to. Most of us prefer knowing to not knowing, or at least we prefer letting others believe we are knowledgeable. **Guesstimate**, people reason, adds intelligence and respectability to their wild **guess**, their unsubstantiated **estimate**.*

HAIRBRAINED

Idiotic for **harebrained**. • Hitler can be seen as coming up with all sorts of **hairbrained** schemes, but they all had the virtue that they conceivably could have affected the eventual outcome of the war, and only **hairbrained** schemes had that promise. USE **harebrained**. • The small voices of **hairbrained** ideas are very easy to hear. USE **harebrained**.

> *Harebrained* means foolish; flighty; having or showing no more sense than a hare. People who use *hairbrained* have less sense still.

HANGAR

Misused for **hanger**. • An over the door clothes **hangar** will expand your hanging capabilities. USE **hanger**. • You hang your clothes on the **hangar** and put your shoes in the bag. USE **hanger**.

> A *hangar* is a building that houses airplanes and the like. A *hanger* is a device used for hanging clothes or other items.

HARBRINGER

Misspelling of **harbinger**. • Cirrus clouds are almost always a **harbringer** of bad weather. USE **harbinger**. • I hate to be a **harbringer** of more bad news, but get ready and start saving. USE **harbinger**. • No caution-minded bride thinks of carrying a bouquet made up solely of red and white flowers—that floral combination is a **harbringer** of death. USE **harbinger**. • These struggles in the "developing" world could possibly serve as a **harbringer** of the future in the West. USE **harbinger**.

> A *harbinger* is a herald; someone or something that foretells the future. The barbarous *harbringer* is a slayer of sense, a taker of souls.

HARDLY...THAN

Solecistic for **hardly...when.** • At Rome he had learned Latin and Greek, and **hardly** had he left the school of rhetoric **than** he ventured on a Commentary on Abdias the Prophet. USE **hardly...when.** • **Hardly** had the surgeons opened me up **than** my aorta, an artery which runs from heart to head, ruptured. USE **Hardly...when.**

*The expression **no sooner...than** is correct, but **hardly...than**, despite its currency, is incorrect. This error is also found in the phrases **scarcely...than** and **barely... than**, both of which require **when**, not **than**. SEE ALSO **no sooner...then (when)**; **not hardly (barely; scarcely)**.*

HARDY

Misused for **hearty.** • Menu items include favorite Mexican entrees which will appease any **hardy** appetite. USE **hearty.** • Located in the Blue Ridge Mountains of Virginia, our beautiful stone lodge offers a warm and **hardy** welcome to park visitors. USE **hearty.** • He smiled **hardily** at her. USE **heartily.**

And **hearty** is sometimes misused for **hardy:** • All three are excellent beginner herbs and they are **hearty** perennials that do well in the Chicagoland area. USE **hardy.**

***Hardy** means robust, vigorous; daring, courageous; able to survive difficult or winter conditions. **Hearty** means warm, friendly; enthusiastic; unrestrained; strong, healthy; nourishing, satisfying; needing or enjoying a good deal of food.*

It's a task hardily joined by heavyweights Microsoft and Yahoo, along with an ever-expanding list of smaller players.
—**Steven Levy, *Newsweek***

THE DICTIONARY OF DISAGREEABLE ENGLISH

HARRASS

Misspelling of **harass**. • I'm a teacher and we have noticed the increased incidence of children, especially girls, using the text buttons of cellphones to bully and **harrass**. USE **harass**. • As with most abusers he feels he's done nothing wrong and to this day he continues to **harrass** me. USE **harass**.

> *Harass* has but one *r*. Clever people—those who spell the word correctly, per- haps—pronounce it (hah-RASS); others pronounce it (HAIR-es).

HAWK

Misused for **hock**. • Despite the finance minister's declaration that we are in **hawk** up to our eyeballs, the government continues to ignore the perilous fiscal situa- tion we have created and continue to sustain in land claim settlements. USE **hock**. • Often a new contract, written in a forign language, is forced on the employee once she's in **hawk** for her fees and far away from home. USE **hock**. • If Susan dies, **hawk** her things. USE **hock**.

> *Slang though it may be,* ***hock*** *means to pawn;* ***in hock*** *means in debt.* ***Hawk****, of course, is a bird of prey; a person who preys on others; a person who favors military action.*

H

HEAL

Misused for **heel**. • Thomas, who has been bothered by a slight tear in his Achilles **heal**, said he plans to practice Friday. USE **heel**. • Fragments of a child's shoe **heal** attached with wooden pegs were also recovered. USE **heel**.

> *To* ***heal*** *is to make well or restore health; to cause a wound to be repaired; to recover or reconcile. A* ***heel*** *is the back part of a foot; the part of a stocking or shoe that covers the heel; something that resembles a heel; a cad.*

HEALTHY

Misused for **healthful**. • Thus, when New England travels to Denver to open its season next Monday night, Drew Bledsoe will be healthy and Terry Glenn will be healthy and Bruce Armstrong will be as healthy as a guy can be after he's played pro football for nearly a dozen years and Ben Coates will be healthy and everyone else on offense who matters will be healthy, and that is a **healthy** situation. USE **healthful.** • What's more, Mrs. deBarra always thought that granola bars and popcorn were **healthy** snacks. USE **healthful.**

*The difference in these two meanings is worth observing. Let us use **healthy** to mean enjoying good health, and **healthful** to mean contributing to or promoting good health. SEE ALSO **peaceful.***

HEART RENDERING

Misused for **heart rending.** • These **heart-rendering** statistics might lead you or a friend to adopt some simple preventive measures that could save your lives. USE **heart-rending.** • The loss of life is described with **heart rendering** details of loss and mourning. USE **heart-rending.**

*To **rend** means to tear something apart; to cause emotional pain or distress to. To **render**, quite a different word, means to provide or give; to make; to depict; to translate; to perform; to melt down fat; to process an animal carcass.*

Whether it is a singles or seniors meeting, a women's or men's conference, or a family church event, Venna keeps the excitement of accomplishment alive with entertaining stories and heart rendering messages that touch the soul.

—Venna Bishop, speaker

Speaker Venna Bishop "delivers dynamic programs that improve attitudes, strengthen character, create vivid visual images, instill patriotism, address overcoming fears, cultivate teamwork," and promote the maltreatment of the English language.

HEARTSHIP

Idiotic for **hardship**. • Your financial **heartship** may be their crucible to true adulthood. USE **hardship**. • We each have to write a letter telling what **heartship** there would be to us if he doesn't get the visa. USE **hardship**. • In spite of **heartship**, she was a happy woman, content and thankful for all she had. USE **hardship**.

This misusage further signals the future of the English language. If people continue to heed laxicographers and descriptive linguists (fascinated as they are by this kind of "new usage"), the words will not matter. "Any spelling, any usage, any meaning"—the motto of all ding-a-linguists.

HECTICITY

Idiotic for **frenzy** (or similar words). • By now I am accustomed to all the **hecticity** of these events. USE **stir**. • Since the concept of alienation is too wide and varied, I refined my goal by concentrating on the **hecticity** of contemporary urban life, and the artist's role in creating cultural change in the form of public works that can find a larger audience. USE **franticness**. • But even if I was miserable and discouraged— in the **hecticity** of departure I'd left my warm jacket at home, so I had to bundle up as best I could with every shirt I'd brought and a paper-thin rain shell—many others weren't. USE **disorder**. • Amid the **hecticity** of existence, we perceive the celestial bodies as phenomena that calm and reassure. USE **chaos**. • With people around the globe suffering from what we here call **hecticity**, a pace and schedule so hectic it hurts, here is a book that considers the "disease" to be one which organizational leaders must recognize as serious—yet addressable. USE **tumult**.

*This is an abominable word—one that a silly celebrity or a descriptive linguist might love. As you see, many words readily mean what **hecticity** struggles to. That this word is used by a few impressionable people is hardly reason for more discriminating ones to embrace it. Not all words are worthy.*

HEIGHTH

Misused for **height** • In the high jump, senior Matt Kenny of Red Cloud placed sixth with a **heighth** of 6-2. USE **height**. • This perspective from the center of the Lorenz barn gives an idea of the **heighth** and breadth Dan Otto and Bruce Conley talk about when envisioning a Country Cathedral. USE **height**. • In the case of doll house furniture, your main concern will be the size of the table top and the **heighth** of the legs. USE **height**.

> Though **heighth** has a history, today the standard spelling is **height**, and the correct pronunciation is (HIGHT), not (HIGHTH).

HEINOUS

> The pronunciation of **heinous** is (HAY-nes), not (HEE-nes).

HEREINAFTER

Misused for **hereafter**. • Consciousness is the key assuredly; who made it, to what end is of less importance in our present tense as we'll have plenty of time to debate it in the **Hereinafter** however we choose to define it. USE **Hereafter**.

> **Hereinafter** means in the following part of a document or speech. **Hereafter** means the state after death; after or following this; in the future.

HEROINE

Misused for **heroin** • All **heroine** that is available in Europe is of Afghan origin. USE **heroin**. • It's easy to overdose on **heroine**, which can cause a coma and/or death. USE **heroin**.

> A **heroine** is the principal female character in a novel or story; a woman of outstanding courage and strength of character. **Heroin** is a highly addictive drug derived from morphine.

My distracting point with drugs was during my second year in the faculty of commerce and by the second term I was constantly injecting myself with cocaine and occasionally sniffing heroine.
—**Reham Wafy, Teen Stuff Online**

*That ending **e** makes quite a difference. All who believe that meaning matters little, that spelling matters less, that usage matters least, consider our fair **heroin**.*

HEY

They talk about what a steal that was, but—**hey!**—that was almost forty years ago. DELETE **hey.** • Hey, I'm not saying Zambrano and Clement are bad. DELETE **Hey.** • Converse is drawing heat from anti-gun folks for its new sneaker called Loaded Weapon. **Hey,** it could be worse; could be the name of a new diaper. DELETE **Hey.** • **Hey,** why abandon a game plan that appeals so beautifully to the baser instincts of fellow Americans? DELETE **Hey.**

Certain words do not belong to the realm of writing, or at least nonfiction writing: **Hey** *is clearly one of them.*

Hey, I'm hardly against men pitching in around the house and helping with kids, or listening to their wives' concerns (in fact, as a mother of three with another little one on the way, I'm all for it).

—Betsy Hart, *Jewish World Review*

Hey, in a country where not actually winning the popular vote can lead to the Oval Office, it pays to aim low.

—Kimberly Reyes, *Entertainment*

Hey *is exclamatory, but only less than able writers (note also the period preceding the parenthesis in Hart's sentence)—however friendly they wish to appear—would use it, in effect, as an inverted exclamation mark with which to capture our flagging attention.*

H

HIATUS

The pronunciation of **hiatus** *is (hi-A-tes), not (he-A-tes).*

HIM (ME) ...-ING

Misused for **his (my) ...-ing.** • Aside from **him** being an athlete and **me** being an athlete, he's my husband and I'm here to show support for him. USE **his; my.** • Senator Lugar, I very much appreciate **you for** joining us. USE **your.** • So what name do you belong to, if you don't mind **me** asking? USE **my.** • I do vaguely remember **him** being badly spoken. USE **his.** • Any chance of **me** being sent that $1,400 before the end of the month? USE **my.** • Do you mind **us** going? USE **our.** • There is no prohibition against **them** making this information available either to FDA or to their customers. USE **their.**

*Use the possessive pronoun, not the personal pronoun, before verbal nouns ending in **-ing**.*

HISTORIC

Misused for **historical.** • Imperiled by habitat loss, invading species and other known and unknown dangers, up to a third of U.S. amphibians have disappeared in part of their **historic** ranges. USE **historical.** • Mexico's peso currency fell to a new **historic** closing low on Wednesday, weakened by fears of a jump in inflation. USE **historical.** • Partisan differences over both national security and domestic issues are at a **historic** high a year before Election Day, according to an in-depth voter poll by the Pew Research Center for the People and the Press. USE **historical.**

And **historical** is sometimes misused for **historic:** • The highly publicized murder was a **historical** turning point in New York's fight against lawlessness, prompting police programs that led to dramatic crime reductions. USE **historic.** • This was a **historical** day for Antrim midfielder Edel Mason as she became the first player to have won an Intermediate medal with two counties, namely Down and Antrim. USE **historic.**

*__Historical__ means relating to history; **historic** means having importance in history.*

It's especially unsettling when the word **historic** is used to describe events that are hardly **historical,** indeed, wholly unimportant or forgettable: • It is a **historic** piece of mail; it's the most ambitious single piece of political mail ever undertaken. DELETE **historic.** • Sampson wouldn't reveal proposals, but says the meeting will **be historic and** address recent scandals in college basketball. DELETE **be historic and.** • All the scoring chances didn't mean much, though, even if it was a **historic** night with some of Hollywood's pretty people. DELETE **historic.**

HOI POLLOI

Misused for **hoity-toity** (or similar words). • And, can the Knights exact a whangy-twangy revenge on the snobby **hoi-polloi** society group that caused Tubby's to be closed down in the first place, while eluding the doofus cops who are hot on their trail at every turn? USE **hoity-toity**. • Soon nurses, handing out programs, are seating tuxedoed and fur draped members of the **hoi polloi**. USE **elite**.

> *Greek for the many, **hoi polloi**, which has come to mean the common people or the masses, is sometimes confused with **hoity-toity**, dialectal for snobbish, pompous, or pretentiously self-important. That is, some people use **hoi polloi** thinking it means the opposite of what it actually does mean.*

HOLD UP

Misused for **holed up**. • Plans take a turn for the worse when everyone is forced to spend the night **hold up** inside the diner at the hands of ruthless prison escapee. USE **holed up**. • Russian forces bombarded the tiny town from the ground and the air Monday to dislodge dozens of Chechen fighters **hold up** inside the local police station. USE **holed up**.

> *To **hold up** is to rob, often at gunpoint; to prevent from falling; to halt or delay; to remain vital or strong or lasting. To **hole up** is to hibernate or hide oneself.*

HOMAGE

Webster's II University Dictionary indicates that *an* is used before words beginning with vowels or unpronounced *h* words. This same dictionary indicates the word *homage* uses the pronounced *h* as its preferred pronounciation. But I have also heard *an homage*. I know most newscasters and newspapers use *an* before any *h* word, pronounced or not, but to me it is merely an affectation rather than grammatically required. What's right?

I think **homage** is better pronounced OM-ij, as **heir** is better pronounced AIR and **herb**, ERB. Most dictionaries today do indeed show HOM-ij as the first listed pronunciation, but this may mean only that it's how the word is most often pronounced, not that it's necessarily preferable to OM-ij. Either pronunciation, OM-ij or HOM-ij, is acceptable.

- Merriam-Webster's Collegiate Dictionary *shows 'ä-mij first and 'hä-mij second but in their Explanatory Notes writes "A second-place variant is not to be regarded as less acceptable than the pronunciation that is given first."*

- The Oxford American Dictionary, *which shows '(h)ämij, writes "The more common pronunciation is listed first, if this can be determined, but many variants are so common and widespread as to be of equal status.*

HOMOPHOBIA

When did the word *homophobia* appear on the scene? It would seem to mean "fear of sameness"--a morbid horror of monotony or boredom--a fine concept and a needed word.

So why do I keep seeing it used to mean "fear of faggots"?

No dictionary defines **homophobia** as "fear of faggots," no dictionary defines **homophobe** as "a hater of faggots"—but the word **faggot** identifies a homophobe.

Homophobia, a late 1960s coinage, has had only one meaning: a morbid dislike or fear of homosexuals. The prefix **homo**, here, is short for **homosexual**; it does not mean "same."

HONE

Misused for **home**. • Several companies **hone** in on web performance. USE **home**. • UCSF researchers develop a faster way to **hone** in on cancer genes. USE **home**.

*To **hone** is to sharpen or perfect, whereas to **home in** is to move or be guided toward a goal or destination. No dictionary that maintains that **home in** is synonymous with **hone in** ought to be consulted further.*

It was a simpler recommendation to simply say everyone over age fifty get vaccinated than to try to hone in on the specific chronic illnesses that would be in that group.
—Dr. Julie Gerberding, Director, CDC

*Home in, not **hone in**, is what Dr. Gerberding means to say. One must wonder what other words, what other data, she and the CDC have spoken or written that are not quite correct, not quite accurate, not quite meant.*

H

HOPEFULLY

Solecistic for **I hope** (or similar phrases). • I'm really enjoying it at the moment and **hopefully** that will carry on. USE **I hope**. • Unfortunately, it happened; **hopefully**, he won't have to regret it for the rest of his life. USE **we hope**. • But a few are like me—**hopefully** a future professor who will go on into grad school. USE **I hope**. • This time, **hopefully**, people realize we have more time and resources and money. USE **let's hope**. • Hopefully this helps people see what Susquehannock soccer is all about. USE **We hope**.

*Hopefully means in a hopeful manner; it does not mean **I hope**, **let's hope**, or **it is to be hoped**. Incorrectly using **hopefully**—all most people have any knowledge of—tells a good deal about a person's relationship with the English language. A person who uses **hopefully** correctly—as in "So much of nature speaks **hopefully** to me, from the singing of the birds, the laughter of children to the occasional straight drive on the golf course."; "United substitute Diego Forlan ran **hopefully** towards* *it but collapsed under Martin Keown's challenge.";* "*More often the white crowned sparrow sang* **hopefully** *in the night"—is clearly conscious of how he speaks and writes; he who uses it incorrectly, as in the earlier examples, is likely unconscious of a good deal more than this one misusage. SEE ALSO* **thankfully**.

HORDE

Misused for **hoard**. • A gang of Wakamba tribesmen raided one of the Yaaku villages, killing many and stealing their **horde** of ivory. USE **hoard**. • But, we also understand that most companies will **horde** their knowledge and refuse to share it for fear of losing some of that control. USE **hoard**. • The idea behind it was to create discussion on why people **horde** possessions and the meanings attached to the objects. USE **hoard**.

> A **hoard** *is a hidden stock of something; a cache. As a verb,* **hoard** *means to accumulate a hoard; to keep hidden or private. A* **horde** *is a large group of people; a crowd; a nomadic tribe.*

HUMONGOUS

Idiotic for **huge** (or similar words). • There are lengths of natural cherry and red and white cedar, and three pine tie beams 23 feet long, the center one **humongous** at 13 by 15 inches, with two sets of step dovetail pockets cut into it. USE **huge**. • Surfing the online GTS scene you'll find giantesses galore—in reality, photos of normal-size women manipulated to appear **humongous**. USE **gigantic**. • Somehow the Prides found time (and a vacant computer) in this madhouse to compile their evaluations in a **humongous** and amazingly complete atlas to all educational software available for personal computers and CD-ROM platforms. USE **mammoth**.

> *Not quite a misusage,* **humongous** *is altogether a monstrosity. It is a hideous, ugly word. And though it's not fair to say that people who use the word are hideous and ugly as well, at some point we come to be—or at the least are known by—what we say and what we write. SEE ALSO* **conversate**.

HUNG

Misused for **hanged**. • Engram, a Black repeat felon, attacked Laurie (a White woman), raped her, and **hung** her by an electrical extension cord until she was dead.

USE **hanged**. • Both were pregnant, and by the law of those times they could not be **hung** until they had their babies. USE **hanged**. • Those who continue to protest will have their businesses confiscated and will be brought to justice and could be **hung** by their necks until they are dead. USE **hanged**.

*Today, the word **hanged** is used only in the sense of to execute by suspending from the neck; in our slipshod society, however, **hung** is used just as often to mean this—our only solace can be that fewer hangings occur today.*

He went upstairs and, using belts to fashion a noose, hung himself from the door in his bedroom, Don Hooton said. ... In August 1989, Eric Elofson of Bakersfield, Calif., hung himself from a tree in his front yard.

—**Jere Longman**, *The New York Times*

*Even the sad horror of someone's hanging himself is made bathetic when we are told he **hung** himself.*

HURDLE

Misused for **hurl**. • Ward inadvertently deflected the ball into the path of Abbey, who had no problem **hurdling** the ball past Warner from close range, for his fourth goal of the season. USE **hurling**. • A blazing fireball came **hurdling** toward him. USE **hurling**. • Without these, it would be difficult, if not impossible, to detect a round object, like a baseball, **hurdling** toward you at 90 miles per hour. USE **hurling**.

*To **hurdle** is to run in a race while jumping over hurdles; to clear a barrier; to over-come a difficulty. To **hurl** is to throw something, such as a ball, with great force; to push or shove violently; to yell; to vomit. SEE ALSO **hurtle**.*

HURTLE

Misused for **hurdle**. • It's the last **hurtle** between me and 100 percent Linux on the desktop at work. USE **hurdle**. • One major **hurtle** Lipinski has been working on

is making the building's computerized utility system more efficient. USE **hurdle**.
• Federal legislation that would curb pre-existing condition exclusions in health care policies, cleared a huge **hurtle** in the U.S. Senate and is confronting a new and ominous obstacle in an expanded health care bill, HR 995. USE **hurdle**.

And **hurdle** is misused for **hurtle**: • They also project the path of the clouds of particles and magnetic fields **hurdling** through space at a million miles or more an hour. USE **hurtling**.

In the world of Hollywood action movies, hoist ropes are never far from snapping in two, sending the car and its passengers hurdling down the shaft.

The basic idea of a seatbelt is very simple: It keeps you from flying through the windshield or hurdling toward the dashboard when your car comes to an abrupt stop.

—Tom Harris, Howstuffworks.com

For all Mr. Harris does know, he seems not to know that ***hurdle*** *means something quite different from* ***hurtle***. *Would he similarly confuse a hoist rope for a drawstring, a seatbelt for a black belt?*

I (HE)

Solecistic for **me (him)**. • If you have a problem, please see **Dana or I.** USE **Dana or me.** • He does not jump but can, at times, challenge **her or I.** USE **her or me.** • You can use the CWA Constitution and file charges against **he, she or them.** USE **him, her, or them.**

Some people, people who think rather highly of themselves, perhaps, tend to use a nominative pronoun (such as I) instead of an objective pronoun (such as me).

Last December, **him and President Clinton** came up with another solution. USE **President Clinton and he.** • He even spends the night every day but I don't mind because **she and him** always go somewhere for a few hours every day so I get time to myself. USE **she and he.** • My thought on this one is that **they, or him or her or whoever,** is a religious fanatic. USE **they, or he or she or whoever.**

*Whereas others, people who do not think much at all, use an objective pronoun instead of a nominative. SEE ALSO **it's me.***

In the meantime, me and my friends and my conservative colleagues will continue to use legal organizations to advocate that point of view.

—U.S. Representative Tom DeLay

You teach a child to read, and he or her will be able to pass a literacy test.

—U.S. President George W. Bush

It takes an extraordinary mind to mix nominative with objective personal pronouns. President Bush, it is clear, may not be able to pass a literacy test.

IDLE

Misused for **idol**. • I've done tons of research about Billy the Kid; I guess you could say he's my **idle**. USE **idol**. • Inundated as we are by rival pop **idle** shows, it ought be self-evident to the record-buying public that the whole purpose of manufactured pop bands is simply to separate fools from their money. USE **idol**.

> **Idle** *means having no value or significance; unfounded; unemployed or unoccupied; lazy; not in use.* **Idol** *means an image of a god; a heathen deity; someone who is very highly admired.*

I.E.

Misused for **e.g.** • Also, unlike other popular diet books, *Metabolize* does not focus on one dietary component to the exclusion of others (**i.e.**, all protein, no carbohydrates). USE **e.g.** • Do you find that you use sex as a way of dealing with feelings (**i.e.**, stress, loneliness, sadness, fear, anger)? USE **e.g.** • Up until two decades ago, "awesome" was reserved for the sublime: **i.e.**, an F5 tornado or God. USE **e.g.**

> *The difference between* **i.e.** *and* **e.g.** *is the difference between the phrases* **that is** *and* **for example***; the first is for stating an equivalence, the second for stating an illustration. Only scientists and academicians (who have their own perverse rules of style and composition, and seldom seem able to write a readable sentence) have any reason to use* **i.e.** *(or* **e.g.***); the rest of us should use* **that is** *(or* **for example***).*

IF

Solecistic for **whether**. • The biopsy will determine **if** Kailee's anemia is transforming into myelodysplasia. USE **whether**. • It makes not a whit of difference **if** they are Jewish or American. USE **whether**. • People will have sex **if** it's legal or not. USE **whether**. • It almost seems silly to ask **if** Valdosta can win the state championship. USE **whether**. • By monitoring how hard the heart is beating, the device can figure out **if** the patient is resting or climbing stairs and adjust the flow of blood accordingly. USE **whether**. • The Messenger of Allah, may Allah bless him and grant him peace, said, "Let me know **if** she dies." USE **whether**.

> *Traditionally,* **if** *introduces a single condition, whereas* **whether** *(or* **whether or not***) introduces two or more possibilities. Today,* **if** *or* **whether** *is permissible though*

whether is the better choice when describing two or more alternatives. Just remember that *if* should not be used when doing so may cause misunderstanding.

IF...THEN

Solecistic for **if.** • If the nation's indicators of economic progress are obsolete, **then** they consign us to continually resorting to policies that cannot succeed because they aren't addressing the right problems. DELETE **then.** • If he is re-elected, **then** we will all suffer further. DELETE **then.**

In certain mathematical or computer expressions, ***if...then*** is the necessary expression; in prose, the understood ***then***, when explicitly stated, is often an encumbrance to grace and elegance.

ILLICIT

Misused for **elicit.** • It is interesting to note that sugar placed directly over the diaphragm or on the Crown Chakra will not **illicit** a reaction of any kind in a balanced body. USE **elicit.** • I love any film which can **illicit** debate and *Session 9* is one film which will have anyone who has seen it talking for some time. USE **elicit.** • Several vaccine strategies have been designed in order to **illicit** a heightened immune response that use HPV type-specific epitopes (components of viral surface antigens) involved in viral replication and transformation. USE **elicit.**

Illicit means forbidden by law or custom; unlawful. ***Elicit*** means to call forth, draw out, or provoke; to arrive at by logic.

I

ILLITERATE

Idiotic for **iterate.** • I could **illiterate** them here but I think you and most other thinking people know exactly what those crimes might be. USE **iterate.** • This is a good example of how I try to take things and **illiterate** them so that they can stick in your mind. USE **iterate.**

Occasionally, **illiterate** is meant to mean **illustrate** or **mention:** • As I **illiterated** in my earlier post, N. Korea is probably close to economic collapse. USE **illustrated.**

Iterate, *a verb, means to repeat.* *Illiterate*, *an adjective, means uneducated or ignorant.*

Illiterated, by the bye, is an obsolete (a senseless) formation: • From comments from other computer-**illiterated** people, blogging is easier than any computer application—even easier than email. • Never man has listened to the simple, the children, the righteous, the **illiterated** and the powerless. • You're obsessed with your hatred of Bush, and anyone who disagrees with you, are labeled **illiterated**, stupid, ignorant.

Mrs. Malaprop. There, Sir Anthony, there sits the deliberate simpleton who wants to disgrace her family, and lavish herself on a fellow not worth a shilling.

Lydia Languish. Madam, I thought you once--

Mrs. Malaprop. You thought, miss! I don't know any business you have to think at all--thought does not become a young woman. But the point we would request of you is, that you will promise to forget this fellow--to illiterate him, I say, quite from your memory.

—Richard Sheridan, *The Rivals*, 1775

ILLUSION

Misused for **allusion**. • There are several ways to begin your paper. You may begin with: 1. A paradoxical or intriguing statement. 2. An arresting statistic or shocking statement. 3. A question. 4. A quotation or literary **illusion**. USE **allusion**. • Even in the description of the drawbridge and passing barges it makes a literary **illusion** to the mythological River Styx. USE **allusion**.

And **allusion** is misused for **illusion**. • This house is run by a command central computer system that vacuums, cooks, cleans, creates optical **allusion** vacation scenes on your family room wall. USE **illusion**. • This is what intrigues me about photography: the compelling **allusion** of reality. USE **illusion**. • Holograms are a great way to trick people. They look so real, but in reality there is nothing there. Parabolas play a big part in creating this magical **allusion**. USE **illusion**.

Allusion is an indirect or passing reference; a hint. *Illusion* is an incorrect perception of reality; a false belief or idea; a mirage, hallucination, or trick. SEE ALSO *delusion*.

IMAGINATE

Idiotic for **imagine** (or **imaginative**). • It is the place where you want to be, place that you **imaginate**, place you are in when you dream. USE **imagine**. • I **imaginate** many people took the Friday off as well. USE **imagine**. • *Down to Earth*, by Gavin Chafin and Steve Wood: an extremely funny and **imaginate** strip that takes place, at various times, in Heaven, Hell, and a small diner out in the middle of nowhere. USE **imaginative**.

Imaginate is not a word in the English language. Not a few people apparently believe that adding a suffix to a word somehow increases the value of the word or enhances its meaning. *Imaginate*, instead of *imagine*, sounds absurd and means nothing other than its user is a dullard.

IMBIBE

Solecistic for **eat** (or similar words). • Generally, you should be living a clean life, and only **imbibing** food substances which are fresh, light and pure. USE **eating**. • Because of the scarcity of staff and the lack of time to properly **imbibe** food, I resorted then to giving myself an IV shot of vitamin C with calcium. USE **ingest**. • If we **imbibe** these "substantial," higher calorie meals on a regular basis, we'll pack on the pounds in stored body fat. USE **consume**.

To *imbibe* is to drink; to take in as if by drinking; to absorb or assimilate. It does not mean to *eat* or *consume*.

I

IMMANENT

Misused for **imminent**. • The truth is Iraq did not have weapons that represented an **immanent** threat. USE **imminent**. • Here the yips of a few autograph-seekers and the flashes of a few bulbs might be enough to convince viewers of Alex's **immanent** celebrity. USE **imminent**. • The threat is real. It's not **immanent**, but there are still terrorists out there who would like to repeat what happened on September 11. USE **imminent**.

Immanent means inherent or existing within. ***Imminent*** means about to occur; impending; threatening. SEE ALSO **eminent**.

Again, in U.S. Senate and House Committee hearings, the FDA conceded that the packaging and recalled drug violations were minor and posed no **immanent** health hazard to the public.

—W. Lloyd Eldridge, The Tullahoma News

The **imminent** hazard, if not to our health, is to our humanity. Using the English language badly is hazardous to our humanity.

IMMERGE

Misused for **emerge**. • As far as personality disorders there are theories that there are some personality traits that we can either exhibit automatically or will **immerge** under some stimulus. USE **emerge**. • We are those stubborn little caterpillars that given the grace of God, we may **immerge** beautiful butterflies. USE **emerge**.

Immerge means to submerge or immerse in or as if in a liquid; ***emerge***, much the opposite of ***immerge***, means to rise from or as if from immersion; to come forth or become evident.

IMMUNITY

Confused with **impunity**. ***Immunity*** means exemption from legal prosecution; freedom from something unpleasant or burdensome; resistance to or protection against a disease ("A Northampton County judge has granted **immunity** from prosecution for a reluctant witness in the John Hirko Jr. trial, making it more likely *he will testify"; "He cited a study conducted several years ago in which 85 percent of children who had one shot without the booster developed protective **immunity** against the flu"). **Impunity** means exemption from punishment or harm ("At times he has operated with the **impunity** of a man who has nothing to lose"; "In too many cases, these crimes have been committed with **impunity**, which has only encouraged others to flout the laws of humanity").*

IMMURE

Misused for **inure**. • Violence today seems to have become a hallmark of modern society; it is so pervasive that many children are becoming **immured** to it. USE **inured**. • We can even get **immured** to low-level constant pain because our brain starts to presume it is a constant that it need not process. USE **inured**.

*   **Immure** *is to enclose within or as if within walls; to imprison or confine.* **Inure** *is to make used to something difficult, painful, or unpleasant; to habituate.*

I love horror movies, but there is so much excessive violence in many of them that you become immured to it and it doesn't affect you any longer which is disturbing in itself.

—Trevor Schmidt, as quoted in *See Magazine*

*Schmidt, until he knows the meaning of **inured**, should be immured in the "Castle wall of the ultimate Shade."*

I

IMPACTFUL

Idiotic for **influential** (or similar words). • Positive and **impactful** progress requires confidence, strategic vision, and the energetic change agents who will lead the way to new paths of success. USE **effective**. • Let Exclusive show you how our motivational, **impactful**, focused campaigns can translate into revenue growth and expanded opportunities. USE **powerful**. • Since his arrival on the scene over four years ago, Dave has been an **impactful**, respected member of the USA team. USE **influential**. • He said his job is to attract audiences with quality content; it's the advertisers' job to make their marketing messages **impactful**. USE **memorable**. • This could be the most **impactful** Congress in thirty years. USE **influential**.

*The verb **impact** is criticized, and rightly so, but the adjective **impactful**, often used by businesspeople and marketers, is condemnable.*

IMPASSIBLE

Misused for **impassable**. • Some beach segments of the route can be **impassible** at high tide. USE **impassable**. • There are hundreds of yards of trails that are **impassible**. USE **impassable**.

***Impassible** means unable to feel pain or suffering; impassive. **Impassable** means impossible to pass or travel over. SEE ALSO **passible**.*

IMPATIENT

Misused for **inpatient**. • A study of two programs in Washington state found that for every $1 the state spent, $9.70 was returned through **impatient** treatment while $23.33 was garnered through outpatient programs. USE **inpatient**. • When home is not enough, hospice **impatient** care is available for short-term symptom management and respite care. USE **inpatient**.

*An **impatient** person is irritable; edgy; intolerant. An **inpatient** is a person hospitalized for treatment.*

IMPERMEABLE

Misused for **impervious**. • We are the best of the best, **impermeable** to disease and age. USE **impervious**. • It does not matter how much he hurt me because I love him; he is strong, powerful, **impermeable** to pain and to love. USE **impervious**.

*Both **impermeable** and **impervious** mean impenetrable, but **impermeable** also means not allowing fluids to pass through; **impervious** also means not affected by.*

IMPETUOUS

Misused for **impetus**. • This gave the market a bid into the close Friday, and provided the **impetuous** for the positive numbers seen in the market this week. USE impetus. • The main **impetuous** of the contract was to prepare and then implement a move of over three hundred computers from a San Francisco office to a Concord office. USE **impetus**. • So, there is an **impetuous** to move forward according to schedule. USE **impetus**.

> ***Impetuous***, *an adjective, means acting impulsively or rashly; moving with force and energy.* ***Impetus***, *a noun, means the force or momentum to accomplish something; a stimulus.*

IMPLY

Misused for **infer**. • What does it mean that Zaccheus was a chief tax-collector? What can we **imply** about him for that? USE **infer**. • What can we **imply** from Rav Sheishes initial statement that bar Pivli fulfilled Rebbi Yehudah's Torah obligation? USE **infer**. • You cannot **imply** from this that I reject all forms of control on liberty. USE **infer**.

> *To* ***imply*** *is to suggest; to* ***infer*** *is to conclude. Speakers* ***imply****; hearers* ***infer****. Some dictionaries, continuing their disservice to us all, consider these two words synonymic, defining one with the other. The first thing we do, let's kick all the laxicographers.*

IMPUT

Misspelling of **input**. • We learned it is too late to have much **imput** once the plan has been set and the funding is in place. USE **input**. • Members of the board want the Vero Beach City Council to have their **imput** before the plan is implemented. USE **input**. • The league also received **imput** from WCHA observer Denny Davis of Duluth. USE **input**.

> ***Imput*** *is a misspelling of* ***input****.*

INCENT

Idiotic for **encourage** (or similar words). • How do you **incent** a CEO to innovate? USE **encourage**. • Reduce prices by 20 percent for standard configurations and 10 percent for non-standard configurations to drive more volume and to **incent** cus-

I

tomers to buy standard configurations. USE **motivate**. • A compensation program needs to be developed to **incent** employees to retire at an older age. USE **persuade**. • The VSI bonus program is designed to **incent** a person to join, to stay with VSI over a long period of time and to tell friends about all the benefits a VSI membership provides! USE **inspire**.

> *Incentivize* instead of *motivate* or *encourage* is quite bad enough, but *incent*— for those who cannot manage to utter a polysyllabic word—is execrable. SEE ALSO *incentivize*.

INCENTIVIZE

Solecistic for **motivate** (or similar words). • Just as public shareholders seek to align their interests with management, private owners can also use options to **incentivize** management. USE **motivate**. • In the face of diminished competitive barriers and an economy where profitability depends on a broad customer base, companies of necessity will offer frequent customer awards to **incentivize** repeat business. USE **stimulate**.

> *The English language often welcomes nouns being made into verbs—for instance, computerize, jeopardize, and criticize. However, other -ize formations are less welcome—finalize, prioritize, and incentivize—especially if words already exist that have much the same meaning. Moreover, incentivize sounds idiotic; motivate, incite, inspire, stir are far more euphonious.*
>
> *More frightful still is the frightful disincentivize, instead of, say, discourage or deter. SEE ALSO incent.*

INCIDENTLY

Misspelling of **incidentally**. • **Incidently**, most people seem to think that the simple edition is just as good as the more expensive travelers' edition. USE **Incidentally**. • **Incidently**, many women consider affection and conversation to be preconditions for sexual fulfillment. USE **Incidentally**.

> *Incidentally* means as a minor or less important matter; parenthetically, by the way. *Incidently*, though usually a misspelling of *incidentally*, is a word meaning so as to depend on something else; concomitantly. SEE ALSO *accidently*.

INCIDENTS

Misused for **incidence**. • It is in the interest of everyone in the county that the **incidents** of disease and unwanted pregnancy be minimized or eliminated. USE **incidence**. • A recent study by the Minnesota Department of Health reveals higher **incidents** of cancer and cancer-related death in the state's minority population. USE **incidence**.

Incidents is the plural of incident, which is an occurrence; a minor disturbance. Incidence is the frequency or rate of an, often undesirable, occurrence.

INCLIMATE

Idiotic for **inclement**. • O'Dell pointed out that the large room can also be used as a gym for P.E. classes forced inside by **inclimate** weather. USE **inclement**. • Indeed, the facility bustles, especially during the winter months, when **inclimate** weather forces many climbers and athletes away from outdoor sports. USE **inclement**.

If laxicographers continue to compile dictionaries, inclimate will soon be listed as a variant spelling of inclement.

The ceremony was rescheduled for the following Sunday, but had to be cancelled again due to inclimate weather.

—**Luke O'Neill,** *Hyde Park Townsman*

Rebuke Luke, the Townsman's *editors should, for in one sentence, he manages to make four grammatical errors.*

I

INCOMPATIBLE

Misused for **incomparable**. • I have never seen anything like it, so the view was **incompatible** to me. USE **incomparable**. • She wonderfully combined **incompatible** beauty with cleverness and common sense and was always very kind toward her close friends. USE **incomparable**.

Incompatible means unable to get along or live together; unable to coexist. *Incomparable* means without equal; unable to be compared.

> Still, a science fiction novel by the incompatible Ms. McCaffrey is always a winning treat and readers will relish and crave the next book.
>
> **—Harriet Klausner**
>
> As bad as the novel is this review of it by the *incomparable* Ms. Klausner.

INCREDULOUS

Misused for **incredible**. • It is **incredulous** that we learned about the third American Media employee from a televised news conference rather than from appropriate governmental agencies. USE **incredible**. • The class is designed to introduce the **incredulous** ways acrylics can be used! USE **incredible**. • Really, how do action-thrillers get away with the most **incredulous** and unbelievable scenes pitting humans against a gazillion bullets, C4 mushroom-shape explosions, super-durable sports cars, and deranged killer robots? USE **incredible**.

Incredulous means unwilling to admit or accept what is offered as true; not credulous; skeptical. *Incredible* means hard to believe.

INDIGNITY

Misused for **indignation**. • "A Dwarf has no business acting as nurse-maid to an Elf!" he stated firmly, beard bristling with **indignity** at the suggestion. USE **indignation**. • What they have done has aroused the **indignity** and strong dissatisfaction of the Chinese people. USE **indignation**. • The story's strengths are its elaborate paintings of righteous **indignity**, pompous historical pride, professional jealousy and nonstop conflict. USE **indignation**.

Indignity is something that wounds one's self-respect or dignity. *Indignation* is anger or contempt for a perceived injustice or unfairness.

INDISPENSIBLE

Misspelling of **indispensable**. • Holmes said the Yoders, beyond their natural athletic talent, played an **indispensible** role for this year's team. USE **indispensable**. • A water chart is **indispensible**, and a bird chart helpful. USE **indispensable**.

*Only able spellers know that **indispensable** ends in **able**, not **ible**.*

The problem is that Arafat was and is the indispensible Palestinian political figure; recent polls show that his popularity remains undimmed.
—**Cameron W. Barr, *Christian Science Monitor***

In his indispensible history, "In Nevada: The Land, the People, God, and Chance," David Thomson describes the burgeoning of Las Vegas to big-city status.

—**Richard Corliss, *Time***

Even the mighty Monitor, *the unshakable* Time *do not know their **i**'s from their **a**'s, one vowel from another.*

INDITE

Misused for **indict**. • Three Mountain State University student athletes are out on bail after being **indited** on federal drug charges. USE **indicted**. • Unfortunately, he lacks the power to **indite** her and put her behind bars. USE **indict**. • The police arrested the performers of the play **inditing** them under article 159 of the Turkish penal code, under the grounds that the play was an insult to the Turkish armed forces. USE **indicting**.

*To **indite** is to put in writing; compose. To **indict** is to charge with the commission of a crime; accuse.*

INFANTALIZE

Misspelling of **infantilize**. • To argue that the "very occasional inconvenience" which contemporary racism represents for many blacks is enough to deter black students from pursuing their educational goals is, according to McWhorter, to **infantalize** an entire race. USE **infantilize**. • "Compliant" isn't much better—it still puts the patient in a one-down, **infantalized** position. USE **infantilized**.

> *To treat someone as, or reduce someone to, an infant is to **infantilize** him. A person may be **infantile** (or **infantine**), but not **infantale**.*

INFECT

Misused for **infest**. • Crabs, or pubic lice, are insects that **infect** pubic hair, hairy parts of the chest, armpits, upper eyelashes, and the head. USE **infest**. • Fungi (wood rot) and subterranean termites **infecting** wood are retarded in their growth when the moisture content of the wood is lower than 20 percent. USE **infesting**.

And **infest** is sometimes used for **infect**: • She urged the participants to be polite in delivering the message to the people and advised female students to be content with what their parents provide for them and desist from soliciting help from men who could take advantage of them and **infest** them with the HIV virus. USE **infect**.

> *__Infect__ means to affect or contaminate with a disease-producing organism; to affect or instill with one's feelings or beliefs. __Infest__ means to overrun or be present in large numbers.*

INFINITESIMAL

Misused for **infinite** (or similar words). • We are also part of a macrocosmic world of planets and stars and **infinitesimally** huge distances of space and time to which we are connected in vitally important ways. USE **infinitely**. • Everything we see within the universe is made up of an **infinitesimally** large number of combinations of the one hundred different kinds of atoms. USE **infinitely**. • Having that passion, having that religion, having the maxims to live and love by, is the key to embracing life's **infinitesimal** beauty. USE **infinite**.

> *__Infinitesimal__ means extremely small, not, like **infinite**, extremely large or limit-less. SEE ALSO **miniscule**.*

Each play produces a small loss, but in an extraordinarily rare event, the payoff is infinitesimally large.

—Dr. Bill Brody, President, Johns Hopkins University

INFLAMMABLE

*Confused with **nonflammable**. **Inflammable**, like **flammable**, means easily set on fire. **Nonflammable** means not easily set on fire. Since the consequences of not knowing the definition of **inflammable** are potentially severe, most people quickly learn the meaning of this word. SEE ALSO **masseur**.*

INFLUENCE

*The pronunciation of **influence** is (IN-floo-ence), not (in-FLOO-ence).*

INFUSEMENT

Idiotic for **infusion**. • Unfortunately, selling a sister station is a one-time **infusement** of capital. USE **infusion**. • He's generally not a fan of federal involvement, but he hopes that the Byrd grant will provide an **infusement** of energy. USE **infusion**.

And there are examples in which the intended meaning of **infusement** is a little less clear: • The goals of the GeroRich Program include: To provide faculty with educational resources in gerontology to promote ease of **infusement** within existing curricula. • There are (at least) three types of rituals: those with spiritual **infusement**, those that act as a rite of passage, and those that are merely repetitious.

*The word is **infusion**, the introduction of a new element or quality into something. **Infusement** means nothing at all—though, to those who say nothing at all, it might indeed mean something.*

I

Theoretically, this four-year infusement of money would be enough to get the new system up and running with state-of-the-art equipment.
—**John Fox, Cincinnati CityBeat**

*Mr. Fox might improve his credibility as a writer were he, on occasion, to look up the meaning of words he is shamelessly sure of. He would not have found **infusement** in his dictionary, though if he—along with others as careless—continues to use the "word," we one day will.*

INGENIOUS

Misused for **ingenuous**. • One day she is childlike, naive, **ingenious**, a girl of ten. USE **ingenuous**. • When his work succeeds, it appears artless and **ingenious**, and intimate rather than regional. USE **ingenuous**. • Is this intended as an **ingenious** but misguided fantasy for middle-aged women who want to believe someone like Jack Nicholson could fall for an experienced woman like Diane Keaton and never look back at the twiggy twentysomethings who came before? USE **ingenuous**.

> ***Ingenious*** *means brilliant or clever;* ***ingenuous****, naive or artless.*

INIMICAL

Misused for **inimitable**. • John also had a one-year run as the host of a daily three-minute syndicated radio rant called "Rotten Day" commenting on rock history in his unique and **inimical** style. USE **inimitable**. • But before that, the well-known TV gardener Jeff Turner will keep the audience entertained in his own **inimical** way. USE **inimitable**.

> ***Inimical*** *means tending to harm or injure; unfriendly; hostile.* ***Inimitable*** *means defying imitation; matchless.*

And **inimicable**, a nonword, not a nonce word, is mistaken for **inimical** by some and for **inimitable** by others: • In general, however, anti-Semitism refers to the denouncement in speech or writing of Jewish culture, traditions and attitudes as being **inimicable** to a nation's welfare. USE **inimical.** • Firstly, he was born with an **inimicable** name, one of a kind. USE **inimitable.**

IN MEMORIAM

Misused for **immemorial.** • No other part of Europe can match either the "new" or the "old" Ireland, an island that's been here since time **in memoriam.** USE **immemorial.** • From time **in memoriam,** we have been dysfunctional peoples within the family of countries that make up our world. USE **immemorial.**

Immemorial means extending beyond the limits of memory or recorded history. *In memoriam* means in memory of; an obituary.

INNOCULATE

Misspelling of **inoculate.** • You may wish to experiment with Sulphur Shelf on Cherry Logs and **innoculate** pine tree seedlings with Chanterelle spawn. USE **inoculate.** • We are faced with the real possibility of attack with biological weapons, and have drawn up plans to **innoculate** the entire unvaccinated segment of this country. USE **inoculate.**

Inoculate has one *n*, not two.

IN REGARDS TO

Solecistic for **in regard to.** • PalmGear.com will assume no responsibility for software submitted by any developer **in regards to** usability and or damage that it may cause. USE **in regard to.** • I also encourage you to contact any of my clients for a recommendation **in regards to** my performance, competency, support and service levels. USE **in regard to.** • **In regards to** the development or recovery of binocular vision, vision therapy is much more successful than surgery or glasses alone. USE **In regard to.** • Please exercise good judgement **in regards to** what information you wish to transmit to Hyatt via this medium. USE **in regard to.**

In regards to, like *with regards to*, is an example of egregious English. That these forms can be found in the writing and speech of some otherwise articulate people is ever startling. SEE ALSO *anyways*.

INSIDIOUS

Misused for **invidious**. • Space is sold to the advertisers for the purpose of making announcements concerning their own business and may not be used for attacking or making **insidious** comparisons with other advertisers, firms, institutions or persons. USE **invidious**. • Genetic information can be used as the basis for **insidious** discrimination. USE **invidious**.

Insidious—which means treacherous; harmful but enticing; spreading slowly and in a subtle manner—is not infrequently confused for the less often used *invidious*—which means provoking ill will or animosity, giving offense; discriminatory.

INSIGHT

Misused for **incite**. • This book will rock the comfortable mainliner, anger the traditional independent, **insight** to riot the hard-core bureaucrat, and motivate to action those who hunger to see what God is about in this world. USE **incite**. • Amazon spokesperson Dale Cheeseman stated that the company did not want to be linked to any publications that might **insight** terrorism, or those who harbor terrorists. USE **incite**.

Insight, a noun, is an intuitive understanding of a person or situation; a deep perception of something. *Incite*, a verb, is to stir or rouse; to urge on.

Isn't Moore concerned about insighting the same fear in people that he criticizes the media for creating?
—**Anna Kaufman, *The Daily Californian***

The Daily Californian *"is run entirely by current or recently-graduated UC Berkeley students,"* but perhaps Kaufman should return to grammar school.

INSURE

Misused for **ensure**. • What we must do is **insure** that Mr. Taylor is the last president of Liberia to enjoy unlimited authority. USE **ensure**. • The time off will likely **insure** that the injured throwing shoulder will make a hundred percent recovery while Plummer is out with the foot injury. USE **ensure**.

> *Ensure means to make certain. Insure is best reserved for matters of insurance: to issue or acquire insurance for. SEE ALSO ensure.*

INTENSE

> *Confused with intensive. Intense means in a high degree; zealous; showing strong emotion ("Capturing fabulous moments and behind-the-scenes dramas, these pictures reflect the filmmaker's intense personality"; "Gamers applaud the Midway Sports trademark arcade-style gameplay and intense action but also want to experience their favorite teams, players, and stadiums in an authentic professional sports context"). Intensive means increasing in degree or amount; concentrated or thorough; especially attentive care ("The Duchess of York's former aide Jane Andrews is in intensive care after being rushed to hospital in a critical condition"; "And foreign students enrolled in Lewis & Clark College's intensive English language program dropped 30 percent since last fall").*

INTERESTING

> *The pronunciation of interesting is (IN-trah-sting), not (IN-tah-res-ting).*

I

INTERPRETATE

Solecistic for **interpret**. • Doesn't it take legal debate in court between two opposing sides to **interpretate** that law, when it comes under question? USE **interpret**. • In conclusion, data on ketamine were inconsistent and difficult to **interpretate** with only one of four trials showing improved analgesia with pre-emptive treatment. USE **interpret**.

> *Though interpretation is the noun form, the correct verb form is interpret, not interpretate.*

INVESTIGATABLE

Solecistic for **investigable**. • Solecistic for **investigable**. • I wished them to explore, then define **investigatable** questions, conduct experiments, and write a conclusion reporting what they had learned. USE **investigable**. • Ask questions, both **investigatable** and non-**investigatable**, about objects and events observed. USE **investigable**. • Statistics are not easy to find in the book but it appears that the PCC rejects far more complaints as "outside its remit" than does the Australian Press Council (in 1995 for example only 476 of 2,508 complaints were deemed **investigatable**). USE **investigable**. • The cruelty case must fit a certain criteria before it is deemed **investigatable**. USE **investigable**. • The sphere of modern science is the systematizable, the organizable, and the empirically **investigatable**. USE **investigable**.

Investigable is correct, as is *investigative*. Incorrect is *investigatable*.

IN WHICH

When is *where* correct, and when should *in which* be used instead?

The word **where** is permissible, though not always desirable, in place of the phrase **in which**.

• We have a situation **in which** there were opportunities, apparently, to be able to ward off this terrible blow.

• The games weren't tightly scripted Homeric epics **in which** warriors dropped their weapons every four years to honor the twin virtues of amateur sport and brotherhood.

• It is a world **in which** everything has already happened; **in which** there never can be anything new again.

In these sentences, and in most careful or deliberate writing, **in which** sounds better than the casual **where**.

INVISIBLE

Solecistic for **indivisible.** • I pledge allegiance to the flag and to the republic for which it stands one nation **invisible** with liberty and justice for all. USE **indivisible.**

Invisible means unable to be seen. Indivisible means unable to be divided.

IRREGARDLESS

Solecistic for **regardless** (or similar words). • **Irregardless** of trees they should be cleared a minimum of once a year because of birds and animals depositing debris in your gutters. USE **Regardless.** • Would you like to have one email address **irregardless** of how many times you switch jobs or Internet providers? USE **regardless.**

*Using **irregardless**, a nonexistent word, is the sign of a shoddy speaker, a third-rate writer, a thoughtless thinker.*

Every single moment of your life you are faced with a choice irregardless of your station in life, irregardless of your status, irregardless of your circumstances or your limitations.
—Diana Rogers, Crystal Clear Reflections

Irregardless is nonstandard used once, illiterate used twice, barbarous three times.

I

IRRELEVANT

Misused for **irreverent.** • It was full of **irrelevant** fun almost to the point of Marx Brothers-style of antics, with a small dose of the horrors of war thrown in. USE **irreverent.** • Andy Armstrong takes an **irrelevant** look at motoring and motorsport. USE **irreverent.** • His **irrelevant** style of humour is both witty and makes us think of how we see ourselves. USE **irreverent.**

Irrelevant means not relating to the subject; not pertinent. Irreverent means lacking reverence, disrespectful; critical of what is generally accepted; satirical.

IRREVOCABLE

*The pronunciation of **irrevocable** is (i-REV-ah-kah-ble), not (ir-ah-VOH-kah-ble).*

ISSUEIZE (ISSUEIZATION)

Idiotic for **become a concern** (or similar words). • The overuse of antibiotics, though a problem for many years, has only become **issueized** in the past ten years. USE **an issue.** • Whether we like it or not, whether it makes prudent development sense or not, in the donor countries increasingly we see **an issuization of funding strategies.** USE **funding strategies becoming a concern.** • That's how citizens make change; they take something they're upset about and they **issueize** it. USE **make it an issue.**

> *Many people object to the frequent use of **issue** and **has issues with** instead of, for example, **problem, difficulty,** or **dislike**. Consider then how disagreeable a word like **issueization** is to sensible people. **Issueization** (or **issuization**), like **issueize** (or **issuize**), is apparently meant to mean turning (something) into an issue, a problem, concern, or worry. Occasionally, it may also mean issuance or issuing though, in other instances, it's not altogether clear what the word is meant to mean—a very good reason not to use it.*

IS WHEN (IS WHERE)

Misused for **during, with.** • Parent Week **is when** parents come to the school and get a taste of what their children are doing. USE **During Parent Week.** • A bribe **is when** I offer to give you something and in return you give me something. USE **In a bribe.** • Spring **is when** the pond begins to awaken from its long winter dormancy as signs of life reappear with longer days. USE **With spring.** • A case in point **is where the Talmud says** that Jesus of Nazareth was a student of Yehoshua ben Perahia, a sage who died at least one hundred years before. USE **is the Talmud's saying.**

> *Is when (like is where), when introducing a definition or explanation, is a device that only the least able writers use.*

ITERATE

Exactly how does prefixing the word *iterate* with *re-* modify its meaning, and when is it correct to use each?

*Strictly, **iterate** means to say or do a second time; **reiterate**, to say or do a third or more time. **Iterate** is seldom used, but when it is, it is usually as a synonym for **reiterate**, which most often means to repeat or to repeat again.*

IT'S

Misused for **its**. • By now, even the most out of touch among you must realize that the government of the United States is at war against **it's** own people. USE **its**. • Freemasonry requires that **it's** members confess a belief in a supreme being. USE **its**. • Our customers have been absolutely spellbound by **it's** results. USE **its**.

*Most often, this confusion is simply a matter of carelessness, but in the end, all good writing is careful writing. **It's** is a contraction for **it is** or **it has**; **its** is a possessive pronoun meaning pertaining to or belonging to.*

I

IT'S ME

Solecistic for **It's I**. • It's **him**! How can it be **him**? USE **he; he**. • If circumstances had been different, it might have been **them** here today—not **us**. USE **they; we**. • We logged on using a different name, so Blue Nile wouldn't know it was **us**. USE **we**. • It was **us** looking at them looking at us. USE **we**. • How do you know it is **her**? USE **she**.

*A pronoun that refers to the subject of a sentence or phrase and that follows a form of the verb **to be** is correctly nominative. SEE ALSO **I (he)**.*

I have listened to English professors argue about this question: When you answer the phone,
is the correct response "It's me"
or "It is I"? (Personally, I get
out of the entire dilemma by
just saying "Speaking.")

People do argue for both expressions: **It** or **This is me** and **It** or **This is I**. When I answer the phone, I say, **This is he** or, more often, the startlingly correct **I am he**.

Less formal, and not necessarily thought incorrect, is using **me** instead of **I** (or **he** or **she**).

The rule, however, is to use a nominative pronoun after some form of the verb **to be**, but as **It's me** and many other similar expressions make clear, the rule is infrequently observed.

JAUNDRA

Misspelling of **genre**. • All ephemera is inspected by three experts in the appropriate **jaundra**. USE **genre**. • That's why I can't wait to have it playing 24/7 so I can really experience yet another **jaundra** of thought and music. USE **genre**. • He goes on to detail the characters in the movie and why he chose to make a film in this **jaundra**. USE **genre**.

> *Genre, not **jaundra**, is the correct spelling of the word that means a type or class, a style of artistic composition.*

JEWELERY

Misspelling of **jewelry**. • No matter which team wins the 2003 World Series, a former Tulsa Drillers player will be wearing new **jewelery** next year. USE **jewelry**. • This site includes beaded **jewelery** and hemp **jewelery**. USE **jewelry**. • The line will include jeans, T-shirts, **jewelery**, lingerie and a fragrance. USE **jewelry**.

> *Jewelry is the American spelling, not **jewelery** or **jewellery**.*

JUDICIAL

> *Confused with **judicious**. **Judicial** means relating to judges and courts of law; befitting a judge; fair and unbiased ("The **judicial** branch hears cases that challenge or require interpretation of the legislation passed by Congress and signed by the president"). **Judicious** means showing good judgment or wisdom; careful ("**Judicious** use of insecticides is essential for natural enemy conservation and for the enhancement of natural biological control").*

KNOTICAL

Misused for **nautical.** • This third S/V Olapa Survey spent five weeks looking for NF at sites every six **knotical** miles along the Atlantic reef crest. USE **nautical.** • As a tropical disturbance strengthens, pressure drops and winds increase to 20 **knotical** miles per hour, it becomes known as a tropical depression. USE **nautical.**

> *Though the speed of a ship is measured in **knots**, the distance traveled is specified by the word **nautical** (relating to ships, sailors, or the sea), not **knotical**.*

KUDO

Misused for **kudos** (or similar words). • It is obviously Formula One influenced—he deserves **a great kudo.** USE **kudos.** • **Another kudo** for Congress, I guess. USE **More kudos.** • Incidentally, Art's award was presented to the best journalist of any size paper competing, quite a **kudo.** USE **an honor.**

> ***Kudos*** *is praise or acclaim for an achievement; the word is singular. The spelling* ***kudo*** *exists only in some descriptive dictionaries, the nether regions of English usage, which certainly does not legitimize its use.*

Despite rain, cold, lack of outhouses and "three large vultures circling" the camp, he receives the ultimate kudo: "You made my life larger."
—**Gayle Keck, *The Washington Post***

The "ultimate kudo" belongs to cuckoo Keck, who makes our lives smaller with her sloppy writing. Bad usage atrophies our thoughts and feelings; it shrinks our ability to speak clearly and withers our ability to write well.

LACONIC

Idiotic for **emotionless** (or similar words). • His tone of speech is **laconic** and pithy. USE **dispassionate**. • "Death Watch," a **laconic** litany of medical patients who were given faulty terminal diagnoses, delivers a shorthand version of hope and fatalism run awry because of human error. USE **unemotional**. • Glenn behaved in the familiar way of the sexist Australian pig and the fact he was a bushie (speaking with a dinky-di **laconic** Aussie voice, vowels as wide as the brown plains are endless) made it worse. USE **emotionless**. • She may not be pushing comedic boundaries, but her irreverence and **laconic** delivery make you feel you are in the company of the best kind of pub raconteur. USE **deadpan**.

> *When a word takes on a new meaning—often a wholly incorrect and inappropriate meaning—laxicographers and ding-a-linguists, bungling, clumsy arbiters of the language, call it a "semantic shift" or "semantic drift."*
> *The meaning of the word **laconic** is terse, concise; using few words. It does not mean unemotional, affectless, or dispassionate.*

LAMBLASTE

Misspelling of **lambaste**. • In just the past decade, America was **lamblasted** for not doing more to prevent atrocities in Somalia, the Balkans, Zaire, etc. USE **lambasted**. • Not only was he being **lamblasted** by the press, there were people at NBC who were questioning his ability to portray Charles Ingalls, happily married frontiersman and devoted father. USE **lambasted**. • Do I not **lamblaste** Brahmins for having become a degenerated class? USE **lambaste**.

> *To **lambaste** (lam-BAST) is to criticize someone severely, to scold or berate. **Lamblaste** means nothing other than that its user is an inattentive listener, an infrequent reader.*

Bush lamblasted "activist judges"--presumably those justices from Vermont, Massachusetts and New Jersey--for "redefining marriage by court order, without regard for the will of the people."
—Cornell Daily Sun

LATER

Misused for **latter**. • The real confrontation came in the **later** sixteenth century, as the church faced the radical challenge of Protestantism. USE **latter**. • But Bloomberg reported that investors sold the shares and bought those of arch rival Foundry Networks, Inc. as the former's sales growth slowed to the **later's** level. USE **latter's**.

> *Later means at a later time; subsequently. **Latter** means near the end; the second of two people of things mentioned. **Latter**, however, ought not to be used to mean the last of three or more people or things mentioned.*

LAUDATORY

Misused for **laudable**. • Kansas earned a **laudatory** No. 15 ranking, while Missouri came in blah and blaher at 28. USE **laudable**. • While maintaining "family values" is a **laudatory**, if ambiguous, goal, we have to wonder if it is worth rewriting the Constitution for. USE **laudable**.

> *Laudable means worthy of being lauded; praiseworthy. **Laudatory** means expressing praise; eulogistic.*

LAXADAISICAL

Misused for **lackadaisical**. • Winstone is a good actor but here he seems **laxadaisical**, as if he isn't much interested in what's going on. USE **lackadaisical**. • The Kaphatype person is slow, methodical, and thorough; if imbalanced, they can become **laxadaisical** and inert. USE **lackadaisical**.

*Though some people might, on occasion, allow, even applaud, the spelling **laxicographer** (a hopelessly descriptive dictionary maker), no one should allow the misspelling **laxadaisical**.*

LEAD

Solecistic for **led**. • Not only did she have a successful career on stage, screen, radio, and television, she **lead** the way for many women to become leaders in their fields of endeavor. USE **led**. • The Pirates **lead** 6 to 2 going into the top of the 4th before the Astros' bats came alive with 9 runs in that inning and 6 more in the top of the 5th. USE **led**.

> ***Led*** *(LED) is the past tense of **lead** (LEED): to direct the course of; to guide; to be in charge; to be at the forefront of. **Lead** (LED) is a heavy, soft, bluish-gray metal.*

LEARNINGS

Idiotic for **lesson** (or similar words). • And the **learnings** we get from our employee telework program are embedded in the networking services we sell to customers. USE **knowledge**. • The early days are certainly handing us some painful **learnings**, but then sport is not about instant gratification. USE **lessons**. • Many of these "skills" fit in with the "essential **learnings**" the district wants the kids to take with them when they graduate from high school. USE **aptitudes**. • For journalists, change brings new challenges and new **learnings**. USE **insight**.

> ***Learning*** *no one can find fault with, but **learnings** is a different word, and a ridiculous one. **Learning** has been made plural so as to include the meanings of a dozen other words, more precise words. People are impatient with, even intolerant of, exactitude and nicety. We are no more careful of our words than we are caring for one another. The less exact our words, the less clear our thoughts, the less sincere our sentences, the less honest our behavior.*

LEAVE

Misused for **let**. • Since the parsley has seen its best days already, I'm just going to **leave** him be and watch what he does. USE **let**. • Do me a favour and **leave** me be. USE **let**. • Until we hear some more facts, I'd be inclined to **leave** it lie, rather than assume it's operational. USE **let**.

L

Leave means to go away from, whereas *let* means to permit or allow. *Leave* to mean *let* is incorrect (except in the phrase "leave me alone," which, because it is popularly used, few grammarians bother to grumble about).

LENSE

Misspelling of **lens**. • It's a quick step-by-step process to remove the cataract and insert a manmade **lense**. USE **lens**. • Administrators call this information another **lense** to view how schools are doing. USE **lens**. • A really good **lense** is a polarized **lense**. USE **lens**.

Lens, not *lense*, is the correct spelling. The plural of *lens* is *lenses*.

LEAPT (LEAPED)

Have you noticed that journalists, both print and broadcast, no longer write or say something like "The witness leapt to his feet" or "She knelt in prayer"? Instead, they use *leaped* or *kneeled*. Is this acceptable?

Either **leapt** or **leaped**, **knelt** or **kneeled**, or as a further illustration, **blest** or **blessed** is correct though using **-t** instead of **-ed** to form the past tense or past participle of these verbs may sound quaint, if not incorrect, to modern ears.

Other verbs insist on the **-t** ending. We say, or should say, **swept**, never **sweeped**, and **kept**, never **keeped**.

LESS

Misused for **fewer**. • In a survey of 132 jumpers, **less** than half had complaints. USE **fewer**. • The number of car repossessions has doubled in just five years; home foreclosures have more than tripled in **less** than twenty-five years. USE **fewer**. • When we looked at that and the fact in this economy there are **less** investment bankers flying, **less** lawyers flying, we made the very difficult, but prudent decision to retire the Concorde. USE **fewer**.

And **fewer** is misused for **less**: • With the current number of members, even if **fewer** than 1% of the total membership post a link each day, it's far too many links to take in. USE **less**. • She noted that close to 200 US students are enrolled in academic programs at Hebrew University this year, 40 percent **fewer** than before the violence. USE **less**.

*The distinction between **fewer** and **less** (like that between **number** and **amount**) centers on what can be counted and what cannot. **Fewer** we use for numbers; **less** we use for amounts. SEE ALSO **amount**; **much**.*

Even the confusion between these two words is being encouraged by lexicographers, for many dictionaries now offer one word as the synonym of the other. In the end, lexicographers who suppress or discourage the distinctions between words reduce our ability to see clearly and reason convincingly.

LESS

Misused for **lest**. • **Less** we forget, we won the national championship in football in 1998 and made it to the Final Four in basketball, holding the top rank for most of the season. USE **Lest**. • In these days of great scientific advances, some people get scared, **less** we discover something which makes God redundant or irrelevant. USE **lest**.

*Lest** means for fear that. **Less** means not as great in amount or quantity; lower in importance.*

Do you prefer *fewer* or *less* for percentages? For example, "Fewer (or less) than 10 percent of the people surveyed like politicians."

*Percentages deal with amounts, not numbers, so the correct word is **less**. Even in your example, when we might know, or imagine, that "**fewer** than 10 percent of the people" amounts to 50,000 people, the word should be **less**. If, however, your sentence did read "**Fewer** than 50,000 of the people surveyed like politicians," it, then, would be correctly worded.*

L

> I thought I would ask what you think of "10 items or less." Bill Walsh, a copy editor at the *Washington Post* and until now a reasonable guy, has caved and accepts it. I was quite startled when I visited my sister in Iowa City and saw that all stores--grocery stores, even the Wal-Mart--have signs in their express checkout lanes that say "10 items or fewer."

*If Wal-Mart's signs say "10 items or **fewer**," it may indeed be time to embrace "10 items or **less**."... No, if Walsh accepts it, I think that's unfortunate. Some of our worst dictionaries maintain that **less** is synonymous with **fewer**, and **fewer** with **less**. It is not time to acquiesce, as Walsh apparently has done; it's time we all loudly complain.*

LEVY

Misused for **levee**. • Experts have warned since the late 1990s that New Orleans' **levies** couldn't withstand the storm surge of a major hurricane. USE **levees**. • The gates of your communities are about to burst like the **levies**. USE **levees**. • Schumann looked at images of the flooding from the breached **levy** and said, "In this duffel bag is everything I own." USE **levee**. • The helicopter then passed over the break in the **levy**. USE **levee**.

*There are three words, all pronounced the same, and two of them are spelled **levee**. A **levee** (LEV-ee) is an embankment alongside a river or body of water designed to prevent flooding; a landing place or pier. It is also a formal reception; a reception held by a sovereign or person of rank. A **levy** (LEV-ee) is a tax or the collection of a tax; property seized to satisfy a judgment; a compulsory enlistment, often for military service.*

LIABLE

Misused for **libel**. • It's unfortunate, but in this country, if you're successful or famous, many courts will allow defamation, slander and **liable** to go unpunished. USE **libel**. • Most clubs and officers do not know how vulnerable they are to **liable** suits. USE **libel**. • Right now, your only recourse is to sue for **liable** damages. USE **libel**.

Libel (LIE-bel) is a noun that means a published or written false and defamatory statement that damages a person's reputation. Liable (LIE-ah-bel) is an adjective that means legally bound or responsible; likely though undesirable.

LIABLE

Misused for **likely**. • Because information is **liable** to change from time to time you should not rely on the information on this web site but should check the accuracy of the information with the relevant supplier. USE **likely**. • There are a lot of kids, including my own, who are **liable** to start a grade proficient in standards at that grade level. USE **likely**. • These days, goods are just as **liable** to travel by air or truck as they are to travel by sea. USE **likely**.

Liable means undesirably likely, not likely alone; legally obligated.

LIASON

Misspelling of **liaison**. • Drivers and **liason** officers had not been paid their allowances, and were only given limited money for petrol throughout the Tour. USE **liaison**. • It also reports results to issuer and participating broker dealers and acts as a **liason** among trustees, issuers, broker dealers and security depositories. USE **liaison**.

Remember, liaison is spelled li, ai, and then son.

LICENCE

Misspelling of **license**. • Webevents is able to offer **licence** agreements for its online exhibition software. USE **license**. • Shop needs an experienced designer who can also perform landscaping tasks, provide good customer service and possesses a valid Massachusetts driver's **licence**. USE **license**.

In the United States, license is the correct spelling.

LIE

Misused for **lay**. • Many times I had to **lie** the book down and control my breathing as I found I would be holding my breath without realizing it! USE **lay**. • **Lie** him on his back on the floor with a play gym over his head. He will not only love watching

L

the bright objects but will try and raise his hands to touch them. USE Lay. • The government wanted to attain revenue for **lying** pipeline from Turkmenistan, Iran and India via Pakistan. USE **laying**. • He **lay** the bicycle down by the side of the road. USE **laid**. • They're all there among the 65,000 **lain** to rest over the generations beneath the baked, sandy surface of El Paso's Concordia Cemetery. USE **laid**.

And **lay** is, even more often, misused for **lie**: • We hear a big boom and turn and see a freshman **laying** on the field. USE **lying**. • She just **laid** down on the floor, alongside her cot, and we couldn't get her to respond. USE **lay**. • This reflects a throwback to the early days of the gathering, when a generation of flower children brought about the resurgence of handmade crafts—a specialty that had **laid** dormant through 1950s commercialism. USE **lain**.

And not uncommonly, the word **lied** is thought to be the past tense of **lie** or **lay**: • Zinka **lied** down on her bed and didn't go to lunch, drifting in and out of sleep until dinner. USE **lay**. • After his talk to all of the third- and fourth-graders, he **lied** down on the gym floor and arm-wrestled Alexandra Ritchie, 9. USE **lay**. • She **lied** it down on the coffee table and picked up her glass and walked into her bedroom. USE **laid**.

*The verb **lie** means to assume or be in a reclining position. The verb **lay** means to put or place something. The verb **lay** often takes an object; **lie** doesn't.*

Present	Present Participle	Past	Past Participle
lie	(am) lying	lay	(have) lain
lay	(am) laying	laid	(have) laid

Then she danced suggestively with two black female dancers taking their shirts off, and then they laid on top of her on the chaise.

—L. Brent Bozell, journalist

*The syndicated L. Brent Bozell should know that **lay** (that is, **lie**), not **laid** (that is, **lay**) is the correct word, which may be why he prefers the initial **L**.*

LIER

Misspelling of **liar**. • Bustamente is a **lier** and a racist. USE **liar**. • How can you trust a **lier**? USE **liar**. • Most MT solvers had a two-step approach where they first ask a question to establish whether the person they are talking to is a **lier** or truth speaker. USE **liar**.

Liar, not *lier*, is the correct spelling.

LIGHTENING

Misused for **lightning**. • The pages loaded **lightening** fast. USE **lightning**. • Check-21 is a **lightening** rod for the banking industry, and smaller banks and credit unions are at the greatest risk of getting burned. USE **lightning**. • Those harsh conditions have included everything from major flooding, **lightening** storms, hail, 110-degree heat, forest fires and an earthquake. USE **lightning**.

*Though **lightening** once was the spelling to describe an electrical storm, today the word is **lightning**. Lightening means to make lighter; to make less heavy or less burdensome. Lightening also describes when the fetal head begins to descend into the mother's pelvis.*

LIGHTING

Misused for **lightning**. • After a couple of dry winters, Hawaii has become unaccustomed to the drenchings and the occasional thunder and **lighting** of the winter storms like the one that put a damper on the end of the Thanksgiving weekend across the state. USE **lightning**. • Strong winds and **lighting** storms are occurring around the Grassy Plains, the Puppy Field, and the Battle Field. USE **lightning**.

Lighting is a certain kind of light; the lights that produce illumination; illumination. Lightning is a flash of light in the sky caused by a discharge of atmospheric electricity; very fast and sudden.

LIKE

Solecistic for **as**. • The Vatican now says the marble shines **like** it did in the early part of the century. USE **as**. • It's going to revitalize the downtown—much **like** Quincy Market did for us. USE **as**. • **Like** I said, some men don't remember they

L

put the mask on in the first place. USE **As.** • Other countries wouldn't be ripping us off **like** they're doing. USE **as.** • I don't know if we'll ever have people riding the trains **like** they do in Europe. USE **as.**

*No solecism is as ubiquitous as this one. Though to the misguided masses, the cachet of using **like** instead of **as** may be appealing, to others it is nothing less than appalling. Knowing when to use **as** instead of **like** is the mark of conscientious people who still value one of the hallmarks of being human: Using the language well.*

So if you feel passionate about "spider hole," I would suggest you vote early and vote often, like they do in Chicago.
—John Shibley, Lake Superior State University

*Shibley, co-compiler of Lake Superior's Banished Words list, not only uses **like** instead of **as**, he uses the word in the sense he banished it in 1986. Shibley should know his shibboleths.*

LIKE

Solecistic for **as if** (or similar words). • I just remember feeling **like I was** on eggshells all the time. USE **as though I were.** • It's **like they're** taking out of your hand what you worked for the whole year. USE **as if they were.** • It makes it look **like** you cheated on a test, and everybody got the same grade. USE **as though.** • It's not **like we're** destroying their property or breaking out windows down here. USE **as if we were.** • She looked at me **like I was** insane. USE **as though I were.** • He would sing **like he was** praying. USE **as though he were.**

***As if** or **as though** is the proper expression to use when a verb in the conditional form follows (or should follow). The use of **like** in these instances is uneducated.*

LIKELY

*Confused with **apt**. **Apt** suggests a natural tendency ("The Fed is more **apt** to raise rates if it believes that the economy is growing too quickly"), and **likely**, something* expected or probable ("Most riders who use the Metro bus system within the city of Cincinnati **likely** won't have to pay a fare increase next year").

LIKEWISE

Idiotic for **so do I** (or similar words). • I cannot abide his behavior. **Likewise**. USE **Nor can I**. • It's nice to meet you. **Likewise**. USE **As it is to meet you**. • I love being with them. **Likewise**. USE **So do I**. • Happy holidays. Thank you and **likewise** to you as well. USE **happy holidays**.

In the sense of similarly, in the same way, or in addition ("I invite others to do ***likewise****"; "****Likewise****, the nesting activities of house wrens, cardinals, chickadees, and other common birds can stimulate a lifelong interest in nature"),* ***likewise*** *is a perfectly good word. In the sense of* ***so do I*** *(or the juvenile,* ***me too****) or* ***same to you****, it's ungrammatical.*

LINEAGE

Misspelling of **linage**. • Dow Jones told investors at the UBS Warburg media conference that November ad **lineage** was down 12 percent, and that total ad **lineage** in December would be down about 30 percent from a year before. USE **linage**. • Increase your print **lineage** by running a directory ad that lists the businesses in town with web sites. USE **linage**.

Linage *(LIE-nij) is the number of lines of printed, usually advertising, material.* ***Lineage*** *(LIN-ee-ij) is direct descent from an ancestor. Though some dictionaries offer the spelling* ***lineage*** *is a variant of* ***linage****, this practice is less than helpful, and doubtless little other than the result of people confusing one word for the other.*

LITANY

Misused for **list**. • Iverson listed a whole **litany** of reasons for a debacle that left the crowd booing the 76ers throughout the second half. USE **list**. • In his annual State of the City address, Reed recited a **litany** of accomplishments that he said have taken place during those years. USE **list**.

A ***litany*** *is a prayer consisting of a series of petitions recited by a leader alternating with fixed responses; a tedious recital or repetitive series. A* ***list*** *is a number of items, typically printed one below another.*

A litany of guests appeared on "Blueprint," including banjo master Bela Fleck, Dobro virtuoso Jerry Douglas (who plays with Krauss in Union Station) and upright bass genius Edgar Meyer.

—Kira L. Schlechter, *The Patriot-News*

Some people do prefer the polysyllabic to the monosyllabic word, but if they do not know the meanings of the words they use, they impress no one who matters.

LITERALLY

Misused for **figuratively** (or similar words). • I have been reading about indigenous tribes whose members have very few possessions and live very simple lives, yet they **literally** radiate happiness. DELETE **literally**. • Ted Heller's diabolically witty debut novel, *Slab Rat*, is a **literally** bloody farce about life and death in a too-fancy New York magazine office housed in a slablike tower. DELETE **literally**. • We are not only a society that is **literally** drowning in a sea of sexual evil, but we seem to be enjoying it. DELETE **literally**.

*The misuse of **literally**, which in these examples, means actually or in fact, occasions more mirth than does the misuse of many other words.*

Characters from books literally leap off the page in this engrossing, action-packed fantasy by the author of *The Thief Lord*.

—Sharon Rawlins, *School Library Journal*

*The characters, of course, do not **literally** leap off the page. Since **literally** is the wrong word, we might easily wonder whether the book is indeed engrossing and action-packed or, more likely, tedious and mind-numbing.*

LITERATELY

Solecistic for **literally**. • The Fulton County Playhouse is a non-profit theater located about a mile out side of Byrant, Illinois. It is **literately** in an old barn. USE **literally**. • Since **literately** anyone can stand up as representatives, there is room for entrepreneurs. USE **literally**. • Alex will have you **literately** in stitches every time he emerges on the screen. USE **literally**. A properly crafted worm could **literately** hit millions or tens of millions of IM clients very quickly. USE **literally**.

> **Literately** *is the adverb of* **literate**, *able to read and write.* **Literally** *means in a literal or strict sense; word for word. SEE ALSO* **alliterate**.

LOAN

Misused for **lend**. • The nation's largest union-owned life insurance company says it's willing to **loan** more than $110 million toward a new stadium for the Florida Marlins. USE **lend**. • The equipment is owned by the U.S. Forest Service, but can be **loaned** indefinitely to state forestry departments. USE **lent**. • We have money to **loan**. USE **lend**.

> **Loan** *is a noun.* **Lend** *is a verb. Today,* **loan** *is also used as a verb because banks and mortgage companies are concerned with making loans, and the verb* **loan**, *better than the more casual* **lend**, *reminds people that they owe money. If we were to use* **lend**, *we might not feel so compelled to pay back the money. Use* **lend**; *usurers* **loan**.

LOATHE

Misused for **loath**. • In a culture based on a deep understanding of such interconnectedness, individuals would be as **loathe** to hurt their neighbor, or the ecosystem, as we are now **loathe** to stub our toe. USE **loath**. • New Zealand's wind power potential is vast, writes James Weir, but wind farms are something that many kiwis are **loathe** to have in their line of sight. USE **loath**. • Remembrances of you litter my apartment here and there, and so I am **loathe** to clean—and you linger still. USE **loath**. • Winter visitors have been **loathe** to leave this year. USE **loath**.

L

> **Loathe** *(LOATHE), a verb, means to dislike greatly, hate, or detest;* **loath** *(LOTH),*

an adjective, means disinclined, reluctant. If people could grasp the difference in pronunciation, perhaps they could grasp the difference in meaning. Here, too, dictionary makers lie, cheat, and steal by suggesting the same pronunciation (and, some, even the same spelling) for both words. SEE ALSO **cachet**.

LOSE

Misused for **loose**. • The slogan "**lose** lips sink ships" was popularized during World War II in Britain, when the entire country was mobilized, to increase security awareness in the population. USE **loose**. • She is a **lose** woman so any player who is able to role play it well enough could leave early. USE **loose**. • As the election saga in Florida winds up, the Bush and Gore legal teams tie up **lose** ends, including putting a stop to all legal initiatives. USE **loose**.

> **Lose** *(looz) means to lack the possession of; to mislay.* **Loose** *(loos) means not fastened or restrained; not taut; without moral restraint; idle; not exact.*

LUXURIOUS

Misused for **luxuriant**. • Instead of keeping a **luxurious** growth of photosynthetic tissue from ground to crown, the typical palm sheds leaves as it grows, retaining only a tuft of greenery at the very top. USE **luxuriant**. • Such **luxurious** growth signals high productivity, and modern scientific measurements confirm this. USE **luxuriant**. • Its organic botanicals and minerals act like a conditioning tonic, insuring fuller, thicker, more **luxurious** hair. USE **luxuriant**.

> **Luxurious** *means characterized by luxury; splendid, rich, or extremely comfortable.* **Luxuriant***, characterized by a lush or abundant growth; excessively florid.*

-LY

Not only did the little boy get away **safe**, he also called the police. USE **safely**. • She learns very **quick**. USE **quickly**. • Women usually treat me **terrible**. USE **terribly**. • He is behaving very **irrational**. USE **irrationally**. • You're doing **fantastic**. USE **fantastically**. • They showed us how to build the product as small and as **cheap** as possible. USE **cheaply**. • Your position on taxes is so **screaming** loud, we can't help but know it. USE **screamingly**. • Don't take this **personal**. USE **personally**. • Didn't they take you **serious**? USE **seriously**.

*An adverb (often ending in -**ly**), not an adjective, modifies a verb.*

They never called in and said he was acting belligerent.

—Kenneth Lawson, lawyer

Listening to lawyer Lawson speak might make anyone act ***belligerently***.

L

MANOR

Misused for **manner**. • It is perfectly possible to take the changes we are going to recommend in a revenue neutral **manor**. USE **manner**. • His **manor** of deliverance, was almost Shakespearian. USE **manner**. Rape is a power driven, violent assault that is acted out in a sexual **manor**. USE **manner**.

> A **manor** is a mansion; the principal residence on an estate. **Manner** is a way of acting; a way in which something is done; kind or sort.

MANTEL

Misused for **mantle**. • Our Lady was clad in a robe of dazzling whiteness, over which she wore a **mantel** of heavenly blue. USE **mantle**. • Johnson kept his illness out of public view and struggled to wear the mask and the **mantel** of the corporate executive. USE **mantle**. • Thus, when a strongman passes from the scene, there is often a dearth of qualified candidates to assume the **mantel** of leadership. USE **mantle**.

> A **mantel** is a shelf above a fireplace. A **mantle** is a cloak or shawl; something that covers or conceals; an important role or responsibility that passes from one person to another.
>
> Some dictionaries maintain that **mantel** is a variant spelling of **mantle**, and **mantle** of **mantel**. Let the distinct spelling of each word denote the distinct meaning of each word.

MARRAGE

Misspelling of **marriage**. • Janie's **marrage** to Logan Killicks is an unhappy one for her, as she looses many of her girlish fantasies about love and **marrage**. USE **marriage**. • A sham **marrage** is better than no **marrage** at all. USE **marriage**.

> The word **marriage** contains **iage**, "I age"—a suitable mnemonic. SEE ALSO **adultry**.

MARSHAL

Misused for **martial**. • Then-Mayor Dewey Archambault declared **marshal** law and summoned National Guard troops and Works Progress Administration workers to help clear roads and maintain order. USE **martial**. • If charged, punishment will range from anything to no punishment at all to a court **marshal**, which brings the case to trial in a military court. USE **martial**. • Rapier combat is a **marshal** activity enjoyed by many in the Society for Creative Anachronism, both as an exciting active pursuit and as a very entertaining spectator sport. USE **martial**.

*The noun **marshal** means an officer; a military commander; an official in charge of ceremonies. The verb means to arrange in order; to array; to manage; to guide or usher someone ceremoniously. **Martial** means relating to war or military forces; warlike; characteristic of a warrior. SEE ALSO **marshall**.*

MARSHALL

Misspelling of **marshal**. • Be discreet, be respectful at all times, be on time, dress appropriately, follow the directions of the parade **marshall** and you will be welcome next time. USE **marshal**. • Illustrious Master John D. Schaeffer served as **Marshall** of Ceremonies, Dorsey B. Reynolds was the Toastmaster, and Joseph V. Gaddy delivered the after-dinner address. USE **Marshal**. • The Alabama Fire **Marshall's** office, along with the ATF, are investigating the cause of the explosion since no power or gas was hooked up to the house. USE **Marshal's**.

*The correct spelling of **marshal** has one **l**, not two. SEE ALSO **marshal**.*

MARTIAL

Misused for **marital**. • The purpose of the Women's Resource Center is to educate women on all pregnancy options, while promoting the values of the sanctity of human life, premarital abstinence, and **martial** fidelity in our community. USE **marital**. • Just ask for our wedding package and you'll be well on your way to **martial** bliss. USE **marital**. • If you had **premartial** sex during your engagement period is that still a sin? USE **premarital**.

And **marital** is occasionally misused for **martial**: • The Konasari Regulars represent the bulk of the Undercity's **marital** forces. USE **martial**.

M

Adjectives both, **marital** *means of or relating to marriage or to a husband, and* **martial** *means of or relating to war or the armed forces.*

MASONARY

Misspelling of **masonry**. • She said forty-five people were evacuated, but the station "stayed on the air" during the fire, which originated in an office in the middle of the one-story, **masonary** building. USE **masonry**. • We have been in the **masonary** business over fifteen years and we have insurance. USE **masonry**.

A mason's trade, brickwork or stonework, **masonry** *(MA-son-ree), not* **masonary** *(MAY-son-air-ee) is the correct spelling (and pronunciation).*

MASSEUR

Misused for **masseuse**. • Being a qualified back **masseur**, she's bound to release all of your tensions! USE **masseuse**. • She is an excellent sports **masseur**. USE **masseuse**.

Masseurs *are males who give massages;* **masseuses** *are females who give massages. Perhaps lexicographers will agree that this is a distinction that ought to be respected. SEE ALSO* **inflammable**.

MASTERS

Which is correct: *Masters* or *Master's* (with apostrophe)? Possible contexts: "I have a Master's of Science" or "It's a Master's program in communications."

Bachelor, **master,** and **doctor** *are capitalized when they follow a person's name (Samuel Smithson, Doctor of Divinity); otherwise, they should be lowercased with an apostrophe ("I have a* **master's** *degree"; "It's a* **master's** *program in communications").*

MASTICATE

Misused for **masturbate**. • You can **masticate** at the beach, on a boat, in an airplane or while you are driving a car. It is best if you keep your mouth closed while **masticating**. USE **masturbate**; **masturbating**.

*Old jokes are always new to some people. A person who doesn't smile or smirk on hearing this one may need to be told the punch line: **masticate** means to chew food; **masturbate** means to stimulate one's own or another's genitals for sexual pleasure.*

MAUNDER

*Confused with **meander**. **Maunder** (MON-der) means to talk incoherently; to move or act aimlessly ("Music makes me write this sort of **maundering** adolescent nonsense without embarrassment"; "This of course invokes the image of the **maundering** gypsy near an abyss with a sack tied to a staff hoisted over his shoulder"). **Meander** (mee-AN-der) means to follow a winding course; to wander leisurely ("If you were to explore almost any **meandering** river you would find the landforms that are shown in the diagram to the right"; "Included here is Doughty's **meandering** but strange hymn in praise of desert camels"). As you see, **maunder** and **meander** have similar meanings—to move about or express oneself aimlessly—but someone who **maunders** is being disparaged, and someone who **meanders** is not.*

MEDIAS

Idiotic for **media**. • When suicide bombers attack schools, bus stations, marketplaces, or other highly populated civilian areas, the biased liberal **medias** of the world all turn a blind eye. USE **media**. • Her art covers many aspects and **medias**, but today she is most widely noted for her sport action figures, portraits and pet portraits, but also does seascapes, landscapes, or still life should a client request them. USE **media**. • I want extra batteries for the remotes, an extra bulb for the projector, two backup copies of the presentation (naturally, in two different **medias**). USE **media**.

*As **data**—not **datas**—is the plural of **datum**, so **media**—not **medias**—is the plural of **medium**. Though **media** is sometimes used and allowed as a singular word, **medias** as a plural is insupportable.*

M

MENDICITY

Confused with **mendacity**. **Mendicity** (men-DIS-i-tee) means begging or beggary ("In 1814 an Institution for the Relief of the Poor of Douglas and the Suppression of **Mendicity** was established based on voluntary subscriptions whose aim was to help the needy poor"); **mendacity** (men-DAS-i-tee), untruthfulness, lying ("Bush's **mendacity** on economic matters was obvious even during the 2000 election, but lately it has reached almost pathological levels").

MERETRICIOUS

Misused for **meritorious**. • I informed her that that was a **meretricious** plan except for the fact that it involves lying. USE **meritorious**. • If the Other Side is Wrong, their arguments, however **meretricious**, will not in the end survive exposure to ours. USE **meritorious**. • Judges believed her coverage of the Port Lincoln bushfires was especially **meretricious** as she managed to cover an event that demanded immediacy within the restrictions imposed by a weekly newspaper. USE **meritorious**.

Meretricious means of or relating to a prostitute; falsely or vulgarly attractive; pretentious. It does not mean **meritorious**, having merit, deserving of honor.

MERITOUS

Idiotic for **meritorious**. • It is **meritous** to proceed to renew the ablution after having made an obligatory prayer or a supererogatory prayer and having gone round the Kaaba. USE **meritorious**. • The **Meritous** Circle of Honor is given to a member whose achievements in the field of battle, both in terms of leadership and servitude are exemplary and unable to be fathomed. USE **Meritorious**. • But for society to be able to reward a **meritous** person in right measure, society must first measure his merit. USE **meritorious**. • In 1990, it received the ACS Award for Outstanding Performance by Divisions in recognition of its service to its members and its **meritous** contributions to the profession and the public understanding of chemistry. USE **meritorious**.

Meritous, at best, is but a mumbler's way of pronouncing **meritorious**. SEE ALSO **superity**.

I am grateful to President Chirac for hosting this
historic event, and for once the word historic is
indeed meritous.
—U.K. Prime Minister Tony Blair

MESSAGE

Idiotic for **write** (or similar words). • "The third quarter is looking great," Lay **mes-saged** an Enron worker on Sept. 26, three weeks before the company announced $638 million in third-quarter losses. USE **told.** • "Was your idea meant as tongue-in-cheek or are you serious?" **messaged** one reader. USE **wrote.** • Clyde went to check out the tractors the day before the sale and **messaged** John that both of them started easily, although it had been a couple of years since either had run. USE **emailed.**

*In the sense of to send a **message**, the verb **message** is disagreeable; in the sense of to mail, email, write, or tell, it is abhorrent.*

METAL

Misused for **medal.** • I am the first male squash player from the U.S. to earn a **metal!** (Mark Talbott won a **metal** eight years ago, but he did not earn it, it was by default). USE **medal.** • Sara Gray and Sheena Bohn both **metaled** in the 800 meter run. USE **medaled.**

*A **metal** (MET-el) is typically hard, shiny, malleable, and a good conductor of electricity and heat. A **medal** (MED-el) is often, though not always, made of metal and is given as an award or in recognition of some achievement or event. SEE ALSO **mettle**.*

METRIC

Idiotic for **measure** (or similar words). • Has TSA sought to develop a **metric** for the average time required to effectively and efficiently process passengers and baggage at each airport? USE **measure.** • Don't look at just one **metric**, such as the price-to-book value ratio, when researching a stock. USE **measure.** • Earnings are the single

M

most important **metric** for a company. USE **measure.** • Sales at stores open at least one year—an industry **metric** called same-store sales—rose 4 percent, have the company's expectation 8 percent growth. USE **measure.** • And what I would look at is not the **metric** of the bombings and the casualties, as tragic as they are, but some **metrics** which I would say would be a little more objective. USE **magnitude; measurements.**

*Among the self-important and empty-headed, **metric** is displacing **measure** or **measurement**. This use of **metric** does not refer to metric weights and measures, not to the metric system, not to metric tons, not to metric miles. It is simply a scientific-sounding word that people, uneasy with their own understanding of words and numbers, use instead of a perfectly understandable word like **measure**.*

And then secondarily, what you see is there's obviously been a metric and a measurement of the Iraqi forces and their ability to take over, because I think most of the forces involved in Operation Thunder will be Iraqi forces.

—Brig. Gen. James "Spider" Marks

METTLE

Misused for **meddle.** • As I **mettled** with the system I encountered a new firewall, which immediately locked the key functions. USE **meddled.** • I do not **mettle** in affairs of the heart. USE **meddle.**

And **meddle** is misused for **mettle:** • He proved his **meddle** with a good qualifying effort at his home Grand Prix only to have the boat banged up in the 2nd qualifying session. USE **mettle.**

***Mettle**, a noun, is quality of character or temperament, especially, highly regarded qualities like spirit and courage. **Meddle**, a verb, is to interfere in; to tamper with. SEE ALSO **metal**.*

MIGHT

*Confused with **may**. **Might** is used to express a possibility that is less likely than that expressed by the word **may** ("The looming deficit **might** be important, but it has no moral implications of any kind"; "A labor dispute will destroy any inroads the game has made into non-traditional hockey markets and it **might** just be the final straw for some of the loyal fans"). **Might** is also the past tense of **may**. SEE ALSO **can**.*

MILLENARY

Misused for **millinery**. • Karamu Performing Arts Theater seeks a **millenary** to make costume hats for its Black Nativity show. USE **millinery**. • In most cases **millenary** wire is sewn to the edges of buckram pieces to add extra stiffness and to be able to shape the final hat. USE **millinery**. They must have had a great **millenary** shop at the time. Not your basic hats! USE **millinery**.

***Millenary** means of or relating to a thousand; a thousand years. **Millinery** means women's hats or the business of a milliner. Both are pronounced (MIL-ah-ner-ee).*

MINISCULE

Misspelling of **minuscule**. • It should be noted that these three N.Y. organizations are not small time "mom and pop" groups that raise **miniscule** amounts at weekly church bake sales. USE **minuscule**. • Several **miniscule** but high-capacity drives from different manufacturers have been produced or are about to be, and some appeared at the recent Consumer Electronics Show (CES) in Las Vegas. USE **minuscule**.

***Minuscule** is so often misspelled **miniscule** that some dictionaries, bent as they certainly seem to be on promoting the dissolution of the language, allow the misspelling—which, of course, makes it more likely that people will continue to misspell the word. SEE ALSO **infinitesimal**.*

MINUTIA

Misused for **minute**. • Midway through his junior year, Rick switched majors ("I enjoy business," he said, "I didn't enjoy the sort of **minutia** study of it") and trans-

M

ferred to Calvin College, where he majors in mass media. USE **minute.** • A million-and-a-half dollars for a city is **minutia.** USE **minute.**

> **Minute** *(my-NOOT), an adjective, means exceptionally small; insignificant; extremely thorough and meticulous.* **Minutia,** *a noun, is a small, trivial detail. Perhaps more disturbing than the misuse of* **minutia** *for* **minute** *is the mispronunciation of it.* **Minutia** *is better pronounced (mi-NOO-shee-ah), not (mi-NOO-sha), as the lazy ones would have it. The plural of* **minutia** *is* **minutiae,** *whose only pronunciation is (mi-NOO-shee-ee). Though people may mean* **minutiae** *(mi-NOO-shee-ee), they invariably spell it* **minutia** *and pronounce it (mi-NOO-sha).*

It's the basic framework of government, not the day-to-day **minutia that is** involved in statutory law. USE **minutiae that are.** • They're all reminders—tangible or imagined—of the lives he touched, the people he knew and loved, the **minutia** that made up his life. USE **minutiae.** • Often in discussions like this people get bogged down in the **minutia** surrounding such attacks. USE **minutiae.**

MISCELLANY

> *Miscellany.* I've heard it pronounced MIS-ah-lay-nee and mi-SEL-ah-nee. Are both correct, and do you have a preference?
>
> *Both are correct though mi-SEL-ah-nee is the British pronunciation.*

MISCHIEVIOUS

Misspelling of **mischievous.** • They alleged that the construction of Kalabagh Dam was merely a **mischievious** act on part of the co-Musharraf ruling party to divert the attention of public from the current national issues. USE **mischievous.** • The insinuation that three prostitutes were found in the rooms of our client and his colleague, Garfield Smith, is false, **mischievious** and malicious. USE **mischievous.**

Two *i*'s, not three, are used to spell **mischievous**. Though at least one dictionary does include the pronunciation (mis-CHEE-vee-es) as an alternative to the correct (MIS-chi-ves), only adolescents and descriptive linguists pay much attention to this extra *i*.

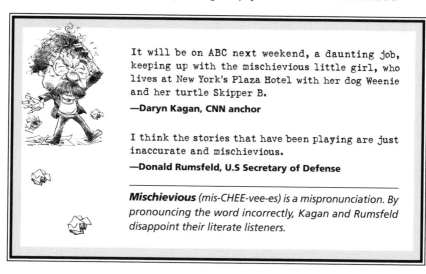

It will be on ABC next weekend, a daunting job, keeping up with the mischievious little girl, who lives at New York's Plaza Hotel with her dog Weenie and her turtle Skipper B.

—Daryn Kagan, CNN anchor

I think the stories that have been playing are just inaccurate and mischievious.

—Donald Rumsfeld, U.S Secretary of Defense

Mischievious (mis-CHEE-vee-es) is a mispronunciation. By pronouncing the word incorrectly, Kagan and Rumsfeld disappoint their literate listeners.

MISCONSCREW

Misspelling of **misconstrue**. • You take a comment about the privacy of a family's pain and **misconscrew** it into something completely off topic and wrong because you can't refute my original argument. • USE **misconstrue**. Why do you always **misconscrew** what I say? USE **misconstrue**. • If you are someone who may **misconscrew** it that way, then I suggest skipping this sight and checking eBay for Lawrence Welk albums. USE **misconstrue**. • I think it is safe to say that my inner beauty outshines my outer beauty, but just so that you do not **misconscrew** that as meaning I must be a dog: I have pictures to exchange, so if you are interested and would like to learn more. USE **misconstrue**.

Misconstrue, to misinterpret or mistake the meaning of, is the correct spelling.

MISPELL (MISSPEL)

Misspelling of **misspell**. • One common error in writing function is to **mispell** the function, in which case, either Excel effectuates an unwanted function or does not

M

understand the function. USE **misspell.** • Enter kelley blue book **mispelled** kelly sometimes in the search box below and press the green arrow button. USE **misspelled.** • She lives in Kenya and manages to **misspel** my name every time. USE **misspell.**

__Misspell__ is spelled correctly when it has two __s__'s and two __l__'s; all other spellings are misspellings.

MITIGATE

Misused for **militate.** • But this is only one side of the story; inner cities are also rich in culture, institutions, and other resources that can **mitigate** against adversity and promote healthy development and learning. USE **militate.** • NUTRI-RICE has been known to increase energy, improve general health, **mitigate** against numerous degenerative diseases and slow the aging process. USE **militate.** • Other factors also **mitigate** in favor of appellant. USE **militate.** • Personality traits of activists **mitigate** in favor of and against archivists' adoption of marketing as a strategy for advancing the archival service to society, but the reference archivist must use character strengths to overcome the weaknesses. USE **militate.**

The phrases __against__ and __in favor of__ invariably follow __militate__, not __mitigate__. To __militate__ is to work or fight against (or sometimes for), whereas to __mitigate__ is to lessen or alleviate, to improve.

MOMENTARILY

Confused with __momently__. __Momentarily__ means for a moment ("Then came a play that __momentarily__ disrupted the mood"). __Momently__ means from moment to moment; at any moment ("We expect him to arrive __momently__").

MONGERER

Misspelling for **monger.** • George Bush is a war-**mongerer** in my opinion. USE **monger.** • I wonder how much of this climate of revenge against him he created by being a hate **mongerer** himself. USE **monger.** • I'd heard about this from Carlo, who is a **mongerer** of conspiracy theories and other misinformation. USE **monger.** Utah's second-leading scorer has noted *New York Post* rumor **mongerer** Peter Vecsey to thank for his heartburn. USE **monger.**

__Monger__, as either a verb or a noun, is the correct spelling; __mongerer__ is incorrect.

I thought of this a few weeks ago when Burt Reynolds was raked over the scandal-monger's coals for "hitting" a CBS producer.

—Steve Penhollow, *The Journal Gazette*

No matter whom--Al Smith or Jose Maria Sert
Or Clemenceau--veins standing out on her throat
As she yelled *War mongerer! Pig! Give us the vote!*,
And would have to be hauled away in her hobble
skirt.

—James Merrill, "The Broken Home," 1966

MORALE

Misused for **moral**. • The **morale** of the story is to start celebrating backwards decision making. USE **moral**. • They have no **morales** when it comes to customer satisfaction. USE **morals**. • Street racing knows no **morales**, but if you think this is a bit too stealthy or deceiving, I'm sure more than one of us has been unceremoniously smoked by a nitrous-fed car that looked innocently stock. USE **morals**. • So he chooses his own **morales**, his own beliefs and among those **morales** and beliefs are he should help save humanity. USE **morals**.

> *A **moral** is a lesson or principle taught in a fable, story, or event; **morals** are standards, principles, or habits of right or wrong conduct. **Morale** is a state of mind or spirit with respect to courage, confidence, disciple, endurance, and the like.*

MORAYS

Idiotic for **mores**. • Finally, citing the existence of religious social **morays** has no bearing on the validity of atheism. USE **mores**. • In Amsterdam's Red Light District, social **morays** are cast aside. USE **mores**. • It is simply amazing that Ms. Whitney would find it amusing to denigrate the social **morays** of both the Valley and the University of Alabama in a single article, and that the editors considered and approved it as "newsworthy." USE **mores**.

M

The word for the customs, conventions, or traditions of a community or society is **mores**, not **morays**. People who misspell the word **morays** reveal they do not read, or if they read, they do not think.

Mores is pronounced MOR-az, not MOR, despite the second pronunciation that some dictionaries, and others who have no notion of the word, offer. The singular of **mores** is **mos**, pronounced MO.

In some issue areas where social morays are still being defined, such as the use of genetic engineering in food production, the Social Values funds take a precautionary approach by avoiding firms who expect to derive substantial revenues from products relying on acceptance of these technologies.
—**Acuityfunds.com**

Never do business with a company whose literature is execrably written ("morays," "issue areas," "firms who"). If they take no time to prepare their wording, they'll take no time to please their customers.

MORE PREFERABLE

Solecistic for **preferable**. • Like the gender approach, staff often regard participation as a more inclusive, and therefore **more preferable**, strategy for benefiting women. USE **preferable**. • It's possible to change the question to accommodate the answer, but in this case, it's much easier and **more preferable** to change the answer instead. USE **preferable**.

More preferable is redundant. *Preferable*, which means more desirable than an alternative, is all the comparison that is needed.

MORE...RATHER THAN

Misused for **more...than**. • Many of the problems I present are more sociological and marketing related **rather than** technical. USE **than**. • More office space was vacated **rather than** leased in 2001. USE **than.** • African-American teens also were more likely to identify figures known through the media **rather than** family or friends. USE **than.** • For Microsoft, the post release debate centered more on the product registration mechanisms of the new OS **rather than** on any of its other features. USE **than.**

*After the word **more**, do not use **rather than** when **than** alone is required.*

MORESO

Misused for **more so.** • While it may not be killing trees, it is alienating to be endlessly pitched to, even **moreso** when they have you figured out. USE **more so.** • We still get the best of the old standards—even **moreso** in some cases. USE **more so.** • It's partially because of the wacky plots and situations Mike Allred likes to put his characters into but **moreso** because the book seems to vary in strength. USE **more so.**

*Despite the frequency with which some people use **moreso**, it is necessarily two words, **more so**, meaning to an even greater degree or extent.*

MORESOME

Idiotic for **more** (or similar words). • The Couples Group is for couples and individuals who are part of a couple, triad, foursome or **moresome.** USE **more.** • Now Cockshutt, now Moline, now John Deere and Fordson! Then Oliver, Allis, Massey, and **moresome!** USE **others.** • Spanish style Hacienda home appr. 6,000 sq. ft. built with high quality construction large lot approximately 450' x 450' excellent landscaping, gazebo in rear and much much **moresome** furniture included. USE **more.**

*Although meant to describe more than a two-, three-, or foursome—and often used by the sexually ever unsatisfied—**moresome** is finding its way into popular usage. Like the equally odious **moreso**, **moresome** is an abomination.*

*And then there are instances where the intended meaning of **moresome** is, if not **awesome**, or perhaps **fearsome**, elusory: ("Its extremely fruity bouquet, with that delicate touch of woodiness, makes it extraordinarily **moresome**.";*
*"In the case of Satanic Verses we had a book and an author. But the **moresome** Muslims hit that author the stronger that author became.")*

M

Calm has entered. Big big Calm, announcer. It is most ernst terooly a moresome intartenment. Colt's tooth! I will give tandsel to it.

—James Joyce, *Finnegans Wake*, 1939

MORIBUND

Misused for **morbid**. • Park seamlessly sutures relentless violence, a **moribund** fascination with death, and the carnivalesque into shots bursting with perfection of color, angle, and composition. USE **morbid**. • HCPCS 43842, gastric restrictive procedure, without gastric bypass, is for **moribund** obesity. USE **morbid**. • A **moribund** curiosity has overtaken him recently, causing the unearthing of old notebooks, letters, photographs, and the usual detritus of existence. USE **morbid**. • My own favorite is to Buster Keaton, whose visual gags and **moribund** humor are clear precedents. USE **morbid**.

> **Morbid** *means unhealthy or diseased; having an unhealthy interest in disturbing or gloomy subjects; gruesome or grisly; pathological.* **Moribund** *means dying; at the point of death; having little vitality.*

MUCH

Misused for **many**. • They're talking about as **much** as twelve inches of snow. USE **many**. • The Dow Jones Industrials Average rose 57 points, or 0.6%, to 9,930 after being up as **much** as 53 points earlier in the session. USE **many**. • **Much** of these developments have their origins in the gradual developments in earlier prehistory within the region itself. USE **Many**.

> *Like other words,* **much** *is used with amounts or quantities, and* **many** *with numbers or that which can be counted. SEE ALSO* **amount***;* **less***.*

MUCHLY

Idiotic for **very much** (or similar words). • Thank you **muchly**. USE **very much**. • I love you **muchly**. USE **very much**. • Thanks to the **muchly** revered Edward Norton and his performance in *Fight Club*. USE **much**. • She is annoying me **muchly**. USE **a good deal**. • Luckily my **muchly**-tattooed roommate Dan came along with me to his regular tattoo artist to get this done, so he kind of prepped me for what to expect. USE **much**.

*The correct adverb is **much** or **very much**. Anyone who uses the obsolete **muchly**—whether or not trying to be jocular—we can be reasonably sure has nothing to contribute to thoughtful discourse. SEE ALSO **thusly**.*

MUSICAL

*Confused with **musicale**. A **musical** (MYOO-zi-kel) is a theatrical production featuring dialogue and a musical score. A **musicale** (myoo-zi-KAL) is a party or social gathering that features a musical program.*

MUTE

Misused for **moot**. • For the bolts there were a few good individual performances in Tempe but the subpar play of the team as a whole makes it a **mute** point. USE **moot**. • This is the requisite "if I were stranded on a desert island I would take" list; of course, it's a **mute** discussion since desert islands have no electricity. USE **moot**.

*__Mute__ (MYOOT) means unable to speak; not speaking or not spoken; a silent, or unpronounced, letter in a word. **Moot** (MOOT), as an adjective, means open to discussion; debatable. It has also come to mean not worthy of discussion because the matter has been settled or is too hypothetical.*

M

NAUSEOUS

Misused for **nauseated**. • Why do I sometimes feel **nauseous** fifteen minutes after a workout? USE **nauseated**. • Many women feel **nauseous** at some point in pregnancy, usually in the first trimester. USE **nauseated**. • Praying the rest of the drinks wouldn't make me **nauseous**, I took a right off of Huntington and walked to the Espresso Royal Caffe. USE **nauseated**.

*Nauseous means causing nausea or stomach distress. **Nauseated** means suffering from nausea. In these examples, working out, being pregnant, and drinking cause nausea; they are **nauseous**. And the result is feeling **nauseated**. The words **feel** or **make me** often precede **nauseated**, not **nauseous**.*

NAVEL

Misused for **naval**. • Israeli **navel** forces also kidnapped the fishermen Mahmoud Ahmed Hussein and Hussein Qaour. USE **naval**. • The Communists in Korea, he declared, can be stopped by air and **navel** forces instead of ground forces. USE **naval**.

*Naval, an adjective, means relating to a navy. **Navel**, a noun, is the belly button, the depression in the middle of the abdomen that marks where the umbilical cord was attached to the fetus.*

NIGGARDLY

*Niggardly (used as an adjective or an adverb) means stingy; parsimonious; meager and inadequate. The noun (or adjective) **niggard**, a miser or stingy person, is seldom seen. Some dictionaries idiotically maintain that **niggardly** (and **niggard**) ought to be used very carefully, if used at all, because many people (no brighter than the average laxicographer) believe that the word means negro (or nigger) and that it is therefore offensive. SEE ALSO **racial**.*

NOISOME

Misused for **noisy** (or similar words). • Gaahl has a revolting screech, and somehow manages to be just as **noisome** when actually holding a note. USE **loud**. • Produced to a metallic sheen by Deftones boardmaster Ulrich Wild, the group's debut album, *Wisconsin Death Trip*, is a pogo spectacular of the highest order, throbbing with industrial clangs, gritty electro beats, and **noisome** guitars. USE **raucous**.

> **Noisome** *means offensive or foul, harmful or damaging; it does not mean* **noisy**.

NONE

I've been twisted in knots about the proper case of the pronoun *none*. When I was in school, I was always taught that the word was singular if it referred to a singular antecedent (e.g., "None of the butter is melted"), but plural if it referred to a plural antecedent (e.g., "None of the eggs are broken"). However, I've noticed recently that everyone, from the *LA Times* to my textbooks, seems to use the singular form, no matter whether the antecedent is singular or plural. Even the *Princeton Review*'s SAT-preparation book marked my student wrong when he used the plural form with a plural antecedent. Deciding that either the language had evolved or that my junior high grammar teacher had been mistaken, I visited Merriam-Webster's web site for confirmation of the rule and was startled to see that Merriam-Webster classifies *none* as a pronoun that can be singular or plural, depending upon the antecedent. So who is right? The *LA Times* and the *Princeton Review*? Or my junior high grammar teacher and Merriam-Webster?

The proper number (not "case") of **none** *has befuddled people for years, especially since, as you know, there is some disagreement on the matter.*

*Whether to use **none** as a singular or plural depends on how you use it in a sentence—that is, **none** may be singular or plural. **None** might mean "not one" or "no one," in which case it would likely be used as a singular word:*

- *There hasn't been a major new refinery in the United States since 1976, and experts say **none** is on the horizon.*

*Or it might mean **not any** or **no amount**, in which case it would likely be used as a plural word:*

- ***None** are of Ukrainian descent; all are of Jewish descent, which means they may have come from Ukraine.*

NONPLUSSED

Misused for **undisturbed** (or similar words). • Media workers are **nonplussed** with their working lives, with 40% describing their jobs as "ordinary" and 30% going as far as saying they were "dispiriting." USE **unexcited**. • Outside the parliament building, thousands of protesters chanted and waved signs reading "Bush is an Evil Guy," and "War Criminal." Bush appeared **nonplussed**, pausing in his remarks and gamely injecting after one interruption: "I love free speech." USE **unmoved**.

*   **Nonplussed** *(not **nonplused**) means bewildered or confused; to surprise so that one is unable to speak or act. It does not mean, as the **non-** may suggest to some, unruffled or calm.*

Although Clark appeared nonplussed by Gore's decision--"I don't pay attention to endorsements, unless they're for me," he said--political observers suggested that former vice president's move may have altered the dynamic of the Democratic race.

—Daniel J. Hemel, *The Harvard Crimson*

*If Clark had been, or had appeared, **nonplussed**, he would not have uttered an intelligible word. But since he was not **nonplussed**, it is Hemel himself who does not write intelligibly.*

N

NORMALCY

Solecistic for **normality**. • They really appreciate any semblance of **normalcy**, because they've been removed from it. USE **normality**. • The foes of the U.S.-led occupation want to slow down and stop the progress toward **normalcy** in Iraq. USE **normality**. • In exchange for America's admiration, the stars preach the importance of **normalcy**, gratitude and above all hard work. USE **normality**.

*Though both words are in common use, **normality** is considered preferable to **normalcy**.*

NORTH OF

Idiotic for **more than** (or similar words). • After **north of** 30,000 live performances, one tragic accident is an anomaly. USE **more than**. • These emerging applications, plus renewed growth in existing markets, will help propel the global GPS market **north of** $22 billion by 2008, according to technology market research firm ABI. USE **beyond**. • Such powerful branding is practically priceless, but, based on conversations with industry sources, we estimate that Google's brand alone is worth **north of** $2 billion. USE **upwards of**.

__North of__, an obtuse term for __more than__, __beyond__, and __upwards__, is popular among directionless writers and dizzy speakers.

The heavyweight has gone north--as in, north of 250 pounds. A kid who's 250 pounds and reasonably coordinated is better off being a football player.

—Burt Sugar, boxing writer, as quoted in the *Los Angeles Times*

Mr. Sugar, like some of the boxers he writes about, has apparently had his ear deformed, his brains addled.

NO SOONER...THEN (WHEN)

Solecistic for **no sooner...than**. • **No sooner** had the words left my mouth **then** the geometry of the circumstance sunk in. USE **No sooner...than**. • Because **no sooner** had we gotten General Motors, **then** I went to New York to talk to William Zeckendorf, who was their major moving force in a lot of their real estate endeavors. USE **no sooner... than**. • Corporate Apple had **no sooner** popped the champagne cork at the Expo **when** the king of the clone makers Power Computing of Round Rock, Texas, took the wraps off their latest new bomber, the Power Tower G3/275. USE **no sooner...than**.

> *It used to be that critics carped about the expression **no sooner...when**, but today the expression **no sooner...then** (as well as, oddly, **no sooner...that**) seems the more popular. The only correct expression is **no sooner...than**. SEE ALSO **hardly...than**.*

NOTARY REPUBLIC

Misspelling of **notary public**. • If you would like additional information on how to become a **Notary Republic** please contact the Secretary of State at (916) 653-3595 or visit their web site. USE **notary public**. • We do offer the services of a **Notary Republic** through our office. USE **notary public**.

> *The correct, and only, spelling is **notary public**. SEE ALSO **affidavit**.*

NOT HARDLY (BARELY; SCARCELY)

Solecistic for **hardly (scarcely)**. • There is **not hardly** a point on the river, below Franklin, that the sound of the steam whistle of the furnace engine cannot be heard. DELETE **not**. • So, do we now have all of the answers so we know what to expect Thursday at Kobe Bryant's scheduled preliminary hearing? **Not hardly**. DELETE **Not**. • Now, this is an idea with merit, though **not scarcely** original. DELETE **not** or **scarcely**.

However, these sentences, in which **not** and **scarcely** and **not** and **hardly** are juxtaposed, are perfectly good: • Lemke infiltrates your brain whether you it like or not, and whether you think it is "good" or **not scarcely** matters. • Debt collection has become a very insidious task which is time consuming and more often than **not hardly** cost-effective.

Hardly and *scarcely* are negative words. To use *not* with them means the opposite of what you intend. Not everyone who uses the phrase *not hardly* is illiterate; people use *not hardly* (though not *not scarcely*) to emphasize, humorously they feel, their distaste for or disagreement with what is being discussed. But the unwitting misusage is never amusing. SEE ALSO *hardly...than*.

NUCLEAR

The pronunciation of *nuclear* is (NOO-klee-er), not (NOO-kyah-ler).

OBFUSTICATE

Idiotic for **obfuscate**. • It isn't true encryption, but a fast and easy online tool to **obfusticate** the source code of your own web pages, to prevent thieves from jacking your html. USE **obfuscate**. • These terms **obfusticate** what is really happening, but it does not matter; they are both useful metaphors, and both valid but only to a point. USE **obfuscate**.

> *Some people would have you believe that **obfusticate** (a word doubtless born of mispronunciation) means to darken, becloud, make obscure, confuse, or make unintelligible. Other people know this is the definition of **obfuscate**, truly a word. Proclaiming the validity and usefulness of **obfusticate** is behavior worthy of a half-wit—or a laxicographer.*

OBLIGE

Misused for **obligate**. • Failure to meet these conditions would **oblige** the IAEA to take the matter to the United Nations Security Council, where sanctions could be imposed. USE **obligate**. • Bern fears the article could be extended to cover tax evasion, which would **oblige** Switzerland to lift banking secrecy if it received a request for legal assistance from an EU country. USE **obligate**. • We only heard about the allegations today and we are **obliged** to investigate. USE **obligated**.

> ***Obligate** means to bind or compel by duty or obligation. **Oblige** means to make grateful for a favor or kindness ("The center is much **obliged** to them for their support and advice"); to do a service or favor for ("Council members wanted county governments to play a bigger role in the new local transportation system, and the Senate **obliged**"). In decreeing no distinction exists between these two words, lexicographers and linguists would have us all wondering what sense is meant. To lose the distinctions between words is to strip us of complexity and nuance, of understanding and clarity. Ultimately, any word will do; all words mean all things.*

O

OCCURENCE

Misused for **occurrence**. • He also said it is a common **occurence** for politicians to test other options when the election season nears. USE **occurrence**. • The court has also appointed a lawyer to examine whether sexual harassment of women in state government offices was a common **occurence**. USE **occurrence**.

> **Occurrence** has two **c**'s, at the beginning of the word, and two **r**'s, not one. SEE ALSO **reoccur**.

OCULIST

Misused for **occultist**. • William Butler Yeats, a renowned Irish poet, used poetry as an outlet for his mystic and **oculist** beliefs. USE **occultist**.

> An **oculist** (OK-yah-list) is an optometrist or an ophthalmologist. An **occultist** (ah-KUL-tist) is someone who believes in, studies, or practices magic or the supernatural.

ODIFEROUS

Misused for **odoriferous**. • The reasons lay in the **odiferous** piles of moldering, rodent-infested clothing, furniture, books, expired coupons, bikes and bike parts. USE **odoriferous**. • In reality, he is like the Roman toilet entrepreneur who famously remarked of his **odiferous** enterprise that "money doesn't smell." USE **odoriferous**.

> **Odiferous**, called a variant spelling in some dictionaries, is actually a misspelling of and incorrect for **odoriferous**. Very likely, **odiferous** endures because people fail to pronounce all five syllables. SEE ALSO **odoriferous**.

Signs hanging from lampposts declare it "Hometown USA," railroad tracks cross Middleton Street at the center of town and odiferous livestock trucks rumble though regularly.

—**Estes Thompson,** *The Miami Herald*

Neither sweet nor foul smelling, **odiferous** has no odor—and no meaning.

ODORIFEROUS

Misused for **malodorous**. • Last fall, the city of Philadelphia put eleven tons of **odoriferous** garbage on a plane to Leibstadt, Switzerland. USE **malodorous**. • Skunks use a highly **odoriferous** secretion to deter predation: a yellow oil composed of thiols and thioacetate derivatives of these thiols. USE **malodorous**. • After ingestion, the **odoriferous** sulfur molecules circulate in the bloodstream and escape from your body through exhaled air and perspiration—as any nose will tell you. USE **malodorous**.

> **Odoriferous** means fragrant; having an agreeable smell. **Odorous** also usually refers to a pleasant smell (though the noun **odor** usually refers to an unpleasant one). **Malodorous** means foul-smelling; disagreeably smelly. SEE ALSO **odiferous**.

OFFICE

Idiotic for **lease office space** (or similar words). • Our staff has been identified as the main reason companies select Front Office over our competitors and is always the factor when they continue to **office** with us year-after-year. USE **buy office services**. • Should you not need to **office** with us on a full-time basis, we can also offer you a DaySuite. USE **lease space**.

> **Office** is a wholly loathsome verb. It may mean lease an office or hire secretarial staff. Is it that **to office** suggests an office and office services rather than the cost of them? Is it less objectionable than using the word **lease** or **hire**, **buy** or **rent**? No, it is not; it's an objectionable, even misleading, term.

They may want to keep their businesses small, and stay with us a long time, or they may office with us until they get so big that they move on.
—Abby Office Centers

*"Who **offices** with Abby?" their web page further reads. Anyone who has little respect for, or interest in, the English language, that's who. Their secretarial and business services must be truly **abbysmal**.*

OFFICIOUS

Misused for **official**. • Welcome to the **officious** web site of Hamilton, New Zealand, the soggy green heart of the Waikato. USE **official**. • The jeweller also gave Antonio a rather **officious** looking document that indicated the diamond was worth $5,800. USE **official**.

Officious *means meddlesome; offering unwanted or unnecessary advice or services.*
Official *means of or relating to an office or position of authority; authorized or authoritative; formally set or prescribed.*

OFF THE BEAT AND PATH

Solecistic for **off the beaten path**. • The town the resort is located in is **off the beat and path**, so there is almost no shopping or activities near by. USE **off the beaten path**. • Set **off the beat and path**, parking is never a problem, and our Main Street location offers plenty of convenient lunchtime eateries and shopping. USE **off the beaten path**.

The idiomatic phrase is ***off the beaten path****, meaning in a little known or isolated place; unusual or different.*

OFTEN

Even though my dictionary acknowledges both pronunciations of *often* and notwithstanding the fact that "of-ten" is more commonly heard, isn't it preferable to say "of-en"—similar to the silent *t* in, for example, *hasten*, *listen*, and *christen*? Is there any country or region in which it is proper to vocalize the *t* in *often*?

OFF-en *is the preferred pronunciation even though you may, as frequently, hear people pronouncing it* **OFF-ten**. **OFF-en**, *of course, requires less effort to articulate than does* **OFF-ten**. *In a society that seems to value easiness (and entertainment) over all, it may be surprising that the* **t** *burst in* **OFF-ten** *finds such favor.*

OFTENLY

Solecistic for **often**. • Parodies are criticisms and witticsms created by **oftenly** intelligent people, trying to change the world through exaggerating problems or faults of a certain subject. USE **often**. • The in-vitro cultivation is **oftenly** the only reasonable way to propagate big quantities of carnivorous plants in a relatively short time. USE **often**. • There are **oftenly** many concerts organized by FM Radio Rock n' Pop. USE **often**.

> *Though many adverbs do end in **-ly**, **often** never does. How unfamiliar with the English language some people are is made alarmingly clear when they affix **-ly** to words that do not require it and fail to use -ly with words that do. SEE ALSO -ly;* ***seldomly***.

OKAY

Misused at the beginning of sentences. • OK, I'm finally getting around to organizing this a bit. DELETE **OK**. • Okay, let's talk holiday parties. DELETE **Okay**. • Okay, now no one is more respectful than I am of newspaper editors; theirs is a hard and often thankless task, involving hundreds of small decisions every day. DELETE **Okay**.

> ***Okay** as an interjection announcing the end of one topic and the beginning of another is unacceptable written, and prosaic spoken, English. SEE ALSO **hey**.*

Okay, I go to see this *Last Samurai* movie with Tom Cruise over the weekend.
—Bill O'Reilly, Fox News

*Not only, in this trebly embarrassing sentence, does O'Reilly begin his sentence with **okay**, he uses the present tense to describe a past event, and he leaves us wondering if he attended the movie with Cruise.*

ON BEHALF OF

Misused for **in behalf of.** • To correct this imbalance, Operation Sunbeam manipulates karma **on behalf of** all mankind by sending spiritual energy directly to the Mother Earth. USE **in behalf of.** • Representatives of the North Metro Crossing Coalition, the League of Minnesota Cities, the North Metro Mayor's Association, and the Association of Metropolitan Municipalities explained to council members what they do **on behalf of** the city. USE **in behalf of.** • It takes an extraordinary person to speak **on behalf of** people who were once active members of our community and now need your help. USE **in behalf of.**

On behalf of means as the agent of; representing. In behalf of means in the interest of; for the benefit of. Because most dictionaries ignore the distinction between these two phrases (as they do so many others), people are increasingly ignorant of the distinction; and because people are ignorant of the distinction, ignominy is all. Dictionaries decline thus: ignore, ignorant, ignominy.

ONE'S

One should mind *ones* (or *one's* or *ones'*) own business? In other words, is the possessive *ones* or *one's* or *ones'*?

The possessive of the indefinite pronoun **one** *is* **one's**: *"One should mind* **one's** *own business." Better still is "A person should mind* **his** *own business" or "People should mind* **their** *own business" (or* **"She** *should mind* **her** *own business" or* **"They** *should mind* **their** *own business" or* **"You** *should mind* **your** *own business"). The impersonal* **one** *is rarely preferable to a personal pronoun or the word* **person***.*

ONE IN (FIVE) HAVE

Solecistic for **one in (five) has.** • **One in three** adults **have** arthritis. USE **has.** • **One in three** white teen girls **use** tanning booths. USE **uses.** • **One in six** adults **have** neurotic disorder. USE **has.** • **One in five** young Britons **suffer** mental health problems. USE **suffers.** • Nearly **one in three** companies (30 percent) **are** operating without a formal IT disaster recovery strategy in place. USE **is.** • **One in ten** long-haul travellers **risk** deep vein thrombosis. USE **risks.** • **One in five** Chinese entrepreneurs **are women.** USE **is a woman.** • **One in four** immigration "Diversity Lottery" winners **were from countries** considered security risks. USE **was from a country considered a security risk.**

*The expression **one in (five)** takes a singular, not a plural, verb.*

ONE OF THE...(HAS)

Solecistic for **one of the...(have).** • Everyone knows that this was **one of the worst things that has** happened to America since Pearl Harbor. USE **have.** • Carol is **one of the few people who gives** as good as she gets from Melvin. USE **give.** • She was **one of the women who was** charging ahead with the women's movement. USE **were.** • Door-to-door service is **one of the benefits that sets** the Special Transportation Program apart from others. USE **set.** • But it's **one of those words that has** radically altered its meaning down the centuries. USE **have.** • **One of the actors who is** involved in the process will be speaking with us tonight. USE **are.** • **One of the people that falls** under the Scrooge's whip is Bob Cratchit. USE **fall.** • Anticipating God in your future is **one of the qualities that separates** humans from the animals. USE **separate.**

*Do not use a singular verb after a phrase like **one of the...that (which; who).***

ONE OF THE ONLY

Solecistic for **one of the few.** • It is **one of the only** tools available to us where you can express a deeply personal, deeply moral opinion and be held accountable. USE **one of the few.** • Americana is **one of the only** radio formats that actually embraces the legends of country music. USE **one of the few.** • One of the men who got shot the night of the riot was Officer Isaiah McKinnon, **one of the only** black officers on the Detroit Police force. USE **one of the few.**

Only does not mean two or more; it means one, sole, alone. **One of the only** then is altogether nonsensical—and further evidence that people scarcely know what their words mean. SEE ALSO **(very) unique**.

The following is taken from the "NPR Writer's Almanac":

"He was also one of the only generals who loved talking to the press."

Aren't *one* and *only* in contradiction?

Certainly **one of the few** is a better expression. Illogical though **one of the only** is, it's widely used (Google counts more than 650,000 instances of this expression), which in itself is no endorsement.

Of the six dictionaries I evaluated in the Fiske Ranking of College Dictionaries (see Appendix A), Merriam-Webster's Collegiate Dictionary, alone, allows **only** to mean **few**. In fact, Merriam-Webster's clownlike editors use the expression **one of the only** as their justification for and example of **only** in the sense of **few**.

ON TENDERHOOKS

Solecistic for **on tenterhooks**. • Everyone is **on tenderhooks** awaiting a Court of Appeal decision that may or may not resolve the matter. USE **on tenterhooks**. • At present our relations with the national bourgeoisie are very strained; they are **on tenderhooks** and are very disgruntled. USE **on tenterhooks**.

A **tenter** is a frame on which cloth is stretched for drying. **On tenterhooks**, not **on tenderhooks**, means to be uncertain, anxious, or in suspense about something.

OPINIONATION

Idiotic for **opinion**. • We started that trip as the usual collection of walking American egos and **opinionations**, and came back uniformly anti-Soviet, the liberals most of all. USE **opinions**. • The Usenet Bowie discussion group gets this question every week, so it was about time to mount some wild-eyed **opinionations** on the web, covering as much of Bowie's catalog as possible. USE **opinions**.

*Perhaps people who use the regal-sounding, polysyllabic **opinionation** believe it gives more weight to their views than does the plainer **opinion**. If laxicographers ever add **opinionation** to their dictionaries, there will be no reason to consult them further.*

They did not talk much. The nervous loquacity and opinionation of the Zenith Athletic Club dropped from them. But when they did talk they slipped into the naive intimacy of college days.
—**Sinclair Lewis, *Babbit*, 1922**

OPPORTUNISTIC

Idiotic for **opportune**. • However mid-way through the half, an **opportunistic** Edinburgh score seemed to buoy the students. USE **opportune**. • After Medco made its offer in December, Dr. Williams said it was **opportunistic** coming so close to Christmas. USE **opportune**. • It's a very **opportunistic** time for these brands. USE **opportune**.

Opportunistic also is misused to mean seeking or welcoming opportunity: • Now, the Eagles must face an **opportunistic** Carolina team riding an emotional wave after dramatically snapping the Rams' fourteen-game home winning streak. • Be efficient throwing the football, **opportunistic** on defense, sound on special teams, and you can win without a running attack for the ages.

***Opportunistic** means taking advantage, without regard to ethics or consequences, of a circumstance to further one's interests. **Opportune** means right for a particular purpose; occurring at an advantageous time.*

Strong goaltending from Pasi Nurminen, who has won both those games, and opportunistic scoring from Slava Kozlov, Patrik Stefan and JP Vigier were the recipe.
—**John Manasso,** *Atlanta Journal-Constitution*

When did opportunism become a bad word?
—**Darva Conger, on the television program** *48 Hours*

These astonishing sentences reveal how little we know the meaning of the words we use and, even more disturbing, how little meaning matters.

O

ORDNANCE

Misused for **ordinance.** • Matewan is located at the end of Trail #10, where by means of a town **ordnance,** an ATV rider may turn left on Mate Street and enter the Town of Matewan and proceed to a designated free parking lot. USE **ordinance.** • City **ordnance** was written in a manner to prevent the duty weapon from being seen. USE **ordinance.**

Ordinance is also misused for **ordnance:** • The purpose of the survey was to locate and document any military **ordinance** or other debris that may be deposited on the lake bottom. USE **ordnance.** • On the military side, among other uses GPR can be expected to help ferret out underground command and control bunkers, landmines and unexploded **ordinance.** USE **ordnance.**

__Ordnance__ is cannon and artillery; military weapons, including ammunition, combat vehicles, and other equipment. __Ordinance__ is a governmental statute or regulation; an authoritative direction or command.

ORIENTATE

Solecistic for **orient.** • In creating a piece of documentation, we often find it necessary to **orientate** a user by using visuals. USE **orient.** • The meaning of practical training is to **orientate** students for future tasks and offer facilities for working life in general. USE **orient**. • The man was having trouble walking and appeared extremely intoxicated, confused and **disorientated**. USE **disoriented**. • There are a lot of depressed, elderly, mentally **disorientated**, and handicapped folks who can be affected by this vote. USE **disoriented**.

> *By careful writers,* **orientate** *is eschewed. The longer word strikes many as being more unwieldy and cacophonic than the less syllabic* **orient**.

OSCULATE

Misused for **oscillate**. • Songs like "Stay Together" are reminiscent of Funkadelic songs with their **osculating** beat. USE **oscillating**. • If so, you could try directing **osculating** fans towards the leaf zone. USE **oscillating**. • Sometimes a pump thrust with excessive axial clearance will allow the pump and motor shaft to move back and forth, endwise. This **osculating** motion will draw the oil out of an otherwise well sealed motor bearing and deposit it on the windings. USE **oscillating**.

> **Oscillate** *means to swing back and forth with a regular rhythm; to be indecisive; to vacillate.* **Osculate** *means to kiss. Only rarely is* **oscillate** *used where* **osculate** *could be:*
> *How do you titillate an ocelot?*
> *You* **oscillate** *its tit a lot.*

OSTENTATIOUS

Misused for **ostensible**. • Bangladesh was conspicuous by its absence and Dhaka has already expressed itself in favour of a new round of trade talks, though the **ostentatious** reason for its absence is cited to be the general election in the country. USE **ostensible**. • The **ostentatious** reasons for branding women witches are infertility, menopause, matrimonial problems, property disputes, and other related socio-economic problems. USE **ostensible**.

> **Ostentatious** *means showy or pretentious.* **Ostensible** *means apparent; professed; seeming.*

OTHERWISE

Misused for **other**. • Spam—fraudulent and **otherwise**—continues to skyrocket, clogging overtaxed networks. USE **other**. • Future events and actual results, financial and **otherwise**, may differ from the results discussed in the forward-looking statements. USE **other**.

*This usage is all but lost. The word **other**, as a noun or adjective, is certainly correct; less so the word **otherwise**—even though few people today do not use **otherwise** in these constructions where **other** seems the better choice. Only the punctilious use **other** instead of **otherwise**, and only they say what they actually mean.*

OUGHT NOT

Solecistic for **ought not to**. • I think Democrats **ought not** be afraid of their roots. USE **ought not to**. • We **ought not** be executing people who, legally, were children. USE **ought not to**. • **Oughtn't we rather** be tearing our clothes in deep shame for our own great sins? USE **Oughtn't we rather to**.

*Ought not, as anyone knows who reads well, requires **to**: ought not to.*

Similarly, though a less frequent mistake, **ought** alone requires **to**: • The motors and engines Americans rely on for transportation **ought** run only when there is good reason for them to be running. USE **ought to**. • A doctor was speaking common sense, but also telling his younger colleagues that they **ought** go on the record morally with patients. USE **ought to**. SEE ALSO **didn't** (**hadn't**, **shouldn't**) **ought**.

And there are some people who ought not run.

—Soledad O'Brien, CNN anchor

*Would anchor O'Brien also intone, "And there are some people who **ought run**"?*

Is the preposition *to* required with the use of *oughtn't*? For example, "We oughtn't to think poorly of all lexicographers" vs "We oughtn't think poorly of all lexicographers"? My British editor inserts the preposition; my American editor deletes it. Is it a U.K. vs. U.S. thing? Is one of them dead wrong?

Ought not, like **ought** alone, requires **to**. If your American editor recommends your not using **to**, recommend he find a new line of work.

OUT LOUD

Did I read *out loud* to my children or *aloud*?

This is largely a question of personal preference. **Read out loud** is slightly less sonorous than **read aloud**, but beyond that one expression is as good as the other.

In years past, it's true, use of **read out loud** was discouraged by grammarians who maintained the phase was colloquial, but today, it does not seem to suffer from that stigma.

OUTMOST

Misused for **utmost**. • The primary focus of the audit profession should be to faithfully use and enforce these auditing standards and accounting principles with the **outmost** diligence and integrity. USE **utmost**. • All information that you provide will be treated with **outmost** confidentiality. USE **utmost**. • Since all books were highly prized during this period, protecting them was of **outmost** importance. USE **utmost**.

> Although **utmost** may mean **outmost**, **outmost** does not now mean (though, some centuries ago, it may have meant) **utmost**. **Outmost** means outermost, farthest out; **utmost**, which in some contexts shares this meaning, more often means of the greatest degree, amount, or intensity.

O

PALATABLE

Solecistic for **palpable**. • If only we could capture that **palatable** feeling in a bottle so that it can touch us on a more regular basis, it would do so much good. USE **palpable**. • About six months later I remember thinking that we were headed for a full-fledged recession, there was an almost **palatable** uneasiness in the air. USE **palpable**. • The tension was **palatable** between the girls as break-up rumours started swirling in the British press. USE **palpable**.

And **palpable** is misused for **palatable**: • The curly fries were the only **palpable** food that we ordered. USE **palatable**.

Palatable means agreeable to the palate or taste; acceptable to the mind or senses. *Palpable* means tangible or capable of being touched; easily perceived, noticeable.

This is just the sort of idiocy that laxicographers delight in. Within a few years, dictionaries will show **palpable** as a synonym for **palatable**, and **palatable** as a synonym for **palpable**.

I believe that there is only one palpable solution to how attendants of a church, whether long-standing members or first-time visitors, can freely attend a service that God has so decreed.

—Shandon L. Guthrie, professor of philosophy at the University of Nevada

Yes, Gutherie is *palpably* a foolosopher. The language does change over time, but language that changes largely or exclusively owing to people's ignorance or illiteracy should not necessarily be admired or embraced. Let the language change for good reason, not for unreason.

PALETTE

Misused for **palate**. • A delightful wine, it excites the **palette** without being too sweet. USE **palate**. • Until he sought medical help, Boyle had no idea that as he'd aged he had developed an enlarged **palette**, the hard and soft tissue making up the roof and sides of his mouth. USE **palate**. • Begin to focus on inhaling deeply through your nose, abdomen rising, and exhaling forcefully through your mouth, tongue resting gently at the top of your **palette**. USE **palate**.

P

Palette—*a board used by artists for mixing colors; a range of colors used by an artist or in a painting; a range of qualities in other art forms such as music*—*does not mean* **palate**—*the roof of the mouth in some vertebrates; the sense of taste.*

The cardamom carrot syrup was an exotic complement to the dish, and the mildly bitter water crest salad revived and refreshed the palate.
—Michael J. Reiss, FoodandWineAccess.com

Michael J. Reiss's credentials as a food and restaurant critic might easily be questioned given that he does not know a **palate** *from a* **palette**. *And like the* **watercress**, *his remarks leave a bitter aftertaste.*

PARAMETER

Misused for **perimeter**. • Firefighters have been having some success drawing a **parameter** around the flames. USE **perimeter**. • Our parliamentary committee refused to authorize 400 million of public resources for Janet's UWESO office renovations and **parameter** wall. USE **perimeter**. • The fence now built along the western **parameter** of the city was begun a year ago. USE **perimeter**.

Parameter is also carelessly used to mean any number of other words: • Perhaps the most exciting **parameter** of success has been the extraordinarily high number of acquisitions that have taken place within the past year. USE **measure**. • The newspaper said Rashid-Merem acknowledged a supplier could lose its GM contract, saying: "Yes, that's the case, but everyone will work **in that parameter**." USE **under these terms**.

*A **perimeter** (pah-RIM-i-ter) is the outer boundary of a figure or area; the length of this boundary; the border of a military encampment or defended area; a limit or guideline. **Parameter** (pah-RAM-i-ter), a mathematical and statistical term, is a constant in an equation whose value varies in other equations; a quantity calculated from data that describes a population.*

PARTIALLY

Misused for **partly**. • Andy Mullins, executive assistant to the chancellor, said he remembers one game where someone was parked **partially** on the grass and **partially** in a handicap spot next to the Lyceum. USE **partly**. • Terry A. King, 43, of 20206 Township 306, was driving his 2000 Jeep Wrangler on an unnamed haul road when he hit a **partially** opened gate. USE **partly**.

And **partly** is misused for **partially**: • The major sources of trans-fatty acids in the diet are from **partly** hydrogenated vegetable fat. USE **partially**. • Most academic information appears in print, so blind and **partly** sighted students rely on a support network for access. USE **partially**.

Sometimes it is difficult to decide which would be the better word: • He was found by staff **partially** (or **partly**) clothed and attempting to sexually assault a male resident. • **Partly** (or **partially**) cloudy skies are expected, with a 30 percent chance of showers and thunderstorms. If both words work equally well, use **partly**.

*Much like the distinction between **number** and **amount**, **partly** is best used when a whole can be considered to have distinct parts, and **partially** is best used in the sense of to a degree.*

PASSIBLE

Misused for **passable**. • They arrived at the Allegheny near Sharpsburg to find the river only partially frozen over and not **passible** on foot. USE **passable**. • Road "A," however, has fewer obstacles and is **passible**; road "B" has no obstacles and is **passible**. USE **passable**. • In junior high school my depression and anxiety was so great that my grades dropped from high marks to low but **passible** grades. USE **passable**.

Passable means able to be passed or traveled on or over; adequate or satisfactory. *Passible*, a theological term, means able to feel or suffer. SEE ALSO **impassible**.

PAST

Misused for **passed**. • Time **past** slowly as he sat waiting for her to acknowledge that the discussion as far as he was concerned was over. USE **passed**. • He indicated that nearly eight to ten months **past** before the municipality objected to the hydronic system and the lack of insulation. USE **passed**. • Roman found Belle **past out** on the floor of the penthouse and gave her a shot to counteract the penicillin, for Belle was just as allergic as her mother. USE **passed out**.

> *Passed* is the past tense and past participle of the verb *pass*. *Past*, a noun, adjective, adverb, or preposition, is never a verb. If this confusion continues, lexicographers and linguists all will sanction it; usage, they maintain, not some notion of correctness or clarity, dictates meaning.

PATIENCE

Misused for **patients**. • Carleton Place hospital selects Zycom to implement new mission critical server environment to run hospital **patience** records system. USE **patients**. • After you have become an established pediatrician, the number of **patience** that come to you depend on your reputation. USE **patients**.

> *Patience* is calm self-control despite suffering, delay, boredom, and the like. *Patients* are people under a doctor's or other professional's care.

PAWN OFF

Solecistic for **palm off**. • People who bag animals in the wild undoubtedly get healthier meat than the plastic-wrapped flesh supermarkets **pawn off** on the paying public. USE **palm off**. • The leather store tried to **pawn off** a piece of cowhide that was too thick, saying it was the same thing as kangaroo. USE **palm off**.

> To **palm off** is to pass off something inferior by fraud or deceit; to misrepresent. To **pawn off** is incorrect.

PEACEFUL

Misused for **peaceable**. • Unless irritated or attracted by blood, sharks are **peaceful** animals. USE **peaceable**. • I am concerned about increasing frustration among Iraqis and I am telling everyone that they are a **peaceful** people. USE **peaceable**.

And **peaceable** is misused for **peaceful**: Tens of thousands of protesters jammed central London on Thursday in a **peaceable** demonstration against President Bush. USE **peaceful**.

> **Peaceful** means tranquil; undisturbed by strife or turbulence. **Peaceable** means inclined to peace.

PEDALOGICAL (PEDILOGICAL)

Idiotic for **pedagogical**. • The beauty of a Jewish school is that it wraps up all the values both **pedalogical** and religious which parents want for their children into one neat convenient package. USE **pedagogical**. • What is there can radically change the **pedalogical** approaches used by teachers to reach their learners. USE **pedagogical**. • I was not looking for psychological, **pedilogical** nor philosophical discussions. USE **pedagogical**. • They do this by setting up institutes for professional training that teach both at the **pedilogical** level and at the content level for teachers. USE **pedagogical**.

> Dictionaries have yet to list **pedalogical** (or **pedilogical**) as a "variant spelling" of **pedagogical**, but sham scientists (lexicographers, descriptive linguists, and others equally misguided) will likely soon begin excusing, justifying, and promoting these sham spellings.

PEDDLE

Misused for **pedal**. • This then poses the question—should we let our foot off the campaign **peddle**? USE **pedal**. • It seems like when this team smells a little blood, we get going and put the **peddle** to the floor. USE **pedal**.

And **pedal** is misused for **peddle**: • However, with this knowledge in hand, it's up to those **pedaling** goods and services to get through to the right person. USE **peddling**.

To **pedal** *is to move or operate by the use of a pedal or pedals. As a noun, a* **pedal** *is a lever used to power a bicycle, car, drum, piano, or other mechanism. To* **peddle** *is to sell items from place to place; to hawk goods; to promote a view.*

PEEK

Misused for **peak**. • The clouds break apart and a mountain **peek** stares through. USE **peak**. • Recorded on July 13th, 1991, this awesome display of pure rock emotion captures the band at the **peek** of their fame. USE **peak**.

And **peak** is misused for **peek**: Take a few moments and sneak a **peak** at just some of CaterXpert's powerful features. USE **peek**. • I still could not control myself from stealing one last **peak** up her skirt. USE **peek**.

> A **peek** *is a furtive glance. A* **peak** *is a summit of a mountain; the highest point of something; a pointed end.*

PEEK

Misused for **pique**. • Paint Branch is presenting a few distinct courses that hopes to **peek** interest in the student body. USE **pique**. • I'm looking for someone who can stimulate my inner most thoughts and **peek** my curiosity. USE **pique**.

> To **peek** *is to glance at quickly and often secretively. To* **pique** *is to arouse; to cause to feel resentment.*

PENULTIMATE

Solecistic for **last** (or similar words) or **best** (or similar words). • The **penultimate** (last) chapter is about the growing crisis of baroque armaments. USE **last**. • The New Economy's successful leaders understand this permanence, too. Consider the **penultimate** computer lord, Bill Gates. USE **ultimate**. • Helena Bonham Carter has for most of her career been the **penultimate** corset girl. USE **quintessential**.

> **Penultimate** *means next to last, not as some people assume, last, ultimate, best, definitive, or quintessential.*

The penultimate in performance and appearance, our Centaurus line of systems have no equal.
—**Directron.com**

The people at Directron.com might be mortified to learn they're boasting that their systems are second rate, next to last in performance and appearance.

PER; AS PER

Idiotic for **as** (or similar words). • Write a rough draft for essay one **per** instructions in "Analyzing a magazine advertisement" and "Preparing a draft for peer conferences" in the Class Notes. USE **according to.** • **As per your request**, this cover letter keys the Registrant's responses to the comments expressed in the above referenced letter of comments and also provides any supplemental information requested by your staff. USE **As you requested.** • **As per usual**, all the wallrats were out in force chalking up and taping various bodily parts. USE **As usual.** • **Per our discussion** in class on Thursday, below you will find two essays on racial profiling—the practice of using race as probable cause in policy work. USE **As we discussed.**

> *(**As) per** is commercialese—which is to say, an expression at once hideous and comical—and means nothing more than **as** or **according to**.*

PERMANENTIZED

Idiotic for **make permanent** (or similar words). • Once the cognitive elements are manipulated in the desired direction, the programmed conditioning and behavior becomes **permanentized**. USE **permanent.** • Instead, I find myself repeatedly disappointed to meet women who insist they want the traditional vagaries, supposedly **permanentized** with a superstitious ceremony. USE **made permanent.** • That is why the half million people would come here; to rub some of the (muddy) fame off on themselves, participating as first-hand witnesses, **permanentized** in a moment of history. USE **immortalized.**

*We know a concoction like **permanentize** is objectionable when it's scarcely pronounceable. **Make permanent** or, perhaps, **immortalize** does nicely; the ungainly, needless **permanentize** does not.*

PERMISCUOUS

Misused for **promiscuous**. • We certainly haven't been as **permiscuous** in licensing our content as some other news and news wire providers, but it's actually a pretty decent revenue stream for us. USE **promiscuous**. • A fourteen-year-old school girl who had **permiscuous** sex is not a woman. USE **promiscuous**. • What was offensive in this movie was the continuous use of alcohol and **permiscuous** sex (some of which would be considered violent sex). USE **promiscuous**.

*The people who misspell and mispronounce **promiscuous** seldom have liberal views and values. Descriptive linguists, who generally are liberal thinking, would probably be mortified to mispronounce or misspell this word, but they allow, even encourage, others to do so. Only the small-minded embrace illiberal thoughts and actions, and only the dull-minded embrace ignorance and nonsense.*

And he sang, very slowly and dolefully, this
side-splitting ballad:

"We met at the corner, Marire and me.
Quite permiscuous! Who'd ha' thought of it?
She took and invited me 'ome to tea;
Quite permiscuous! Who'd ha' thought of it?
I sat in the parler along with her,
Tucking into the eggs and the bread and but-ter,—
When in come her Par with the kitching po-ker!
Quite permiscuous! Who'd ha' thought of it?"

—Various, *Punch Among the Planets*, 1890

PERQUISITE

Misused for **prerequisite.** • He said peace is a **perquisite** for development, adding that, until countries ensure equitable distribution of wealth they would continue to suffer from wars and host refugees. USE **prerequisite.** • Trust is a necessary **perquisite** for cooperative moral action. USE **prerequisite.** • Course 1 is a **perquisite** to course 2; course 2 is a **perquisite** to course 3. USE **prerequisite.**

> *Perquisite* (commonly called a **perk** by the ever-monosyllabic, ever-hasty everyman) is something additional to regular pay; a privilege or benefit; a tip or gratuity. *Prerequisite* is something required beforehand; a requirement.

PERSECUTE

Misused for **prosecute.** • When you remember that the Court's mandate is to **persecute** crimes against humanity and genocide, it becomes much clearer why some countries have declared their acceptance of this international body while others have sought to reject it. USE **prosecute.** • Forgery, other fraudulent acts and any other dishonest use of any part or whole of this web site are strictly prohibited and can be **persecuted** in a court of law. USE **prosecuted.**

And **prosecute** is sometimes misused for **persecute:** • Why did Hitler **prosecute** the Jews? USE **persecute.**

> To *persecute* is to harass or oppress continually; to annoy constantly. To *prosecute* is to institute legal or criminal proceedings against; to carry on or follow to the end.

PERSONNEL

Misused for **personal.** • A complete exercise and fitness program will be designed and implemented by a certified **personnel** trainer. USE **personal.** • I know, however, from **personnel** experience, that it may not be the battle of choice in the war of issues our kids are facing. USE **personal.** • In his **personnel** life, Keith enjoys boating, water skiing, working on his home, and playing with his children. USE **personal.**

And **personal** is misused for **personnel:** • This site is aimed at human resources **personal** at major companies. USE **personnel.**

Personnel *is a noun meaning the people employed by or associated with an orga-nization or other group; people.* **Personal** *is an adjective meaning of or relating to a particular person; concerning a person's private relationships or concerns.*

PERSPECTIVE

Misused for **prospective**. • Personality profiles of **perspective** jurors and other courtroom players are prepared as part of the pre-trial and jury selection process. USE **prospective**. • Advertisements in newspapers or national publications may generate leads to **perspective** investors. USE **prospective**.

> **Perspective**, *a noun, is the viewing or drawing of objects or a scene in a particular way; a point of view; a judgment of something; a vista.* **Prospective**, *an adjective, means likely to happen or be; expected; relating to or effective in the future. SEE ALSO **perspectivize**.*

The best thing we can do is to send our counselors out and visit perspective students.

Students at Simpson have mixed feelings about com-mercials and how they impact perspective students.

Every step must be positive for perspective students to want to become a part of the Simpson community.

—Shelly Zeller, *The Simpsonian*

*If Simpson College (an inauspicious though apparently apt name) finds its **prospective** students dwindling, we need not wonder why.*

PERSPECTIVIZE

Idiotic for **put into perspective** (or similar words). • The course intends to **perspec-tivize** some of the issues that have been at the center of the debates in pragmatics over the past few decades. USE **put into perspective**. • This atheist is simply saying that real faith would **perspectivize** one's life in terms of eternity; even grief, he says, "would occupy hardly a moment of my thoughts." USE **clarify**.

*Even more benumbing than **finalize**, **prioritize**, and **incentivize**, **perspectivize** finds favor with academicians and others who think their intelligence is most accurately measured by how unintelligible their writing is. SEE ALSO **perspective**.*

PERUSE

Solecistic for **skim** (or similar words). • My intention was to **peruse** the book quickly and then gossip with the good folks behind the bar. USE **skim**. • The Standard CV allows employers to **peruse** quickly and easily without having to turn a page for further information. USE **scan**. • A quick **peruse** through the flashy liner notes gives a hint of what's in store for the poor listener. USE **look**.

*Some people incorrectly maintain that **peruse** has two opposite meanings: to read thoroughly and to read hurriedly. **Peruse**, however, means only to read with great care. It does not mean to glance over or to read quickly. Nor is it—no matter how grand someone wishes to appear—a synonym for the word **read**.*

The difference allows Williams to peruse works of art he doesn't own by visiting various museums around the country.
—**Eric R. Danton, *The Hartford Courant***

A locker away, Hawkins would talk about the great Satchel Paige and peruse his collection of throwback jerseys.
—**Jim Souhan, *Minneapolis Star Tribune***

Though thousands head down U.S. Route 20 to Rockford this time of year to peruse Cherryvale Mall and the many chain stores lining East State Street, area residents don't have to travel at all to find unique and personal gifts.
—**Gary Mays, *The Journal-Standard***

*Danton, talking of artwork, Souhan, talking of jerseys, and Mays, talking of a mall, all foolishly, stupidly, idiotically misuse the word **peruse**. **Peruse** does not mean to look at or to examine something; it means to read painstakingly, to read carefully, to read thoroughly.*

PET

"He pet the dog" or "He petted the dog"? The dogs don't mind which way we say it, but my husband and I disagree on which is appropriate. I say, "He bet $5 on the line" makes *me* right. My other half says "He jetted half-way around the world" makes *him* correct.

*Though many irregular verbs exist for us to struggle over conjugating, **pet** is not one of them. Further, neither **bet** (which also permits the past tense **betted**) nor **jetted** matters one bit to the past tense of **pet**.*

*Your husband is correct this time: **petted** is the past tense of **pet**. Even Google, not necessarily an arbiter of good usage, agrees: 160 results show "He **pet** the dog," whereas 516 results show "He **petted** the dog." All the same, before long, I bet dictionaries (which simply—and, if you ask me, absurdly—compile how people use the language) will show **pet** as an alternative past tense.*

PHASE

Misused for **faze**. • Valencia, who were league-leaders coming into this game, were not **phased** by the early setback and pushed hard for the equalizer. USE **fazed**. • Although Bracco had issues with the $26 million police station design that initially came to City Council, he is not **phased** by 80 percent of every tax dollar being spent on public safety. USE **fazed**.

*Faze, a verb, means to embarrass or disconcert. **Phase**, as a noun, means a stage or period of something; an aspect or part. As a verb, **phase** means to do in stages; to synchronize.*

PHENOMENON

Misused for **phenomena**. • You write about three **phenomenon** that helped shape women's role in this country. USE **phenomena**.

Occasionally, **phenomena** is used instead of **phenomenon**: • Legs Diamond, Marcus Gorman, and Billy Phelan also figure in *Roscoe*, a work that magnifies **this phenomena** yet further. USE **this phenomenon** (or **these phenomena**).

*The plural of **phenomenon** is **phenomena** or, less often, **phenomenons**. SEE ALSO **criterion**.*

PICARESQUE

Misused for **picturesque**. • Maybe it's the **picaresque** view, but the bridge is a popular end-of-the-line stop for the suicidal. USE **picturesque**. • In Michigan, the surprisingly **picaresque** town of Kalamazoo has a brewery making no fewer than half a dozen porter or stout variations. USE **picturesque**.

Picaresque *describes a sort of literature involving the adventures of a picaro, or rogue; relating to a rogue or scoundrel.* ***Picturesque*** *describes something attractive enough to be a picture; vivid.*

PLAINTIVE

Misused for **plaintiff**. • The judge's decision was against the **plaintive**, Seiko, who was suing Nu-kote which had been marketing replacement cartridges at half the regular price. USE **plaintiff**. • Rep. Bob Barr (R-Ga.), another **plaintive** in a lawsuit seeking to overturn the law, said he was not surprised. USE **plaintiff**.

Plaintive *(PLANE-tiv), an adjective, means expressing sorrow or melancholy; mournful.* ***Plaintiff*** *(PLANE-tif), a noun, is a person who brings a suit in a court of law.*

PLASTICATE

Misused for **plasticize**. • If auto manufacturers would build rather than **plasticate** everything, we would be safer. USE **plasticize**. • He is wearing a plastic cover over his Kangol cap, much as people **plasticate** their three-piece suits or their car seats to keep them good as new. USE **plasticize**.

*In the plastics industry, the verb **plasticate** means to make a plastic material malleable by heating or kneading: ("Use the entire cooling time to **plasticate** the next shot"; "A low-compression screw should be used with polycarbonate in general, but even more so with the metal fleck because it tends to **plasticate** more evenly").*

* **Plasticate** in the sense of to make, become, or cover with plastic is incorrect; that is the definition of **plasticize**. And even though plastic, factually and figuratively, overwhelms us, one word, **plasticize**, is quite enough to describe this unpleasantness.*

P

PLAYWRITE

Misspelling of **playwright**. • Besides being a novelist and a **playwrite**, Camus was an active journalist, writing hundreds of articles and editorials for newspapers. USE **playwright**. • I have worked as an actor, model, **playwrite**, director and producer. USE **playwright**.

*The **wright** of **playwright** means one who builds or makes something, not one who writes. SEE ALSO **writing**.*

PLUS

Solecistic for **and** (or similar words). • **Plus**, there are a ton of nighttime concerts that are happening around the city. USE **And**. • Those donating their hair will get a free styling, free round of golf, a rock sculpture, **plus** before and after photos. USE **as well as**. • **Plus**, I was curious to see how a guy would be struck by this explicitly women-focused network. USE **What's more**. • **Plus** we're deepening Cooking 101 with more guides and glossaries. USE **Moreover**. • **Plus**, why are senators and congressmen from other states suddenly authorities on the laws of California? USE **Besides**.

*Whether used as a conjunction (**and**) or an adverb (**besides**), **plus** is casual and hardly suitable for most published writing. Of course, most published writing is hardly suitable for publication.*

POISE

Misused for **pose**. • Then, realizing each of these pamphlets was inaccessible, I **poised** a question still not adequately answered. USE **posed**. • To many of us the mosquito is only a small insect which **poises** a danger to human beings because of its malaria virus. USE **poses**.

> **Pose**, as a noun, is a bodily position, especially one held for an artist or photographer; a way of speaking or behaving. As a verb, **pose** means to adopt a posture; to pretend to be someone else; to be pretentious; to ask a question; to present, especially a problem, danger, or threat. **Poise** is ease and grace of manner; composure; self-assurance; a state of balance or equilibrium. As a verb, **poise** means to be balanced or perched.
>
> It could very well be that if you lack grace and dignity, if you lack **poise** (POIZ), you spell it **p-o-s-e** and pronounce it (POZ).

POPULACE

Misused for **populous**. • They may not have the background and the time to do the necessary research, even if it involves the "biggest" running story of the second most **populace** country in Latin America. USE **populous**. • The strip is the most **populace** area in the world and it would have put up a fierce resistance, which would have caused a real massacre in case of an Israeli occupation. USE **populous**.

> **Populace** means a population; the masses. **Populous** means crowded or thickly populated.

POUR

Misused for **pore**. • We **pour** over hundreds of books and book reviews to pick twelve of the most interesting titles we can find. USE **pore**. • And they evoke the most wonderful memories, of afternoons spent **pouring** over coloring books and pictures. USE **poring**. • Beads of sweat begin to flood from every **pour** in my body and I feel as if my temperature skyrockets to around 110 degrees! USE **pore**.

And **pore** is sometimes used for **pour**. • A true friend is a person to whom you can **pore** out your heart. USE **pour**.

Pour means to dispense from a container; to give full expression to. *Pore* means to read or study carefully; or, as a noun, a minute opening in tissue.

PRACTICABLE

Misused for **practical**. • It is full of old-fashioned **practicable** advice and is equipped with easy-to-use indexes to help find answers to questions. USE **practical**. • It has proved to be the most wholesome, the most comprehensive and the most **practicable** guide for all sectors of human life. USE **practical**.

> **Practicable**, *a word that cannot be applied to people, means capable of being done or put into practice; feasible.* **Practical** *means useful; suitable for use. The difference, though slight, is important, for from such distinctions we know subtlety of thought. And without subtlety there can be little society.*

PRECEDENTS

Misspelling of **precedence**. • Any announcements made at the lake take **precedents** over written rules. USE **precedence**. • This Chapter shall take **precedents** over and supersede any other provisions of this Title which appear to regulate charitable solicitations. USE **precedence**.

> **Precedence** *is the condition of being more important than something else; priority; the order of importance of people having different rank.* **Precedents**, *the plural of* **precedent**, *is an act or statement that serves as an example or justification in a legal case; an earlier instance or occurrence of something regarded as a guide or archetype for later events.*

Keep in mind that scholarly activities take precedents over all other activities for which we use the computers.

—Salem Academy

Although we are told that "Academic achievement is at the center of" Salem Academy, this sentence from one of the academy's web pages makes us question their activities and academics.

PRECEED

Misspelling of **precede**. • For Canadian symbols, **preceed** the symbol with the letters CAN. USE **precede**. • When addressing mail to an Assemblyman, the title Honorable should **preceed** his full name, i.e., "The Honorable firstname lastname." USE **precede**. • A special pre-concert "informance" will **preceed** this entertaining and educational concert experience. USE **precede**.

> In confusion with **proceed**, the word **precede** is sometimes—quite regularly—misspelled **preceed**.

Preceed is also a misspelling of **proceed**: • At this point you can verify the quantity and costs of your order and either modify, delete or **proceed** with your purchase. USE **proceed**. • Without writing a thick volume on angels, demons and Satan, let's **proceed** with some answers from the only reliable source that God has given mankind—the Bible. USE **proceed**.

> And a little less understandable, the word **proceed** is sometimes misspelled **preceed**.

PRECIPITOUS

Misused for **precipitate**. • In what Johns Hopkins believes to be an unwarranted, unnecessary, paralyzing and **precipitous** action, the Office of Human Research Protection (OHRP) has today suspended all federally supported medical research projects involving human subjects at almost all of our institutions. USE **precipitate**. • In the absence of **precipitous** behavior on the part of the subject, negotiators should initiate dialogue in English, working on the assumption that the subject might take the opportunity to talk. USE **precipitate**.

> **Precipitate**, as an adjective, means moving rapidly; done abruptly or rashly; occurring suddenly. **Precipitous**, like a precipice; very steep.

PREDOMINATE

Idiotic for **predominant**. • But of course, the magnificent flag of the U.S.A. flies in the **predominate** position on the Giant Stride. USE **predominant**. • While central station power will continue to be the **predominate** delivery system for our industry for years to come, Consumers Energy is exploring the use of on-site generation. USE **predominant.**

The adjective is **predominant,** *not—despite what some dictionaries now suggest—* **predominate.** **Predominate** *is a verb meaning to prevail or dominate. That this word is now sometimes used to mean the adjective* **predominant** *(having superior strength, authority, influence, or force; most common or conspicuous) is due to people confusing the words and, what's worse, to laxicographers endorsing people's ignorance. SEE ALSO* **dominate.**

> Among Middle East experts, it has become the predominate wisdom that real progress toward peace can only be achieved if not just Palestinian Leader Yasser Arafat, but also Sharon, step down as leaders of their nations.
>
> **—Richard Gwyn, *Toronto Star***

> Wolfson also seems to buy into "personhood theory," the predominate view in bioethics that people with severe cognitive impairments are less than fully equal persons, and hence, have fewer rights.
>
> **—Wesley J. Smith, *The Weekly Standard***

The adjective is **predominant.** *These writers—all writers—ought to know that dictionaries chronicle the dissolution of the language; they are the new doomsday books. Without sensible words and dependable meanings, there can be no sane world.*

PREFERABLE

The pronunciation of **preferable** *is (PREF-er-ah-ble), not (pri-FER-ah-ble).*

PREJUDICE

Solecistic for **prejudiced.** • I think the main reason why some people dislike other people is because they are **prejudice.** USE **prejudiced.** • Since **prejudice** people cannot deal with their inner frustrations, they stereotype, blame, and attack less powerful groups. USE **prejudiced**. • I walked with him for a moment not saying anything, then I asked if he was **prejudice** against Starbucks. USE **prejudiced**.

> **Prejudice** *is a noun or verb. The adjectival form of* **prejudice** *is* **prejudiced***; the past participle is also* **prejudiced***. SEE ALSO* **cliché***;* **copyright***.*

PREMIER

Misused for **premiere**. • Paceline Systems co-sponsors the **premier** of the InfiniBand Association's IT Roadshow. USE **premiere**. • A world **premier** of the play *Nobody Knows You're a Dog* will take place on the WPI campus on November 16-18. USE **premiere**.

And **premiere** is sometimes misused for **premier**: • One of those was the **premiere** of the Soviet Union who extended an invitation to the artist to visit Moscow as a guest of the Union of Artists of the U.S.S.R. USE **premier**. • Paul Okalik, the **premiere** of Canada's Nunavut province, has his finger directly on the denial button. USE **premier**.

> **Premier***, the noun, means a prime minister or a chief administrative officer.* **Premiere** *is the first public performance, as of a movie or play.*

PRESCRIBE

Misused for **subscribe** • Further, we do not **prescribe** to the theory that increased regulation will lead to an appreciation of the local currency. USE **subscribe**. • No longer will students feel shut out or underrepresented just because they **prescribe** to a certain philosophy. USE **subscribe**. • Whoever would like to have information about sporting and cultural events and what's going on here on a regular basis, should **prescribe** to our free newsletter. USE **subscribe**.

> **Prescribe** *means to lay down as a rule or direction; to recommend; to issue as a medicine.* **Subscribe** *means to contribute a sum of money; to sign one's name to a document; to authorize someone to receive access to a publication or service; to express approval or assent to. SEE ALSO* **ascribe***;* **proscribe***.*

P

The purpose of language is to communicate, rather than prescribe to rules and standards.
—**Scott Kapel,** *Solecisms of Mechanics and Grammar*

*The correct word is **subscribe**, not **prescribe**, though the author of this sentence, an English teacher and a so-called descriptive grammarian—who further writes, "rules were either created or sternly upheld by those insecure, upper-class intellectuals who insisted upon them to prove their education over that of the lower elements"—might try to rebut this.*

PRESENTLY

Misused for **currently** (or similar words) • Is lava **presently** flowing out of Mauna Loa? USE **now**. • I am **presently** an undergraduate student at Northern Arizona University. DELETE **presently**. • John Jeter is **presently** in his seventh season as the Music Director and Conductor of the Fort Smith Symphony. DELETE **presently**. • Our site is **presently** under re-construction and some links or shopping cart functions may not be working. USE **currently**.

***Presently** is best used to mean soon or in a short time. In the sense of now or currently, it is less defensible.*

PRESUMPTIOUS

Misspelling of **presumptuous** . • It would be **presumptious** of me to consider my life to be significant enough to warrant an autobiography, and I am not a **presumptious** person. USE **presumptuous**. • Isn't it a little **presumptious** of us humans to think we can be the arbiters of design everywhere in the Universe? USE **presumptuous**.

*If we would pronounce **presumptuous** (pri-ZUMP-choo-es) correctly, perhaps we'd be more likely to spell it correctly.*

PRESUMPTIVE

Misused for **presumptuous.** • It's also quite **presumptive** of him to assume that all 25,000 of those students have never heard of Christianity. USE **presumptuous.** • I was taught that addressing a stranger by his first name was **presumptive** and rude and too personal, that a stranger should always be addressed formally as Mr. or Mrs. or Miss if and until a friendship is established. USE **presumptuous.**

> *__Presumptive__—which often refers to heirs, political nominees, and criminal sentences—means giving grounds for belief; based on probability. __Presumptuous__ means presuming, excessively forward, arrogant, or bold.*

PREVARICATE

Misused for **procrastinate.** • But if you continue to **prevaricate**, your window of opportunity will close. USE **procrastinate.** • In the prevailing climate, President Habyarimana and the extremists who surrounded him hoped that if they could **prevaricate** until UNAMIR's mandate expired on April 5, 1994, the Security Council would lose patience and withdraw the force. USE **procrastinate.**

> *To __prevaricate__ is to stray from the truth; to equivocate; to lie. To __procrastinate__ is to put off; to postpone or defer.*

PREVENTATIVE

Why do we require both *preventative* and *preventive*?

We don't. __Preventive__ is preferable because it has one fewer syllable. What's more, it very well may be that the origin of __preventative__ (ca. 1676) was simply people mispronouncing __preventive__ (ca. 1639). Oxford English Dictionary also says that __preventive__ is the "preferable formation."

PREVERT

Misspelling of **pervert**. • I think you're some kind of deviated **prevert**. USE **pervert**. • Why am I not surprised that a NAMBLA **prevert** like you is defending a child molester like Jackson. USE **pervert**. • But you clicked on the link, so obviously you are a filthy **prevert** and only found DrF because you were searching for free porn, weren't you? USE **pervert**.

P

> And **preversion** is a misspelling of **perversion**. It may be that **prevert** is sometimes used to add a sense of **perversion** to the noun **pervert**, to emphasize the **perversion**, but all the usage truly unveils is a stupid, often repugnant, person.
>
> **Pervert** is a perfectly good verb, the meanings of which are not often heard: to lead away from what is right, correct, moral, or good; to debase; to misconstrue or distort: ("Google is not going to **pervert** its search results, regardless of any contract language"; "A second count alleged that he conspired to **pervert** the course of justice by providing false evidence about the allegations").

PREY

Misused for **pray**. • **Prey** for help from whatever power is greater than you. USE **pray**. • **Prey** to God for mercy because you will find none from us. USE **Pray**. • We all hope and **prey** for his return to good health. USE **Pray**.

> To **pray** is to hope for; to make supplication; to recite a prayer; to worship God or another deity. To **prey** is to hunt or kill other animals; to rob or plunder; to swindle or exploit someone; to weigh heavily on.

PRINCIPLE

Misused for **principal**. • We are delighted to have the generous support and assistance of our **principle** sponsors. USE **principal**. • Today, the Russians are our **principle** partner in space exploration, a fact inconceivable in 1957. USE **principal**. • Students also must complete the highest level of math offered at their high school before taking a college math class unless an exception is made by the high school **principle**. USE **principal**.

> A **principle** (always only a noun) is a truth, law, standard, or rule. **Principal**, as an adjective, means chief or highest in importance. As a noun, it means a person

who holds a high position or has a main role; a sum of money that is owed and on which interest is charged.

> Then there's the Muslim practice of not charging explicit interest: that opens the door to having creditors write off interest but not principle.
> —*The Wall Street Journal*

If The Wall Street Journal—*three times in one editorial—does not know the difference between **principle** and **principal**, let us mistrust their numbers as much as we must their words.*

PRIVLEGE (PRIVLEDGE)

Misspellings of **privilege.** • Authentication does not give you any **privlege**, it only provides a basis for deciding **privlege**. USE **privilege.** • For tax purposes, income is defined by the Supreme Court as a gain or profit earned by **privlege**. USE **privilege.** • To earn a Fun Friday, the children must earn the **privledge** to participate. USE **privilege.** • Is Bush about to withhold information, by invoking executive **privledge**, from the 9-11 investigation? USE **privilege.**

*Privilege (PRIV-i-lij or PRIV-lij), neither **privlege** nor **privledge**, is the correct spelling. The **d** that people so often want to include in **privilege** is found in the adjectival form: **privileged**.*

PROBLEMSOME

Solecistic for **problematic** (or similar words). • These non-unique solutions are **problemsome** and we appeal to additional considerations to find the one(s) that actually will appear in nature. USE **problematic.** • Even with this joint underlying mission, the relationship between these two agencies has often been **problemsome** and on some past occasions the size and scope of the altercations were legendary, such that stories still circulate. USE **problematic.**

*Despite the existence of **worrisome**, **troublesome**, and **fearsome**, **problemsome** is not in the English lexicon. **Problematic** (as well as **problematical**) is.*

PROCTOR

People ask me if *proctor* is a verb. I tell them no. They use it anyhow. They ask me which is correct, "proctor the students" or "proctor the test"? I tell them to *supervise* both, but they won't listen, they're stuck on *proctoring*. Are they beyond all help?

Proctor *is given as a verb in:*

- *1982* American Heritage Dictionary *(Houghton Mifflin): to supervise (an examination)*

- *1960* Webster's New World Dictionary *(World): to supervise (an academic examination)*

- *1947* American College Dictionary *(Random House): to act as a proctor (one appointed to keep watch over students at examinations)*

- *1940* Webster's New International Dictionary, *Second Edition (Merriam-Webster): to act as a proctor (for, in, or toward)*

*What's more, **proctor** is useful because it means more than **supervise** does alone; it means, as some of these definitions show, "to **supervise** an academic examination" or "to keep watch over students taking an exam."*

*Perhaps, sixty or more years ago, the argument against the verb **proctor** was more cogently made, but today, the cause is lost and the word beyond reclamation.*

PRONE

Misused for **supine**. • Sex/Homosexuality lost the intermediate level of points per instance once due to a woman straddle-sitting on the pelvic region of a man while he was **prone**, face-up. USE **supine**. • One interesting note: cockroaches affected by this product will die **prone** (**face up**) rather than on their backs as is the norm for other control products. USE **prone** (**face down**).

*Prone means face down; **supine**, face up.*

PRONOUNCIATION

Misspelling of **pronunciation**. • With the landslide selection of Arnold Schwarzenegger as the state's newest governor, local politicians had more to mull Wednesday than the **pronounciation** of "Kawleefornia." USE **pronunciation**. • Also, not that you asked but now that I'm offering **pronounciation** guidelines, Warre is pronounced "war." USE **pronunciation**.

People who spell the word incorrectly may also pronounce it incorrectly: (pro-nun-see-A-shen), not (pro-NUN-see-a-shen).

PROOFREADING

*Misused for **copyediting**. **Proofreading** means only one thing: comparing one document (an edited manuscript or galley) to another (a typeset galley or page proof) to ensure all changes have been correctly made. **Copyediting** means reviewing a manuscript for grammatical errors, spelling, punctuation, and the like. Proofreaders are not copyeditors.*

Pity the poor proofreader. Imagine wading through the thicket of contemporary written English, uprooting such verbal weeds as misplaced whos and whoms, hopeless hopefullys, singular data, whatever.
—**Robert Siegel, *All Things Considered***

*Mr. Siegel nicely illustrates the incorrect, the common, use of **proofreading**.*

PROPHESY

Misused for **prophecy**. • Gaze into our crystal ball for the predictions and **prophesy** made by ancient millennium prophets and modern experts concerning the fate of our planet and the future of mankind. USE **prophecy**. • Some Churches try to use the successes of futuristic **prophesy** to justify faith, particularly faith in the infallibility of Scripture. USE **prophecy**.

> **Prophesy** (PROF-i-si) is the verb, **prophecy** (PROF-i-see) the noun; not misspellings, they are different parts of speech.

P

PROPORTION

Misused for **portion**. • Don't get me wrong, I'm not anorexic, I just eat small **proportions**. USE **portions**. • In general, Thai eat several small meals throughout the day and evening and nowhere near the large **proportions** of food that farang (i.e., westerners) eat. USE **portions**.

> **Proportion** refers to a part considered in relation to a whole or a comparative relationship between things or parts of things with respect to size, amount, or degree. **Portion**, in the sense discussed here, refers to a helping of food.

So what are the best ways of staying healthy? Eat small proportions.

—Dr. Mallika Marshall, television news correspondent

---

*Dr. Marshall is quite lovely, but her **proportions** are a good deal larger than our **portions**.*

PROSCRIBE

Misused for **prescribe**. • We are on record to abide by the 1949 Geneva Conventions and their relevant sections that **proscribe** the rules of war. USE **prescribe**. • They often **proscribe** rules of behavior which we must follow to attain rewards or avoid punishment in this or the after world. USE **prescribe**.

> To **proscribe** is to prohibit, forbid, or disallow; to **prescribe** is to set down, order, or recommend. SEE ALSO **prescribe**.

PROSTRATE

Misused for **prostate**. • Eating tomatoes, ketchup, tomato sauce and tomato paste-topped pizza more than two times a week can reduce the risk of **prostrate** cancer by 21 to 43 percent, according to Dr. Edward Giovannucci of the Harvard University School of Public Health. USE **prostate**. • Preventing **prostrate** cancer is easier than fighting **prostrate** cancer. USE **prostate**.

> **Prostate** means of or relating to the prostate gland; the prostate. **Prostrate** means lying face down; overcome.

PROVEN

Misused for **proved**. • Has the existence of extraterrestrial life finally been **proven**? USE **proved**. • SalesLink has **proven** our success with hundreds of satisfied customers. USE **proved**. • Chairman of the Forum for Unity, Cohesion and Justice in East Timor, Domingos MD Soares, has maintained that the partisanship of the U.N. Assessment Mission in East Timor (UNAMET) with the anti-integration camp has been **proven** beyond doubt. USE **proved**.

> **Proved** is the verb form; **proven** the adjectival form.

PUBLICALLY

Misspelling of **publicly**. • The university's chapter of NAACP held a rally Tuesday during lunch to **publically** show its support of the decision to change the on-the-field mascot. USE **publicly**. • Even on the U.S. Supreme Court there are several who have **publically** stated that we must look to foreign legal systems for our legal precedents and ignore our own constitution. USE **publicly**.

> The people who spell **publically** (instead of **publicly**) are the same people who spell **accidently** (instead of **accidentally**)—dupes all. SEE ALSO **accidently**.

(IS) PURPORTED

Misused for **purports**. • I've seen what **is purported** to be the preliminary report on the autopsy. USE **purports**. • Even China **is purported** to be headed down the flat-tax road. USE **purports**. • It is tough to vote against anything that **is purported** to be property tax relief. USE **purports**.

> *The verb **purport** should not be used in the passive; it is regarded as passive, and means is supposed or is represented. **Purports**, not **is purported**, is correct.*

P

What's more, the subject of **purport** ought not to be a person: • Will Martin write this book, revealing to the world, the "monstrous, appalling things," his great-grandfather **is purported to have** done? USE **is accused of having**. • It is also clear that as brilliant a man as Clark **is purported** to be, running for president requires its own special set of skills. USE **is said**. • The Iraq War was initially justified because Hussein **was purported** to have weapons of mass destruction and ties to the al-Qaeda. USE **was thought**.

PURPOSEFULLY

Misused for **purposely**. • None of these worthies could give any explanation as to why they had **purposefully**, deliberately and grossly violated the building code. USE **purposely**. • While you are waiting to register the name, it is often worthwhile to temporarily reserve the name with a name reservation form so that it is not accidentally or **purposefully** obtained by a competitor or unwitting third party. USE **purposely**.

> ***Purposely** means on purpose or deliberately. **Purposefully** means with a specific purpose in mind: ("He had a relatively quiet first half, but played more purposefully in the second and scored Bayern's first goal").*

QUANDRY

Misspelling of **quandary.** • Lost in all the nonsense about the Steelers' quarterback **quandry** is that the defense was downright horrendous against the Oilers. USE **quandary.** • Singapore's **quandry**: Use the Internet, but only use it responsibly. USE **quandary.** • The restrictions have put some legislators in a **quandry**. USE **quandary.**

*Though **quandary** (KWON-dah-ree; KWON-dree) may sound like **laundry**, it is spelled **d-a-r-y**, not **d-r-y**.*

QUITE

Misused for **quiet.** • We are on stage, in costume. The audience has **quitened**. USE **quietened.** • The genius within is waiting **quite** and still for an opportunity to guide our path. USE **quiet.** • How come Microsoft, Cisco and Lucent were all deadly **quite** last week? USE **quiet.**

__Quite__ is an adverb meaning to the fullest extent, completely; actually; to a degree, rather. __Quiet__ is an adjective meaning silent; calm or peaceful; untroubled; not showy; understated.

QUOTATION

Misused for **quotient.** • Cognitive testing and neurobehavioral measures can also be used, although caution is in order with full-scale intelligence **quotation** (I.Q.) scores because they can mask subtle neuropsychologic patterns of abnormality. USE **quotient.** • We pay particular attention to stimulating the intellectual curiosity and increasing the emotional **quotation** of the child. USE **quotient.**

And unsurprisingly, some people misuse **quotient** for **quotation:** • Try a Google search with "Fiber Edge + garden" without the **quotient** marks. USE **quotation.** • **Quotient** marks " " are used to phrase a sentence whether whole or partial when showing someone speaking. USE **Quotation.**

> **Quotation** (which is preferable to the noun **quote**) refers to words repeated or reproduced by another; the estimated price of a job or service. **Quotient** refers to the result obtained when one number is divided by another; the amount of a specific quality or characteristic.

Q

RACIAL

Misused for **racist**. • The suspect, who is white, made a derogatory **racial** comment against Watson, who is black. USE **racist**. • Mr. Howard's resignation was prompted by reports that he made an inappropriate **racial** comment. USE **racist**. • As appalling as his **racial** remark was, it is not enough of a reason to destroy a man who has contributed so much to the black community, this university and this state. USE **racist**.

> *People once were accused of making **racist** comments; today, they are as likely to be accused of **racial** ones. A **racial** comment is not necessarily discriminatory or reprehensible; a **racist** one is. A "derogatory" racial comment might more accurately be called a racist comment; an "inappropriate" racial comment, a racist one; an "appalling" racial remark, a racist one. **Racial** is for people who are afraid to use **racist**. SEE ALSO **niggardly**.*

RACQUET

Misused for **racket**. • Why don't you make a loud **racquet** and embarrass them? USE **racket**. • And to get you geared up for an energetic day, the Pro AM crew, PJ and Spanky from local radio station Lantern FM, will be on site making a **racquet** with sounds of the latest moves and grooves. USE **racket**.

> *Racket means, as **racquet** does, a light bat or paddle used in a game; a game. But only **racket** is an uproar; loud or noisy confusion; a means of obtaining money illegally; a livelihood of some sort.*

RATIONAL

Misused for **rationale**. • What is the **rational** for having many secondary schools when the existing National High Schools have served that purpose well? USE **ratio-**

nale. • Our **rational** is if you don't use a dictionary you only use the words you already know. USE **rationale.** • The board's mission is to provide Chamber members with a clear indication of the business **rational** for funding or failing to fund charitable requests. USE **rationale.**

Rational *(RASH-ah-nel) means having the ability to reason; reasonable or logical.*
Rationale (rash-ah-NAL) means the rational basis for a course of action or belief.

RAVAGE

Misused for **ravish.** • The first scene involves a homeless Vietnam veteran and three red, white and blue painted figures who **ravage** a woman painted with symbols and messages wearing a Native American headdress while a man in "black-face" sings the National Anthem. USE **ravish.**

And **ravish** is misused for **ravage:** • In addition, the incursion of illegal Israeli settlements that displace Palestinians and **ravish** the landscape must be prohibited. USE **ravage.**

*Ravage means to destroy; to plunder and sack. **Ravish** is to seize and carry away;*
to rape; to enrapture.

REALATOR

Misspelling of **realtor.** • Because it has been so slow, a serious seller would have been very foolish to give one **realator** an exclusive on his property. USE **realtor.** • Whether you are a **realator,** travel agent, tour guide, contractor, or wedding coordinator, immersive imaging can help your business. USE **realtor.**

*The correct spelling is **realtor,** not **realator;** thus, the correct pronunciation is*
(REAL-ter), not (REEL-ah-ter).

RE- BACK

Solecistic for **re-.** • Under the lease agreement, if LRMC did not use the building for that purpose, ownership would **revert back** to the city. DELETE **back.** • Next, the officers are heading to Long Island to visit another base and will **return back** to South Africa on Saturday. DELETE **back.** • The results are saved so that patients and doctors can **refer back** to them at a later date. DELETE **back.** • This is a day we can **reflect back** on the long and rugged journey from where we came. DELETE **back.** • After receiving the message you will have to **reply back** to confirm your subscription to the list. DELETE **back.**

Revert back, return back, refer back, reflect back, reply back, and similar expressions are all redundant. SEE ALSO *convey back.*

It looks like they're having a big reverting back to pre-freedom times.
—**Martha Zoller, radio talk show host**

That this unexceptional talker has an audience is disquieting: It must be that her listeners are no brighter, and speak no better, than the host herself.

REBOUND

Misused for **redound.** • Another obstacle dream, but this one pertains to personal behaviour and is a warning that you should try to avoid giving false impressions which could **rebound** to your discredit. USE **redound.** • Our Christian young men, having broken way from fear of evil spirits and their animistic practices, are rejoicing that they can see ways of co-operating with the progressive party which will evidently **rebound** to the praise and glory of the Lord Jesus Christ. USE **redound.** • No good deed goes unrewarded. If you help someone, it will somehow **rebound** to your credit. USE **redound.** • But the exposure of Danish artists to New York City's own historically vibrant culture will also **rebound** to their benefit and therefore to their audiences on both sides of the Atlantic. USE **redound.** • In addition, the Howes were opposition Whigs and reluctant to win a victory which would **rebound** to the credit of the Tory government. USE **redound.** • Morgan Stanley, eager to ensure the highly profitable BGI relationship stayed in place, was all too happy to join in any conversations that might **rebound** to their advantage. USE **redound.**

Redound means to have an effect or consequence; to contribute or lead to. **Rebound** means to spring or bounce back after hitting or striking something; to recover as from a setback or illness. Laxicographers, further disaffecting careful writers and speakers, assign the meaning **rebound** to the definition of **redound**.

RECALL (RECOLLECT)

Confused with **remember**. To **remember** something is to do so effortlessly, or without much difficulty. To **recall** or **recollect** suggests a harder time of remembering. That said, the word **cannot** is best used with **recall** and **recollect**; the words **do not** with **remember**.

RECIEVE

Misspelling of **receive**. • Welcome to rock-web and rock365.com free subscriptions. Keep in touch with us and **recieve** a regular news letter about our latest features and free services. USE **receive**. • For more info on diving in Southern Maine and to **recieve** our Northeast Dive Resort Video, contact York Beach Scuba. USE **receive**.

Some people seem unable to remember the spelling of **receive**. You can therefore be sure that some dictionaries will, one day, list **recieve** as a variant spelling of **receive**.

REFER

Misused for **allude**. To **refer** is to mention something or someone directly ("They **refer** to all other women as boy-women, implying that they are dense and oafish like little boys, woefully short of their own fabulous womanliness"; "These bands are technically **referred** to as drum and bugle corps, not marching bands"). To **allude** is to mention something or someone indirectly without naming it or him ("Reports of the time **allude** to the fact that, with the help of prominent business families, Methodism was established here"; "He also talked of expanding access to health care and **alluded** to his proposal to add personal investment accounts to Social Security"). SEE ALSO **allude**.

REFUTE

Misused for **rebut** (or similar words). • The Red Sox have said they will not confirm or **refute** trade rumors. USE **deny**. • Few **refute** that purposeful exercise-walking is beneficial, and golf is yet another opportunity for low-impact, recreational fitness. USE **disagree**. • The panel is expected to **refute** the school board's request at the next state board of education meeting this month. USE **rebuff**. • Because Ashcroft has not attempted to **refute** the racist inclinations and pronouncements of such Christian evangelists as Franklin Graham, Jerry Falwell and Pat Robertson, American Muslims are deeply frightened by these born-again, mostly Republican right-wing fundamentalists. USE **rebut**. • Amid the mounting suggestions on the market bubbles, the Bank of Korea has doggedly **refuted** the proposal to raise the interest rate. USE **rejected**.

> **Refute** *means to prove to be wrong; confute; disprove. It does not mean to rebut, deny, contradict, rebuff, disagree, dispute, or reject.* **Rebut** *means to contradict, counter, or argue against.* **Rebuff** *means to reject an offer; to repel an attack.* **Reject** *means to dismiss; to refuse to agree with; to rebuff.*

REGIME

Misused for **regimen**. • Subjectivity requires intersubjective relationships mediated through a **regime** of possessing, enjoying, and exchanging an object of desire. USE **regimen**. • With a regular **regime** of exercise, the aches and pains will be minimized or even disappear. USE **regimen**. • Metformin works much better if combined with a strict **regime** of diet and exercise. USE **regimen**.

> *A* **regime** *(ri-ZHEM) is an authoritarian government; a way of doing something. A* **regimen** *(REG-i-men) is a program of exercise, medical treatment, or other activity to achieve a benefit. SEE ALSO* **regiment**.

REGIMENT

Misused for **regimen**. • Shay plans to take some time away from education by traveling to Europe, visiting family and starting up an exercise **regiment**. USE **regimen**. • It is any impatient treatment or any medical condition that incapacitates them for more than three days provided that they have seen a doctor and they are under a continuing **regiment** of medical care. USE **regimen**.

> A **regiment** is a unit of an army; a large number of things or people. A **regimen** is a course of medical treatment, exercise, or other activity. SEE ALSO **regime**; **regimentate**.

REGIMENTATE

Solecistic for **regiment**. • We must pre-arrange our material control and **regimentate** our production lines in such a manner that we may fulfill your requests as soon as possible. USE **regiment**. • It is important to **regimentate** strong efforts in the region by promoting the cooperation among the public and private sectors. USE **regiment**. • Policy and polity refer to attempts to **regimentate** or to regulate politics as an action and motion. USE **regiment**.

R

> To **regiment** means to systematize; to subject to uniformity and order. **Regimentate** is misspelled, mispronounced, misused—just the sort of word that laxicographers long for. SEE ALSO **regiment**.

REGISTRAR

Misused for **register**. • To **registrar** call Dee Morton, the center market manager, at 794-2011. USE **register**. • I would like to **registrar** as a Certificate Student. USE **register**.

> A **registrar** (REJ-i-strar) is a person responsible for keeping a **register** (REJ-is-ter), an official list of names or other data. To **register** is to enter a name or other data into an official list.

REGRETFUL

Misused for **regrettable**. • She said FIDA in its twenty-five years of operations in Ghana has been consistent and unrelenting in its gender empowerment endeavours but it was **regretful** that its operation essentially remained an urban phenomenon. USE **regrettable**. • When asked about causalities in Iraq, Mr. Cheney responded that though human loss is always **regretful**, figures are extremely low in comparison to other warfield scenarios in the defense of freedom. USE **regrettable**.

Regretful means feeling or showing regret; sorry or sorrowful. **Regrettable** means giving rise to or deserving regret; undesirable. People are **regretful**; events, **regrettable**.

REIN

Misused for **reign.** • I'd like to find the place where happiness **reins**, where life is free and there are not restraints. USE **reigns.** • Darkness **reined** and many evil things happened led by her wicked brother. USE **reigned.** • Though fear **reined,** Jesus perceived everything through the eyes of love. USE **reigned.**

> And **reign** is sometimes misused for **rein,** especially in the expression **free reign** (or **full reign**). **Reins** are the straps that control a horse; someone or something given **free rein** is freed of restraint and has, at least, some measure of control. **Free reign** is thus quite senseless, for **reign,** as a noun, means rule or dominance; as a verb, it means to rule or to be predominant.

RELIVE

Misused for **relieve.** • Understanding the range of choices that are available to **relive** anxiety and discomfort makes you a well-informed dental consumer. USE **relieve.** • Opiates help to **relive** pain by acting in both the spinal cord and brain. USE **relieve.**

> **Relive** means to experience a past event again. **Relieve** means to ease, lighten, or reduce.

Our mission is to provide individuals and families with assistance to lighten the load and relive the stress caused by financial burdens.

—**Christian Debt Management**

CDM means what it writes. Those who have the misfortune of somehow being on their spam list do indeed relive the stress.

RENUMERATION

Misspelling of **remuneration**. • The Prime Minister said he was not against doctors getting decent **renumeration**, which they well deserved, but there had to be a limit in a poor country to one's ambition and greed. USE **remuneration**. • Wolper Jewish Hospital offers **renumeration** packaging, free food and parking for staff as well as the opportunity to work in a friendly and supportive environment. USE **remuneration**.

*The word is **remuneration** (ri-myoo-nah-RA-shen), not **renumeration**. To remu-nerate means to pay or compensate, not to repay or recompense.*

```
MedWorld is currently recruiting editors, writers,
and contributors from medical schools and hospi-
tals across the world. All positions on MedWorld
are volunteer-based, without renumeration or com-
pensation.
```
—MedWorld

Stanford University's MedWorld clearly does need editors and writers—though perhaps not from this group:

```
Article 3--Renumeration and Rewrites. There shall be no minimum
Script Fee. All Script Fees are negotiable.
```
—Writers Guild of Canada

R

REOCCUR

Misused for **recur**. • Reading your Aug. 27 front-page article, "Tending to teens' need to sleep," irritated a **reoccurring** wound. USE **recurring**. • If you want the appointment or meeting to **reoccur** on a daily basis, then tap on the Daily tab. USE **recur**. • The Top Ten Periodic Frequency graph displays the top ten numbers that are due to come up because of their tendency to **reoccur** in a periodic manner. USE **recur**.

Reoccur** and **reoccurrence** are errors for **recur** and **recurrence**. Some critics and dictionary makers maintain that **recur** means to happen repeatedly, and **reoccur

*to happen, merely, again, but this is a specious explanation for what was at first, and will be to the last, nothing but a blunder. SEE ALSO **occurence**.*

As still further evidence, consider these examples of virtually identical sentences: • Midwestern quake won't **recur** soon. • A Midwestern quake is not likely to **reoccur** soon. USE **recur**.

And then there are those who use **reoccurrence** instead of **recurrence**: • Basically, what this study is doing is looking at state-of-the-art treatments for depression and looking at how well they work in the short term, but also how well they prevent **reoccurrence**. • USE **recurrence**. • Gross margins for the three months ended October 31, 1999 increased to 35% from (5%) in the prior year, primarily due to the **non-reoccurrence** of inventory related charges that resulted in the negative margin for the second quarter of last year. • USE **non-recurrence**.

*Neither **reoccur** nor **reoccurrence** should exist in any reputable English-language lexicon. The use of **reoccur** has nothing at all to do with nicety, everything to do with nescience.*

REPARTEE

Idiotic for **joke** (or similar words). • Phong quickly **repartees**: "Happiness is like an ostrich, for the longer you bury your head the more happy you will be." USE **returns**. • Sir Martin **repartees** with a wicked smile: "I think Tony should worry about his own group." USE **retorts**. • The four men behind us flirt pointedly with the waiter, who good-naturedly **repartees** back. USE **jokes**. • Hughes, in fact, scared the crap out of me by just how sharp she was and how she very skillfully **reparteed** Jon's barbs. USE **replied to**.

***Repartee** is a noun; it is not a verb.*

REPEL

Misused for **rappel**. • You must **repel** down the side of the building in the midst of explosions and flames until you get to a lower rooftop, a few hundred feet down. USE **rappel**. • Homicide detectives spent several hours at the scene before an emergency rescue crew was allowed to **repel** down the shaft to remove the boy's body.

USE **rappel**. • For ice rescue, we use the same half-inch line we use **repelling** off a building. USE **rappelling**.

*To **rappel** (rah-PEL) means to descend a mountain, building, wall, or other vertical surface by means of a rope. To **repel** (ri-PEL) is to reject; spurn; turn or drive away.*

Although upon reaching the top of the wall, many climbers choose to repel down, park officials said.
—**The Kentucky Post**

This writer is best left unacknowledged, as the Post, for its own reasons, itself decided. Until misused, misbegotten words are no longer to be found, we all might prefer being no-name writers.

REPLETE

Solecistic for **complete**. • Steve Jobs, Apple's interim chief executive, unveiled on Wednesday the company's new low-cost computer: the iMac, a translucent teal and white plastic box, **replete** with monitor, keyboard and mouse, that sells for $1,299. USE **complete**. • Finding himself the only Scot in Cannes without a kilt last year, former pop idol Rod Stewart had one—**replete** with family tartan and sporran—flown all the way from his favourite kilt maker in Glasgow for an evening concert. USE **complete**. • Gonzalez said the performance is "in a sense like a Broadway show," where you are entertained throughout by dancing, huge sets, costumes, and an original musical score **replete** with violin accompaniment. USE **complete**.

*Ludicrous are the laxicographers who promote **replete** (which means abundantly full) as a synonym for **complete**. Dictionary makers, we must remember, simply document how the language is used; they are not keen thinkers; they do only as they are told.*

REPRESENTATED

Solecistic for **represented**. • If the student is represented by an attorney, UCSD may be **representated** by the Office of the General Counsel, or other appropriate representative. USE **represented**. • For all of the schematics below, the phosphorylated FixJ is **representated** by the green wireframe and the unphosphorylated FixJ is **representated** by the white wireframe. USE **represented**. • Swanwick helped pioneer the League of Nations Society, **representated** Great Britain at the International Conference of Women, and was appointed by Ramsey MacDonald to be a member of the British government delegation to the League of Nations Assembly in Geneva in 1924 and in 1929. USE **represented**.

*The past tense of **represent** is **represented**, not, as is seen so often, **representated**.*

REPRESS

*Confused with **oppress**. **Oppress** means to subjugate; to tyrannize; to worry or trouble ("Establishing democracy in Iraq will deprive terrorists of their main theme of propaganda—that Western powers want to **oppress** the Middle East"; "Unfortunately, it does not provide clearly for the human rights of Afghan women or mandate a change in laws used to **oppress** women in the past"). **Repress** means to restrain; to subdue ("By all means, don't try to **repress** your feelings of anger, guilt, or sorrow"; "There are governments that still fear and **repress** independent thought and creativity in private enterprise").*

RESPECTIVELY

Misused for **respectfully**. • Choose complimentary close according to formality required: Use Sincerely for most business letters. Use **Respectively** yours when writing to the President of the U.S. USE **Respectfully**. • Graduates of St. Clare School will act **respectively** towards self and others. USE **respectfully**. • Behave **respectively** to adults and each other. USE **respectfully**. • I urge you to consider them carefully and I think you will agree that they meet the objectives of the Commission without the negative implications of the proposed wording. **Respectively** yours, Jeffrey W. Pruett, CPA. USE **Respectfully**. • I invite you to visit this site often and join us as we wade deeper into the Arts! **Respectively** yours, Mrs. Marian Yarus. USE **Respectfully**. • We assure that all calls are handled in a professional manner aimed at helping the consumer to use products effectively. **Respectively** yours, Frances White, President. USE **Respectfully**.

* **Respectively** means in the order designated or mentioned: ("Women's soccer players Paul McGinn of Lynn and Caitlin D'Amario of East Longmeadow were named to*

the NCSAA second and third teams, **respectively**"). **Respectfully** means characterized by or showing respect or deference. Even though, in Shakespeare's day, **respectively** apparently meant **respectfully**, the word in that sense has long been obsolete.

  Despite the rather widespread misuse, no present-day dictionary has yet suggested that **respectively**, once again, also means **respectfully**.

RESTLESS

Misused for **restive**. • Now there is talk of intervening in the turmoil afflicting Serbia's **restless** province of Kosovo. USE **restive**. • Rural folk are **restless** over petrol prices, housing and poor public services—and Labour can no longer afford to ignore their concerns. USE **restive**.

  Restless means uneasy or unquiet; unable to rest or relax. **Restive** means impatient or fidgety under pressure, restraint, or opposition.

More disheartening still is the use of **restive** to mean the near opposite of what it does mean, to mean **restful**: • I hope to have a **restive** Saturday…and tomorrow should be leisurely productive…that is my goal…now let us see if I can stick to it. USE **restful**. • Set atop elevated ground, SouthLinks has tall, balmy trees, luxuriant shrubs and tropical plants which create a **restive** and relaxing environment. USE **restful**. • Now situated on fourteen acres of the original property, the Stone Mansion offers an elegant and refreshing alternative for a secluded office retreat, a relaxing picnic or a **restive** holiday party. USE **restful**.

  Descriptive dictionaries, which feed on this sort of foolishness, will surely one day insist that **restive** does mean **restful**.

RETICENT

Misused for **reluctant** (or similar words). • Despite the seemingly endless challenges, Gallup appears **reticent** to give up either of his jobs. USE **reluctant**. • Without this information, leaders are unclear about where to invest resources and thus are **reticent** to do so. USE **reluctant**. • More enterprises have been less **reticent** to gamble on Linux during the last eighteen months. USE **disinclined**.

  Reticent means disinclined to speak; taciturn; quiet. **Reluctant** means disinclined to do something; unwilling; loath. Because some people mistakenly use **reticent** to mean **reluctant**, dictionaries now maintain **reticent** does mean **reluctant**. Dictionaries actually promote the misuse of the English language.

RIFLE

Misused for **riffle**. • We **rifled** through the book for recipes and found one called Roast Pork Tenderloin with Leeks and Whole Grain Mustard Sauce. USE **riffled**. • And having **rifled** through all the cards in our warehouse, I can understand why the price point for the Ultimate Memorabilia sits where it does. USE **riffled**.

*To **rifle** (RI-fel) means to ransack or pillage; to steal; to cut spiral grooves on the inside of; to hurl with great speed. To **riffle** (RIF-el) means to leaf through a book; to shuffle cards.*

RIPE WITH

Misused for **rife with**. • Pivotal scenes between Tony Soprano and his lady "shrink" are **ripe with** moral ambiguities. USE **rife with**. • Nastier-than-thou tracks "P-Poppin'" and "Blow It Out" are **ripe with** adult content that would make Howard Stern blush. USE **rife with**. • What the show inadvertently says is that in the Bay Area, artists are creating chairs, tables and lighting **ripe with** symbolism and metaphor. USE **rife with**. • It never took long to find company at places like this, and the Dragon's Inn in particular was **ripe with** men looking for companions. USE **rife with**.

*Ripe means ready to be harvested; mature; fully grown or developed; pungent or foul smelling. Rife means widespread; plentiful. Rife with means full of. Infuriatingly, some dictionaries—the worst of them—claim that **ripe with** also means full of. Once we confuse the meanings of words, little is left for us to depend on.*

The debate, ripe with accusations, interruptions, barbs and knee-slapping ripostes, was more entertaining than any game show.
—**Karen Breslau, *Newsweek***

*Ms. Breslau apparently does not know the difference between the words **ripe** and **rife**. If her dictionary says **ripe** means the same as **rife**, she's as much of a fool for believing it as the dictionary's editors are for writing it.*

RISE

Misused for **raise**. The verb **rise** means to assume a standing position or to move to a higher position. The verb **raise** means to move something to a higher position. **Raise** often takes an object; **rise** does not. SEE ALSO **sit**.

Present	Present Participle	Past	Past Participle
rise	(am) rising	rose	(have) risen
raise	(am) raising	raised	(have) raised

R

-'S

Solecistic for **-s**. • In the **1870's**, the Japanese emperor wanted to move away from that traditional approach and make Japan a secular nation, which it is today. USE **1870s**. • Plump **banana's** on sale. USE **bananas**. • So we muddled through the purchase by the seat of our **pant's**. USE **pants**. • We provide free **gift's** to all our riders and if there is something we can do for you, please don't hesitate to ask. USE **gifts**. • Where wood is likely to come into direct contact with fish, it is essential that the preservative used does not taint **foodstuff's** and is nontoxic to humans. USE **foodstuffs**. • If you have any questions or comments about our **chat's**, then please contact us. USE **chats**. • When putting mustard on your **hotdog's** use American mustard and not hot English mustard. USE **hotdogs**.

Use an apostrophe to show possession, not to show plurality (except in a few specific instances such as with numbers, 1's, 2's, and letters, a's, b's).

SACRELIGIOUS

Misspelling of **sacrilegious**. • It almost felt **sacreligious** that my first gondola ride was not with someone that I was actually in love with. USE **sacrilegious**. • The one scene that I could really do without would be, of course, the extremely **sacreligious** scene in the middle of the show. USE **sacrilegious**.

*The adjectival form of **sacrilege** is spelled **sacrilegious**, not **sacreligious**.*

SALUBRIOUS

Misused for **salacious**. • Grab yourself a nice stiff drink, preferably a martini, and check out the **salubrious** sounds of Sexy Diablo. USE **salacious**. • He also appears to feel warranted in partaking in the **salubrious** joys of a swinging single life. USE **sala-**

cious. • An absolute must for the girl on the move, this excellent love shortie is in the style of the one worn by the **salubrious** Jennifer Lopez. USE **salacious**. • It was a long, **salubrious** kiss with twisting exploring tongues darting in and out. USE **salacious**.

*Salacious means lustful or lecherous; obscene. **Salubrious**, though it sounds rather sexy (compare **lubricious**) means something quite different: conducive or favorable to health or well-being; wholesome.*

British actor Hugh Grant's hopes of buying a luxury retreat off France's Cote d'Azur could be scuppered by locals who disapprove of his salubrious past.
—**Contactmusic.com**

SANCTION

*Confused with **sanction**. **Sanction** has nearly opposite meanings: either to authorize or approve ("Since receiving that prize, Arafat has continued to **sanction** and even order terrorist attacks against Israeli Jews") or to penalize or punish ("A judge's decision to **sanction** one of Denver's premier law firms last week could lead to stern discipline for some of its lawyers but is unlikely to damage the firm's reputation or bottom line").*

SANGUINE

Misused for **sanguinary**. • A monastic life was utterly incompatible with the intensely worldly activity of the warrior, nor could the promised peace of mind in secular life be attained, even with the purest faith in his capacity, amid the **sanguine** warfare that was his vocation. USE **sanguinary**. • The proliferation of light weapons in the country was an enabling factor in prolonging a particularly **sanguine** war. USE **sanguinary**.

*Sanguine means cheerful and optimistic; ruddy; of the color of blood. **Sanguinary** means accompanied by bloodshed and carnage; bloodthirsty.*

Being sanguine, I've been lucky in having had a
steady donor, who is my husband.
—**Barbie Cantu, Vampire Church**

*Barbie, managing director of the Texas Vampire Association, is hardly **sanguine**; she is **sanguinary**. By confusing the words, she gives vampires a very bad name indeed.*

SANS

Idiotic for **without**. • And most of that air is getting pulled right through your mouth—**sans** filtering—into your lungs. USE **without**. • Walter Cronkite was once named the most trusted man in America because he could be relied on to report the facts fairly and **sans** bias. USE **without**. • The event takes place at the Agenda restaurant, and tickets are $150 ($75 for show and party, **sans** dinner). USE **without**. • He's a man **sans** a plan. USE **without**.

*There is no need at all to use the Gallicism **sans** instead of **without**.*

SCURRILOUS

I thought *scurrilous* meant using foul
language, but the only sense I hear
the word used these days is exempli-
fied in sentences like these:

"Of course, the Bush campaign's *scurrilous* lies about Kerry's record as a
war hero must be challenged forcefully."

"But given the *scurrilous* campaign
of radical feminists to undermine the constitutionally protected
right of due process, perhaps it is they who owe a letter of apol-
ogy to Mr. Bryant."

Scurrilous (SKUR-ah-les) *does mean expressed in, or given to, coarse or vulgar language. But **scurrilous**, which originally meant speaking the language of a buffoon, has taken on still another meaning, which only some dictionaries now recognize: making defamatory claims about someone. My suspicion is that people confuse **scurrilous** with **scandalous**, and thus, today, many dictionaries foolishly maintain that **scurrilous** is a synonym for making scandalous or defamatory remarks.*

*There is no need for **scurrilous** to mean scandalous since we have that word and others, but to lose, or be about to lose, **scurrilous** in the sense of expressing coarse language is a shame, for with the loss of that meaning there is increasing, if unspoken, permission to use foul language—about which I complain not for senseless moral reasons but for sound linguistic ones.*

S

SEGUAY

Misspelling of **segue**. • I think many people are looking to **seguay** from 9 to 5, time constraints and traffic, into being able to develop an income producing situation that mirrors their values and beliefs. USE **segue**. • That story is only useful as a **seguay** to one of my favorite geek poems, "Abort, Retry, Ignore." USE **segue**.

*Segue, not **seguay**, not **segway**, means to transition from one part to another; to continue without pause from one musical theme to another.*

SEIZE

Misused for **cease**. • Farming the way we know it has changed dramatically, but it will **seize** to exist if we don't do something to increase our income without government help. USE **cease**. • I never **seize** to be amazed by the sheer hugeness of biological complexity and the beauty and elegance of biological design. USE **cease**.

And **cease** is misused for **seize**: • Ian tries to combine that idea with "carpe diem" or "**cease** the day." USE **seize**.

*To **seize** means take hold of suddenly and forcibly; capture using force; confiscate; take eagerly and decisively; to fuse with another part as a result of high pressure or heat. To **cease** means put an end to; discontinue.*

SELDOMLY

Solecistic for **seldom**. • We held this local rally for those who can't go to a large city protest, and to gather members of the community we see so **seldomly**. USE **seldom**. • Kerry is seen as a loner in Washington, **seldomly** socializing out on the town and keeping most acquaintances as just that. USE **seldom**. • Bartow left the press podium with a **seldomly** seen smile. USE **seldom**. • If you are going to eat sweet foods, try to eat them **seldomly** and in small amounts, then have them with a high fiber meal rather than alone. USE **seldom**.

> *The adjective (meaning rare or infrequent), though archaic, is **seldom**, and the adverb (meaning rarely or infrequently) is **seldom**, not **seldomly**. SEE ALSO -**ly**; **oftenly**.*

-SELF

Misused for **me** (or similar words) • Richard and **myself** are going to lunch. USE **I**. • Very large people like **yourself** can eat tiny amounts of food and not lose an ounce. USE **you**. • Let's hope someone comes along, like **myself**, to take his place. USE **me**. • We feel Mr. Roedler's comments do an injustice to collectors like **ourselves** who currently pay $1,500 to $2,000 for radios of this type. USE **us**. • Neither the mayor nor **myself** desires to comment on the status of the matter. USE **I**.

> *Some people, uncertain of which pronoun (**I** or **me**, **he** or **him**, **she** or **her**, **we** or **us**) to use, depend on -**self** pronouns; others, still less deliberate, apparently have no idea that these reflexive pronouns are improperly used in the contexts shown here. A relexive pronoun is used either to refer to another word in a sentence (She injured **herself**") or to emphasize another word ("He **himself** is at fault").*

But while I confided in Sally a lot about the distress between my mother and myself, she never did the same with me.

—Susie Bright, Salon.com

A heartrending story, from which this sentence comes, is made less moving when bad grammar encumbers the telling of it.

I copied the following sentence from my school's superintendent's newsletter:

"Over 150 senior citizens, including myself, are scheduled to watch the dress rehearsal for *Les Miserables*."

Is this the correct use of the reflexive pronoun? I think that "including me" is correct.

*People of all ages and stations in life make grammatical errors. Here, **myself** is indeed incorrect.*

*Some people are reluctant to use the word **me**, considering it a humble substitute for the more stately sounding **myself**. Others rely on reflexive pronouns like **myself** when they are unsure of which case to use—the nominative (**I**) or objective (**me**).*

*Far from sounding regal, however, **myself** (or **I**), when used where **me** is required, sounds clownish, whatever a person's age or profession.*

S

SELF-DEPRECATE

Misused for **self-depreciate**. • In almost every role he takes on, Stiller is the poster boy for **self-deprecation** and disaster. USE **self-depreciation**. • That wry, **self-deprecating** humor is one of the pleasant surprises of *Unvanquished*, an otherwise bitter account of the United Nations' struggles with a hostile United States. USE **self-depreciating**.

*The distinction between **self-deprecate** and **self-depreciate** has been almost wholly eroded by careless writers and speakers—and, of course, the dictionaries that record their errors so that others can make them as well. **Deprecate** means to disapprove of, whereas **depreciate** means to belittle. The confusion is most often found when **self-deprecating** is used instead of **self-depreciating**.*

SENSUAL

Misused for **sensuous**. • Heads turn and diners salivate as the waiter at New York's Zenith restaurant brings a sizzling plate of mushroom steak, steaming with the lusty scent of garlic and **sensual** Asian spices. USE **sensuous**. • The Eid, which occurs this year on or about Dec. 27, ends the month when Muslims abstain from food, drink and other **sensual** pleasures from daybreak to sunset and concentrate on God's commandments. USE **sensuous**. • We all live in a **sensual** world, but often we are too busy to realize the joy in life. USE **sensuous**.

And **sensuous** is sometimes misused for **sensual**: • How long have you been searching for erotic sex with stimulating babes, seductive girls and **sensuous** women? USE **sensual**.

*The word **sensuous** is used in reference to the senses, especially those concerned with aesthetic pleasures such as art or food; **sensual** is properly restricted to the physical senses, especially sexual pleasure.*

SEPARATE OUT

Solecistic for **separate** (or similar words). • We're trying to **separate out** what happened with the helicopter from what happened to our people out there. DELETE **out**. • The oak on the Chardonnay seems to **separate out** into a resinous slick, while the fruit tastes fat, almost rancid, instead of buttery. DELETE **out**. • UPS will **separate out** the packages that are to be delivered to the rural areas and turn them over to the local post office for final delivery. DELETE **out**. • We define "play in Peoria" but didn't **separate** it **out** from the rest of the entry, so we didn't specifically look for the earliest example of this phrase. DELETE **out**.

*We don't need the **out** in **separate out** any more than we do in **stress out** or **print out**. Separate, stress, print, alone, all express the meaning fully.*

SEPERATE

Misspelling of **separate**. • There might be a chapter for each class and a **seperate** section for each method. USE **separate**. • Hotel Vianen A2 has 222 hotel rooms, all with bath, **seperate** shower and toilet. USE **separate**.

*People who do not read or, much the same thing, who read only to be told a story, are likely to spell **seperate**. These people do not attend to words or sentences, to how they are spelled or fashioned. The tale interests them, not the telling.*

SERIAL

Misused for **cereal**. • My host family always eat **serial** or toast for the breakfast, but on Saturday and Sunday they always eat a hot cake for breakfast. USE **cereal**. • Eat this brand of soda, or this burger, or this breakfast **serial** and you too could turn out just like me, naively, selfishly, greedily and arrogantly flogging a dangerous product to kids. USE **cereal**.

*Though this misusage is well known among punsters and clowns ("Could crop circles be the work of a **cereal** killer?"), others less clever do indeed confuse the words.*

SHERBERT

Misspelling of **sherbet**. • Pat beeng-soo (**sherbert** dish) is a kind of Korean sundae with ice, fruit and syrup. USE **sherbet**. • Orange Freeze: 4 cups orange **sherbert**, 2 cups orange juice 1/4 cup Sue Bee Honey 1/2 cup milk. USE **sherbet**.

*Even though some dictionaries maintain that **sherbert** (SHUR-bert) is acceptable, **sherbet** (SHUR-bit) is the only correct spelling (and pronunciation). Dictionaries have virtually no standards, offer scant guidance, and advance only misunderstanding.*

SHIBBOLETH

*Solecistic for **truism** (or similar words). A dictionary or two holds that **shibboleth** (SHIB-ah-lith) means a truism; a commonplace saying. But this is simply what people have mistakenly come to believe **shibboleth** means. And dictionaries, ignominiously pandering to the public, record the definition. A **shibboleth** is an identifying word, phrase, custom, or belief that distinguishes a sect, group, or class; a password or watchword.*

SHOP (IT) AGAINST

Idiotic for **compare (it) to (with)**. • Most will **shop it against** the Contour, Malibu and Altima, which are really small cars positioned between those segments. USE compare it with. • **Shop it against** the Audi A4 or BMW 325i and it seems like a bargain. USE **Compare it to.** • And by all means, **shop one against** the other. USE **compare one to.**

> *Apparently created by marketing people,* **shop against** *is an ugly phrase. Though using* **against** *instead of* **with** *or* **to** *in the phrase* **compare against** *is common (and quite wrong), using* **shop** *instead of* **compare** *is contemptible for it insinuates—certainly more than* **compare**—*you should buy. SEE ALSO* **gift...(with).**

SHUTTER

Misused for **shudder.** • I hope to have another baby in a few years, but the thought of going through this again makes me **shutter** with fear. USE **shudder.** • Just the name of Jesus caused the demons to **shutter** and tremble and run and flee in a hundred other directions. USE **shudder.** • Knowing this, we **shutter** to realize that surely this is not the last of their diabolical deeds. USE **shudder.** • Can we distort what God designed with His own hands anymore than this? I **shutter** to think about it. USE **shudder.**

> *A* **shutter** *is anything used to cover a window or other opening. To* **shudder** *means to tremble or quiver.*

SHORT-LIVED

Which is the correct pronunciation of *short-lived*: is it LIVED with a short-sounding *i* or LIVED with a long-sounding *i*?

Even though most people today pronounce the word with a short **i** *sound, the long* **i** *is correct. The lived of* **short-lived** *derives from the word* **life**, *not the word* **live**.

SIGHT

Misused for **site**. • It does not do any good to advertise on our web **sight** if no one knows about it, so our web **sight** is advertised locally through business cards, signs, brochures and other means. USE **site**. • We were also impressed with the fact that you are on the building **sight** a great amount of time during the construction. USE **site**.

Sight is the ability to see; seeing; something seen; the foreseeable future; mental perception. Site is a place or location; a web site. SEE ALSO site.

SIT

Misused for set. The verb sit means to assume or be in a sitting position. The verb set means to put or place something. Set often takes an object; sit seldom does. SEE ALSO rise.

Present	Present Participle	Past	Past Participle
sit	(am) sitting	sat	(have) sat
set	(am) setting	set	(have) set

SITE

Misused for **cite**. • Pedestrians, bicyclists and any other highway user can be **sited** for failing to comply with these signals. USE **cited**. • The night Norman Wickes and his son were **sited** with the ticket that landed them in court, it was 28 degrees outside and all the shelters were full. USE **cited**. • All information **sited** and given on this site is copyright its original owner and author in full. USE **cited**.

The verb cite means to quote or refer to; to commend for meritorious action; to enumerate; to call before a court of law. The verb site means to locate, and the noun means a location. SEE ALSO sight.

SLACKARD

Misused for **slacker**. • I cannot empathize with a **slackard**, a shirker, and a coward. USE **slacker**. • I challenge anyone to observe one of my lessons and call me a **slack**-

ard; I am a professional—not a **slackard**. USE **slacker**. • It makes no distinction between young and old, good or evil, **slackard** or enthusiast, phylum, species or sub-species. USE **slacker**.

> Though **laggard** and **sluggard, drunkard** and **dullard** are words, **slackard** is not; it is inadmissible.

SLANDEROUS

Misused for **libelous**. • He has routinely abused his position by writing **slanderous** statements and in some cases, blatant lies about me. USE **libelous**. • Fortune magazine has launched an invective, vitriolic, **slanderous** campaign against the Vatican by committing the major sin of journalism—assuming facts that aren't there and condemning with no proof in regards to a scam manipulated by a priest singlehandedly. USE **libelous**.

> The difference between **slander** and **libel** (at least in the United States) is the difference between spoken and written (or recorded) calumny.

SLIGHT-OF-HAND

Misspelling of **sleight-of-hand**. • But despite a little late-game **slight-of-hand** that led to the Patriots tying the score with only 1:16 to play, it was the Cougars who pulled a rabbit out of the hat along with a 2-1 win in overtime. USE **sleight-of-hand**. • WorldCom used a basic accounting **slight-of-hand** to inflate profits. USE **sleight-of-hand**.

> **Sleight of hand** is the skillful use of one's hands to perform tricks or magic; legerdemain; the trick or tricks performed; skillful deception or trickery.

The leaked letter brought to light a host of touchy subjects for the administration, necessitating yet more feats of rhetorical slight-of-hand.
—*Mother Jones*

*Rhetorical **sleight-of-hand** is nothing we could charge this clumsy "mishandler" with.*

SLUFF

Misspelling of **slough**. • He will **sluff** off any questions about whether it actually works. USE **slough**. • These diseased cells inside the gut **sluff** off, are excreted, and can infect other pigs. USE **slough**. • They can't **sluff** off responsibility by blaming God or the Devil. USE **slough**.

> To **slough** means to cast off or shed. **Sluff** (SLUF) is the pronunciation of **slough**, nothing more.

Sluff off is also sometimes used to mean goof off, be idle, or malinger. • You can use the weight room at St. Ben's all you want, but there are times when it's easy to **sluff off**. • He did his work and didn't **sluff off**.

And to some school administrators and their students, the word means tardy: • Unexcused absences are considered a **sluff**. • Students who are more than twenty minutes late to class will be marked as a **sluff**.

S

SO DON'T I

Idiotic for **so do I**. • The crowd liked that number and **so don't I**. USE **so do I**. • You live in Vermont, don't you? **So don't I**. USE **So do I**. • I know you hate me. **So don't I**. USE **So do I**.

> By **so don't I** (or, say, **so doesn't he**), people mean **so do I** (or **so does he**). If you do not use the contraction (if you use **do not** instead of **don't**), you quickly see how silly the expression can be.

SOLUTION

Idiotic for **solve** (or similar words). • They talk about the events that are important to them: love, financial situation, brainstorming about **solutioning** problems, etc. USE **solving**. • I explain my problem because if it isn't possible maybe there is a workaround or another way to **solution** the problem. USE **solve**.

> **Solution** is a noun, not (though many businesspeople and others equally ill-advised may demur) a verb. **Solution** makes a very bad verb indeed.

SOME

Solecistic for **somewhat**. • Fishing has slowed **some** but there are still some good fish to be caught. USE **somewhat**. • I still think these are great magazines, though *CGW* has fallen off **some** in the past few years. USE **somewhat**. • It rained **some** this morning. USE **somewhat**. • While they might respect and even love her **some**, they had no regard for her quest. USE **somewhat**. • This felt really great but also frightened me **some**. USE **somewhat**.

*In sentences such as these, use **somewhat**, not **some**, as an adverb.*

SOMEWHAT OF A

Solecistic for **something of a** or **somewhat -ing**. • One wonders why a film with such high quality production values, a solid young cast, and such timeless themes can prove **somewhat of a bore**. USE **something of a bore**. • Getting there was **somewhat of a challenge**, but Tammara Cole, Mike Doosey, David Mathis and Trey Cavin all agreed that the view was spectacular. USE **somewhat challenging**. • Her extremely sexy voice has become **somewhat of a trademark** that she exploits very well. USE **something of a trademark**. • It is **somewhat of a surprise** that this works. USE **somewhat surprising**.

***Somewhat** is an adverb (meaning rather; to some extent or degree); do not use **somewhat** as a pronoun (meaning something).*

SOMULENT

Solecistic for **somnolent**. • Managers have very different ways of managing portfolios—from fast and loose to slow and **somulent**. USE **somnolent**. • Rather than still and **somulent**, these guys are bright-eyed and bushy-tailed—so to speak. USE **somnolent**. • Approximately seven hours postoperatively, the patient became significantly **somulent**, and was not responsive to verbal stimuli. USE **somnolent**.

***Somnolent** (SOM-nah-lent)—meaning sleepy; inducing sleep; soporific—is the word, not **somulent**.*

SORTED

Misspelling of **sordid.** • Tasteless paintings of nudes engaged in all sorts of **sorted** behavior adorn the walls. USE **sordid.** • Now, with this **sorted** story coming to light, it only serves to call Allstate's motives and methods further into question. USE **sordid.** • Not at anytime in my life did I ever think that the God of Heaven was behind the **sorted** behavior exhibited to me throughout my stay in the Church of Jesus Christ of Latter-day Saints. USE **sordid.**

Sordid means base or ignoble; squalid or filthy. **Sorted** is the past participle of **sort**.

SPADE

Misused for **spayed.** • The adoption fee for a neutered and **spade** dog is $200, and $175 for a non-neutered and **spade** dog. USE **spayed.**

Spade is a tool to dig with; one of the four suits in a deck of cards. **Spay** is to remove surgically an animal's ovaries.

SPIRITUAL

Confused with **religious.** **Spiritual** means relating to the soul or spirit; relating to religion or the sacred. **Religious** means relating to religion, the church, and worship; pious. A **spiritual** person is not necessarily **religious** any more than a **religious** person is necessarily **spiritual.** SEE ALSO **spirituel; spirituous.**

SPIRITUEL

Misused for **spiritual.** • Helena Tornberg Malpana offers you services in mental and **spirituel** well-being and health care. USE **spiritual.** • I am able to relate through the **spirituel** world the path you need to be on and the direction you need to take to achieve happiness, prosperity and success. USE **spiritual.**

Spiritual (SPIR-i-choo-el) means relating to the spiritual rather than the material world, to the church or god, to the supernatural. **Spirituel** (spir-i-choo-EL), in English, means having a refined intellect. **Spiritual** people (or people who contend they are) are mundane, in abundance, whereas **spirituel** ones scarcely exist; for that reason, the use of **spirituel** is most often a mistake for **spiritual.** SEE ALSO **spiritual.**

SPIRITUOUS

Confused with **spiritual**. **Spirituous** means alcoholic or distilled ("You don't need to go see half-naked ladies or indulge in **spirituous** liquor on the weekends to have a good time"). **Spiritual** means relating to the human spirit or soul rather than to material or physical concerns; relating to religion. SEE ALSO **spiritual**.

SPLITTING IMAGE

Misspelling of **spitting image**. • My daughter is the **splitting image** of my mother. USE **spitting image**. • I found a web site of a different actress named Katie Stuart who is also a young teen girl and just happens to be the **splitting image** of Kitty Pryde. USE **spitting image**. • A revamped 2005 Nissan Frontier is the **splitting image** of the company's Mississippi-made truck. USE **spitting image**.

Spitting image, not *splitting image*, is the correct expression.

STALACTITE

Confused with **stalagmite**. Both words refer to icicle-shaped calcium deposits that form inside caves. The difference is that a **stalactite** is a column of deposits that hangs from the roof, whereas a **stalagmite** rises from the floor.

START OFF (OUT)

Solecistic for **start**. • Many people **start off** with good intentions, but the resolve for the resolution soon fades. DELETE **off**. • Here are some of the millionaire's tactics to **start off** the New Year in a great new way. DELETE **off**. • His plan is to **start out** slowly and be inconspicuous for a while. DELETE **out**. • But the year certainly did not **start out** well, dominated as it was by the war in Iraq. DELETE **out**.

*Neither **start off** nor **start out** says anything more than **start** itself does. SEE ALSO **first off**.*

STATIONARY

Misused for **stationery**. • Shop for your favorite greeting cards and **stationary** in the comfort of your own home. USE **stationery**. • Digital 2000 is the leading supplier of office consumables and **stationary** to businesses throughout the U.K. USE **stationery**.

> **Stationary**, an adjective, means not moving; the noun **stationery** means writing paper.

What's more, **stationery** is also misused for **stationary**. • With Ballard focusing on PEM units for **stationery** power plants and transportation applications, and Plug Power focusing on homes and small businesses, we expect DCH Technology to be the leader in the portable power application. USE **stationary**. • If the treadmill, stairmaster, rowing machine or **stationery** cycle doesn't excite you, sample some group activities that strike your fancy. USE **stationary**.

> Wherever they're trying to fly, they'll never arrive and I think of mailing a letter to my neighbors on government stationary demanding the removal of all metaphors from lawns....
>
> **—Bob Hicok, "Middle Age," Poetry**

S

STATUE

Misused for **statute**. • AAUW will support efforts to extend the legal **statue** of limitations in cases of gender discrimination, harassment, and retaliation. USE **statute**. • Students attending the Nevada campus are required by Nevada Regulatory **Statue** to complete course work in the essentials of the Constitution of the United States and the Constitution of the State of Nevada. USE **Statute**.

> A **statue** (STACH-oo) is a figure of a person, animal, or abstract design made of wood, bronze, or other material. A **statute** (STACH-oot) is an established regulation; a law passed by a legislative body.

STATURE

Misused for **statue**. • My love of New York City inspired me to create replicas of the Empire State Building, the **Stature** of Liberty and the World Trade Center. USE **Statue**. • It is the only **stature** erected to honor the memory of Tennessee's famous hunter, frontiersman, soldier, legislator, statesman, patriot and Hero of the Alamo, Colonel David Crockett. USE **statue**.

> *Stature* *(STACH-er) is the height of a person or animal; a person's status or level of success. A* *statue* *is a sculpted, carved, molded, or cast figure.*

STAUNCH

Misused for **stanch**. • Soldiers wore rubies to **staunch** the blood of wounds received in battle and as a talisman against getting shot by arrows. USE **stanch**. • Local children vow to **staunch** the flow of drugs and alcohol. USE **stanch**. • As carriers take desperate measures to **staunch** their losses, cargo initiatives are in danger of dying because of lack of commitment and resources. USE **stanch**.

> *Stanch, a verb, means to stop the flow of blood or other liquid.* *Staunch, an adjective, means firm, faithful, loyal, steadfast; strong or solidly made; substantial. Since so many people confuse one word, or spelling, with the other, dictionaries offer one word as the variant of the other.*

STEP FOOT IN

> *Step foot in sets my teeth on edge--should be set foot in--but I hear it all the time. Ditto for to no end in phrases such as "He bothered me to no end"--where to my ear (or mind) the to simply does not belong. Do the phrases that bother me qualify as variant usages, or are they simply mistakes?*

> *The correct, well-established idioms are, as you know,* *set foot in* *(meaning go into) and* *no end* *(meaning very much; to a great degree). The phrases*

you complain of are bastardizations born of mishearing and nurtured by imitation. Those who embrace a descriptive approach toward language will certainly maintain that—since these expressions are indeed found in our speech and, even, writing—they are acceptable usages. These are the same people who are disinclined to reject **for all intensive purposes**, **beckon call**, and other equally monstrous expressions.

STIGMATISM

Misused for **astigmatism**. • Soft lens to correct **stigmatism** was a big breakthrough in the '80s. USE **astigmatism**. • I went to an eye exam yesterday to find out that my **stigmatism** has gotten worse yet again. USE **astigmatism**.

Stigmatism *is normal vision;* *astigmatism* *is a visual defect.*

S

STRAIGHT-LACED

Misspelling of **strait-laced**. • He's as healthy and **straight-laced** a guy as you'll meet, and in today's society, that is amazing. USE **strait-laced**. • Anyone who's worked in advertising knows it's not exactly a **straight-laced** environment. USE **strait-laced**. • There were those in the media who, **straight-laced** and rigid in their ways, objected strongly and publicly to the use of a seventeen-year-old as a sex symbol. USE **strait-laced**.

Strait-laced *means having strict or severe moral views.* (*Strait* *is from the Latin* strictus, *strict.) The variant spelling, as descriptive dictionaries label* ***straight-laced****, is, in truth, a misspelling. (Descriptive dictionaries seldom label usage mistakes honestly.) The responsibility they had as arbiters of language, dictionaries long ago abnegated. And since they no longer espouse correctness or clarity in language, we obviously can no longer regard them as having much authority in these matters.*

STRAIT

*Confused with **straight**. **Straight** means having no curves or angles; not crooked; upright; undeviating; honest; in a row; and several other meanings ("The Bengals came in looking to enhance their turnaround season with a fifth **straight** win"; "This site provides some **straight** talk about developmental verbal dyspraxia"; "The Y intercept of a **straight** line is simply where the line crosses the Y axis"). **Strait**, as a noun, means a narrow waterway connecting two bodies of water; (usu. plural) distress or difficulty. As an adjective, it means narrow or confined. ("The U.S. has repeated a call for both sides to back off from their rhetoric to assure stability in the Taiwan **Strait**"; "The bridge district has been in such severe financial **straits** that it slashed bus service by a third last month").*

SUBLIMINAL

*The pronunciation of **subliminal** is (sub-LIM-ah-nel), not (sub-LIM-in-ah-ble).*

I don't think there is a plot to try to put subliminal messages in the people's minds.
—U.S. President George W. Bush

*Bush, here, couldn't seem to manage the proper pronunciation of **subliminal**, for he said sub-lim-in-ah-ble— repeatedly.*

SUPERCEDE

Misspelling of **supersede**. • It also determines that basic laws **supercede** regular laws. USE **supersede**. • All amendments **supercede** the initial bylaws and all later (more recent) amendments **supercede** earlier amendments. USE **supersede**.

*   ***Supersede** is the correct spelling; **supercede**, whatever your dictionary may suggest, is not an acceptable spelling.*

To be fair, the future that the robot symbolizes hasn't arrived because it has been superceded by an alternate future: the age of soft machines.

—Red Herring

This is only one of (at least) three instances in one issue of Red Herring *magazine where* **supercede** *is used instead of* **supersede**.

SUPERITY

Idiotic for **superiority** (or **superior**). • Since then, Chinese movies have had a total **superity** over the western. USE **superiority**. • This market **superity** has placed Nasdaq ahead in name recognition even though ECNs execute roughly 30 percent of all Nasdaq stock trades. USE **superiority**.

To eeyores, **superity** *is a gloomy collection of letters, too few to mean anything. "Nobody minds. Nobody cares. Pathetic, that's what it is." SEE ALSO* **meritous**.

SUPPOSABLY

Solecistic for **supposedly**. • Everything God has ever **supposably** said is in the Bible. USE **supposedly**. • **Supposably** people can't figure this out for themselves. USE **Supposedly**. • The vet gave him an injection of antibiotics or some such thing **supposably** to help the tendons and bones form together better. USE **supposedly**. • He was killed in action, but he **supposably** saved his whole platoon. USE **supposedly**.

Supposably means capable of being thought or supposed. Supposedly means presumably or seemingly. Supposably is not a synonym for supposedly; indeed, it exists as such only in the minds of muddled speakers and failed writers. SEE ALSO **supposingly**.

SUPPOSE TO

Solecistic for **supposed to.** • Midland was **suppose to** play Calamus-Wheatland Friday night in basketball. USE **supposed to.** • As long as these Marines keep doing their jobs the way they are **suppose to**, HMH-363 should be celebrating 40,000 and even 60,000 mishap-free hours in the years to come. USE **supposed to.**

Supposed to, *not* **suppose to**, *is the correct expression. SEE ALSO* **use to**.

SUPPOSINGLY

Solecistic for **supposedly.** • Hazel had a brother named James McCoy who died in Redford, Michigan, and a sister, Pearl, who **supposingly** is still living, **supposingly** in Texas. USE **supposedly.** • Come experience a self guided tour of a **supposingly** abandoned corporate facility where a strange unearthly discovery slaughtered everyone who was in contact with it. USE **supposedly.**

Like **supposably**, **supposingly** *is incorrect for* **supposedly**. *The ignominy that people experience from using these incorrect words is well deserved. SEE ALSO* **supposably**.

SURE AND

Solecistic for **sure to.** • Be **sure and** translate the META tags and title too. USE **sure to.** • As you browse, be **sure and** visit the Useful Links page for resources and reviews on computers and technology. USE **sure to.** • Hey parents, make **sure and** visit the Magazine Rack for magazines just for parents! USE **sure to.** • Be **sure and** check out these other sites to find more women looking for relationships. USE **sure to.**

Like **try and**, **sure and** *is ungrammatical, and more evidence (along with, for instance,* **congradulate***) that how people speak is not necessarily how they should write. SEE ALSO* **try and**.

SYMPATHY

Confused with **empathy**. **Sympathy** *is compassion or pity for another person ("Today is World AIDS Day. The members of public will offer some* **sympathy***. But, everything will be forgotten tomorrow"; "U.S. Secretary of State Colin Powell has* telephoned Japan's foreign minister to express his **sympathy** for the killings of two Japanese diplomats in Iraq"); **empathy**, the ability to imagine how another person feels ("Studies show that around two years of age, children start to show genuine **empathy**, understanding how other people feel even when they don't feel the same way"; "Let's face it, they personify every ugly suspicion you've ever had about the very rich: the overwhelming arrogance, the shocking ignorance, the absence of **empathy** for anyone whose background differs from theirs").

SYRUP

The pronunciation of **syrup** is (SIR-up), not (SURP).

S

TAUNT

Misused for **taut**. • The details became more vivid after the obvious action details were listed because students began looking for facial expressions, subtler interactions, and emotional/sensual detail such as "the **taunt** rope burns the clutching hands," and "the tall photographer with the open, unloaded camera stares at his missed shot." USE **taut**. • He watched her walk toward the bathroom, her **taunt** belly bouncing with the movement. USE **taut**. • Using a very complex system of weights and counterweights forces the hammer to strike a stiff, **taunt** string. USE **taut**. • When a patient develops a distended and **taunt** abdomen, the measurement of abdominal compartment pressure can help with early recognition of organ dysfunction. USE **taut**. • Still, a movie that offers such beautiful acting, such well considered direction and such **taunt** writing is a movie simply asking to be considered on its own terms. USE **taut**.

> To **taunt** means to mock or insult in a contemptuous manner; to ridicule. **Taut**, an adjective, means pulled or stretched tight, not slack; tense, not relaxed; concise and controlled.

TEMPERMENT

Misspelling of **temperament**. • Hicks said Denley has the even **temperment**, sense of humor and ethics needed to be a high school principal. USE **temperament**. • I believe I have both the **temperment** and experience to help meet these challenges and to insure that our children get the best education possible. USE **temperament**.

> Though the correct pronunciation is (TEM-per-ment), the correct spelling is **temperament**.

TENANT

Misused for **tenet**. • These **tenants** of faith are the basic foundation for Word of Life Center, as well as for all Christianity. USE **tenets**. • These religious **tenants** are legitimate for the good Father and for those members of his church who choose to accept them. USE **tenets**. • On the whole it will adhere to the time honored Republican **tenants** of limited government, limited taxes and freedom as defined by the Constitution and the Bill of Rights. USE **tenets**.

*A **tenant** (TEN-ent) is a person who holds a lease or rents land or property. A **tenet** (TEN-it) is a belief or principle held to be true.*

More recently the concept of humanism has been incorporated into the tenants of Unitarian Universalism, which is practiced by over 160,000 people in the U.S. alone, and many more globally.

—Cynthia D. Trombley, *Observer-Tribune*

*Neither Trombley nor her editor seems to know the meaning of **tenant**. What other words do they not know? What other words do they confuse the meanings of? What thoughts do they not think because they do not know the words to think them with? And of the thoughts they can think, how many are muddled or mistaken because they confuse the words they use to think them?*

Is it merely careless pronunciation, or is it an accepted shift in meaning, that accounts for the now common use of *tenant* in place of *tenet*?

*It's careless pronunciation, careless spelling, careless reading, careless thinking, all of them the ingredients of and the truth behind modern-day dictionary making. No dictionary that I am aware of holds that **tenant** means **tenet**, but every one of them soon will if people do not use the language carefully. As democracy falters when we neglect it, so does language fail.*

TENOR

Misused for **tenure.** • Gus is a college English professor, who has just been granted **tenor.** USE **tenure.** • Navajo should be the center piece of a strong Native American program with **tenor**-track professors. USE **tenure.**

And **tenure** is sometimes misused for **tenor:** • In an Op-Ed, he argued that the **tenure** of the debate has shifted away from free trade policies unconnected to labor or the environment. USE **tenor.** • Our minds, our thinking, govern the **tenure** of our lives. USE **tenor.**

> **Tenor** *has several meanings, including a singing voice between baritone and alto; a singer with such a voice; an instrument such as a saxophone; the general sense or meaning of something; the course of something, such as a person's life.* **Tenure** *is the conditions under which real estate is held; the time during which something is held; the holding of an office; guaranteed permanent employment.*

THANKFULLY

Solecistic for **I am thankful** (or similar phrases). • These folks spent more time on Japanese beetles, a pest that **thankfully** hasn't yet moved into our region. USE **we are thankful.** • Thankfully, this didn't keep him from composing some of the greatest music ever written. USE **Let us be thankful that.**

> **Thankfully** *means* **in a thankful manner***; it does not mean, as in these examples,* **I am thankful** *or* **let us be thankful** *or* **we feel grateful***. The incorrect usage of* **thankfully** *(like* **hopefully***) is virtually all we encounter today. To see either word properly placed in a sentence would be no less than startling, nothing other than joyful ("The producers, Chris Moore and actor Matt Damon, spoke thankfully about HP's generosity in providing equipment and tech help"). SEE ALSO* **hopefully***.*

THAT THERE

Idiotic for **that** • I believe that every living word in **that there** book is as true as gospel. DELETE **there.** • Boy, those girls are sure having a good time washing **that there** car. DELETE **there.** • Can you cite some code for **that there** law? DELETE **there.**

> *Though* **that book there** *is perfectly good English,* **that there book** *is not. SEE ALSO* **this here.**

THAT (THIS) WOULD BE

Unnecessary phrase. • So, how much carbon does a typical car add to the atmosphere each year, anyway? **That would be** about thirty pounds. DELETE **That would be**. • Who is the tour guide? **That would be** me. DELETE **That would be**. • Do you recognize the handwriting and initials? **That would be** my handwriting. **That would be** my initials. USE **That is; These are**. • What is the first storm of the season? **That would be** Arthur. DELETE **That would be**.

*Only people who ape others—people who do not think or listen to what they say—could possibly utter the nonsensical, the comical **that (this) would be**.*

CNN's Charles Lavadera is in one of the hardest hit communities--that would be Port Charlotte.
—Wolf Blitzer, CNN anchor

T

THEIR

Is it ever acceptable to use *their* when referring to a singular corporate entity (e.g., "their awful customer support practices" when referring to the phone company)?

*Yes, you may use **their** to refer to a corporate entity or other group. Corporations, in particular, are increasingly it-like in my view, but good grammar dictates you may refer to **them**—a group of people in the end—in the third-person plural. **It** or **its** is often used when referring to a company or organization, of course, but I wouldn't recommend you write, "I'll never do business with **it** again."*

THEN

Misused for **than**. • There is no science or anything that proves that men are smarter **then** women or women are smarter **then** men. USE **than**. • A good idea lost is no better **then** not having an idea in the first place. USE **than**. • But if you want to guarantee that your parcel packages arrive to their destinations on time, you need to have them in the post office no later **then** Thursday. USE **than**.

And **than** for then: • **Than** we will drive to Bursa, which was the first capital of the Ottoman Empire. USE **Then**. • If the Packers are going to be down three wide receivers this Sunday against the Lions, as it appears they will, **than** somebody has got to budge. USE **then**.

> *Than is used in comparative statements; **then**, which means at that time or next in time or at another time, in temporal ones. **Then** also means besides or moreover; therefore or consequently.*

THERE

Misused for **their**. • Tell them you're not **there** friend any more. USE **their**. • They are already calling for a White Homeland, and have shown **there** willingness to use terror tactics against blacks, with recent bombings in Johannesburg. USE **their**. • They did a few of **there** well known songs, a couple old ones, and a couple new ones. USE **their**.

There is also misused for **they're**: • I think **there** made out of marble. USE **they're**. • Don't turn your back on them, **there** smarter than they look. USE **they're**.

> *Though pronounced alike, **there**, **their**, and **they're** have distinct meanings and uses. **There**, as an adverb, means at, in, or toward that place or point; and, as a noun, that place or point. **Their**, the possessive of **they**, is a word that shows ownership or possession. **They're** is a contraction of **they are**.*

THEREFOR

Misused for **therefore**. • We disagree with both courts and **therefor** reverse and remand the case to the trial court for further proceedings. USE **therefore**. • Responsive tumors are generally fast growing but have normal cell-death mechanisms and **therefor** are susceptible to cancer therapy. USE **therefore**.

Therefor (ther-FOR), a legal term, means *for that*; **therefore** (THER-for) means *hence or consequently*.

THERE IS (THERE'S)

Solecistic for **there are**. • Where we are located **there's** a million people within reach that probably will never get downtown. USE **there are**. • I could write a book about it, but **there's** no hard feelings. USE **there are**. • We're still looking for identity this year, because **there's** so many young guys. USE **there are**. • **There's** just no goals. USE **There are**. • **There's** many, many people that are homeless. USE **There are**.

The plural **are** is necessary when the subject of the sentence is plural; otherwise, **is** is correct. You can often avoid this solecism altogether by not using the word **there**: • Where we are located **there's a million people** within reach that probably will never get downtown. USE **a million people are**. • **There's many, many people that** are homeless. USE **Many, many people**.

This caution also pertains to **there appears** and **there seems**: • In terms of the information that you've got, though, **there seems** to be some inaccuracies. USE **there seem**. • Overall, **there appears** to be more ducks in the west Tennessee area than last year and hunting has been good in several areas. USE **there appear**.

Don't play politics. There's too many people's lives at stake.
—Bono, musician

We're in the airport and there's these two women.
—U.S. Representative Dick Gephardt

Many people apparently do not understand that the verb to use in constructions like these is decided by the words that follow the verb. That is, neither musician Bono nor congressman Gephardt thinks before he speaks.

THESE (THOSE) KIND

Solecistic for **these (those) kinds** (or similar words). • These aren't the **kind** of negotiations where you can predict when the ending will be. USE **kinds**. • These are the **type** of results you can expect when you have the whole team playing well. USE **types**. • They're easy to sell because they're the **sort** of products every household wants and needs, and they're reasonably priced. USE **sorts**.

> *Kind (**sort** and **type**) are singular and should not be used with the word **these**, **those**, or **they**.*

We're going to hear more of these kind of attacks against the president.

—Ed Gillespie, Republican National Committee

Quite clearly you do not need to know basic English grammar to be chairman of the Republican National Committee.

THEY (THEM; THEIR)

Idiotic for **he** (or similar words). • This user has chosen to not list **their** email publicly. USE **his** or **her** or **his or her**. • If you let a student post **their** personal web page, you need to post all students' personal web pages. USE **his** or **her** or **his or her**. • An informed consumer needs to know what **their** choices are for local service and long-distance and bundled service. USE **his** or **her** or **his or her**, or **informed consumers need**. • As a courtesy to the deaf-blind person let **them** know immediately when you arrive and what you or others must be doing. USE **him** or **her** or **him or her**, or **deaf-blind people**. • If you see your child does have those symptoms, keep **them** home. USE **him** or **her** or **him or her**, or **children do**.

> ***They, them,*** *and **their** are plural pronouns; never, neither in spoken nor in written language, should they be used as singular pronouns. Only imprudent people who cannot be bothered to think about what they say (or impudent feminists consumed with resentment over what others say) use (or insist on using) these pronouns as singular.*

He/she and similarly intolerable eyesores are never acceptable. As some of the preceding examples show, rewriting a sentence with a plural, rather than a singular, subject is often a good solution.

Each of the women during this eight-week program developed **their** body as well as **their** mind and emotions. USE **her; her** • Everyone has **their** own story. USE **his** or **her** or **his or her.** • No one wants **their** name and information given to anyone and we at Elante Luggage hold this to be paramount to good business. USE **his** or **her** or **his or her.** • A quick email to thank somebody for **their** time goes a long way. USE **his** or **her** or **his or her.** • How do you tell someone that you love **them?** USE **him** or **her** or **him or her.** • It's time for anyone who still thinks that singular "their" is so-called bad grammar to get rid of **their** prejudices and pedantry! USE **his** or **her** or **his or her.** • When you love somebody, you have to marry **them** and make a family. USE **him** or **her** or **him or her.**

*Also avoid using the plural pronoun **their**, **them**, or **they** following words like **each** and **one**, **every** and **any**, **everyone** and **everybody**, **anyone** and **anybody**, **someone** and **somebody**, and **no one** and **nobody** when the antecedent is clearly singular.*

```
Then the murderer turned their attention to Hey-
ward Brown.
```
—ABC News correspondent

---

*That the English language has no pronoun that neatly includes both genders is a shame, but so it is. **Their** is not the word to use here; **his or her**, cumbersome though it may be in this instance, is better. Of course, it is well established that the masculine form alone applies to both sexes.*

```
If your child won't wake up or they won't drink enough fluids; if your
child seems to be so irritable, they don't want to be held or touched;
or if your child gets sick, gets better, and they get sick again, that's
a sign that a bacterial infection may have set in.
```
—Holly Firfer, CNN

---

*Firfer might have saved herself some embarrassment had she spoken of **children**. Better still, she could have deleted every **they** and made better sense with fewer words.*

You can take a Russian teenager and say recite some poetry, and they will give you strophes of Pushkin.
—**John McWhorter, in *The New York Times***

Linguist McWhorter, though he, unlike many of his colleagues, regrets the decline of the English language, also furthers it.

It is clear there is someone among us who we cannot trust--that one coward, that one sniveling, spineless, gutless coward, that one person who doesn't have the courage to say that they went to the press.
—**James H. Fagan, state representative**

*After all those **ones**, however can this twisty Fagan allow **they** to follow?*

THINGIFY

Idiotic for **objectify** (or similar words). • Anytime we **thingify** another person instead of valuing and honoring the whole individual, that's wrong. USE **dehumanize**. • Lots of us love to **thingify**, just like all of us love generalising. USE **hypostatize**. • Regardless of the social spin-offs here, legalising prostitution would inevitably **thingify** women. USE **objectify**. • The image, be it of electrons, or plants, or animals, or man, is not that of a pack of cards being shuffled. In thinking that way, we too readily **thingify** the universe. USE **secularize**. • Where this most democratic form of government known to man died out almost completely in Europe, it survived even the slave trade in Africa—the worst testament of man's inhumanity to man, the **thingification** of African women and men. USE **commodification**. • I do not believe our understanding is enhanced through the **thingification** of dynamic, meaning seeking processes as if they are static and definitive. USE **reification**.

*As piteous as the word **thing** usually is, it's not nearly so distasteful as **thingify** (and **thingification**). Though the concept is, in many contexts, repugnant, so, too, is this word used to describe it.*

THINKING OUTSIDE THE BOX

I was wondering if you have any views or information about when the phrase *thinking outside the box* infiltrated the language--and what its origins are.

I don't know the origin of the phrase **thinking outside the box**, *but the origin scarcely matters. That people do not tire of this phrase matters, for it has quickly become a hackneyed expression for* **be clever, be creative, be inventive, be original, be innovative**. *People who use this phrase nicely illustrate the antithesis of what it means.*

THIS HERE

Idiotic for **this** • **This here** lady says a victory is more than possible. DELETE **here**. • I thought my candidate would do a better job as governor of **this here** state. DELETE **here**. • It's been a long time since I've written one of those "The Greatest…of All Time" columns, and a topic came up awhile back that I couldn't refuse mentioning in **this here** little column. DELETE **here**.

> The adverb **here** only calls attention to the person who fatuously uses it. SEE ALSO **that there**.

THO

Idiotic for **although** (or similar words). • Online is fine, **tho** I hope you grow large enough and rich enough to offer a mail subscription version, too. USE **although**. • Chrome's music score **tho** should really get some kind of an official award. USE **though**. • On the other hand **tho**, I've never actually seen one in that condition. USE **though**.

> The people who use **tho** are the same people who use **um** and **ah** and **er**; the same people who use **you know** and **I mean** and **whatever**; the same people who use

if you get my meaning and *let me tell you something* and *can I ask you a question?*; the same people who use **trepidacious** for **fearful** and **alot** for **a lot** and **inimical** for **inimitable**. SEE ALSO **altho**.

THREW

Misused for **through**. • She came **threw** with flying colors. USE **through**. • You were one of the best people I ever knew, I will always remember you **threw** and **threw**. USE **through**. • The festival will begin with camp set up and continue **threw** the weekend, finally ending on Sunday night. USE **through**.

And even **threwout** is used instead of **throughout**: • Brad and Mike both were friends **threwout** junior high and high school. USE **throughout**. • The plot is thick and keeps you guessing as to what's going to happen **threwout** the whole book. USE **throughout**.

Threw is the past tense of *throw*. It does not mean *through*. SEE ALSO *through*.

THRONGS

Misused for **throes**. • When the movie opened, the shot of Will Smith in a tub with a woman, obviously in the **throngs** of passion, should have been my first clue this was not going to be appropriate for my nine-year-old. USE **throes**. • The animations of the characters and the monsters are quite realistic; the death **throngs** of many creatures will force a smile on your face, trust me. USE **throes**. • This book reads like a call to arms that must have had quite an effect on a regional community that was already in the **throngs** of economic devastation after the war. USE **throes**.

And from a University of Michigan web page on the nineteenth-century English novel: • From the slaughterhouse, Pip immediately is thrown into the **throngs** of death at Newgate Prison, which was rebuilt between 1780 and 1783.

Throngs, large crowds of people or animals, and *throes*, severe pain or agonizing struggle, have neither sense nor spelling nor sound in common. SEE ALSO *throws*.

THROUGH

Confused with *thorough*. *Through* (THROO) means from end to end; among; during; around; by means of; because of. *Thorough* (THUR-oh) means complete; painstaking; absolute. SEE ALSO *threw*.

THROUGHFARE

Confused with **thoroughfare**. • Hicks Avenue is a **throughfare** with a posted speed limit of 30 mph, not 25 mph like a residential street. USE **thoroughfare**. • This creates a traffic problem, which is compounded by the fact that there is only one major **throughfare** passing through town. USE **thoroughfare**.

*A **thoroughfare** is a main road or highway; a **throughfare** is a dead end, the result of people confusing **thoroughfare** and **throughway**.*

THROWS

Misused for **throes**. • Design software specialist, Macromedia, is in the final **throws** of appointing a select band of resellers for the Australian market. USE **throes**. • When it comes to the instrumental equivalent of an atrocity or the sound of a menacing machine's death **throws**, industrial delights in the terrifying sounds of technology. USE **throes**. • As it turns out I wasn't in the **throws** of a serious heart attack; rather, I was experiencing a severe muscle pull and the inflammation was causing chest pains. USE **throes**. • They slumped there together with Saskia listing the things she has to do in preparation for Friday night, sounding more like a retired couple than lovers in the **throws** of passion. USE **throes**.

*Throws is the plural of **throw**. **Throes**, also a plural, is violent struggle or severe pain, such as often accompanies death or birth or other agonizing experience. **In the throes of** means in the middle of a difficult or painful event.*

Rattoon is in the throws of settling a deal for the sale of 3 million Tattersall's shares for which it will pay $10 million.
—Helen Matterson, *The Australian*

> This kind of coordination in the throws of the act itself astounds you and you get on your knees and bow to him and his composure as he swings above you, soon dead.
> **—Greg Sanders, *Mississippi Review***
>
> ---
>
> *Ms. Helen and Mr. Greg both—*
> *She scarcely reads, he seldom hears*
> *(Some say they pronounce Goethe Goth*
> *Like many of their toss-pot peers)—*
> *Are graceless writers clearly loath*
> *To learn what wrong writing rears.*

THRU

Idiotic for **through**. • During the time period from 1961 **thru** 1969, the standard error of the OECD coefficient was 1.301. USE **through**. • You'll tan right **thru** the medium level sunscreen fabric in cool comfort. USE **through**. • I know the heartache and torture that families and loved ones go **thru** when dealing with this hideous disease. USE **through**.

> *Thru* appeals to people who are fond of abbreviations and acronyms, people who prefer scribbling a note to composing a sentence. And if they abbreviate their words, so they abbreviate their thoughts. SEE ALSO **altho**; **through**.

THUSLY

Idiotic for **thus**. • Because this was described as school shootings and **thusly** presented as gender neutral, the gendered nature of the killing and shooting was ignored. USE **thus**. • It is impossible not to like a movie in which Elizabeth Hurley is cast as Satan, and she is **thusly** cast in *Bedazzled*, about which there is considerable buzz, as they say. USE **thus**.

> *Thusly*, like the equally idiotic **muchly**, is a nonstandard word. *Thus* is the adverb. SEE ALSO **muchly**.

TOWING THE LINE

What does the expression *towing the line* mean?

The idiom is **toe the line** (not **tow the line**) or **toe the mark** or **toe the scratch**, and it means to do as you are told or what is expected of you, to conform to rules or obey orders. The origin of the phrase is likely from the practice of military personnel, who, when standing at attention, have to stand with the tips of their toes touching a real or imaginary line. Others believe the expression was first used in sprint racing, when the starter refused to fire his gun until he was certain no runner had any part of his foot over the line.

TOO (AS WELL)

Solecistic for **moreover** (or similar words). • **Too**, it's a lot of sewing machine for the money! USE **What's more.** • **As well** we offer globes, calling cards, birthstones, and plaques. USE **Moreover.** • **As well**, Already Gone came in at #25, Good Day Ray at #68, and Passenger at #100. USE **Further.** • **As well this is** a place for you to make specific comments and requests. USE **This is also.** • **As well**, I will publish selected questions with my responses from email communications with students of all ages and all levels. USE **Furthermore.** • **Too**, he was that rare politician who never spoke unkindly of his rivals. USE **Moreover.**

*Do not begin a sentence with **too** or **as well** in the sense of also, moreover, or furthermore.*

TORTUOUS

Misused for **torturous.** • Only water can correct this acid imbalance and relieve the **tortuous** pain it causes. USE **torturous.** • His middle childhood years, to be sure, were filled with **tortuous** pain and agony beyond imagination for most of us. USE **torturous**. • It was one of the most horrific, slow, **tortuous** deaths ever invented. USE **torturous**.

> ***Tortuous*** *means marked by repeated twists and turns, winding; complex; circuitous; devious.* ***Torturous*** *means pertaining to or causing torture; strained.*
>
> *If enough people, in their dull-wittedness, confuse one word for the other, lexicographers and linguists will call the words synonymic, and berate anyone who tries to keep the distinction alive.*

TOWARDS

Would you ever use *towards* instead of *toward*? What's the rule?

I would never use **towards** *instead of* **toward***, but many people in Canada and the U.K. would likely never use* **toward** *instead of* **towards***. The American preferred spelling is* **toward***; the British preferred spelling,* **towards***.*

TRADEGY

Misspelling of **tragedy**. • This same route was followed for a candlelight procession on the first anniversary of the Sept. 11 **tradegy**. USE **tragedy**. • Add also Graham Crowden's Player King who is the one other character in the play with whom these two shadowy, Pirandellian onlookers are liable to get their best chance of being importantly involved in *The Tradegy of Hamlet, Prince of Denmark*. USE **Tragedy**.

> *The misspelling* ***tradegy*** *is nothing other than pitiable.* ***Tragedy*** *surrounds us even though social, political, and religious influences try, for their own self-interest not for our sake, to shelter us from much of it. If we can no longer spell the word, it may, in part, be because we scarcely recognize the concept.*

TRAIPSE

Could you tell me something about the word *traipse*? How did it get the negative connotation? Could it be connected to *trespass*?

According to the Oxford English Dictionary, **trapes** (later, **traipse**) first was:

1. an opprobrious name for a woman or girl slovenly in person or habits. 2. an act or course of trapesing; a tiresome or disagreeable tramp.

Later, the word evidently came to mean:

> 1. to walk in a trailing or untidy way; to walk or trail through the mud; to walk with the dress trailing or bedraggled; to walk about needlessly or aimlessly (usually said of a woman or child). 2. to walk or tramp about.

Webster's New International Dictionary, *Second Edition offers this:*

traipse, trapes: *v.* **a** *to walk; trudge.* **b** *to wander or flaunt about idly; to gad.* *n.* **a** *a slattern.* **b** *a fatiguing walk; a long dusty or muddy tramp.* **c** *a gadabout.*

Among the six dictionaries in the Fiske Ranking of College Dictionaries (Appendix A), only the Oxford American College Dictionary *mentions the archaic sense of* **traipse**, *a slovenly woman. And only the* American Heritage College Dictionary *suggests* **traipse** *may have derived from* **trespass**.

TRANSPIRE

Solecistic for **occur** (or similar words). • After years of research of the Pierce County elections, these skills were necessary to capture an incident that took only a few minutwes to **transpire**. USE **happen**. • Publishing is in an intense state of flux—which means no one has a clear handle on how to best publish books, what distribution will be like in two years, or what unexpected corporate shifts and mergers will **transpire**. USE **occur**.

Transpire has also come to mean, to a wayward few, to unfold or to pass: • The light-welter match is all set for November, but the champs' recent shared double-header provided little insight into how their eventual meeting might **transpire**. USE **unfold**. • How many minutes **transpired** there? USE **passed**.

> **Transpire** *means to pass through a surface; to leak out; to come to light; to become known. Unfortunately, its better known meaning—to come about, happen, or occur—is also its worse one, for no other word means quite what the word's less common usage does. The fewer words we know, the fewer thoughts we have.*

TREPIDACIOUS, TREPIDATIOUS

Solecistic for **fearful** (or similar words). • Together, they decide to write a biography of France and arrive in Galen on a slow, summer day; expectant, delighted, and a little **trepidacious** of what they might find. USE **fearful**. • In these **trepidacious** times for investors, we at Vanguard believe that discipline and patience are more relevant now than ever. USE **anxious**.

> **Trepidacious** *(or* **trepidatious***) is not a word.* **Trepidation**, *meaning fear or apprehension, is a word, as is* **trepid** *(the antonym of the more familiar* **intrepid***), meaning timid or fearful.*

Howe laughed off a suggestion that homeland security officials were trepidacious about venturing into northern climes during snow season.

—**Steve Orr, *Democrat and Chronicle***

Meanwhile, the Elgar estate, which controlled the copyright to the sketches, became trepidacious about anyone continuing work on them, and thus violating their great uncle's deathbed wish.

—**Jonathan Yungkans, writer, editor, former English teacher**

Even though people use it (horrible to hear, ridiculous to read though it is), no major dictionary, remarkably, has yet included **trepidacious** *in its listing.*

TRIUMPHANT

Misused for **triumphal**. • Lawyers are often like the workers who clean the streets when the elephants and horses have left after the **triumphant** procession. USE **triumphal**. • This massive, beguiling, sorrowful, **triumphant** poem is about the idea of Homer and the idea of poetry written on a homeric scale. USE **triumphal**. • For many, this beautiful **triumphant** arch is the single most important symbol of Greenwich Village. USE **triumphal**.

> *Triumphal* *means relating to a triumph; celebrating or commemorating a triumph or victory.* *Triumphant* *means victorious; rejoicing in victory or success. Most often, people are* *triumphant**, events,* *triumphal**.*

TROOP

Misused for **troupe**. • Because of his mainstream success, Waters has the money and the clout to get a great **troop** of actors who play his characters truly. USE **troupe**. • They've been coming to Cherry Valley and performing with Studio B dance **troop** for the past for years. USE **troupe**.

> *Troop* *means a group of people, animals, or soldiers; a great many.* *Troupe* *means a group of performers such as actors, dancers, or singers.*

T

TRY AND

Misused for **try to**. • Experts say **try and** manage your time. USE **try to**. • I would like to **try and** get a summary of the questions and the points that are made, and then at the next meeting to **try and** see if we can't incorporate some of those suggestions in the premium support model. USE **try to**. • It is interesting to **try and** understand which way the encapsulation is running. USE **try to**.

> *Though* *try and* *is probably more often heard than* *try to**, it is nonetheless incorrect. Public figures and spokespeople who use the unassuming, easy-to-ignore* *try and* *will never be considered eloquent. The same holds for* *sure and**, which should be* *sure to**. Some people even maintain that* *try and* *has a meaning different from* *try to**. It does not. SEE ALSO* *sure and**.*

TURGID

Misused for **turbid**. • As is fitting, the boys make their way due east into a **turgid**, turbulent beach front, not the placid harbor stockpiled with schools of fish they had expected. USE **turbid**. • The end result is five ounces of a liquid that looks like **turgid** urine and smells exactly like the musk from a dragon in heat, only amplified a hundredfold. USE **turbid**.

> *Turgid* means swollen or distended; bombastic or grandiloquent. *Turbid* means muddy or cloudy; thick or dark; confused or muddled.

TWIN

The city in England where I live, Bath, is "twinned" with Braunschweig, Germany. I believe this involves student exchanges and so on. However, Bath is also "twinned" with Aix-en-Provence and at least one other European city.

Merriam-Webster still confines the meaning of *twin* to one of two similar or identical items. Should the dictionary catch up with the language, or should the local government employ smarter administrators? Are other dictionaries similarly conservative? Are American cities (outside Minnesota) "twinned" with equal carelessness?

---

*We all long for commonality, for family. In England, you speak of **twin** cities; in the United States, we speak of **sister** cities.* The Oxford American College Dictionary *offers this definition of **twin**: "forming a matching, complementary, or closely connected pair." It also defines **twin city**: "either of two neighboring cities lying close together." No dictionary that I know of allows for three or more twins (nor, of course, should any), but Bath's administrators likely consider Bath and Aix-en-Provence as one "pair" of twin cities, and Bath and Braunschweig as a second pair.*

TWO-YEAR ANNIVERSARY

What is a *two-year anniversary*? I keep seeing and hearing phrases like this from journalists and radio/TV announcers who should know better. Doesn't *anniversary* mean that a year has passed? Isn't *second anniversary* valid anymore? *Two-year anniversary* is tautology, isn't it?

Two-year anniversary is inferior to and tautological for **second anniversary**. **Anniversary** does mean a date that returns yearly, so you're quite right: **two-year anniversary** is used by people who are unfamiliar with the meaning of the word **anniversary**.

T

UBIQUITOUS

Why has *ubiquitous* become ubiquitous? Until this year, this word tickled my eyes and ears a handful of times.

Now and then, people are especially attracted to using a particular word— perhaps because they have heard a celebrity or other well-known person use it, or perhaps because the sound of it appeals to them as much as or more than the meaning—which soon seems everywhere heard and read. About this same time, the definition of the word becomes less exact or incorrect. If **ubiquitous** is today much or more used, you can be sure some people are not using the word well:

- The Pentagon persuaded Congress to spend $8.7 billion on 2,096 Strykers because of their ability to be loaded into the **ubiquitous** C-130 cargo planes. USE **numerous**.

- "The whole album has been like a road map for me," says Clark, her **ubiquitous** cowboy hat on the table beside her. USE **inseparable**.

- The **ubiquitous** struggle in Iraq is not nearing a conclusion. USE **continuing**.

- One thing that is certain, however, is that when you have a product as **ubiquitous** as Google has become, everyone is going to have an opinion about its every move. USE **popular**.

- Korea is a country where Microsoft literally dominates with its dreadfully **ubiquitous** Windows operating system. USE **inescapable**.

• The other thing is that as the Internet becomes a **ubiquitous** part of our lives, people are making a wider breadth of online purchases. USE **big**.

• Want evidence that the **ubiquitous** claim that Minnesota is a battle-ground state in the presidential election is not just a bunch of hot air? DELETE **ubiquitous**.

Ubiquitous means omnipresent, found everywhere. It does not mean **popular**, **numerous**, **continuing**, **inescapable**, **big**, or other words. When a word is thought to have so many meanings, we can hardly be surprised that it is often used.

UNAWARE

Misused for **unawares**. • Set up a process to handle late requests to take an examination at an alternate time so that you are not taken **unaware** by these requests. USE **unawares**. • Pedestrians are caught **unaware** as a giant wave lashes a popular promenade in Bombay, India. USE **unawares**. • Floodwaves more than thirty feet high have occurred many miles from the rainfall area, catching people **unaware**. USE **unawares**.

Though **anyways**, **anywheres**, **nowheres**, and **somewheres** are the words of nitwits, **unawares** is sometimes correct. **Unaware**, an adjective, means not aware, unconscious. **Unawares**, an adverb, means by surprise, unexpectedly.

U

UNDER THE AUSPICIOUS OF

Idiotic for **under the auspices of**. • The accountants from Australia **under the auspicious of** the CPAA were active on many fronts. USE **under the auspices of**. • The Grand Assembly should take place **under the auspicious of** the United Nations. USE **under the auspices of**. • The undersigned further agrees to participate in all functions and promotional activities conducted by and managed **under the auspicious of** the Pageant Committee and Chinese American Civic Council (CACC). USE **under the auspices of**.

Auspicious, an adjective, means marked by a good omen; conducive or favorable to success; propitious. **Auspice**, a noun, means a promising sign for the future. The *correct idiom, **under the auspices of**, means with the help or support of; under the protection or backing of.*

The Office on Aging, which falls under the auspicious of the Department of Human Services, seeks to help improve the quality of lives of our senior citizen population.
—**Department of Human Services, Perth Amboy, New Jersey**

*On the other hand, it could be that the Office on Aging encourages the mental deterioration of its elderly population by muddling them with expressions like **under the auspicious of**.*

UNDOUBTABLY

Solecistic for **undoubtedly**. • You will **undoubtably** be thinking for much less time, so you cannot expect to find all the best moves. USE **undoubtedly**. • I will **undoubtably** seek to speak at such a meeting and put the party line across. USE **undoubtedly**. • For door to door service this is **undoubtably** the way to go. USE **undoubtedly**.

***Undoubtably** is incorrect for **undoubtedly**.*

UNINDATE

Solecistic for **inundate**. • I am now **unindated** with these little tiny dimples which was very disturbing to me. USE **inundated**. • Meanwhile, I have truly watched the field of exercise become **unindated** with terrible and misleading myths and false hopes. USE **inundated**.

*The word meaning to deluge or overwhelm with something is **inundate** (IN-un-date), not **unindate** (UN-in-date).*

We can no longer quote fares or respond by email; our posted addresses are being unindated by spam, viruses, worms, and forwarding via address spoofs.

—**Los Angeles Yellow Cab**

*We sympathize with Yellow Cab's plight, but not with its inuntelligent use of **unindated**.*

(VERY) UNIQUE

Misused for **unique.** • Willkie is **somewhat unique** in that its partnership is diverse. DELETE **somewhat.** • This is a **rather unique** look at Europe that traces the history of ethnic groups, their affinities, and languages. DELETE **rather.** • In terms of song-writing, the song is very interesting, not just because of the **sort of unique** lyrics, but also because of the **sort of unique** chord progression. DELETE **sort of.** • Due to its isolation in the Bay, Alcatraz has developed **very unique** flora and fauna. DELETE **very.** • They have cards for special occasions like birthdays, holidays, graduation, and **more unique** ones like crossword puzzles, word searches, and more. DELETE **more.** • Our range of pewter-based motorcycle sculptures are **quite unique,** and have proved to be our most popular line. DELETE **quite.**

> *Unique, it has long been said, ought not to be modified with **very** or **truly** or **more** or **most** or **quite** or **somewhat**, or any other qualifier. In a society, however, where imitation is supreme and cliché crowned, it's hard indeed to claim anything or anyone is unique.*

USE TO

Solecistic for **used to** (or similar words). • When my older brother and I were young, we **use to** go back in the woods and check out our "muscadine tree" in early spring. USE **used to.** • I **use to** work in a big German company, but now I am a housewife, cooking for my husband. USE **used to.** • They were not the kids we were **use to** meeting; they had the look of battle experience. USE **used to.**

*The correct phrase is **used to** since **used** is the past tense of, as well as the adjectival form of, **use**. SEE ALSO **suppose to**.*

Didn't use to (and **did…use to?**) are cumbersome phrases best avoided: • People **didn't use to** think of butterflies as wildlife. USE **never used to.** • He **didn't use to be** like that. USE **was never.** • What sort of clothes did they **use to** wear? USE **once.**

Illiterate are **used to could** and **used to would:** • I **used to could** do it with the bike unloaded but not on the centerstand. DELETE **could.** • We **used to could** do anything, not even lock our doors, but people will steal anything now. DELETE **could.**

USUAGE

Misspelling of **usage.** • Jargon of war quickly crosses ideological gulf to daily **usuage.** • USE **usage.** • The subscription fees, **usuage** charges and other fees for the service will be as stated in Brain NET Price List. USE **usage.** • A classic in the making, this **usuage** guide gives friendly, useful advice for anyone who needs to write. USE **usage.**

***Usuage**, like **mispell** and **grammer**, is a misspelling that no respectable writer would ever wish to make.*

VEHEMENT

*The pronunciation of **vehement** is (VEE-ah-ment), not (vi-HEE-ment).*

VENAL

Misused for **venial**. • During that talk show, Jakes said he asked the cardinal whether police brutality is a sin, and if it is, whether it's a mortal or **venal** sin? USE **venial**. • A mortal sin, which is more serious than a **venal** sin, that has not been absolved in confession prior to one's death condemns one's soul to hell. USE **venial**.

And, of course, **venial** is misused for **venal**: • The London premiere had Denis Quilley as the sinister Todd, the legendary barber and serial murderer (our doctors were formerly barber-surgeons!) not to be deflected from the pursuit of vengeance for wrongful suffering at the hands of a corrupt and **venial** judge. USE **venal**.

> ***Venal** means characterized by, or open to, bribery or corruption; marked by corrupt dealings. **Venial** means pardonable or easily forgiven; pertaining to a minor offense that can be overlooked or pardoned.*

VERBAL

Misused for **oral**. • A **verbal** contract is legally valid—but as Sam Goldwyn once stated, a **verbal** contract isn't worth the paper it's written on, because it's hard to prove a **verbal** contract. USE **oral**. • Remember, your **verbal** agreement to buy may become an immediate legal contract in some states. USE **oral**. • However, many magazine subscription companies do not honor **verbal** cancellations; to make sure your cancellation notice is honored, it's best to submit it in writing and within a certain time period. USE **oral**.

*Oral means by mouth; **verbal** means, simply, in words—whether by mouth or by hand, spoken or written. Choose between **oral** and **written**, not between **verbal** and **written**. SEE ALSO **aural**.*

VERBIAGE

Idiotic for **words** (or similar words). • Children don't lie about these things; they don't have the knowledge or the **verbiage** about that sort of thing. USE **words**. • Continuing their meeting from Tuesday night, the CCU met Wednesday afternoon to put the finishing touches on **verbiage** that will constitute a recommendation to the Governor. USE **wording**. • But then in Mr. Bush's interview with Fox News anchorman Brit Hume, the president did give his reaction to Kennedy's **verbiage**. USE **words**.

__Verbiage__ means excessive use of words, wordiness; not words, wording, diction or the way in which words are expressed. What's more, people who don't know its proper meaning also do not know its proper pronunciation (VUR-bee-ij, not VUR-bij) and may not know its proper spelling (__verbiage__, not __verbage__).

VERSING

Idiotic for **playing against** (or similar words). • The first was a game of pairs between Pole Cole and Pam Lucas **versing** Betty Carroll and Jean Gill. USE **playing against**. • It doesn't matter who I'm **versing**, I want to win. USE **competing against**. • The funniest episodes were Garth Brooks **versing** Marilyn Manson, the *Knight Rider* guy **versing** John Tesh, and Arnold Schwarznegger **versing** Sylvester Stallone. USE **fighting against**.

As a verb form of the preposition __versus__—which we know means against or in contrast with—__versing__ is popular among schoolchildren and other intellectual tyros, like descriptive linguists who feel that any word used in any way is a further marvel of language.

VERY

• Palmer was **very** fascinated with Innate Intelligence and its relationship to the nervous system. DELETE **very**. • Whether it is someone who uses C-SPAN with students every week or just once a year, but in a **very** unique way, these selected teachers share their expertise with C-SPAN in the Classroom members and staff. DELETE **very**. • They should be sprinkled with cinnamon sugar or dipped in cinnamon sugar for a **very** exquisite North African taste. DELETE **very**. • I was able to watch more of the cast this time, and they were all **very** terrific. DELETE **very**. • The great cutting of the Glenbrook deviation is a **very** stupendous engineering work. DELETE **very**. • The trout caught in the Zap Stream are **very** delicious. DELETE **very**. • This board is **very**, **very** dead. DELETE **very**, **very**.

*Do not use **very**—one of the least useful yet most used words—to modify words that clearly do not need to be so modified.*

VILIGENT

Solecistic for **vigilant**. • News Channel 19's Dan Satterfield, the Area's most **viligent** and trusted Meteorologist, is also a part of our morning team. USE **vigilant**. • Ever **viligent** of art, record company executives fruitlessly scavenge around looking for the next "Seattle." USE **vigilant**. • Aside from abortion, which women's issues do you think will require the most **viligent** protection given the administration for the next four years? USE **vigilant**. • The arching steel beams vault, as **viligent** protectors, towards a central gate composed of panels to honor those who lost their lives in the September 11th disaster. USE **vigilant**.

*Vigilant means watchful, alert, attentive. **Viligent** is a solecism, a misspelling. Lexicographers give credibility to solecisms like this by citing misusages; that is, if dictionary makers cared to, they likely could find many instances of **viligent** in writing over the last several centuries. Use alone is often enough for these blackguards to admit a word to their increasingly useless dictionaries.*

V

I asked a question from the floor as to whether we boxed ourselves in to this point by not being viligent enough in denouncing some of the lyrics.

—Curtis Harris, LiterateNubian.com

*If Harris meant **vigilant**, perhaps he also meant Illiterate-Nubian.*

VILLIAN

Misspelling of **villain**. • We can now crack straight into setting up the narrative tension of *ROTK*, which features Sauron as the **villian**. USE **villain**. • I have maintained that the principal **villian** in the failure to see news accounts of war dead is the media. USE **villain**. • Where cinematic productions constantly contort Christian themes with some deranged persona, such as the movie *Seven*, where the **villian** embarks on a murderous, judgmental rampage against victims who epitomize the seven deadly sins. USE **villain**.

Villain, not *villian* (Ian is not the villain), is the only correct spelling.

VITAMEN

Misspelling of **vitamin**. • For decades, we've known that **vitamen** D helps preserve bone strength. USE **vitamin**. • Brewer's yeast (a supplement) has traces of **vitamen** B1. USE **vitamin**. • Gerber makes **vitamen** drops that are supposed to be apple flavored. USE **vitamin**.

Vitamin is so spelled because it derives from the Latin *vita* (life) and the word *amine* (vitamins were once thought to be amines).

VOCIFEROUS

Misused for **voracious**. • He was a **vociferous** reader, a superb writer—and was able to make a distinctive contribution to American sociological theory especially in the area of class, power and social structure. USE **voracious**. • A **vociferous** reader, he had a fondness for all books, but particularly those slanted towards international history. USE **voracious**. • At the age of eighteen she opened her own studio and began to teach; a **vociferous** reader, she read everything she could about dance and took master classes from all the recognized leaders. USE **voracious**.

Vociferous means characterized by vehement outcry; clamorous. *Voracious* means greedy in eating; gluttonous; insatiable. Neither homonyms nor synonyms, these words are being used by people who only think they know their meanings.

VOCIFEROUS

Idiotic for **ferocious** (or similar words). • That's why they're fighting so **vociferously**. USE **ferociously**. • Why do you think the Musharraf regime has been so **vociferous** in fighting the Da'wah carriers there? Why do they arrest, kidnap and beat those who carry the Da'wah for Islam? USE **fierce**.

*Though **vociferous** has long been confused with **voracious** ("Having become a **vociferous** reader in Grade 4, he became a **vociferous** reader of religious materials in Grade 8"), it is now, by the remarkably dull, being misused for **ferocious** or, perhaps, **vicious**. **Vociferous** means noisy or boisterous. **Ferocious** means savagely fierce or violent, and **vicious**, savage or characterized by violence.*

In the morning session specifically, a tackling drill that involved a ball carrier, a blocker holding a small pad and a defender became a vociferous battle between the blue-clad defenders and the white shirts of the offense.

—Andy Hart, Patriots.com

*Mr. Hart confuses **vociferous** with **ferocious**—which is about all we can expect from a fumbling namby-pamby like Andy.*

V

VOLUMPTUOUS

Idiotic for **voluptuous**. • Our glamour sets are for the woman who wants to create a **volumptuous** lip. USE **voluptuous**. • On October 8, 1997 an astonishingly large, **volumptuous** pumpkin appeared nestled atop Cornell's McGraw Tower. USE **voluptuous**. • Sensual, **volumptuous** actress Gina Lollobrigida was a sex symbol in her native Italy before becoming a Hollywood star. USE **voluptuous**. • I'm 5 feet tall, blue green eyes, long brown hair, and **volumptuous**. USE **voluptuous**.

***Voluptuous** means full of, characterized by, or producing delight or pleasure to the senses; suggesting sensual pleasure by fullness and beauty of form; fond of or directed toward the enjoyments of luxury, pleasure, or sensual gratifications. **Volumptuous**, except among lumpen lexicographers, means nothing.*

-WARE

Misspelling of **-where.** • A large human-edited directory is not going to just pop up out of **noware;** it's going to be constructed from over a year of research and development. USE **nowhere.** • It was ruled a suicide even though there were several packed suitcases, as if she were going **someware.** USE **somewhere.** • Forced Witness features the most shocking content available **anyware** on the web. USE **anywhere.**

*Some people misspell **where ware**; others misspell **wear ware**: ("Last week, similar restrictions were imposed by the U.S. on cotton trousers, knit shirts, and **underware**.")*

WARRANTEE

Misused for **warranty.** Toyota's hybrid battery has a seven-year or 100,000-mile **warrantee.** USE **warranty.** • But the money still doesn't get you a guarantee, a **warrantee** or a buyer's protection plan. USE **warranty.**

***Warrantee**, a legal term, means the person to whom a warrant is given. **Warranty** means official authorization; justification for an action; a guarantee.*

WARY

*Confused with **weary**. **Wary** (WARE-ee) means cautious, circumspect; watchful ("Based on the tone of those questions and the reaction to several of them, the audience appeared **wary** and unconvinced"). **Weary** (WEIR-ee) means fatigued, worn-out; tiresome ("The crowd broke into applause when a **weary**-looking John Paul was wheeled out to the altar in his throne-like chair, dressed in golden vestments and a bejeweled miter").*

WAVE

Misused for **waive**. • They have special deals with some of the airlines to **wave** the fee for changing return flights at the last minute. USE **waive**. • The "to be" new registered agent promised the client the registrar would be persuaded to **wave** the requirement for Certificates of Good Standing. USE **waive**. • The suspicion of cheating does not **wave** the obligation to confirm a battle. USE **waive**.

*To **waive** is to give up or forgo; to refrain from insisting on; to postpone. To **wave** is to move up and down or back and forth in an undulating motion; to signal with a movement of the hand.*

WAY

Idiotic for **much** (or similar words). • It's **way** too early to tell what this means for Apple, but a lot will depend on when the new company is spun off and how it fares. USE **much**. • The City Council is **way** too involved in the details and nit-picking versus providing leadership for long-term issues. USE **far**. • There's no question that what we're doing is **way** better than all the schools around here. USE **a good deal**.

But it gets worse: • It's joining the superior original and **way** awful sequel on DVD on December 11. USE **especially**. • The food was **way** good. USE **very**.

*The widespread, if witless, use of **way** to mean **much** or **far**, **exceedingly** or **especially** reveals how people favor simplicity over precision, easiness over elegance, popularity over individuality.*

WEARAS

Idiotic for **whereas**. • Original toys have Takara Japan stamped on them, **wearas** the reissues have China stamped on them. USE **whereas**. • Even though he missed a lot of the 3rd and 4th quarters he still had a chance to get a vote, **wearas** Hird didn't. USE **whereas**. • So if you were wearing plate boots and walking on a flagstone road, it would make metallic clinks, **wearas** if you were wearing leather, you wouldn't hear it as much. USE **whereas**.

***Wearas** is a pathetic misspelling. SEE ALSO **assume**.*

W

Wear as the Canadians have repeatedly booed the American National Anthem at sporting events in Vancouver, Toronto and Montreal and government officials have repeatedly insulted the great President of the United States and impugned the integrity of its people.

—**Gregg Henson, Boycott Canada**

Not only does Mr. Henson not know what a sentence is, he doesn't know what a word is, and least of all does he know what reason is. People who do not write well are people who do not think well.

WEATHER

*Confused with **whether**. **Weather** is the atmospheric conditions regarding temperature, cloudiness, sunshine, rain, wind, and so on. **Whether** is a conjunction meaning if, either, or in case.*

WENT MISSING

Idiotic for **disappeared** (or similar words). • The boy **went missing** Monday, the day after his birthday. USE **disappeared**. • The estranged husband of a woman who **went missing** five years ago has been charged with her murder. USE **vanished**. • When a $250,000 boat **went missing** while docked at the foot of Grand Street in Alameda, police seemed lost at sea. USE **was stolen**. • A large and potentially hazardous asteroid that **went missing** almost sixty-six years ago was re-discovered by astronomers on Wednesday morning. USE **was lost**. • Many **went missing** after joining the militant groups, while others disappeared after being picked up by security forces for questioning. USE **deserted**. • She's a grown woman, and reasonable people can and should understand that, if they are going to **go missing**, they are going to cause public outcry. USE **disappear**.

Went missing is the phrase to use if you dislike subtlety and exactitude, honesty and insight. Use it also if you're easily influenced, disposed to speak as others speak and think as others think, receptive to every malodorous term that wafts your way.

Why has the phrase *gone missing*, a primarily British expression to the best of my knowledge, crept into the American mediaspeak? It's as if *missing* is a destination or a recreational activity, like fishing or shopping. Just wondering.

*People are so dull-witted and impressionable that, today, in this country, the popularity of **gone** or **went missing** has soared. Words like **disappeared, vanished, misplaced, stolen, lost, deserted, absconded** are seldom heard today because **went missing** has less meaning, or less exact meaning, than any of them, and people, especially the media, perhaps, are afraid of expressing meaning. What's more, **went missing** sounds willful or deliberate, and, indeed, sometimes that connotation is accurate, but the child who has been kidnapped is hardly agreeable to having been so.*

*   **Went missing** *appeals to people because it's largely meaningless and because it's a fad term. Few people who are conscious of how they speak, of the words they use, say **gone** or **went missing**.*

WET

Misused for **whet**. • The food displays will not only **wet** your appetite but will soak you with the idea of wanting one of everything. USE **whet**. • We asked Rain Station to give us a little information about the creation of this song and both Mark Harvey and Jay Moores sent us a couple paragraphs to **wet** our interest. USE **whet**.

*   **Whet** *means to sharpen or hone; to stimulate.* **Wet***, as a verb, means to dampen or drench; to urinate.*

WHERE

Solecistic for **that**. • I read **where** Clinton, before he left office, signed another 29,000 pages of executive orders. USE **that**. • He read **where** the commissioner of the NBA said to stay in school. USE **that**. • Unless the Yoda leaped forward and bit you, unless the blindfold burned your cornea, unless your photo and name appeared in the Hooters' employee newsletter under the headline "Gullible Girl With Silly Name Really Believed Oldest Pimp Joke in the World," I don't really see **where** you have a case. USE **that**. • It is wonderful, although I can see **where** they might have thought it went on too long. USE **that**.

*Do not use **where** instead of **that** to introduce a noun clause.*

WHERE

Solecistic for **whereas**. • It's the Libra in this coupling that desires to express and create many social outings and friends, **where** on the other hand the Capricorn desires a quiet evening at home. USE **whereas**. • Thus, **where** on the one hand it portrays grandeur, on the other hand, an eagle tearing out the meat of its prey can present a gory sight. USE **whereas**. • It has been forecasted for Portsmouth that there will be a significant decrease of jobs demanded in the manufacturing sector, **where** on the other side of the coin, the number of residents within the labor workforce will increase. USE **whereas**. • **Where** some people consider risk a problem, others see it as an opportunity. USE **Whereas**.

*Whatever a dictionary may say, the word **where** is incorrect for **whereas**. **Where** refers to a place or situation. **Whereas** means in contrast or comparison to or, in an opening remark, inasmuch as or since.*

WHERE AT (TO)

Solecistic for **where**. • So, the question is, **where** are they **at** so there will be the motivation to improve. DELETE **at**. • It took awhile to remember **where** the car was **at**. DELETE **at**. • Dante is at a certain place in his life when he has this vision of hell, explain **where** he is **at** and why he must make this journey. DELETE **at**. • **Where** have they gone **to**? DELETE **to**. • And **where** have you been **to** in England? DELETE **to**.

*Neither **at** nor **to** is necessary after **where** in the preceding examples. Avoid **at** when **where** refers to a location; avoid **to** when **where** refers to a destination.*

WHEREFORE

Solecistic for **where**. • Sony 24x firmware: **wherefore** art thou? USE **where**. • You want me to believe that blocking access to my kitchen phone is a blow against the First Amendment? **Wherefore** art thou, Thomas Jefferson? USE **Where**. • Before Bears fans fall in love with Romeo, they would want to know **wherefore** art thou, offensive genius? USE **where**.

*Properly used, **wherefore** asks an existential why or for what reason. It does not mean a mundane **where**.*

WHETHER

When using *whether*, do I also need to use *or not*? For example, "to determine whether any employees should be fired" or "to determine whether or not any employees should be fired." What's your thought on that one?

Whether or not often says nothing more than **whether** does alone. When **or not** is unnecessary to write, it is also unpleasant to read:

• **Whether or not** we get to fifty dollars will probably depend on **whether or not** anything else goes wrong.

In the largely British **whether or no**, the **or no** is often just as superfluous. If, however, you want to emphasize both possibilities, the **whether** and the **not** (or **no**), then do use the full expression. In your example, generosity and fairness recommend that you use **whether or not**.

In other sentences, **whether** alone does not work:

• Kerry basically supports Bush's war to overthrow Saddam— **whether or not** the facts and arguments employed by Bush to persuade the Congress and nation to go to war were at all truthful or made any sense.

WHICH

Solecistic for **and** (or similar words). • The transfer could take years because both state governments and Congress must approve. **Which they should, says a Utah state senator.** USE **The transfer could take years because both state governments and Congress must approve, and says a Utah state senator, they should.** • Gambling indirectly hurts children, they argue. **Which is true.** USE **Gambling indirectly hurts children, they correctly argue.** • His vision, his integrity, his strength, his dignity, his honor will be the standard by which American presidents are measured for decades to come. **Which is as it should be.** USE **His vision, his integrity, his strength, his dignity, his honor will be the standard by which American presidents are measured for decades to come, which is as it should be.** • But there are those who believe that the doctrine of Original Intent has the capability to solve all present-day problems. **Which is nonsense.** USE **But there are those who believe that the doctrine of Original Intent has the capability to solve all present-day problems, which is nonsense.**

*Separating a subordinate clause that begins with the word **which** from the sentence in which it belongs is the writing style of juveniles—and, of course, journalists.*

WHICH

Solecistic for **that.** • A massive double car bomb **which** devastated a Riyadh compound of Arab expatriates, killing at least thirteen people, struck close to homes of Saudi royals. USE **that.** • Actually, the bill undermines the entire Medicare program, pushing people into the very HMOs **which** contribute heavily to Republican lawmakers and barring the government from negotiating for lower drug prices. USE **that.** • It is merely an ample illustration of the kind of structures in place **which** organizes, limits, and controls American cultural output. USE **that.** • Studies have shown that activities **which** exploit a person's natural abilities, be it dribbling a basketball or making good conversation, generate more satisfaction than pricier yet mindless endeavors such as lounging on a yacht. USE **that.** • Parody is not the only thing **which** is confused with satire—sarcasm is another relative of satire **which** can be. USE **that.**

*In the United States, the restrictive, or defining, **that** is used when the clause it begins is necessary to the meaning of a sentence; the nonrestrictive, or nondefining, **which** is used when the clause is not necessary, when it is parenthetical, to* *the sentence.* **Which** *clauses are generally separated by commas (or preceded by a comma);* **that** *clauses are not. Observing the distinction between these two words and their clauses is indispensable to understanding clearly and effortlessly the sentences in which they appear.*

WHO

Misused for **that** or **which**. • The fund will be administered by individuals and organizations **who** are not connected to Siemens. USE **that**. • She became an activist after a 1986 conference revealed the perilous future of the animals, **who** are hunted (for food and as pets) and are ill-treated in medical research. USE **which**. • But spokesman Bob Carolla acknowledges that the group receives substantial funding from drug firms, **who** provide most if not all of the anti-discrimination campaign's $4 million annual budget. USE **which**. • He leaned down to pat the dog, **who** wiggled gleefully and then dashed off in pursuit of some small creature that darted before him. USE **which**. • Animal shelters across the country are full of companion animals **whom** their guardians couldn't keep, and many of these animals are killed. USE **that**. • The car **who** Ford introduced was a modern follow-up to the Le Mans winner, the Ford GT40. USE **that**.

In standard, nonsolecistic English, **who** *is used to refer to people,* **that** *to both people and things, and* **which** *to things alone. Further,* **which** *is the preferred word to begin nonrestrictive (or nondefining) clauses (those that use a comma before the word* **which***), and* **that** *to begin restrictive (or defining) ones.*

For now it's the Ericsson T28 World cell phone (the cost, depending on the service provider: from nothing to $199; www.ericsson.com) with VoiceStream Wireless or Cingular Wireless, who include international service.

—Real Simple

*This magazine is true to its name, for it doesn't let the apparent complexity of using correct grammar (***which includes** *instead of* **who include***) interfere with its mission.*

WHOA

Misspelling of **woe.** • This isn't a "**whoa** is me" plea; I am blessed beyond measure in countless ways, and God is indeed good. USE **woe.** • You might share about broken relationships, not to wallow in the mutual **whoa**-is-me of it all, but to be released from pain and anger and move into love. USE **woe.** • This whole **whoa**-is-me, Gen-X attitude is getting a little tired. USE **woe.**

> **Whoa** is a pathetic (and apathetic) misspelling of **woe.** No one who uses the absurdity **whoa** can have much sense of what is meant by **woe:** deep distress, grief, or misery; calamity or affliction. What's more, the correct expression is "**woe** is I" (misery is I; calamity is I), not "**woe** is me."

WHOM

Misused for **who.** • If I did it again, maybe I'd be a little fairer with regard to **whom** the real villains were. USE **who.**

Who is also misused for **whom.** • You all know exactly **who** I am talking about—which is odd considering that we don't have princes. USE **whom.** • This is a man **who** even Republican cohorts sometimes find disturbing, for the way he uses almost anything to his advantage. USE **whom.** • APT's members are public interest groups and individuals, some of **who** historically have been left out of the Information Age. USE **whom.**

> **Who** is used where a nominative pronoun could also be used; if you can substitute **I, we, he, she, you,** or **they** for it, **who** is correct. **Whom** is used where an objective pronoun could be; if you can substitute **me, us, him, her,** or **them, whom** is correct.

Has the use of *whom* been abandoned? I understand that in normal conversation it may be difficult to quickly choose the correct form, *who* or *whom*, but not when writing. A *Daily News* headline read "Who Shot Who?" Any comment?

"She Shot He?" Only presidents and their kind talk this way, ignoring all distinction between nominative and objective pronouns. **Whom** is an objective pronoun, comparable to **me, him, her, them, us**, and thus demands the linguistic respect it is entitled to, meaning it ought to be correctly used.

Showing respect for the word is not enough; let's also deny it to those who would say, or, even more reprehensible, write, a sentence like *"Who Shot Who?"*

Knowing when to use **whom** is more than most people can manage. And if people rarely use **whom** in spoken English, they quickly become disinclined to use it in written English. Clumsy speech influences us more than careful writing does.

If **whom** sounds "stilted" in spoken English, it's surely because we seldom hear it used. People have been prognosticating about the disappearance, the death of the word **whom** for some years, but it endures, here and there, among those who still value elegance in language.

WHO'S

Solecistic for **whose**. • The person **who's** idea we use will receive a free set of Kirlian postcards. USE **whose**. • The grandkids argue over **who's** turn it is to use it. USE **whose**. • Happy birthday to my Dad too, **who's** birthday was a day before mine. USE **whose**.

And **whose** is misused for **who's**: • He was the creator of some of the greatest of the modern blues bands and a list of the various members of his bands reads like a **whose** who of modern blues. USE **who's**.

*Do not confuse **who's** (that is, **who is**) with **whose**, the possessive form of **who**.*

WIERD

Misspelling of **weird**. • Wallace overtook teammate Jeremy Mayfield over the last 100 laps and weathered a couple more **wierd** adventures. USE **weird**. • New science aims to explore systems as wholes and the **wierd** new properties which can emerge as things "switch states" and only apparently go "out of control." USE **weird**.

> *Despite the popularity (and sham purposefulness) of **wierd** on the web, the correct spelling is **weird**. Some people neglect to attend to how letters are arranged; others, however you spell it, are simply deranged.*

WILDFLOWER

Misused for **wildfire**. • Urban legends grow and spread like **wildflower** because it gives people something fun to talk about. USE **wildfire**. • In the last three years Spragga's singles released in Jamaica have burned up the place and spread like **wildflower** into the dancehalls abroad in the States, Canada, the U.K. and Japan. USE **wildfire**.

> ***Wildflowers** do indeed spread, but the correct idiom is **like wildfire**, that is, intensely; quickly.*

-WISE

Solecistic for **in** (or similar words). • It was a step up **careerwise**. USE **in her career**. • If you want to save regularly but aren't yet in the **big leagues moneywise**, bonds can be a good starting point. USE **big financial leagues**. • In Germany, where almost anything goes **TV-wise**, the program is being aired on the struggling private network RTL II, which generally reruns U.S. shows such as *Home Improvement* and soft-core porn. USE **for TV**. • Hopefully he will be back in plenty of time as he is **close enough fitness-wise** to start the game. USE **fit enough**. • What do you think is driving, **issuewise**, college students? USE **What issues do you think are driving**.

> *This suffix is a device that people rely on when they cannot easily think of how to express themselves better. Never is there any need to use these -**wise** words.*

WITCH

Misspelling of **which**. • When booting the PC, I see fast track stating a Striping Raid configuration (witch is correct). USE **which**. • The movie also had points of comedy in it **witch** is strange, but good for war era movies. USE **which**. • Guess **witch** monster survived the biggest building. USE **which**.

*Before long, considering the disrespect and indifference that many people feel for the English language, **witch** may indeed become a variant spelling of **which**.*

WONT

Misspelling of **won't**. • We hope it will stop some of the pockets of resistance out there and that it **wont** be quite as deadly. USE **won't**. • Walsh has to get better or the NBA **wont** even give him a second look. USE **won't**. • Doctors are being very selective and **wont** give just anyone a flu shot. USE **won't**.

*__Won't__ (WONT), of course, is the contraction of **will not**. **Wont** is a misspelling. Another word, **wont** (WANT), is an adjective meaning accustomed to or in the habit of, or a noun meaning custom, practice, habit: ("But Miller, as he is **wont**, made a 3-pointer to thwart the run"; "As is her **wont** each December, Whitfield is ensconced in the Plush Room of the York Hotel, one of the last truly great cabaret spaces in the country").*

WORSER

Solecistic for **worse**. • Is it getting **worser** or is it getting better? USE **worse**. • The war, barely began, is all but finished and grows **worser** than ever. USE **worse**. • Disc number two in Retromedia's optimistically named "Italian Science Fiction Collection" is clearly the **worser** of the two. USE **worse**.

*Some people apparently feel that since the comparative of **good** is **better**, the comparative of **bad** must be **worser**. They are mistaken.*

*Equally mistaken, to put it charitably, are the people who add the word **more** to -**er** (or **most** to -**est**) terms, such as **more better**, **more worse** (**most simplest**, **most happiest**).*

WOULD HAVE

Solecistic for **had**. • I think I would have gotten nervous if I **would have** looked at her. USE **had**. • What would have been the harm if he **would have** published the article without using her name? USE **had**. • None of this would have gone on if the husband **would have** let the parents care for their daughter. USE **had**.

• If you **would have** read the story, you would have seen it had to do with lawn-mower pollution. USE **had**. • If she ever **would have** hit her, I would have fired her. USE **had**.

Would have is incorrect for *had* in a sentence that states or implies a condition.

> If I would have been a publishing house, I would've eagerly taken David's book.
> —**Rich Lowry, editor,** *National Review*

Mr. Lowry's use of ***would have*** *exposes an inability to reason well—as does his imagining he might conceivably have been a publishing house.*

WRACK

Misused for **rack**. • **Wracked** with pain from his advanced form of cancer, Jimmy V courageously reminded us all to cherish every moment of every day. USE **Racked**. • Those who did work were **wracked** with guilt, with 92 percent wishing they were at home with their child. USE **racked**. • There was a large TV set in one corner, a magazine **wrack** propped against a wall, and several sofas arranged around the room. USE **rack**.

To ***rack*** *means to trouble or afflict; to torture; to strain mightily. As a noun, a* ***rack*** *is an instrument of torture; a shelf or structure for storing items. To* ***wrack*** *means to wreck or, as a noun, wreckage; it does not mean to trouble or torture.*

WREATHE

Misused for **writhe**. • For all we know that child is consciously with the One, even as we see the body moan and **wreathe** in pain. USE **writhe**. • The word had spread among all 4,000 of them that a top-track honor student, and one with a reputation (to the extent they had heard of him at all) of being a bit of a wimp, had attacked Big Bill Hal and left him **wreathing** in agony on the cafeteria floor. USE **writhing**.

*To **writhe** (RITHE) is to make twisting movements; to squirm in pain; to suffer emotional distress. To **wreathe** (RETHE) is to coil, twist, or entwine around something; to decorate with wreaths; to cover or surround.*

WRECK

Misused for **wreak**. • Yet with TSC continuing to **wreck** havoc on people's lives, more than 1,500 families in the U.K. now rely on its services. USE **wreak**. • After destroying a liberal weekly modeled on the New Republic and making an enemy of its literary editor Lionel Heftihed, he goes on to **wreck** havoc elsewhere. USE **wreak**. • Lesson IV: How to **Wreck** Vengeance on Anyone Who Has Ever Done You Wrong....and Get PAID FOR IT! USE **Wreak**.

*To **wreak** (REEK) is to inflict upon a person; to vent; to bring about or cause. To wreck (REK) is to destroy or tear down.*

WRECKLESS

Misspelling of **reckless**. • Sixteen-year-old Cordara "Cory" Lewis is charged with **wreckless** use of a firearm and involuntary manslaughter. USE **reckless**. • Prosecutors on Friday charged the child's mother, Amy Detlor, 19, with four felony counts in connection with the baby boy's death, including **wreckless** homicide. USE **reckless**.

*Though **reckless** is a word (without heed to consequences; careless), **reck** is an archaism (meaning to pay heed or be of concern). And though **wreck** is a word (a shipwreck or the remains of one; the remains of anything badly damaged; destruction or ruin; a person physically or emotionally in poor health), **wreckless** is a misspelling.*

Roy Jester Vowell, 31, of 88 Old Homestead Rd in Big Sandy was also charged with criminal attempt to manufacture meth along with wreckless endangerment, three counts, because of the three children in the house.
—**Robert Cobb, *The Camden Chronicle***

In a separate but related incident, Robert Cobb and The Camden Chronicle *have been charged with **reckless** endangerment of the English lanugage.*

WRITTING

Misspelling of **writing.** • Unfortunately, poor grammar used in the **writting** of the character descriptions completely ruins the value of this extra. USE **writing.** • Todd Alsop said the problem was that McCorkle never followed their warranty claim procedure which requires all homeowners to put all requests in **writting.** USE **writing.**

*The noun of **write** is **writing**. SEE ALSO **playwrite.***

He has certain information of this by verbal Expresses; writting beeing absolutely dischargd for fear of discovery. He desires me aquent your Grace of this, that you may lay the whole before His Majesty.
—**Andrew Lang, *Pickle the Spy*, 1897**

YOLK

Misused for **yoke**. • October 24, 1964 signified the breaking of the **yolk** of colonialism and foreign domination, yet thirty-nine years later, we are not any better. USE **yoke**. • The day featured some of the region's finest fiddle groups, sheep dogs at work, **yolk**-oxen, horse-drawn rides, arts, crafts, a farmer's market and a traditional banquet feast. USE **yoke**.

> **Yolk** *is the yellow substance of an egg.* **Yoke** *is a frame that harnesses two oxen together; a pair of harnessed animals; something that binds or bonds; something that oppresses.*

YOUR

Solecistic for **you're**. • However, if you've done the research and feel good about the area, then **your** likely to make the right choice. USE **you're**. • If **your** not a member, consider joining now! USE **you're**. • **Your** with us or against us. USE **You're**.

> *The misuse of* **your** *for* **you're** *suggests a certain contempt for the careful use of language; it's one of the countless mistakes that descriptive linguists and other language liberals wouldn't think of censuring but also wouldn't think of making.*

YOUR'S

Idiotic for **yours**. • Find out how it can be **your's** here! USE **yours**. • Mine is bigger than **your's**. USE **yours**. • Sincerely **your's**. USE **yours**. • Do you want to share your views and ideas? Post **your's** here. USE **yours**. • If you don't see **your's** listed, ask us if it is compatible. USE **yours**. • Do respect the rights and opinions of others, and expect them to respect **your's**. USE **yours**. • If **your's** is over this size, additional fees may apply. USE **yours**. • In the boxes below, please enter the recipient's name and email addresses and **your's**. USE **yours**.

> The possessive pronoun **yours** is never spelled **your's**. Equally incorrect are **her's** (instead of **hers**), **it's** (instead of **its**), **our's** (instead of **ours**), and **their's** (instead of **theirs**).

Z

ZOOLOGY

The pronunciation of **zoology** is (zoh-OL-ah-jee), not (zoo-OL-ah-jee).

Z

APPENDIX A

THE FISKE RANKING OF COLLEGE DICTIONARIES

The Fiske Ranking of College Dictionaries (FRCD) ranks the following six college dictionaries, based on their handling of twenty-five words and phrases:

- *The American Heritage College Dictionary* (4th edition, 2002) (AH)

- *Webster's New World College Dictionary* (4th edition, 2002) (NW)

- *Microsoft Encarta College Dictionary* (1st edition, 2001) (ME)

- *Random House Webster's College Dictionary* (2nd edition, 2001) (RH)

- *The Oxford American College Dictionary* (1st edition, 2002) (OA)

- *Merriam-Webster's Collegiate Dictionary* (11th edition, 2003) (MW)

This ranking does not consider the number of entries or quality of definitions in each dictionary, nor does it consider etymologies or usage notes, the opacity of the paper or clarity of the typeface, or other features. The FRCD is concerned solely with how these six dictionaries treat the words and phrases listed in the table, for how they treat them provides insight into how they regard the language.

The inclusion in a dictionary of a nonstandard word—even though a usage note may accompany it—is reason enough for its being listed in the FRCD. Its inclusion, whatever a usage note might say, is an implicit sanction, an authorization to use the word, not an injunction against using it. Lexicographers understand this perfectly well, as do the people who consult these books, all of whom pay far more attention to definitions and spellings than they do to remarks about usage.

A checkmark (✓) signifies that the nonstandard word or usage in the leftmost column is included in the dictionary named at the head of the column. The higher the total number of checkmarks for a particular dictionary, the more descriptive, that is, the worse the dictionary.

Some of the words designated nonstandard (those not enclosed in parentheses) are not, in themselves, incorrect (*enormity* is a perfectly good word, for instance).

These nonstandard words are incorrect only when they are used to mean the standard word—when *enormity* is used to mean *enormousness*—which is how they are being evaluated here. For example, consider terms 1–5: Two of the dictionaries offer the spelling *accidently* as an alternative to the spelling *accidentally*; all six dictionaries include entries for *alright* and *anyways*; two of the dictionaries maintain that *cliché* is a perfectly good adjective; and five of the six dictionaries record that *disconnect* is a noun meaning a gap or miscommunication.

NONSTANDARD (STANDARD)	AH	NW	ME	RH	OA	MW
1. accidently (accidentally)	✓					✓
2. alright (all right)	✓	✓	✓	✓	✓	✓
3. anyways (anyway)	✓	✓	✓	✓	✓	✓
4. cliché (clichéd)				✓		✓
5. disconnect (miscommunication)	✓	✓	✓	✓		✓
6. enormity (enormousness)	✓	✓		✓	✓	✓
7. fatal (fateful)	✓	✓	✓	✓		✓
8. fearful (fearsome)	✓[a]	✓	✓	✓	✓	✓
9. flaunt (flout)	✓	✓		✓		✓
10. get (get)[b]		✓				✓
11. historic (historical)	✓	✓	✓	✓		✓
12. hone in (home in)	✓					✓
13. in behalf of (on behalf of)		✓	✓	✓	✓	✓

14. infer (imply)	✓	✓	✓	✓		✓
15. less (fewer)	✓	✓		✓		✓
16. peruse (read casually)		✓	✓c	✓		✓
17. precipitate (precipitous)		✓				✓
18. predominate (predominant)		✓				✓
19. publically (publicly)						✓
20. reoccur (recur)		✓	✓	✓	✓	✓
21. reticent (reluctant)	✓		✓			✓
22. sherbert (sherbet)	✓		✓	✓		✓
23. supercede (supersede)		✓			✓	✓
24. where (that)		✓		✓	✓	✓
25. zoology (zoology)d	✓	✓			✓	
TOTAL	**15**	**19**	**12**	**16**	**9**	**24**

a. American Heritage makes no effort to distinguish these two words. The first meaning of both entries is: "causing or capable of causing fear."

b. This entry deals with the pronunciation of **get**: the nonstandard GIT versus the standard GET.

c. Some of these definitions are too entertaining: "to read or examine something in a leisurely or careful way."

d. This entry deals with the pronunciation of **zoology**: the nonstandard zoo-OL-ah-jee versus the standard zoh-OL-ah-jee.

As you see, based on these twenty-five words, *Merriam-Webster's Collegiate Dictionary* (11th edition, 2003) has the highest total score—24 of 25. It is, therefore, the most descriptive, the least useful of the six dictionaries.

Two of the newest dictionaries are also two of the best: *The Oxford American College Dictionary* (1st edition, 2002)—9 of 25—and *Microsoft Encarta College Dictionary* (1st edition, 2001)—12 of 25.

Dictionary publishers might do their readers (and even themselves) a considerable service by labeling their products. As recordings, DVDs, and video games are rated, so let our dictionaries be ranked. Based on the FRCD, *Merriam-Webster's Collegiate Dictionary*'s label would read "Ranked 24 of 25 in the FRCD" (which would clearly please Merriam-Webster), whereas *The Oxford American College Dictionary*'s would read "Ranked 9 of 25 in the FRCD" (which may or may not please Oxford's editors). This essay, or other explanatory notes, could be printed on the dust jacket flap of each dictionary.

NOTES

Had I chosen a different twenty-five words, the scores also would have been different, but I dare say Merriam-Webster's still would have ranked highest, that is, worst (most descriptive), and Oxford American and Microsoft Encarta still would have ranked lowest, that is, best (least descriptive). Of course, had I chosen twenty-five words and phrases that were once controversial but are now largely accepted, the ones prescriptivists have lost hope of reclaiming—transpire (occur), careen (career), disinterest (uninterest), decimate (destroy), enthuse (excite), fortuitous (fortunate), and so on—it's likely that all six dictionaries would have scored very high (that is, very badly) indeed.

APPENDIX B

FIFTY-FIVE BEST WORDS AS IDENTIFIED BY THE READERS OF *THE VOCABULA REVIEW*

1. **aberrant** (AB-er-ent)—deviating from the proper course

2. **animadversion** (an-ah-mad-VUR-zhen)—strong criticism; a critical or censorious remark

3. **borborygmus** (bor-bah-RIG-mes)—a rumbling noise produced by the movement of gas through the intestines

4. **brouhaha** (BROO-ha-ha)—an uproar

5. **cacology** (kah-KOL-ah-jee)—bad choice or use of words

6. **caliginous** (kah-LIG-ah-nes)—dark and gloomy

7. **callipygian** (kal-ah-PIJ-ee-en)—having beautifully proportioned buttocks

8. **chthonic** (THON-ik)—of or relating to the underworld

9. **contumely** (KON-too-mah-lee)—rudeness or contempt; insolence

10. **decorum** (di-KOR-em)—appropriate behavior; propriety

11. **egregious** (i-GREE-jes)—conspicuously bad or ridiculous

12. **ennui** (on-WEE)—boredom; listlessness

13. **euphony** (YOO-fah-nee)—pleasant sound

14. **excoriate** (ik-SKOR-ee-ate)—to censure or denounce; to abrade

15. **feculent** (FEK-yah-lent)—laden or polluted with filth; fecal

16. **floriferous** (flo-RIF-er-es)—bearing flowers

17. **fuliginous** (fyoo-LIJ-ah-nes)—dark; sooty; obscure

18. **hebetudinous** (heb-ah-TOOD-en-es)—dull-minded; mentally lethargic

19. **ichthyophagous** (ik-thee-OFF-ah-ges)—feeding on fish

20. **jejune** (ji-JOON)—not interesting, dull, empty; childish; lacking in nutrition

21. **kakistocracy** (kak-i-STOK-rah-see)—government by the worst or least qualified citizens

22. **lachrymose** (LAK-rah-mos)—inclined to shed many tears; causing tears

23. **logorrhea** (log-ah-RHEE-ah)—excessive, incoherent talkativeness

24. **lucubrate** (LOO-kyoo-brate)—to study diligently; to write in a scholarly way

25. **mellifluous** (mah-LIF-loo-es)—sweetly flowing; smooth and sweet

26. **mulct** (MULKT)—to swindle or defraud; to acquire by trickery; to penalize by fining

27. **obloquy** (OB-lah-kwee)—verbal abuse of a person or thing; calumny

28. **obstreperous** (ob-STREP-er-es)—unruly; noisily defiant

29. **odious** (OH-dee-es)—repugnant; hateful

30. **officious** (ah-FISH-es)—meddlesome; unnecessarily or obtrusively ready to offer advice or services

31. **otiose** (OH-shee-os)—lazy, indolent; useless; ineffective, futile

32. **penultimate** (pi-NUL-tah-mit)—next to last

33. **perambulate** (pah-RAM-byah-late)—walk through, about, or over; stroll

34. **persiflage** (PUR-sah-flazh)—banter; light, good-natured talk

35. **perspicacious** (pur-spi-KA-shes)—having keen judgment or understanding; acutely perceptive

36. **pilgarlic** (pil-GAR-lik)—a bald-headed man

37. **poltroon** (pol-TROON)—a contemptible coward

38. **porphyrophobia** (por-FIR-ah-fo-bee-ah)—fear of the color purple

39. **propinquity** (prah-PING-kwi-tee)—proximity; nearness

40. **pusillanimous** (pyoo-sah-LAN-ee-mes)—timid or cowardly; fainthearted

41. **quidnunc** (KWID-nungk)—a busybody; a nosy person

42. **quixotic** (kwik-SOT-ik)—extravagantly chivalrous or romantic

43. **quotidian** (kwoh-TID-ee-en)—daily; everyday; commonplace

44. **redoubtable** (ri-DOU-tah-ble)—arousing fear or awe; worthy of respect; formidable

45. **salubrious** (sah-LOO-bree-es)—conducive to health or well-being

46. **scalawag** (SKAL-ah-wag)—scamp; rascal

47. **stentorian** (sten-TOR-ee-an)—very loud

48. **syzygy** (SIZ-ah-jee)—a pair of connected things that are similar or opposite

49. **tatterdemalion** (tat-er-di-MAL-yen)—a ragamuffin

50. **troglodyte** (TROG-lah-dite)—a cave dweller; recluse

51. **ubiquitous** (yoo-BIK-wi-tes)—being or seeming to be everywhere at the same time; omnipresent

52. **undulation** (un-jah-LA-shen)—movement in waves; a wavy, curving form or outline

53. **uxorious** (uk-SOR-ee-es)—excessively fond or submissive to one's wife

54. **vicissitude** (vi-SIS-i-tood)—an unexpected change

55. **zephyr** (ZEF-er)—the west wind; a gentle breeze; something airy or insubstantial

Love a word? Tell us what it is (and its definition). There need not be any well-reasoned analysis of your high regard for a word; emotional reactions to the sound or meaning of words are welcome. See www.vocabula.com/forum.

FIFTY-FIVE WORST WORDS AS IDENTIFIED
BY THE READERS OF *THE VOCABULA REVIEW*

1. **action**—A verb created from a noun not previously lacking in a root verb, namely, *to act*. Favored by lazy administrators as a way of making their mundane tasks seem more consequential or deliberate. "When we have received the report from management, we will action their recommendations immediately." Apparently, *act (on, upon)* or *implement* doesn't create enough of an illusion that something will actually happen. By forcing the word *action* into their speech, they foolishly believe it evokes images of thrilling car chases and back-alley shootouts, rather than somniferous pencil-pushing. When one hears *action* used as a verb, one can expect to see very little actual action in the form of a noun.

2. **advise**—In the sense of to tell or to notify. For example, "He advised the committee that the budget was being developed."

3. **anal**—*Anal* (short for anal-retentive): The new all-purpose pop psychology buzzword that's come to replace *fussy, particular, careful, conservative, old-fashioned*, etc. Used extensively by a**holes.

4. **antiquing**—Instead of shopping for antiques. I hate it. When I go to the grocery store, am I fooding?

5. **athalete**—Why must sports announcers continually misspeak this simple noun? From where does the extra syllable (ATH-ah-leet) come?

6. **athleticism**—I have detested *athleticism* from first hearing it, but I am at a loss to account for my own aversion. The concept seems rather handy—something to cover the gap between "athletic ability" and "athletic performance," and a comparatively short word to stand in for such lengthy locutions as "tendency to be very active and physically resourceful in the game." But what is it about the *sound* of this one that makes me grit my teeth and refuse to use it?

7. **awesome**—An all-purpose adjective for *good*. Until two decades ago, *awesome* was reserved for the sublime. For example, an F5 tornado or God. The casual use of this word is more loathsome than *groovy* was in the 1960s.

8. **behaviors**—*Behaviors* is pretentious, entirely unnecessary extension of *behavior*—a word almost never used until about fifteen years ago. Yes, Shakespeare used it, but he could and the rest of us should not.

9. **closure**—What I'll never attain until this word is stricken from the English language.

10. **differential**—Basketball announcers often use this word to describe the difference between the game clock and the shot clock: "There's a three-second differential between the game clock and the shot clock."

11. **dinghy**—I hate the word *dinghy*.

12. **disrespect**—As a verb. It's even worse in the past tense as in, "She disrespected me in front of the kids."

13. **eatery**—It sounds revolting. It is crass American shorthand, and invokes images of gross people stuffing handfuls of unspeakable food into open, salivating mouths.

14. **famously**—Overused and unnecessary. "'Cogito ergo sum,' as Descartes famously remarked." Ugh! He may have said it loudly, but he didn't say it *famously*.

15. **flush out**—Instead of *flesh out*. A gem from a manager making tens of thousands of dollars more than I; it was also news to her that the Chinese language comes in more than one variety.

16. **gay**—At my high school, I continue to hear the word *gay* used incorrectly: "Man, this test is gay," or "The computer class was gay." In this sense of the word, *gay* is a substitute for *dumb* or *stupid*. This incorrect usage drives me crazy!

17. **gift**—Used most frequently in publications created by companies that deal with money, as in "You can gift up to $9,000 to your grandchildren."

18. **gobsmacked**—My vote for one of the least attractive words in the English language today (leaving aside some of the four-letter ones) would have to go to *gobsmacked*. I don't know if it is in use in American English, but it is not uncommon in British and Australian English and is an unappealing alternative for *surprised, astonished, dumbfounded, aghast,* etc.

19. **going forward**—What's wrong with *in the future*? My respect for the speaker plummets when I hear this one. This is business-speak babble at worst, and is redundant at best. *In the future* has worked just fine up to this *time frame* (that's another, but I'll save it for a later rant). Besides, the way most corporate word-manglers use this phrase, it is evident from context that the future is implied. Who cares about changing goals *going backward*?

20. **grow**—Annoying and overly general when used in corporate lingo. "In the second quarter, we expect to grow the business internationally." Also: Grow profits, grow income, grow revenues. *Increase revenue* and *expand business* will do nicely, thank you.

21. **guesstimate**—Use *estimate*, for crying out loud! It's the same word!

22. **healthy**—*Healthy* is a nonsensical synonym for *healthful* (a healthy meal, a healthy lifestyle) that even respected writers and publications use frequently.

23. **impactful**—The quality of attracting attention or creating a positive impression. (Someone in upper management at a publishing company told me, "Well, in the case of impactful, that actually is a word" to reprimand me for mocking co-workers' use of nonwords such as *incentivize* and *gift* as a verb. I was laid off a few short weeks after this comment. The manager had come from a management position in advertising but had given herself the title Executive Editor at our publishing company.)

24. **incent**—It means, in the corporate-speak I've heard, to motivate someone to do something by promising something if they do. Then the thing they get

is an incentive. That word is fine, but it does not automatically beget a verb. My problem with *incent* is that it gives the subject no credit for a decision. They become a perfectly predictable robot, subject to the whims and offerings of the clever, incentive-offering manager.

25. **invite**—The use of *invite* (pronounced IN-vite) in place of "invitation" irritates me.

26. **issue**—*Issue* seems to have supplanted *problem* among the vocabulary deficient as the all-purpose word for anything difficult or disliked. Especially bad is the psychobabble *has issues with*.

27. **key**—Adjectival *key*, once reserved for crucial openers of figurative locks, is now so overused—for the merely somewhat related as well as for the crucial—as to have lost all meaning. Many speakers seem to call just about everything and anyone key. To quote my 1966 edition of *Modern American Usage*: "The interests of good writing suggest that we leave 'key' in actual or conceivable locks and reinstate the simple qualifiers 'chief', 'main', 'prime', 'important', 'outstanding' where the logic of a lock and a key isn't evident." And I find constructions such as "____ is key" particularly awful.

28. **leverage**—I hate it when people use to *leverage* when what they really mean is to *capitalize upon* or to *parlay*. For instance, I have a dollar. I want to turn that into twelve dollars by buying a share of Dizzy.com stock. (I didn't say I was smart.) I tell my stockbroker, "Hey! Buy me a share of Dizzy.com so I can leverage my dollar instead of letting it burn a hole in my pocket!"

29. **liaise**—The worst word that I have come across is *liaise*. Argh!

30. **meaningful**—Usually to describe a discussion or, worse still, "dialogue." Can it even be a discussion if it is without meaning? I was recently involved in a court case where the decision turned on the judge's emphatic view that "meaningful consultation" (the term used in the contract at issue) was more than "consultation."

31. **networking**—It's lost all humanity. Even fish don't want to be in nets.

32. **nice**—The word I dislike the most is *nice* used to mean courteous, amiable, or pretty. Many teenage girls use this word to describe their classmates.

33. **nucular**—I would like to add the nonword *nucular*. One never sees this spelling, of course, but the president of the United States recently pronounced *nuclear* as *nucular* in an address to the nation, so it's time to take a stand.

34. **office**—The most egregious phrase I have come across: "The new way to office!" Ouch. This was posted on a new office building near my office as an enticement to local businesses to rent space. *Office* as a verb gives us: I am officing, You are officing, and so forth. In the subjunctive: If I were to office, then I would partner with them. Gross! I realize that in English we have many words that function as both verbs and nouns. I also realize the language changes, but some of the recent coinages in the business arena are laughable and painful to listen to.

35. **ongoing**—This odious term has been used by bureaucrats, reporters, and other idiots to refer to actions or processes that are of a continuing or even perpetual nature. That which continues to "go on" merely continues and does not have to be *ongoing*. It is unfortunate and disturbing that this alleged word has found its way into some dictionaries.

36. **paradigm**—*Paradigm* has lost its original meaning and become a squishy term for anything having to do with a new way of doing or viewing anything. It sounds pretentious and it is.

37. **parameter**—Used in mathematics involving independent variables. It was not meant as a pseudo-elegant alternative to *perimeter*.

38. **penis and vagina**—(Well, you asked for it.) They stand out as uncomfortable. I asked myself years ago, is it the connotation of the words or the sound? I believe it's the sound. Think about it; *penis* and *vagina* do not rhyme with any other words in the English language, which proves that they do, indeed,

sound different. The only rhyme I can think of is *Venus*. Most every other word can be rhymed with, save for these two.

39. **pick**—I hate this crummy word used instead of *choose*. *Pick* is fine for a guitar or ice or your nose.

40. **piece**—As in, "This is a piece you can wear year-round," referring to an item of clothing, or "These pieces work so beautifully in this room," referring to items of furniture. Don't know why this irks me. Also hate "pant" for "pants," and "shoe" for "shoes": "This pant is so chic, and works with the shoe to create a total look—these are pieces you'll wear forever." Uck! I have *got* to stop watching the Style Network.

41. **portion**—*Portion* is one of those words to which I have a visceral reaction: disgust. *Portion* and its ilk (including *meal*) are mean, stingy little words. They bring to mind slapped hands and lectures about "people starving in China" and also those scary, molded plastic trays with sections for individual foods (slop such as creamed corn and Jell-O and boiled fish). *Portion* is also insidious: a simple, concrete word, it is used constantly by people unaware of its niggardly nature. To me, it is the worst word.

42. **posse**—The word I hate? *Posse*. It looks ugly, sounds ugly, feels ugly, and should never again be used. Ever.

43. **proactive**—As opposed to anti-active?

44. **quantum**—In physics, a tiny change in location, not the overused cliché indicating a large leap.

45. **rationalize**—"We will rationalize our work force." *Rationalize* is used in corporate-speak for *fire* or *lay off*.

46. **reality**—*Reality* is misused as in "but the reality is…." I hear this from my girlfriends (in their mid-forties) when they are trying to explain differences in perception. *Reality* is objective, and yet they use it for truly subjective explanations.

47. **scrotum**—The ugliest word in the English language.

48. **service**—The worst word I've encountered in business-speak of late is *service*, as in, "we service that account." All nouns can be "verbed," but we had a perfectly good one already—*serve*. They may serve me, but servicing is something that a stud does for a mare! When I hear that "I'm getting serviced," I can be assured of being screwed.

49. **share**—Unctuous folks use this word when they mean *tell*, but it's hardly ever used any more to mean "to divide and parcel out; apportion." Perhaps that's because it's so much easier and cheaper to share feelings than to share money or possessions!

50. **smegma**—One of my professors back in the 1960s said that to him the ugliest English word was *smegma*. The word not only sounds gross....

51. **solution**—*Solution* belongs back where it came from: math, chemistry, and logic puzzle books. Sucked dry of all meaning through nefarious overuse by corporate sales and marketing. Is it a kid's book, or a "pediatric text delivery solution"? The second one will surely bring a higher price! For the love of all that's holy, please stop using *solution* and remember: If you're not part of the solution, you're part of the precipitate.

52. **stakeholder**—This refugee from *Buffy the Vampire Slayer* needs to be, well, buried with a stake through its sweet heart.

53. **status**—Culled from an HMO web site: "Click on this link to status a recent claim." The creator of this abomination should be condemned to the fourth level of HMO hell. Just say "Click on this link to check the status of a recent claim."

54. **veggie**—I utterly detest this word. I don't even like to type it or say it. Talked my brother out of using it (and "server," which I also dislike, but not as much) in his restaurant's menus. He doesn't really care, but he humors me. I don't mind "veg" at all, for some reason. It's used routinely in restaurants along with "protein" and "starch" to signify the components of a meal. I think "meat and

two veg" is hilarious, though possibly because I only heard it recently—like any other vulgarism, I imagine it gets boring with repetition. But *veggie*—hate it, hate it, hate it. Have hated it since they made it up in the seventies, or whenever it was. Ick!

55. **verbiage**—I'd like to add *verbiage* to the list of Worst Words. It is used way too often by my supervisors when they mean wording. Worse still, they always mispronounce it as "verbage." It's maddening.

Hate a word? Tell us what it is (and why you hate it). There need not be any well-reasoned analysis of your distaste for a word; visceral reactions to the sound or meaning of words are welcome. See: www.vocabula.com/forum.

*

APPENDIX E

WRITE TO A LAXICOGRAPHER

Robert Hartwell Fiske encourages you to send a letter to the editors of descriptive dictionaries. Copy the letter on the following page, and in the white space below "Do be sensible," please add your own indignation. Mail it to:

Executive Editor
The American Heritage Dictionary
Houghton Mifflin Company
22 Berkeley St.
Boston, MA 02116

Editor in Chief
Merriam-Webster's
Collegiate Dictionary
47 Federal Street
P.O. Box 281
Springfield, MA 01102

Managing Editor
Oxford American
College Dictionary
G.P. Putnam's Sons
375 Hudson St.
New York, NY 10014

Editor in Chief
Microsoft Encarta
College Dictionary
St. Martin's Press
175 Fifth Ave.
New York, NY 10010

Editor in Chief
Webster's New World
College Dictionary
Wiley Publishing, Inc.
10475 Crosspoint Blvd.
Indianapolis, IN 46256

Editorial Director
Random House Webster's
College Dictionary
Random House Reference
1745 Broadway, 15-3
New York, NY 10019

Dear Sir or Madame:

I am appalled by the descriptive posture you take in

_____.

I want a dictionary that helps me write and speak clearly and persuasively, not one that promotes any meaning, any spelling, any usage whatever.

Do be sensible.

Regards,

*

THE VOCABULA REVIEW

If you've enjoyed *The Dictionary of Disagreeable English, Deluxe Edition*, you may want to subscribe to *The Vocabula Review* (www.vocabula.com). Twelve monthly issues of *The Vocabula Review* cost only $15.00.

Mail this page with your check or money order—made payable to *The Vocabula Review*—to:

The Vocabula Review
5A Holbrook Court
Rockport, MA 01966

Name: _____

Email address: _____

(please print clearly)

Once we've received your payment, we will email you a password so that you can read *The Vocabula Review*'s pages.

VOCABULA BOOKS

Vocabula 101 Series Handbooks are slim volumes replete with sound advice on how to use the English language well.

1. *101 Wordy Phrases*—A Vocabula 101 Series Handbook includes some ludicrous, though much used, examples of wordiness. Sentence examples illustrate how wordy phrases can be made more concise. *101 Wordy Phrases* encourages you to speak and write more concisely and clearly.

2. *101 Foolish Phrases*—A Vocabula 101 Series Handbook includes some of the most foolish phrases we speak and write. Incisive, sometimes acerbic, commentary accompanies each entry. *101 Foolish Phrases* encourages you to speak and write more carefully and thoughtfully.

3. *101 Elegant Paragraphs*—A Vocabula 101 Series Handbook includes some prize examples of beautifully written, elegant English. *101 Elegant Paragraphs* encourages you to speak and write with deliberation, style, even beauty.

Read about Vocabula Books here: www.vocabula.com/VocabulaBooks.asp

VOCABULA BOOKS ORDER FORM

VOCABULA BOOKS ORDER FORM

ITEM	QUANTITY	PRICE	TOTAL
101 Wordy Phrases (51 pages; ISBN 0-9774368-0-2)		$9.95 each	
101 Foolish Phrases (53 pages; ISBN 0-9774368-1-0)		$9.95 each	
101 Elegant Paragraphs (78 pages; ISBN 0-9774368-2-9)		$9.95 each	
All three 101 Series Handbooks (*101 Wordy Phrases, 101 Foolish Phrases, 101 Elegant Paragraphs*)		$28.00 for all three	
Postage and handling [$3.00 per order (in U.S. and Canada) except for products sent via email]		$3.00	
		Grand Total	

Mail this page with your check or money order—made payable to Vocabula Books—to:

Vocabula Books
5A Holbrook Court
Rockport, MA 01966

Name: _____

Address: _____

_____

Email address: _____
(please print clearly)

*